THE HUMAN FACE OF D-DAY

THE HUMAN FACE
OF D-DAY

Walking the Battlefields of Normandy: Essays, Reflections,
and Conversations with Veterans of the Longest Day

COL (RET) KEITH M. NIGHTINGALE

CASEMATE

Philadelphia & Oxford

Published in the United States of America and Great Britain in 2023 by
CASEMATE PUBLISHERS
1950 Lawrence Road, Havertown, PA 19083, USA
and
The Old Music Hall, 106–108 Cowley Road, Oxford OX4 1JE, UK

Hardcover Edition: ISBN 978-1-63624-102-9
Digital Edition: ISBN 978-1-63624-103-6

A CIP record for this book is available from the British Library

Printed and bound by CPI Group (UK) Ltd, Croydon, CR0 4YY.

Typeset by Lapiz Digital Services.

For a complete list of Casemate titles, please contact:

CASEMATE PUBLISHERS (US)
Telephone (610) 853-9131
Fax (610) 853-9146
Email: casemate@casematepublishers.com
www.casematepublishers.com

CASEMATE PUBLISHERS (UK)
Telephone (0)1226 734350
Email: casemate-uk@casematepublishers.co.uk
www.casematepublishers.co.uk

Front cover image from author's collection.

Contents

Soldiers, Sailors and Airmen of the Allied Expeditionary Force!

You are about to embark upon the Great Crusade, toward which we have striven these many months. The eyes of the world are upon you. The hopes and prayers of liberty loving people everywhere march with you. In company with our brave Allies and brothers-in-arms on other Fronts, you will bring about the destruction of the German war machine, the elimination of Nazi tyranny over the oppressed peoples of Europe, and security for ourselves in a free world.

Your task will not be an easy one. Your enemy is well trained, well equipped and battle-hardened. He will fight savagely.

But this is the year 1944! Much has happened since the Nazi triumphs of 1940–1941. The United Nations have inflicted upon the Germans great defeats, in open battle, man-to-man. Our air offensive has seriously reduced their strength in the air and their capacity to wage overwhelming superiority in weapons and munitions of war, and placed at our disposal great reserves of trained fighting men. The tide has turned! The free men of the world are marching together to Victory! I have full confidence in your courage, devotion to duty and skill in battle. We will accept nothing less than full Victory!

Good Luck! And let us beseech the blessing of Almighty God upon this great and noble undertaking.

Signed
Dwight D. Eisenhower

The Point of the Spear

The invasion of Normandy in June 1944 was the largest single military operation this planet has ever seen and could be the greatest single event in our civilization to date. And this operation was but a small portion of the much larger efforts going on elsewhere—in the Pacific, the Mediterranean, and in Russia. Despite its rather minor resourcing compared to the whole, its outcome would largely determine the future of the entire Allied effort.

At Arlington Cemetery we all recognize and honor the area reserved for the Tomb of the Unknown Soldier. The constant guard mount and the reverence for the place and what it means leaves a lasting impression on all who visit it. So it is with Normandy. Normandy exhibits the same spirit, honor, and reverence for the sense and purity of purpose that we attest to Arlington.

First out the door on the Cotentin. First off the ramp on Dog White. They, and the thousands that followed them, brought light to a dark place and symbolized what our civilization is all about. It was here, on the sand and in the swamps and villages of Normandy, that we showed the world what we were truly about.

Simply put, Normandy truly is ground where ordinary people did extraordinary things. This action encapsulated all that is good about our society and left a spirit of meaningful service that will live long after all involved have passed away.

It has been my privilege to have walked the beaches, hills, and towns of Normandy with many of those who fought there. They each imparted a unique, highly personal view of their experience. Together, over many years, these vignettes have created for me a great tapestry of their actions there and reinforced the righteousness of the effort.

In my annual terrain walks each June with active-duty troops, I do my best to retell what the veterans have told me and to transfer their sense of service to those that have followed. It is awe inspiring to see the faces of the soldiers as they walk the positions and hear what Private First Class Hall said about his experience at Omaha or Bob Murphy's recollection of Owens holding La Fière.

This book encapsulates my experiences in gathering the story from the "Originals" through their voices and recollections. The staff rides are their voices and descriptions—the human face behind the facts of D-Day. It was and is an honor to be part of the bridge to history joining the old with the new.

Introduction

At the age of 10, I discovered *Life Goes to War, A Picture History of World War II* published by *Life* magazine. For whatever reason, the section on Normandy and D-Day was burned into me. As my interest progressed from adolescent wonder to an adult obsession, the events of that day became a lodestone for my life. In 1984, having become an officer in the U.S. Army myself, I brought the 82nd Airborne back to Normandy for the first time since the war to celebrate the 40th anniversary of D-Day. Ever since, I have led yearly staff rides on all the sites of Operation *Overlord*, recounting what I have learned so active-duty troops would see and feel the bridge between what happened then and their tasks for today.

This book is a reflection of my 50-plus years walking the ground of Normandy and speaking to literally hundreds of veterans about that significant day. I began to learn of Normandy from the Originals on my first trip there in 1977. I walked along Omaha, met a number of veterans, and just listened and questioned them. As an active-duty soldier, they were anxious that I understand what had happened to them at this place. They responded to my questions with specificity. They were not hesitant to discuss casualties or the quality of their associates—things they normally would not relate to a civilian who might not understand.

As an officer in the Airborne and Ranger communities, I gained unique access, both formally and otherwise, to the veterans: I walked Omaha with First Wave veterans and heard their stories. I followed General James Gavin around the 82nd sites, listened to Colonel Terence Otway at Merville Battery, and heard Major John Howard at Pegasus Bridge. They and their associates painted unique, on-site pictures in my mind's eye that I hope to have transferred to these pages.

On my annual trips to Normandy from 1977 through 2018, I met veterans of all elements, and was able to compile a remarkable collection of their personal impressions and descriptions of events on D-Day and throughout the Normandy Campaign. Having served as a unit commander from platoon through brigade in the 82nd Airborne Division, I had already been granted significant one-on-one interviews and had multiple informal discussions with key leaders, even before I returned to France as the task force commander in 1984. These included exchanges with men at the cutting edge like Generals Omar Bradley, Joe Collins, Matthew Ridgway, James Gavin, and Benjamin Vandervoort, the latter two becoming close friends who visited my battalions and spoke to my troops numerous times. I also developed lifelong associations with many lesser-known veterans of Normandy, whose recollections provide a true picture of the grunt thrown into the most significant operation of the war.

I did not initially do any formal interviews, just walk-alongs and listening. Afterwards, I would make notes in my green Army notebook and annotate with a name if I remembered. Some were anonymous/not remembered, but their input was significant. It was only much later—in preparation for the 40th anniversary and during the battle staff rides—that anything approximating an interview was done.

I continued to collect input during my many return trips and simple informal discussions with the veterans. Many of the personalities, Bob Murphy, James Gavin, Ben Vandervoort, Bud Lomell, James Hill, and Bill Sullivan were almost a continual dialogue. Some, such as the British commanders, were one-time affairs but quite academic in nature, e.g., in-depth discussions in a formal atmosphere.

What I found most striking was the very human emotional aspects many of the veterans attached to their experiences. Many had not been in combat before and wondered if they could perform for their buddies. This was a common concern. "I can't fail. I wonder how I will do?" This sort of point they would discuss with me as a fellow soldier who could appreciate the thought.

On the annual staff rides, I would have the troops with me and address the points of the place. If I knew of a veteran on site, I would ask them to speak. Some would go on at length as to actions, others would demur but listen intently. All the veterans were anxious to meet the troops and would readily engage in conversation. I can honestly say that I learned a new fact or nuance to a specific event almost every year as part of this process, such as the Brécourt men recalling how zombie-like they were and how upset they were when told to attack Brécourt. Or Bob Murphy showing exactly where he low crawled to deliver the message to Staff Sergeant Bill Owens at La Fière to hold at all costs. This was and is a humbling experience.

After each staff ride, veterans would seek me out, wanting to talk about their personal experiences at the place we had just visited. It was if each had capped a pressurized well inside himself and suddenly felt ready to open the valve. Most often, they would be accompanied by eagerly listening family members. I would ask one or two basic questions: What unit were you in? Where did you land? What happened? What was your impression?

These questions usually started off a monologue by the veteran, a sudden freeing of a long-carried burden. Details, feelings, and opinions freely coursed, releasing an ocean of hitherto withheld experiences. Finally exhausted, the veteran would stop, gather himself, and fall silent: the troops would applaud, and he and his family would move on. On numerous occasions, relatives returned to tell me they had had no idea until that very day what the veteran had done during the war.

There was a consistent thread with virtually all of them. They had no ego, bravado, or sense of great self-importance. Rather, they were quite humble, but immensely proud of being part of the invasion and what it meant for the world. Many spoke of the American cemetery, their friends who had fallen, and how fortunate they were to survive. It was extremely important to them that I and the troops understood what had happened and the price it took to achieve results. They invariably mentioned the Omaha cemetery in making their point. On more than one occasion, there were tears.

The more senior of the Originals, the colonels and generals, spoke, appropriately, on their level and the command issues or management aspects. They were universally aware of the written histories and often would make corrections or provide the "rest of the story" to an issue. Why General James Hill chose Terence Otway or John Howard for their specific tasks, Gavin emphasizing Owens and Captain John Dolan's exceptional performance, or Vandervoort on Lieutenant Turner Turnbull's actions at Neuville.

Altogether, these interviews, walk-abouts, bar discussions, letters, phone calls, and casual encounters revealed the true human aspects of the invasion and the deeply personal thoughts and feelings of the participants. They well knew the significance of the tasks they had been assigned to do and wanted to ensure that we understood mission accomplishment and the cost.

In totality, these encounters stoked the fire of my obsession and reinforced it as a worthy cause and as something that needed to be remembered as each year more veterans have passed.

The veterans "got it." By that I mean they truly understood what happened there and took pride in what they did and what their history is.

In some future dark place, they will reflect upon what they saw and felt in Normandy and draw on an inner resolve to do likewise.

I cannot speak on the latter, but the former is universal for every year I have participated. I hear it in their voices, but more importantly, I see it in their eyes.

***

If this book stands out from the crowd of publications on Normandy as I hope, it is because it reveals the human aspects of the invasion through the thoughts and feelings of the participants in a uniquely personal way. General Gavin arranged for more than a hundred veterans and their families to attend the events of 1984 and personally led the discussions at La Fière Bridge. Dozens of veterans added their insights to each event; it is their observations, recollections, and comments that I have included in this book.

This book is not a history book—those looking for a definitive and complete history of D-Day need look elsewhere. Instead, it brings together a hybrid of historical facts reinforced by the voices of the veterans and a series of vignettes of specific places and events that the veterans I encountered wished to impart. This book is more about the emotions and the impressions of a given moment than the spare facts associated with the discussion. Theirs are the human faces behind the statistics and cold facts, and their presence, their voices, make all the difference.

Many of the participants commented on multiple aspects of the war, and their voices are heard where appropriate throughout. Their commentaries derive from personal interviews and informal discussions, notes from a presentation (Bradley), and formal interviews or recollections of events (General Maxwell Taylor and Lieutenant Malcolm Brannen), and appear as direct quotations, where possible, or close paraphrase taken from my notes.

My most extensive discussions throughout the years were with Gavin and his daughters, Bob Piper, Ben Vandervoort, Bob Murphy, Bill Sullivan, Frank Norris, Susan Eisenhower, and members of the Renaud family. These were long-held associations and personal friendships that developed over many years as the story of Normandy and the French-American relationship it created was fostered among the original participants and continued to evolve.

I do not address the British beaches or events as I did not talk to British veterans of those locations. But I did have extensive discussions at Merville Battery, Ranville Ridge, and Pegasus Bridge with the principals and other veterans. I do not go into depth regarding units at Omaha or Utah other than what a veteran may have imparted to me. The rest is for other studies.

The invasion is such a huge subject that before one can appreciate what the veterans are saying/have said or what occurred, it is necessary to understand the basic facts behind Normandy and D-Day. I have provided that in a summary form at the beginning. The book is then divided into several major sections:

Part One aims to impart my motivation for writing this book: my first introduction to Normandy as a 10-year-old boy, my subsequent visits there both in and out of uniform, my many discussions with the veterans, and my observations of the Norman people—all created a deep desire to recount the history as I understood it, a history that reflects the purity of purpose and spirit of place that makes Normandy so special.

Part Two covers the background to the invasion: an understanding as to why Normandy was chosen is crucial to understanding what actually occurred there. The place, its geography, and population were manifestly important in how the invasion unfolded. The decision-making process was driven by two key parts: a strategic evaluation of German strengths and weaknesses compared to the Allies, likely German responses coupled with ours, and simple geographical facts.

Part Three looks at the groundwork: once a decision was made as to Where and When the invasion would take place, the How became of paramount importance. This process ranged from command selection to force selection to pre-invasion controversies and personalities and supporting programs. All these had to be identified and managed before meaningful training could take place.

The actual invasion was a compendium of ordinary people doing extraordinary things. Regardless of nationality, rank or location, thousands of our men did what the Germans thought near impossible. They did it with the ingenuity, drive, and initiative that is an inherent characteristic of our culture. Part Four is a glimpse of their story while Part Five addresses memory and commemoration in Normandy since the end of the war.

Due to the way in which I interviewed the veterans, many of my textual quotes are a "best recollection" from the cryptic notes or a particularly memorable direct quote. I understand that this is not a formal academic approach. However, the quotes are exactly to the point and, I believe, represent the personality and nature of the man. There are several types of quoted material: direct quotes as received in a meeting or letter; a reasonable approximation from notes and memory; or narratives as provided to other forums or publications. I do not attempt to differentiate other than acknowledging outside sources.

In writing this book, I found a number of holes in my personal interviews regarding important aspects of the invasion and its results. I simply did not have a direct interview for that specific point. Hence, I used open-source narratives of veterans that described that place or event and I so note.

The Sources section is a listing of all those I interviewed, corresponded with, and/ or discussed the events of the day. There are also many others who gave me insights but I was unable to recall or note their names. I cite "anonymous" in several places, which indicates I made notes at the time but did not record the veteran's name.

The appendices also include material that may be of interest to the reader but would burden the narrative.

The point of the book is to impart the power of place and the people that made it so. Much of it, individually or collectively, is viscerally emotional. That is the point.

PART I
An Obsession with Normandy

CHAPTER I

Zane

Sergeant Zane Schlemmer, Headquarters and Headquarters Company, 1-508th, 82nd Airborne Division, represents to me the "Everyman" of D-Day. His experiences parallel virtually all other veterans I met. Above all, his humanity and appreciation for being part of something larger than himself for a moment in time is emblematical of them all. While the specifics of the life story are unique to him, the overall context of what he experienced is not. He told me his story in Normandy on his last trip there in 2016.

My name is D. Zane Schlemmer. I was born on October 13, 1924, in Canton, Ohio, U.S.A. As of June 6, 1944, D-Day, I was a 19-year-old sergeant in Headquarters Company, Second Battalion of the 508th Parachute Infantry Regiment, 82nd Airborne Division. My military occupation was Forward Observer for an 81mm mortar platoon.

Soon after my 18th birthday in 1942, I enlisted and volunteered for paratroop duty: I had been attending Northwestern University on a work study program. I joined the paratroops because I was attracted by the $50.00 per month jump pay, which would help pay for my postwar college tuition and cost. Also, I really wanted to prove my capabilities, and I also wanted a pair of jump boots and jump wings. And then, a third reason that I joined was that being of German descent, I felt that we had to make a point, and prove our loyalty.

After joining the parachute regiment, basic training, jump school, and following tactical training and maneuvers, we arrived in Northern Ireland by boat in January, 1944, then to Nottingham, England on St. Patrick's Day, 1944, where we became a part of the 82nd Airborne Division. There, we established our tent base camp, which was used as a base camp for both Normandy as well as the Holland invasion parachute jumps. Although it was cold, and we were living in a tent city in Midland England, we were quite comfortable. We would always, always, have a spot in our hearts for Nottingham, England, and its people.

In the Airborne, all being volunteers quite unlike the rest of the military, from the ranks of generals down to the privates, we all jumped together, and all shared the same experiences. In the field, there was unusual camaraderie and mutual respect between the officers of all ranks, many of whom were West Pointers, and the enlisted men.

We spent most of the pre-invasion months in England, doing many tactical combat exercises for which we had been trained.

Most of our training involved jumps, or mock jumps, then assembling and setting up hillside defense positions. All this constant training triggered a great deal of speculation on which country we would be invading. The conjectures and the rumors ranged all the way from Norway down to the Pyrenees Mountains.

We were looking forward to our first combat jump.

In early June, 1944, we boarded a group of ancient English buses with all our combat gear and motored to the airports.

Our battalion assembled at Saltby airfield behind a barbed wire security enclosure. We then all drew combat loads of ammunition. At the time, I was carrying an M-1 Garand .30-caliber rifle, mainly because most of my time was to be spent with the front-line companies as a forward observer. We had been informed that the German troops had been instructed to give priority to eliminating forward observers, officers, and non-commissioned officers in that order. So, by carrying a rifle and wearing my binocular case on the back of my rifle belt, I tried to look as inconspicuous as possible.

Other items that we drew were, of course, the ammunition for our mortars and all of the other crew-serviced weapons. In addition to fragmentation and thermite grenades, we each drew a Gammon grenade. The Gammon grenade was an English invention that was a cotton sock filled with approximately two pounds of composition C-2, a plastic explosive. This, then, was armed with a very simple impact fuse igniter. They were super for attacking any armored vehicles, and we called them our "hand artillery." The Gammon grenade was also very popular with us, because a very small piece of the C-2 plastic, when lit with a match, would burn very fast, very hot, and smokeless, so it was excellent to heat coffee and our K-rations in the bottom of our foxholes. So, in Normandy, the size of our Gammon grenades got progressively smaller each day. Each trooper was also given an anti-tank mine to carry into battle. One of the most puzzling phenomenons that I saw during that time was how each trooper went back for extra ammunition and grenades after everybody had drawn their basic load. Despite the weight of the basic equipment, which we each had to carry, everyone tended to increase their potential firepower, rather than to rely upon re-supply.

Our waiting time was spent on equipment inspections, cleaning and re-cleaning our weapons, sharpening and resharpening our knives, then rolling our mortars, our telephone equipment, and our ammunition all into para-pack bundles that would be dropped from the bottom of the respective planes at jump time.

We then attached small, colored lights to the para-packs, since this was to be a night drop, so that we could locate and identify the respective para-pack bundles that had dropped.

We then went into sand table sessions of our drop areas and objectives. We were then informed that German troops had occupied our originally planned hill and that our mission had been changed.

We were also told that we should jump regardless, under any circumstances, and that we were not to return to England with the plane.

The first session with the sand tables was without any identifying names, just the terrain with the fields, the roads, the rivers, bridges, and villages. The second session was around the same sand tables, but with English-sounding names near the villages. Evansville, (which, in the third session, became Etienville) and Port Abbey, (which, in the third session became Pont L'Abbe) and Pickleville, (which, in the third session became Picauville).

At this third and final sand table session, we were informed that the invasion site was to be Normandy, France, and that our objectives were to block off all German approach routes and their attempts to reach the Utah invasion beach—very much like down-field blocking in a football game. We were then to hold until relieved and to prepare for further sealing off of the Cherbourg peninsula after the beach troops had come through to our positions.

We were then issued additional items, among which were silk escape maps and tiny compasses which we were to sew in each of our gas impregnated jump suits. We were issued "invasion money" in several small French Franc denominations, in the event that we had to purchase anything from the French populace. We were each also issued two Benzedrine tablets to help keep us awake and alert and two morphine syrettes for self-administering in the event that we were wounded. I, of course, had no idea at the time of issuance of the Benzedrine tablets or the morphine syrettes that I would have use for both of them before I left Normandy.

We also were given a small toy "frog" clicker, which we were to use for identification and communication upon landing in the pre-dawn darkness of D-Day. One click was to be answered by two clicks of the clicker. Lastly, we were each issued a yellow life vest. Our M-1 rifles were broken down into several parts and put into felt cloth containers that we commonly referred to as "violin cases." These were then strapped diagonally across our chest under our reserve parachutes, which meant until we cleared the parachute and harness upon landing and assembled our weapon that we had very little personal protection. Because of this, I had brought along a small .32-caliber nickel-plated Smith & Wesson short barrel revolver, which I carried just above my reserve chute, and just under my yellow life vest, in the event that I needed it upon landing.

D-Day, as you know, was originally scheduled for 5 June 1944, but weather caused a 24-hour postponement. Finally, about 8:30 p.m., on Monday 5 June 1944, we assembled by stick. There were 18 jumpers in my stick, and we struggled across the airfield to our assigned planes where we again checked on our para-packs for the last time. We all had our last relief stop, for once we had our equipment on and buckled up it was physically impossible to relieve ourselves.

We then blackened our faces, donned our equipment, put on our main and reserve chutes, then the yellow life vest and our helmets and chin straps. We were then pushed or hauled aboard the plane by the plane crewmen, for our individual combat loads were so bulky and heavy that it was impossible for us to get into the planes by ourselves. The moods of the various troopers ranged from nervous chatter and nervous laughter to almost religiously quiet. All minor personality differences between the men were forgotten and camaraderie prevailed. I recall that I was chewing an entire pack of gum from the time of embarking and to this day, I don't have any recollection of what happened to that mouth full of gum; whether I swallowed it or whether I lost it in drop.

We had some reservations about our plane, which was of C-53 configuration, having a relatively smaller exit door than the standard C-47, but this proved to be no problem. I've often thought about the engineer that designed the bucket seat in the troop transport planes for they definitely were not designed for the combat equipment paratroopers use. Most of the men found that they were better sitting on the floor with all their equipment rather than on the front edge of the bucket seat, which just didn't fit.

The pilot and crewmen asked that we all cram forward for takeoff as much as possible to permit the overloaded plane to become airborne as quickly as possible. We noted that each Allied plane and glider, painted their usual drab military colors, now each had three newly circled white bands around each wing and around the fuselage for immediate identification as an Allied D-Day plane. We were told that any planes without such markings were fair game to be fired upon. Then, in the dusk and coming darkness of the English evening at the airfield, the motors of the planes started cranking up, each coughing, then coming to life, idling, running back up, idling again. The planes then jockeyed into their respective take-off positions.

As the motors on our plane advanced to full take-off power, it seemed that every loose rivet vibrated in harmony with the engine, and the planes struggled down the runway to become airborne. As we lifted off, we could see the airfield personnel all out in the flight line, waving white handkerchiefs, for they then knew, as we did, that the long-awaited D-Day operation was finally underway.

6 June, 1944, 0001 hours, (British time), found us approaching the English Channel. With no door on the plane, the prop wash created a nice cool breeze. As I mentioned before, there were 18 troopers in my stick. Lieutenant Talbert Smith, one of our officers, led the stick jumping, and me, being a sergeant, was jumping last to "push the stick."

As we reached the English Channel, it was getting dark, but below the channel waters were dark with distinguishable wave patterns. It seemed that as we hit the Channel, the mood changed from the chattering bravado, and the stick became very quiet and almost pensive.

In retrospect, it was probably the sobering thought of jumping into combat and the baptism of fire for the first time. The only lights that I saw were several glows of cigarettes.

From where I was, next to the cockpit bulkhead, by standing I could see past the pilot through the cockpit windshield, the blue wing light tips of the formations stacked ahead of us in our serials.

After flying over the dark waters of the Channel for some time, and then a left turn, I saw two small blacked-out islands appearing off our left wing. I later learned that these were the Alderney

Islands off the coast of France. Soon thereafter, our plane crossed the French coast, and though it was dark, we could see the roads, the fields, and some small houses, which stood out in a reddish brown color. We then stood and hooked up our parachutes to the static lines and arranged our equipment in order to be prepared to jump, should any problems arise. The red light had come on. Then, suddenly, and without any warning at all, our plane was engulfed in the middle of a cloud of dense white fog. This really concerned us, because all we could see outside the plane was white; we couldn't even see the blue wing lights at the end of our plane's wings. This, of course, caused the pilots of the planes and the formation to disperse in order to avoid any mid-air collisions with the other planes in the formation.

The time seemed endless with us standing there, going through the cloud or fog, until suddenly it cleared just as rapidly as it had engulfed us. It was at that time that we started to experience the German flak and small arms fire, which, when it hit the plane, sounded very similar to gravel crunching on a metal roof (it was quite an unmistakable sound, and one which once you have heard, you remember it forever). Our equipment check proceeded. We then closed the stick up to exit just as fast as possible, as we awaited the green light while enduring the flak. During this time, I had time for two personal thoughts. The first was to get the hell out of the plane just as quickly as possible, since I was the last one in the stick to jump, and secondly, I found myself asking myself what I had done to find myself in such a predicament, (and I found that I asked myself the same thing many times during the following fateful days).

Generally, through familiarization and instinct, a trooper can anticipate the green jump light, for the pilot will throttle back the plane to jumping speed and will raise the tail of the plane, but not this night. The green jump light flashed on, and out the door went the stick in a very well rehearsed—it almost seemed choreographed—sequence.

The opening shock of my parachute was quite violent, but very much a welcome feeling. My helmet had been jarred forward over my face and I had to push it back in order to see. The sky seemed alive with pink, orange, and red tracer bullets, which would arc up gracefully, then snap by with little tugs as they went through the parachute canopy. I've since wondered what ratio the ordinary bullets were to the tracer bullets that the German Army utilized that night, for just the number of visible tracer bullets criss-crossing was a very sobering sight. In the distance to the east, that's the direction which the planes were flying, I could see a sizable fire burning on the ground—this must have been Sainte-Mère-Église, although I didn't know it at the time.

The one good thing about a night drop is that you cannot see the ground coming up and do not have a tendency to anticipate your landing. We had jumped extremely low, to minimize the defenseless time that we had in the air, and I hit in a hedgerow apple orchard, coming up with very sore bruised ribs from the impact of all the equipment that I had strapped onto my body. I quickly cleared my chute harness assembly, assembled my rifle, and tucked my little revolver away. The moon, at that time, was behind broken clouds and the reflection of the tracer bullets on these low hanging clouds created a reddish sky glow against which I could see a small lane next to the field and a small building with a tiled roof. The flak and small arms, by this time, had been switched to the next flight serial, which was coming across. I could not discern any sign of life, either in the field or in the little house. But, down the lane in a westerly direction, from a group of buildings, obviously a German stronghold, the firing was quite overwhelming. There was no way possible for me to assemble with my stick in that direction nor did I have any possibility of recovering the para-pack bundles.

I later learned that Lieutenant Talbert Smith, who had jump mastered our stick, had been immediately captured and taken prisoner and subsequently killed during an American fighter plane strafing attack.

At that moment, as I went from the field out into the lane, a very large, orange ball of fire appeared overhead, coming in a steeply descending easterly line of flight. It looked very much like a meteor. It was accompanied by the roaring whine of two runaway full-power plane engines, obviously a troop carrier going down, and my immediate thoughts were of the troopers and of the crew who might still be aboard.

I thought it odd that I did not recall hearing this blazing mass hit the ground, but later, during D-Day daylight, I saw a burnt out hulk of a C-47 out in the Merderet River marshes. Whether this was the burning plane that I saw descending, I've never been able to ascertain.

Three factors had been quite unknown to us, and came into reality just about this time. Firstly, the area into which we had jumped was occupied by the German 91st Airlanding Division, which was a very highly rated German unit. Their division command post was located just at the edge of our drop zone, and they seemed to occupy all of the large French farm houses in the area west of the Merderet River.

Secondly, no one had informed us of the immense size of the French hedgerows. We were, of course, told that we would be in hedgerow country, and we had assumed that they would be similar to the English countryside hedgerows, which were like small fences or hedges that the fox hunters on the horses went over.

Thirdly, no one had informed us of the flooded marshes surrounding the Merderet or the Douve rivers, which had been depicted on the sand table merely as streams or narrow rivers. Instead, these flooded marshes, at places, were like shallow lakes, almost as far as you could see. We learned later that the Germans had flooded these river valleys in order to prevent just the type of attack we were conducting. The marsh waters were generally too deep to traverse, there were intersecting drainage ditches dropping off, the water was quite dirty, and with the tall weeds that grew there, it made passage through the marshes almost impassable. I was alone, I had no idea where the hell I was other than being in France. I was unable to assemble with my stick due to the German-occupied farm buildings in my direct path. So, I quickly laid my anti-tank mine in one of the tracks in the lane, covered it over with brush, pulled off the safety ring clip device, thus arming the mine, and headed across the large pasture field in a southerly direction, in order to flank the occupied stronghold.

Near the far edge of the next field, I came across a sergeant from the 101st Airborne Division, who was just as bewildered as I was as to where we were. Both of us were very far from where we should have been. We then heard small arms firing to the southeast and decided that it meant that there were friendlies there, so we headed that way and suddenly came across an east–west running road. In the ditch alongside this road, we found two parallel wires strung along the ground. It was obviously military communications, so we clipped the wire and rolled up about a hundred feet of it, clipped it again, and threw the cut piece of wire over a hedgerow to keep it from being used again.

Just ahead, the road came to a little turn, and rounding the turn, it became a causeway over the flooded marsh, with a large house back in a group of trees from which the firing was originating. It was obviously another German stronghold, so we continued on the causeway some distance, until we came to a small masonry bridge, then some darkened houses along the road, and finally to an intersecting railroad track. I knew then that the only railroad village in our immediate area was a town called Chef-du-Pont. The bridge, the village, and the railroad track all fit in place from our model sand table. That orientation meant that I had landed some one-and-a-half miles southeast of our designated drop zone (which wasn't bad compared to where many the others had dropped) but it also meant that I was now on the wrong side of the Merderet River. The sergeant from the 101st decided to continue southeast towards his divisional operation area, and I, knowing that I was on the wrong side of the river, doubled back over the small bridge. By that time, there was considerably more German fire coming in my direction from the big house, which was a chateau, so I was forced to detour along another partially flooded roadway that went in a northerly direction from the main road that I had originally traversed. There was sporadic small arms fire in all directions, but I wasn't able to tell whether it was friend or foe, or whether it was meant for me. Just as I reached the edge of the flooded marsh, I heard a glider crash into the tall trees bordering a field somewhat distant from me. We had been told that several gliders, each carrying a baby bulldozer, would come in before dawn in order to make landing strips for the later glider landings. The sound of this glider hitting the trees was similar to smashing a thousand match boxes all at once, and I could just visualize the poor glider pilot with a baby bulldozer behind him. I suddenly found myself cold and shivering.

Whether from the dampness of the marsh, the coldness of the night, or whether I was, by that time, just plain scared, I didn't know. Shortly after, by using the frog clicker, I came across three other troopers. One of whom had already been wounded and another who had a broken leg from the jump, so we stashed these two requiring medical assistance in a roadside ditch under an overhanging hedgerow, and the other trooper came along with me.

As dawn came, we left the roads and the lanes and took to the fields, for we had been instructed that as of D-Day morning, we were to stay off the roads and out of any houses or buildings, because artillery generally zeroed in on these. Thus, by conceding these to the Germans, we could better control the battlefield by ambushing, not unlike Indian tactics in the Wild West days.

So, during my stay in Normandy, I never entered a French farm house or building until I was later wounded; then our medical aid station was in a small cattle shed quite some distance to the rear.

We came across additional troopers who were in the various fields waiting to ambush any German activities on the roads and lanes.

Each of these fields seemed to become a separate battle ground. Before entering, we would examine it through the hedgerows. If there were any cows, we were pleased because we could be reasonably certain that these fields, then, were not mined. Also, by watching the cows, who were, by nature, quite curious animals, we could tell whether there was anyone else in that field. The cows seemed to associate people with milking, and they would stand, waiting, facing anyone there in anticipation of being milked. Over all these years, I've had a place in my heart for those lovely Norman cows with the big eyes and the big udders. We too became accustomed to the sound of the German hobnail boots on the Norman back roads, whereas paratrooper jump boots were rubber soled, and made a much different sound. In this manner, we were able to ambush many patrols, merely by the sound on the other side of the respective hedgerows which were too tall and too thick to see through.

Also, we were soon able to distinguish between the different rates of fire of the automatic weapons and machine pistols that identified Germans or friendlies, even without seeing them.

By mid-morning D-Day, more and more troopers—many already walking wounded—assembled, and we found that we had no mortars, few machine guns, few bazookas, fewer radios, little medical supplies (except those which each trooper carried), and few medics to attend to our wounded. We did each have our own weapons and those we took from the wounded. We thus attempted to attack towards our original objective, Etienville, some miles distant, but to no avail. Finally, a message from the colonel informed us that we were to break it off and to assemble on Hill 30, which overlooked the flooded marsh which I had crossed in the dark that morning.

We converged on the hill from which, theoretically, we could control the two causeways across the Merderet River. However, they were covered with tall hedgerows and apple orchards. I was assigned a fighting outpost, and I spent most of the following four days and nights at this fighting outpost on the Hill 30 perimeter with Lieutenant Colonel Thomas Shanley's group. I preferred the outpost, even though we would sometimes receive fire from both sides. Back in the perimeter, we had many wounded and dying and there was no way to evacuate them. It was difficult to listen to their cries and the moans, because we had no medical supplies. We had not received re-supply of ammunition, equipment, food, or water; we could do without these items, but the lack of medical supplies and blood plasma was really felt by everyone.

Several troopers volunteered to wade and swim the flooded marshes and river at night to attempt getting the blood and medical supplies to Hill 30.

We were elated when several days later we were able to call in 75mm artillery fire via radio contact across the marsh.

This fire broke up several German attacks at very critical times for us in the outpost. After one firing to break up a German attack coming up a sunken lane very near our outpost, we captured and retrieved two small German artillery pieces and some ammunition. These we hauled back to Hill 30 to turn around and use again for the next attack.

6 June 1944, 11:59 found me bone weary but mentally alert, (probably helped along by the Benzedrine), dug in with a parachute that was very, very warm, and very luxurious in my foxhole.

We had no knowledge at that time whether the invasion had or had not succeeded, nor did we realize that we would be isolated there for five days until the seaborne troops pushed through to join us. In those five days, I went from boyhood to fighter as only a frontline infantryman could comprehend.

I must also mention that during midday of D-Day, we learned of the death of our Catholic chaplain who had jumped with us, when Germans grenaded a gully where he was attending our wounded. So, we vowed, then and there, to avenge his death with little regard for any proprieties of warfare.

We then continued to fight continuously along the front line until 3 July, 1944 when I was wounded by American artillery fire in an attack up the side of Hill 131, a major fortification above the French town of La Haye de Puits.

The 4th of July 1944 found me aboard an LST hospital ship, bound for an English field hospital. They had to cut off my dirty, bloody, stinking jumpsuit, which I had worn continuously for the past 29 days without a bath. I insisted that they let me keep my jump boots on when they operated on my wounds, for they were my most prized possession there.

I marveled at the incredible luxuries of the navy, with clean blankets, a white sheet, canned peaches, white bread, fruit juice, and real coffee—all of which were both foreign and forgotten by us in those Norman hedgerows in which we had endured.

Our regiment was relieved on 8 July, 1944, and of the 2,055 paratroopers of the 508th Parachute Infantry Regiment that jumped into France on the darkness of the morning of 6 June, 1944, only 918 boarded the LST to return to Nottingham, England, for refitting, replacement, and their next parachute jump. The rest of these men were either killed, wounded, or missing in action. However, many of us later were able to re-join the regiment again. I was fortunate that my wounds responded and that I was able to talk my way out of the hospital (mainly by threatening to take off anyway) in time to jump with my own platoon into Holland on September 17, 1944, even though my left arm was still bandaged and healing from my Normandy wounds.

For many years following my Army discharge in November 1945, I tried to submerge and to black out any and all thoughts of those fateful days and months, but they would somehow subconsciously come out periodically.

In the early 1970s, I suddenly realized that those years were a part of me, that they were now history, that nothing I could do would change these memories which were at best bittersweet.

In 1974, I returned to Normandy and to Europe to re-walk those farms, fields, forests, and towns that I had known in a different capacity so many years before. I searched out and found the apple orchard field in which I landed. I met the French people of Normandy who lived there in those days and who welcomed us into their homes and into their hearts and who will always treasure their liberation. But above all, I found a peace within myself and I discovered to my surprise that indeed all paratroopers can, indeed, shed tears.

In 1977, the very wonderful people of Picauville, France, erected a plaque near the field where I landed and honored me by renaming the adjacent road "Rue Zane Schlemmer." The farmer, Pierre Cotelle, who collected WWII wartime artifacts from his fields and the marshes for many years, named his collection "Museum de Zane Schlemmer." And all this, because one night, many years before, a young American paratrooper returned to give back to them the same thing that their French General, Lafayette, had helped our revolutionary army obtain for us many, many decades prior—liberty.

CHAPTER 2

Chance Encounter

A fortunate chance encounter forever planted the seeds of my obsession with Normandy and its personalities. It began as a simple visit to an historical area with a guided tour by the veterans of the day.

On a rainy 6 June 1979, Lieutenant John Cal and I were trudging toward La Fière Bridge along the road connecting Sainte-Mère-Église to the bridge and Picauville beyond. We were in field fatigues and the red Airborne beret. We both had large rucksacks on our back as we had been camping along the battle sites.

Prior to this, John and I were assigned to the 509th Airborne Battalion Combat Team stationed in Vicenza, Italy. As a major, I was the battalion executive officer and John a rifle platoon leader. We were both coaches on the battalion football team and had developed a close association, fueled in large part by our love of history. We had exchanged several books regarding Normandy and often talked about the events, playing trivia with each other as well as formulating a visit plan. By June of 1979, we decided to take the train to Normandy and walk the battle sites. This would be a road march and camping trip so we packed a full ruck and began our journey.

After several transfers, the train dropped us in Carentan and we rented a small Renault and drove to Sainte-Mère-Église. There was a light misty rain in the town square as we unloaded. Our orientation complete, we began our trek toward La Fière, the most anticipated objective. Omaha, Pointe Du Hoc and other sites would follow, but we wanted to begin here first.

John was holding the *West Point Atlas of Wars* and I had S. L. A. Marshall's *Night Drop*. Per our internal Standard Operating Procedure (SOP), he would find the precise locations and I would recount the actions.

La Fière was greatly anticipated by us both as the penultimate action of the 82nd in Normandy. This was before the surge of present-day tourists and events. The road was empty and the land was flat, broken by several low hedgerows and the occasional quizzical cow. Our berets dripped with the misting rains.

Suddenly behind us, a car approached. It halted beside us and a florid red face draped in white hair leaned out and in a clear Boston accent said, "Are you guys Airborne?"

I replied, "Yes. 509th, Italy. We're going to La Fière Bridge"

Quickly responding, he said, "So are we. 82nd. Get in."

With that, we met the trio that would take us around the area where they had fought, recounted the stories of each site in the first person, and ensured that we were fed, hydrated, and had shelter from the rain. Out from the car came former Private First Class/Pathfinder Bob Murphy (1-505th), Sergeant O. B. Hill (1-508th) and Corporal Dave Jones (1-508th).

Our rucks in the trunk, we piled into the back of an already crowded vehicle and headed toward La Fière. They seemed as excited to be with us as we them. O. B. Hill had a considerable chest and Jones was about 6'4". As clowns in the circus, we contorted ourselves to meet the space available, but were more than happy for the physical inconvenience. The rucks were getting heavy.

Quickly arriving at La Fière, Murphy pulled to the side of the road, stopped the car and we all untangled ourselves. This was the first time I had the opportunity to see the three. O. B. was relatively short, but well-built. Davey Jones loomed over us all and was the tall Jeff to the short, mutt-like O. B. Murphy was the conductor who vigorously slapped our shoulders and was clearly glad to meet us. For the next 40 years, he would be my guide, mentor, and bridge between the Originals and the active-duty troops of today.

Based on the mutual enthusiasm for the engagement, the veterans decided that each would take us to where they had landed and recount the story of their time. Murphy said he would go last. We squeezed ourselves in the car and took an obscure track that carried us west.

Initially, we asked about La Fière as it was the greatest focus of our trip. We had studied the actions and understood this was, perhaps, the most crucial event for the 82nd in Normandy. Bob assured that we would return and he would describe the events. With that, and a clear command directive, we went back to the car.

Winding through a rolling hedgerowed land, we suddenly emerged into the village of Chef-du-Pont—the other key bridge and the principal objective of the 508th Parachute Infantry Regiment. O. B. kept up a rolling commentary as we passed through and along the narrow causeway that coursed the lower Merderet River. We continued toward Picauville when O. B. loudly exclaimed, "That's it. There it is."

That was a large, square two-story house just off of the road. We stopped in front and got out. O. B. proceeded to tell us about it with Jones adding comments.

Nearby, O. B. and Jones had landed in the water on the edge of the flooded ground. Their parachutes had inflated with the wind which providentially blew them toward land where they were deposited on the bank. They could see numerous of their companions who had dropped in the water either struggling or drowning.

They found each other in the gloom and attempted to determine their location, which they knew was not where they were supposed to be. After some careful reconnoitering of the road net, Jones said he believed he knew their location.

As a member of the 508th S2 section, he had intensely studied the imagery of the area, and the road net and farm houses were familiar. They were about 2 miles west of where they should have been and astride the key road leading to the bridge at Chef-du-Pont, the key objective of the 508th. O. B. decided then to fight the war where they were since he recognized key terrain when he saw it.

By 0400, O. B. and Jones, moving along the water's edge, had collected a total of 28 people, all of lesser rank than O. B. At the age of 19, he would be their leader. With the early light of 6 June, O. B. spotted the farm building and determined to make a stand there as well as to block the road. Positions were hastily established and soon German elements began to probe from the west.

Sighting tanks, O. B. told his men to hold their fire rather than reveal their positions. From his position on the second floor, he watched the tanks and infantry approach, wary but unaware. For whatever reason, the lead tank decided to pull off the road and take a defilade position under the extended porch.

The tank commander, dressed in Panzer black, emerged from the turret and looked around. O. B., hiding on the porch, took out a Gammon grenade and stealthily reached over the railing and dropped it. The grenade, highly sensitive, went right down the turret between the commander and the lip of the cupola. It exploded loudly and in O. B.'s words: "He popped out like a champagne cork and came up to me and then down like on an elevator."

The Germans quickly retreated, uncertain as to the American strength.

O. B. walked us around the farm buildings outlining where his men were placed and described the action. From this position, his small force held an effective roadblock until they were relieved by advancing elements of the 90th Division in the afternoon of 9 June. O. B. then showed us a photo of his men by the house. O. B. was in the front with his distinct figure, their leader at the age of 19.

Cal and I were definitely impressed by the initiative taken by these men and could clearly see where they had been emplaced and their excellent fields of fire. This was a professional position that Fort Benning would have approved.

Piling back into the car, we retraced our steps, arriving back at La Fière. Murphy pulled into the narrow farm road accessing Le Manoir, the stone building complex that dominated the scene. Here, he introduced us to Mr. Leroux, the owner at the time of the event.

Like eager puppies, we followed Murphy and Leroux to the stone work sheds next to the main house. Murphy showed us the extensive bullet pocks against the walls and described how elements of the 508th and 505th cleared the area after fierce fighting throughout the morning of 6 June.

Mr. Leroux then invited us into his house, almost leveled between 6 and 9 June. He proudly showed us several shiny copper bullets embedded in the winding staircase where a trooper with a Thompson submachine gun had cleared the final holdouts. He also showed us an album with black and white pictures of his farm and buildings after the battle. The roofs were collapsed, walls blown down, and rubble strewed the courtyard. He was obviously proud of the role his farm played and was eager to show us the place, not as tourists, but as active-duty Airborne troops.

Murphy then led us across the road to the north side of La Fière, a bare hill overlooking the river, now receded from its D-Day flooding. The meadow bounding the river was a lush green as it flowed as far as the eye could see to the north and as far as Chef-du-Pont in the south. The river itself was just a trace of flowing water, less than a foot deep and 10 feet wide.

Murphy moved us across the side of the hill until we were approximately halfway across. He stopped and waved toward the meadow, indicating the original water line, now outlined by a small hedge trace paralleling a small farm road leading to the north. On that trace, 1-505 defended the bridge.

Murphy recounted how the battle ebbed and flowed to defend the area, pointed to where Marcus Heim and Lenold Peterson had stopped three tanks with their bazooka and where Sergeant Bill Owens made what appeared to be his last stand.

Murphy then paused from his rapid fire narration. He pointed toward the high ground behind Le Manoir as the location of Lieutenant John "Red Dog" Dolan, commander of A Company 1-505. By late afternoon of 6 June, Dolan was the effective battalion commander and Owens the ranking survivor of the company defending the ground.

Pointing to it, he said that at a critical point with the position about to be overrun, Sergeant Owens, now the ranking member of Company A, told Murphy to get to Dolan, describe their situation and ask for guidance.

Murphy gestured to where he low-crawled to protected ground and moved to Dolan. There, he briefed Dolan. Dolan took out a message book and quickly wrote on the pad telling Murphy to take it to Owens. He had scribbled,

There is no better place to die.

Murphy related how he moved back with the ground swept by bullets and mortars impacting throughout the transit. Owens read the note and shouted to the small remaining force: "We stay."

With that, they did. Murphy was clearly still in awe of Owens' demeanor and presence of mind under the circumstances. He said that he became closely attached to him throughout the rest of the war and was with him at *Market Garden* and the Bulge. His affection for the man transcended the 34 years since they had last met.

At this time, 1979, the area had no markers or monuments, only the original land, largely untouched. The rough trace of positions could be discerned as well as the narrow winding causeway whose capture would allow the entire western invasion effort to succeed.

The overall apparent insignificance of the land was striking when considering the exceptionally fierce combat that occurred. Ground that the U.S. Army Historian, Brigadier General S. L. A. Marshall called the bloodiest small unit struggle in the experience of American arms. Only these personal tour guides marked the way.

Murphy, O. B., and Jones, with their matter-of-fact descriptions, lack of bravado and sense of detail, eagerly brought us into their fold and we quickly became attached, as only those with a shared experience can. Cal and I were easily able to transcend time, be with them in their positions, and see the events as they lived them. It was a remarkable day and somewhat life altering.

Other experiences with the many veterans would follow, but this day was and always will be uniquely special.

CHAPTER 3

The Open Door

Everyone has a dream or a fantasy. Mine—for many years—was to jump into Normandy as an 82nd trooper. Sometimes dreams become reality and I realized mine on the 40th anniversary of D-Day as the commander of troops for the 82nd Airborne on their first return to Normandy since 6 June 1944. This led to everything that follows.

As Commander of 2-505, I had suggested to Major General Jim Lindsay, that the 82nd return to Normandy for the 40th Anniversary. The division had not been back to France since 6 June 1944 and this was long overdue for the division, the nation, and our Airborne veterans. He approved, and I began a year of preparing the handpicked soldiers from throughout the division for this historic return. We established a reading program as well as historical reviews. Each regimental unit and support element had to study and brief the events and actions of their veteran predecessors. One of my tasks, and most personally rewarding, was to talk to some of the key players of the division on D-Day as well as the enlisted soldiers who did the heavy lifting. On several occasions, they talked to the assembled soldiers who would retrace their path. These talks and the subsequent history lessons transformed this from another task to be accomplished to a personal quest and homage of remembrance to those that had gone before.

General Jim Gavin, though frail and somewhat hesitant in speech, clearly showed the fire and strength that made him the most revered of combat leaders. He addressed our group directly, said what a wonderful honor it would be to return, and that we were going to be successful in any battlefield and any war because we were Airborne and there weren't any better soldiers in the world. When he finished, we knew we would go wherever he directed. Later, a veteran from the 505, Bill Sullivan, told us that his most significant personal moment came when in England, General Gavin stood on a jeep hood to address the 505th Parachute Infantry Regiment and said, "I will not send you to Normandy, I will take you."

Leadership cannot be taught but in the most cursory way. General Gavin was born with qualities in his core that were clear to us and consistently reinforced by the veterans. If he would take us, we would all surely follow.

General Matthew Ridgway was interviewed by me at his home near Pittsburgh. He was in his nineties and still active, engaged and enthused with life. He recounted the training in England and the immense pride he held for the soldiers and their ability to overcome the worst of circumstances. He addressed actions in North Africa, Sicily, Salerno, and Normandy. In his kitchen, he lost 40 years of age and was back on the ground of which he spoke. The immensity of his pride in his soldiers was clear. For all of his titles, ranks, and positions, his time as commander of the 82nd and its soldiers was paramount in his personal honors list. Looking into his dark eagle eyes combined with his direct delivery, there was no doubt you would do what he told you to and that it was the right and only answer. The measure of the man who saved our army in Korea had never changed from what the troopers knew in Africa.

General Ben Vandervoort spoke to us on several occasions as he lived relatively close by in Hilton Head. He was always humble, direct, and matter of fact. You didn't realize he was a god from Olympus unless you were paying close attention. He had a great humanity and an immensity of character as well as a very clear vision of what had to be done and how it had to be done. Any soldier that served with him knew he was in the presence of someone very special and would probably be much better for the association. He didn't advertise as he didn't need to.

By late May of 1984, our group got on the C-130s and headed to England to begin this voyage of remembrance. Each of the 350 soldiers had realized his own epiphany and the legacy he was tracing. More than one soldier told me, referring to the many veterans we had encountered, *We will not fail you.* A sense of purpose and dedication was clear to us all.

Our force of about 350 Airborne soldiers, with the new Division Commanding General, Ed Trobaugh, assembled at RAF Lyneham much as the Originals did on their day of days. Other than a difference in aircraft—C-130s for C-47s—the scene would have been very familiar to the Originals that gave us all a sense of poignancy and reflection. Many veterans had followed us throughout our England tour and were at the airfield to mingle and see us off.

The aircraft were lined on the ramp, doors open, with each stick of fully loaded soldiers sitting under the shade of the wings with their equipment and parachutes in various stages of dress and undress. Ones and twos were lined behind the aircraft on the edge of the grass relieving themselves—an event all the veterans volunteered was a direct reflection of their activities on D-Day eve. Jeeps were running back and forth with crews and messages. For myself, I could close my eyes and relive what must have been and now understood why we had so ardently wished to participate—now we were there.

Slowly, with full gear and a non-historic sunny sky, we loaded through the rear ramp and found our places on the red nylon outboard and inboard seats. I was sitting in the third position on the stick and the commanding general at the eighth—where we guessed he would land mid-drop zone. As the Airborne commander, I had on a headset connecting me with the pilot and crew. As this event was drawing a huge population at Sainte-Mère-Église and we had half the brass and politicos in the world engaged, we were getting constant changes, adjustments, and "suggestions," many of which we ignored. I talked to Captain Dave McNeil from the drop zone and he indicated the largest and most significant issue was people on the drop zone and that the gendarmes were only beginning to deal with the problem.

I was called forward by the pilot just before takeoff. He was an older colonel who shook my hand and introduced himself. He said he had a special request—if it was OK with us, he would like to fly the course with the doors open as they did on the original run. I thought it a good idea but said I had to get permission from the commanding general. General Trobaugh, overcome with an avalanche of public relations issues—not his forte—nodded and said OK. I gave the pilot a thumbs up. I had no idea beyond what he stated as to why this was important. The engines began their rev up to takeoff and with a sudden release, we were rolling down the runway following the path of history.

Though the noise and blurring images through the now open doors were momentarily disconcerting, they brought a strange peacefulness and isolation to each of us. It was clear that this was not an ordinary trip. If anything, we were in a time machine. I looked back on the troops and each was looking out the doors and immersed in the residue of his thoughts, distilled by all that had taken place to this moment. This was a serious moment and not just another jump.

Before the jump, we briefed our plan and that of the original drop and had a number of Airborne veterans—U.S. and British—talk to us on the ramp, among them Lieutenant Colonel Ben Vandervoort, my predecessor battalion commander that night and Lieutenant General Napier Crookenden, who jumped with the British 5 Para on D-Day. There was a consistency about all of their discussions. They displayed no bravado or ego, which would have been expected and accepted in the light of history, but rather joked and made matter of fact comments about the great weights they carried and the difficulty in getting into the aircraft, the problems with relieving themselves once loaded, excited platoon leaders yelling orders, and mass confusion as to who and what went on which aircraft.

One enlisted veteran described the incident where a Gammon grenade went off, destroying an adjacent 82nd aircraft and killing part of the stick on the ground just before takeoff. He related that one of the shaken survivors emerged from the aircraft with remnants of people and explosives on his uniform, struggled toward the closest aircraft occupied by the veteran describing the incident and was pushed in the door by the ground crew—the veteran said, "He wasn't going to stay and we weren't going to leave him."

Said in a quiet, unemotional manner, it made a distinct impact on all of us. Through the many individual veteran recountings, there was a very clear pride in doing what they did and an even clearer conviction that they would succeed. Most of my troopers had never heard a shot fired in anger and most wondered how they would perform in combat. Every participating trooper knew he was taking part in a personally important moment and having the rare gift of being able to walk and talk with the ghosts.

Ben Vandervoort said the 24-hour delay on 4/5 June wasn't wasted on much sleep—rather lots of poker, craps, conversation, letter writing, re-checking gear, and just trying to get to the mess hall and back while eating in the pouring rain. No pub crawl, which was a disappointment to many. The next day was as much an emotional drain as a break. Most of the sleep achieved was under the wing of C-47s in the early evening of 5 June, a fact that they would pay for later.

The invasion aircraft, like ours, took off in almost broad daylight—around 2300 British Double Summer Time, and blended into huge circles until all were airborne and then began to fly in a V of V's south and east. We followed in their wake.

The veterans stood by the runway and waved at us as we passed. What a flood of memories they must have held. A consistent theme from the veterans—from generals to privates—was the tremendous feeling of confidence and personal awe they felt as they looked out the door of their aircraft en route to Normandy. For the first time, they were able to put the true size and resource endeavor together in a personal visceral sense. It was the one binding, overarching impression that uniformly affected them all and provided a tremendous sense of confidence—confidence in themselves and in the mission and was perhaps the single most unifying impression of that night. Generals Ridgway, Taylor, and Gavin, Lieutenant Colonel Vandervoort, Private First Class Murphy, and countless other Airborne veterans had the same view out the door and the same lasting impressions. This was a bonding moment that is so crucial to a soldier's mental state going into combat.

During the invasion, most jump aircraft had their doors removed prior to takeoff from England. This permitted the jump masters (the senior officer or NCO on board) to have an unimpeded view of the sea and land below. For the Airborne, that was virtual daylight as the Pathfinders departed at roughly 2200 British Double Summer Time. For the others, while it was after dusk, the full moon and the receding twilight still provided sufficient visual reference to the horizon and the English Channel below.

As our aircraft ran down the runway with each soldier resting in his personal world, I closed my eyes with those comments in my mind and reflected on this shared moment with those that I had interviewed prior to this flight. Ben Vandervoort, Jim Gavin, Matt Ridgway, Bob Murphy, Bob Piper, Charles Timmes, and Bill Sullivan independently had the same impression and reaction.

In later conversations with veterans I always made a point to ask them what they saw on their flight and their thoughts. Universally, their impression was of the impact of the physical reality of the immensity of the undertaking and their individual immediate absolute confidence in the outcome. Our flight was insignificant compared to that but immensely important to each of us.

Our flight was in brilliant English color—the verdant green of the pastures below, then the white chalky beach, and the deep blue-black English Channel with high patches of bright white Monet-like clouds stretching to the horizon and a brilliant golden rising morning sun burning off the evening dew from the farm fields below—D-Day in our minds was no longer in black and white. D+40 years was in brilliant color.

The 250-knot wind coursed easily by the fuselage, enveloping each of us in a sensory canopy permitting the deepest personal reflections. Unlike all other Airborne movements, I didn't see a single soldier sleeping—like me, each was in his own world taking a trip in which they were well-versed but had never replicated. As I looked down both sides of the aircraft, I could see the intensity in their eyes that had been born by their exposure to this history and their part in it.

As we reached flight altitude, I was called on the headphones and asked for the second time to go to the cockpit. Somewhat bewildered, I struggled there with all my gear and the pilot got out of his chair—highly unusual—extended his hand, looked me in the eye and said, "This is my last flight. I am retiring after this mission as flight lead and from the Air Force Reserve. 40 years ago tonight I was flying a C-47 as flight lead for elements of the 82nd Airborne. Thank you for making this happen. This is one of the greatest moments of my life."

I was stunned speechless but returned his handshake and gave him a salute and said "Thank you," returning to my stick with a much clearer understanding of his original request. I mulled over what he must have seen and carried with him to be remembered at that moment.

The red light came on just before the Channel coast. The other jumpmasters and I stood up, hooked up, and looked at the sticks. My right foot was hooked in the open frame and the wind blew briskly by my uniform and equipment. Each soldier in line—inboard and outboard stick—looked up anxiously and alert awaiting instructions as they had done 40 years before.

The broken checkerboard fields of Normandy swept as a blur past my eyes as we went through the timeless rituals of the jump commands: Stand up. Hook up. Check static lines. Check equipment. Sound off for equipment check. Stand by. Looking at the men and their demeanor, they all knew that not only were they jumping for the sake of history, they were part of it. It was a moment.

At the two minute warning, I placed both feet flush on the fuselage frame, reached out with my left hand, grasped the wind deflector, and leaned out the door into the rush to confirm the drop zone. I was momentarily transfixed by the warm humid air and wind blurred vision. Then the landmarks became crystal clear in my mind—Vandervoort had said he flew his route on the map and aerial photos in his mind a hundred times so he could pick out key route features and ensure his bearings. (This was prescient as he had the pilot turn off the red light once when he saw the pilot had misread the landmarks. Had he followed the sequence, his stick would have landed miles from their intended drop zone).

In the brilliant morning sun, I had it much easier and without ground fire. Clearly distinguishable below were the key 101st objective towns with their distinctive church towers, Saint-Côme-du-Mont and Sainte-Marie-Du-Mont, and further was Utah Beach and the critical causeways. To the north, Omaha Beach and the receding coast toward the British beaches could be readily seen. Then suddenly the patchwork quilt of the Norman fields and small villages and bisecting roads came up. Then dead ahead, Sainte-Mère-Église, distinct on the main Cherbourg–Carentan highway with its dramatic church square. Just in front of it was a small curling stream of yellow smoke marking the drop zone. Clear spot! Thumbs up for the jump master and troops. Stand in the door! The loadmaster stood to my rear with his fingers in front of my face counting the last five seconds... Green light. Go! We were jumping into a time warp. The first two jumpers were away and I inserted myself in the column with the jump master taking the door. I watched my chute deploy, straightened out the lines, and then looked down.

The drop zone was a sea of humanity. Women, children, men, gendarmes, French and U.S. Army personnel running across the narrow fields so thick they blotted out the ground. I couldn't see an open spot to steer to and tried to move closest to the smoke. The drop zone was a series of typical small hedgerow fields designated La Londe and had been theoretically isolated hours earlier by the gendarmes. However, within a couple of hours of the jump, thousands of French infiltrated everywhere in their intense desire to see this return and touch the successors of those that came before and delivered them. In Normandy, the invasion has always been current events and those that participated are truly treated as gods on earth never to be forgotten. As surrogates, the first return en masse was a moment to be remembered by us but to be treasured by them.

In the air, I had this vision which I always carried of the Sainte-Mère-Église church stained glass—of the Airborne soldier suspended with the town on fire with raised knees. I assumed that pose for a moment in homage and then went about my business of looking for a safe spot to land.

Fearing to hurt someone and with no clear spot of ground to see, I tried to twist away from the closest mass but simply slammed into the ground, my parachute collapsing over several milling families. While still lying on my back, I was grabbed by several small boys, a man, and a woman—the man shook my hand and the boys grabbed my chute and helped me roll it up. I couldn't see a soldier for the exuberantly happy humanity surrounding each of us. We were the surrogates for those people whose parents and grandparents could not perform the same act of gratitude 40 years before. The 82nd Airborne had returned to France, but in truth it had never left—nor will it. The cemetery at Omaha Beach attests to that.

CHAPTER 4

Some Shit Happened Here

I begin every staff ride period with an overview of Normandy and events with a large map in the city hall of Sainte-Mère-Église. Due to scheduling issues, this is usually done in the late afternoon of the troops' arrival from the States. They are tired, hungry, and anxious to get some sleep, but like soldiers everywhere, they dutifully follow instructions and sit in front of me.

Standing in front of the room as the troops shuffled in with the normal daze of an 18-hour trip on C-130s from Fort Bragg and Fort Benning, I noticed one sergeant in particular. He had the easy efficiency of one used to leading under stress and with the natural response of men willing to commit themselves. He spoke in a low tone, primarily with gestures. His men immediately responded through their haze and sat down with alert eyes. As he checked his men, our eyes met. Both satisfied with the result, we returned to our tasks.

He and his men were part of what the Army calls a "Good deal trip." Yet after the seemingly endless plane ride, MRE meals, and expeditionary quality bathroom options, he and the troops were not yet ready to call it that.

For whatever reason, I noted his alertness as well as his demonstrated control and response of his men. This was a reliable combat soldier.

The following day, I walked a site with the mass of men, briefing them and taking questions as always. I noted him off to the side in a position where he could see me, his men, and the land. Again, he caught my eye with his presence. I saw he had a combat patch from the Rangers and his current organizational patch. He had probably served from private to platoon sergeant in the Sandboxes and served well with first class units multiple times. He had a Combat Infantry Badge and the sharp analytical eyes of one used to very kinetic moments. He lived on the cutting edge, and even here he had the quick alertness of the combat mind.

As the day wore on, I could see that he was becoming immersed in the place and the moment. He transferred from a person controlling his men as a matter of emphasis to absorbing the story of what had occurred at this time and place. His trained eyes analyzed the terrain, calculated the enemy forces, his own resources, and the necessary resolution. He became the man on the spot 75 years ago. Mentally, he maneuvered his men as if he were Bill Owens at La Fière, Turner Turnbull at Neuville, Bud Lomell at Pointe du Hoc, and John L. Hall at Omaha Beach. Here was a man with multiple hard combat tours who was clearly transfixed by his predecessors' actions. As only one who has experienced the facts of combat, he appreciated the moment. He had bridged the span of time and become part of the place.

Walking back from a site, he moved to the front of his men, an exception from his normal positioning, and tugged on my sleeve.

We slowed our pace and catching my eye, he said with clear reverence, "Sir. Some shit happened here."

That sergeant and that statement made all my visits worthwhile.

PART II
The Where, The When, The How

CHAPTER 5

Why Normandy?

After the Tehran Conference in 1943, the Combined Chiefs of Staff charged General Eisenhower with the following orders:

> You will enter the continent of Europe and in conjunction with other Allied nations, undertake operations aimed at the heart of Germany and the destruction of her armed forces...

Then, the question was where and how. There were limited options that had already been considered before Ike was chosen. Well before Eisenhower's appointment at the Casablanca Conference on 12 April 1943, the Combined Chiefs created a paper planning headquarters called Chief of Staff, Supreme Allied Command (COSSAC), under Lieutenant General Sir Frederick Morgan, to start the planning process. With a robust Allied intelligence and operations staff, he began to search for options.

In this, he was driven by several primary considerations:

This must be a risk mitigation strategy to minimize the ability of the Germans to use their strongest asset—combined arms mechanized forces—against the immediate lodgment. This consideration was based on the experience to date with like German forces that had usually bested Allied elements when operating with maneuver force options. Simply put, the Germans, if marginally better than the Allies on the point of penetration, would likely defeat the invasion. This could not be risked. Consequently, locations that were unfavorable for heavy mechanized forces must be chosen.

This dictated that the physical characteristics of the selected area must minimize German advantages and enhance Allied likelihood of defending it with limited initial forces.

Choice must enhance the significant advantage the Allies held in the application of massed logistics. After a lodgment was secured, the Allies would pour an overwhelming mass of reinforcements ashore that would be unstoppable regardless of German reinforcements. This necessitated one or more deep water ports that could quickly become operational.

Morgan conducted in-depth studies of all options in Europe with these factors in mind. He quickly discarded Norway because "to debouch therefrom southward in battle array would be quite something." Prevailing winds off the North Sea made beach landings in Belgium and Holland very risky. They also lacked outlets through the waterlogged lands that were subject to widespread inundation. Concurrently, Portugal and Spain south of the Pyrenees Mountains were far from objectives inside Germany and would create both major political and logistical problems.

The focus on northern France became the only viable option. The studies indicated that the beaches at Dunkirk and in Brittany were much too small to support amphibious assaults and lacked port capacity. The winnowing process thus "whittled themselves down to two: direction Pas de Calais or direction western Normandy."

Calais at first seemed attractive, because the 22-mile cross-Channel trip allowed maximum fighter coverage, which would be a significant combat multiplier. It would also minimize shipping requirements with very rapid turnaround times between England and the beaches.

From a maneuver perspective, the straight-line routes to the German border measured barely 150 miles. However, this was not a one-sided analysis because defenders could read maps as well, which is why the Germans had made Calais the core of Atlantic Wall fortifications. Beaches were small, widely spaced, and exposed to storms, which meant that a cohesive initial landing would be difficult. Seaports along that stretch of coast were inadequate even in perfect conditions, and actions to seize Antwerp or Le Havre would create open flank opportunities for the Germans for the full distance.

The only remaining option for France was the Bay of the Seine between Caen and the Cotentin Peninsula. It was better sheltered than Calais and had generally contiguous capacities coupled with excellent port facilities at Cherbourg. Best of all, the entire area was judged poor for any mechanized maneuver forces.

The distances, though greater than Calais, were within reasonably supportive air and sea distances from England. Air power, of which the Allies had a decided advantage, could be used to isolate the area and limit reinforcements. In sum, bad for the Germans could be good for the Allies. In this choice, Morgan saw significant physical advantages.

The lodgment area suggested occupied the departments of Manche and Calvados (the equivalent of U.S. counties), both bounded on the north by the Bay of the Seine and on the south by rough, wooded terrain that the locals call "bocage." The term is roughly translated as rolling hills interspersed with creeks, rivers, and woodlands. The dominate feature was hedgerowed fields, seen on photos but not yet fully appreciated for their defensive advantages.

Cross compartments were common, with wide open spaces conspicuously absent. The region has numerous swampy low ground areas and a significant amount called the "Prairies Marcageuses." This was essentially a low swamp complex somewhat similar to Georgia's Okefenokee Swamp, between Carentan and the beach area. Interspersed throughout the Cotentin were dikes, drainage ditches, and locks along inland waterways.

Once settling upon this area as the best option that met the required conditions, the question was: where do we land?

Where Do We Land?

This became a two-part question: What gross physical area was to be the invasion site and what specific beaches would support that decision?

The larger Normandy area essentially self-selected. Any landing in Normandy would be defined by very limited choices, which became a domino effect. Beaches were few and well defined. Key military objectives would drive the ultimate choices.

Key in the planners' minds was the necessity for a deep-water port. The only one available was Cherbourg to the extreme north of the Cotentin Peninsula. Le Havre was deemed too far and too well defended. Cherbourg dictated the Cotentin.

Risk mitigation meant sealing off access by the Germans with their mechanized elements to the entire lodgment area. That meant the Ranville Ridge/Caen complex features to the west must be held. Between the two was about 75 miles of beaches.

Seizure of this broad area would provide reasonably efficient defense in the early stages as well as allow for buildup of forces for an ultimate breakout in the Saint-Lô area and a thrust toward Brittany and the German border.

Once the gross Normandy area was selected, it then became a staff exercise in beach specifics for the posited invasion site. Normandy and the Bay of the Seine had issues that required serious study before specific beaches could be selected.

The first was the tide. The bay tides were severe with the significant currents that usually ran parallel to the southern- and eastern-facing beaches.

Beach gradients in the area were extremely shallow. In some cases, more than 1,000 yards of sand would be exposed at mean low tide.

Exits off the beaches were generally very limited and, in some cases, almost non-existent. Exits were essential to get forces off the beach and, in the interior, to make space for the reinforcements and adequate defensive and maneuver space to secure the force as a whole.

Lastly, the English Channel weather was notoriously fickle and subject to significant rain, wind, and storms.

Intensive studies by the intelligence planners, including human observations, pre-war postcard analysis, and exhaustive photography, made it clear there were limited to no options.

Utah

Utah Beach resolved three requirements: it was close to Cherbourg, the key to the invasion; it had access to the narrow neck of the Cotentin Peninsula, allowing it to be cut off by Allied forces; and it provided a quick severing of the German defensive road network in the area.

Utah had 4 miles of level, firm sand and minimal tide issues. Defenses were weak and multiple access roads emanated from the beach. While these crossed flooded ground, they quickly gained the high ground. Utah became the anchor on which the invasion depended.

Omaha

Omaha Beach provided for three requirements: it connected Utah with the British beaches, sealing the entire lodgment area in a near continuous line; it ensured German forces could not take advantage of a gap and defeat the Utah/British areas in flank; and it provided excellent maneuver force for build-up allowing options in any direction.

Regardless, Omaha also had several issues, recognized by the planners as being very problematic. The immediate Omaha Beach areas (Omaha and Pointe du Hoc) were protected by steep cliffs ranging from 100 to 200 yards in height. Further, Omaha was concave, allowing an enfilade defense in decent depth, the only beach of the five to do so.

The tides were very steep, exposing a distance of 1,000 yards plus from low water to high water obstacles.

The currents ran parallel to the beach, which created significant channels/runnels that could be highly disruptive to the initial assault.

Exits off the beach were very small and easily defended. However, once gained, the land behind was relatively open.

The Germans recognized the crucial nature of the Omaha area if an invasion of Normandy was to be attempted. Hence, they spent considerable time and resources in developing defenses. All daily intelligence noted this emphasis.

Regardless of the issues, Omaha was viewed as absolutely essential and the risks necessitated by the requirements. This was the only beach of the five that had two divisions immediately dedicated to the initial assault with an airborne assault considered on the high ground in support.

Gold

Progressing west, approximately 5 miles separated Gold Beach from Omaha. Gold was viewed as the connective tissue between the three British beaches and the U.S. forces. While it had no major tactical objectives other than Port En-Bessin and

Bayeux, its positioning would prevent German movement along the parallel road network to the beaches.

The nature of the area was similar to the other two British beaches and markedly different from the U.S. landing sites.

The landing beach was quite flat and protected from the worst tidal and current effects. Concurrently, it had a deep-water aspect much closer to shore than either Omaha or Utah. Furthermore, the beach area was bounded by low sand dunes, absent of traditional defensive land forms.

There were extensive built-up areas on and behind the beach. It was highly urbanized and significant quality road networks projected from the beach allowing rapid movement inland.

Juno

Juno Beach was reserved for the Canadian Army with the crucial tasks of seizing Caen (the major urban complex in the area) and the all-important heights behind on Carpiquet Ridge to be used for tactical fighter strips by D+2.

It was very similar in characteristics to Gold, with a greater density of building complexes and an excellent road net. It was this road net that would hopefully allow the Canadian forces to attack Caen on D-Day.

Sword

Sword Beach was unique. The beach area ranged from a half mile at Lion-Sur-Mer to more than a mile at Ouistreham on the extreme western edge. The low water-mark edge just covered a relatively steep drop off that made it very favorable for the planned Mulberry deep-water harbor (Mulberry harbors were temporary portable facilities facilitating the rapid offloading of cargo onto beaches).

The beach area itself was heavily urbanized, consisting of an occupied beach resort area, numerous houses, and a seawall protecting the houses along almost the entire beach.

As would be expected in a resort area, there were numerous well-paved roads leading from the beach inland to the key tactical objectives of Ranville Ridge and Pegasus Bridge.

Planners recognized that the beaches identified were the only options available based upon the objectives selected. Cherbourg, Ranville Ridge, the Cotentin Peninsula, and Sainte-Mère-Église dictated the landing areas.

The reverse/north area in the Bay of Biscay was too far away to be feasible and did nothing to provide for an area unacceptable to armor. While each beach had specific issues, it was thought that with air superiority, naval supremacy, and surprise, all concerns could be mitigated. Accordingly, the forces assigned to each beach were tailored for specific tasks as key terrain dictated.

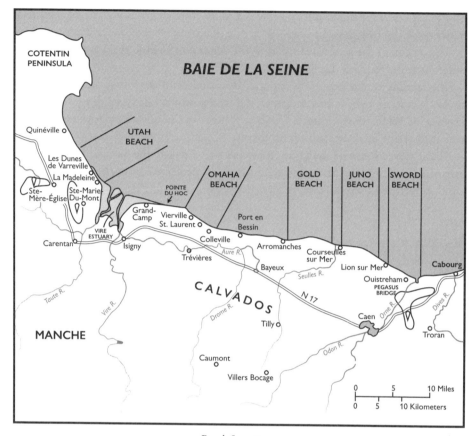

Beach Locations

Key Terrain

Today, the Army identifies a broad engagement area by a given element as Battle Space Management. In 1944, this management meant identification of both enemy elements as well as key geographical terrain. This is ground which, when controlled, markedly enhances the success in that area or provides for follow-on operations. Normandy provided a variety of key terrain features.

Beach Exits

Getting off the beaches with significant force to the inland ground was crucial to succeed. Defense of the thin lodgment area could only be achieved by building depth for artillery, tactical fighter strips, logistics, and armor. All planners envisioned exits to the inland grounds by H+8 hours if not sooner. Under no circumstances could the Germans be allowed to attack the landing forces on the beach.

The exits ranged from well paved in the British sector to almost non-existent in the U.S. sector. In the case of Utah, the causeway exits were more than a mile to the high ground to the west.

Omaha had tightly constricted mixed dirt and macadam tracks, but quickly entered into the high ground and relatively flat terrain.

Dams and Locks

These features were unique to the American sector at La Barquette, north and east of Carentan. The confluence of the Douve and Merderet Rivers were controlled by this complex. Since 1942, the Germans had managed the locks to time with high tide, trapping two plus years of water behind it and flooding an area that coursed more than 30 miles north.

The limited road net between Omaha and Utah was judged as vulnerable to flooding if the Germans controlled the several smaller locks in the area. This could impede operations to join the two forces.

Bridges

Bridges in the lodgment area took on two aspects—those that were essential to immediate control to isolate the area and allow rapid reinforcement, and those that were German controlled that permitted their reinforcing units to move to the beaches.

Key bridges in the British sector were those that controlled the Orne and Caen Canal. Both were located semi-contiguously in an area of less than 200 yards square at Benouville. These had to be seized to prevent German interference at Sword as well as be used later, to transport reinforcements to the west.

The bridges connecting the lodgment area were identified early as requiring destruction to prevent access by German reinforcements. These were over all the primary major river systems deep within the occupied territories. Isolation of the battlefield became a key requirement of the planners and necessitated Eisenhower's forcing the issue, as Air Force leadership did not feel them more important than their strategic targeting of oil fields and industrial facilities. These bridges had to be destroyed prior to the invasion occurring.

Coastal Fortifications

Fortifications of some description were part of all the invasion areas. However, two were viewed as especially crucial and took on special significance and attention: the batteries at Pointe du Hoc and Merville. Failure to seize and hold either would risk the entire venture.

Pointe du Hoc was located approximately 4 miles east of Omaha Beach. It jutted into the ocean and was buttressed by cliffs exceeding 100 yards in height. It had been developed into a formidable artillery position by the French and then by the Germans, very intensively, from 1942 onward. It had five concrete gun positions, three of which were covered and fortified against anything the Allies could use against them. Each position was credited with holding a 150-mm artillery piece capable of ranging both Omaha and Utah beaches.

Infantry defenses were developed with primary focus on the landward side but with interior fighting and living quarters that provided a 360-degree defense from protected positions. The entire position was interconnected by underground tunnels and ringed with an open fighting trench. This trench protected the cliff side.

Merville Battery was a significant physical entity. It was about 2 miles from Sword Beach and just to the north of the town of Merville in an open field.

Unlike Pointe du Hoc, it was purpose built by the Germans and was extremely well constructed. The Organization Todt had applied its best efforts, with Rommel's constant urging. Its four large concrete bunkers were buried in the ground with steel doors and fighting ports. The concrete was more than 6 feet thick in some places and virtually invulnerable to bombs. Living quarters, ammo storage, and support facilities were independently housed in each main bunker.

Surrounding the position were several outer rings of triple strand concertina wire all protected by extensive minefields. The front of the position had a deep tank trap in addition to fencing and mines. Infantry bunkers had been placed throughout to provide interlocking fire against infantry. The entire position was accessed by underground tunnels.

The guns were thought to be Czech Skoda 150-mm pieces and could strike both Sword and Juno beaches. A large concrete observation bunker overlooked Sword to control fire.

Dominate Terrain

Only in the U.S. sector, adjacent to Utah, was the land itself a major factor for planners. In the other beach areas, other than the cliffs at Omaha, the inland ground was considered a minimal problem. This was not so for the Cotentin Peninsula.

This area was dominated by two major ridge lines. One stretched from just north of Carentan to several miles north of Saint-Côme-du-Mont, paralleling Utah. The other forked from a juncture with the latter ridgeline north of Carentan all the way through Sainte-Mère-Église to Cherbourg. Both would have to be contained and managed.

The Utah ridgeline, if held in force, would effectively block exits off Utah and stall the entire effort. The Sainte-Mère-Église ridge was the primary communication link between Carentan and Cherbourg and the lifeline for German reinforcements and control of the entire peninsula.

Urban Complexes

Planners noted three key urban areas that were integral to the short-term purpose of the invasion: Caen, Cherbourg, and Saint-Lô. Each had a key part to play in sequence and specific forces tailored to manage it. Caen was the only major city to be managed in the initial phase. Its occupation would control the major road networks in the area and provide a logistics base for follow-on operations. Cherbourg was the jewel in the crown. The necessity for a large deep-water port complex was the key requirement for the invasion. Cherbourg provided that within the secured confines of the Cotentin Peninsula. Its occupation would follow expansion from Utah and be the hub of the million and half men and equipment for the ultimate breakout to Berlin. Saint-Lô was identified as the point of departure for the breakout from Normandy and the assault to the west to clear Brittany, the rest of France, and thence to the Low Countries and Germany. It marked the beginning of significant mechanized maneuver room and had sufficient road networks to support the thrust from the beaches to the interior. But what then?

When Do We Land?

Once the location for the invasion had been decided, the issue then was "When do we land?" This question had two parts: both in larger sense and also in the more precise timing of the tides.

The first answer determined the second. The specific tide tables were known by day so it was only a matter of picking the date and then examining the tide tables for the desired hour of the invasion.

This could be done without a clear identification of the actual forces other than the notional—naval, airborne, and gliders. Each element had specific needs unique to it that had to be resolved individually and then in combination.

The beach obstacles noted in all reconnaissance imagery had to be cleared to permit reinforcements moving across the beach. This meant that they had to be cleared very quickly, within a single phase of the tide. There was significant early disagreement by the planners regarding a low tide or high tide landing. This was not a trivial argument due to the nature of the tides and their significant locational variance.

The high tide argument by the Army was that it allowed the force to get closest to the defenses at the initial assault and clear them. Then, the engineers could work back destroying obstacles as the tide revealed. The problem was that this required two actual tide flows as the support ships, the large flat bottomed Landing Ship, Tanks (LSTs), Landing Ship, Docks (LSDs), Landing Ship, Infantry (LSIs), and barges needed to offload as close to the beach roads as possible. It was deemed very problematic that all the wheeled vehicles could navigate wet sand in any volume.

The low tide argument by the Navy was that it immediately exposed the obstacles, allowing instant clearance so reinforcements could be brought in with the following tide. The belief being that pre-assault bombardments would eliminate most resistance and allow an engineer-heavy force in the initial phase. Hence, the long traverse from low tide to beach defenses, in some cases in excess of 1,500 yards, was not thought impractical.

The decision was ultimately decided by Admiral Bertram Ramsay, who ruled that the assault would be at extreme low tide, exposing the obstacles to allow immediate reinforcements. The need for a spring tide significantly limited potential invasion dates.

The planning problem for low tide was that it occurred at different times with virtually every beach. Ultimately, ramp down time varied from beach to beach between 0630 and 0730.

The decision to employ significant airborne forces dictated a full or near full moon. The airborne experience in Sicily demonstrated that a moon was necessary for both pilots and troops.

The pilots and jumpmasters needed the moon to illuminate geographic locations in order to ensure proper flight direction and location of the drop zones. There would be electronic assists for the pilots, but they were notoriously unreliable and the drop zones were very precise, small places. Pilot eyeballs would be crucial.

Concurrently, the jumpmasters controlling the drop itself had to be certain of the location when the green light came on. They would be given mosaic photographs of the route and follow the ground looking out the open door.

A full or near full moon, in confluence with favorable tide dates, further restricted scheduling options.

Days with full moon and spring tides were two three-day periods in June and one in July. The first window would be 5–7 June.

Once all these physical and geographical issues were identified and managed, the question for the planners and commanders was who goes and where do they go. These were difficult issues with much discussion and wrangling.

Summary

Planning for Normandy followed a domino pattern. Select an invasion area: Calais or Normandy. Then select the specific landing sites. Then select the date. Then the time. Once the physical aspects and schedule details were identified and the specific needs of the landing forces developed, exactly what forces landing where could be plugged in.

However, the commanders somewhat reversed this process regarding the Who and What.

CHAPTER 6

Ike as a Team Builder

I would rather allow a commander to come to his own conclusion than give an outright order that draws my same conclusion.

—DWIGHT EISENHOWER

No other single personality was as important to the successful invasion as Dwight Eisenhower. His unique and largely untested skills to that point made all the difference in terms of ability to pull together the many nations, personalities, and problems to be solved. As Supreme Commander, Mediterranean, Ike was little more than a figurehead. As Supreme Commander, Allied Expeditionary Force, he was, in fact, the supreme commander, in both title and persona.

Commanding this operation, arguably the most important single operation of the war to that point, was General Dwight Eisenhower. He had been selected by President Roosevelt in order to keep General George Marshall as commander of the entire U.S. Army. In 1940, Ike had been a lieutenant colonel, but by 1944, he was a four-star general responsible for bringing together the largest military operation ever assembled. His unusual character, persona, and management welded the disparate Allied forces into a focused, single-purpose force. It is doubtful any other personality of the moment could have done likewise—a point General Alan Brooke, British Chief of Staff, acknowledged. I think his example is foundational in understanding the composition and nature of the invasion and how such a monumental undertaking could be achieved. His example was and is unique to our experience and worthy of study.

Discussing Ike's attributes will better explain how success on 6 June was achieved. He was the steel that forged the force into a cooperative, coordinated body. It was not easy. He was the ultimate team leader.

Eisenhower and his ability to meld disparate Allies, strong egos, and competing agendas made D-Day and Normandy a success. It is doubtful any other personality could have achieved what he did with a tempered ego and the strategic sense of responsibility to the ultimate objective. He had to manage Field Marshal Bernard Montgomery, Charles de Gaulle, Winston Churchill, and George Marshall, a requirement that would surely test a saint.

I have read a great deal about the man, both positive and negative, from first person sources and analytical historians. Most importantly to me, I have had extensive discussions with his granddaughter, Susan Eisenhower, who had special insights into the man and, as a mature historian herself, studied the man with a balanced and insightful eye.

Within the space of 18 months, Dwight Eisenhower went from a colonel to a lieutenant general—all due to the sponsorship of George Marshall, the U.S. Army Chief of Staff. Marshall saw very quickly that Ike had a great grasp of both the strategic and tactical aspects of situations, was a very quick learner, had excellent communication skills, and possessed the unusual ability to get along with very diverse personalities and temperaments. These qualities would be continuously tried, tested, and honed to the point where, by war's end, the most senior leadership acknowledged that he and he alone had the ability to mold the successful team that he did. How did he do it?

He understood that staffs and units were composed of a grouping of individual thoughts, motivations, and desires. He viewed it as his job to provide them with the necessary confidence and motivation to do the very best job possible. This was especially so with the front-line fighters—the infantry, the Navy, and the Army Air Forces. Throughout his tenure as Supreme Commander, he used visits to these elements to both rejuvenate himself and to provide the most positive reinforcement to them. He told a graduating class of British Officer cadets in 1944:

> That cultivation of human understanding between you and your men is the one part that you must yet master, and you must master it quickly.

And he described his own methodology:

> I adopted a policy of circulating through the whole force to the full limit imposed by my physical considerations. I did my best to meet everyone from the general to private with a smile, a pat on the back, and definite interest in his problems.

With both his very divergent Allied staff and his face-to-face encounters with his operational forces from general to private, he exercised a highly developed listening ability, and wherever he went he asked questions. He welcomed complaints, and if it was in his power, he worked to improve the situation.

In his staff meetings, he listened much more than talked. He expected quality detail as that was one of his key personal traits, as attested to by both Marshall and Douglas MacArthur, who he served under in the Philippines. He restricted his specifics largely to the desired end result rather than paths to get there. His very austere and competent Chief of Staff, Lieutenant General Bedell Smith, was responsible for molding the staff work into a quality final product for his consumption.

A key point to Ike's management style was delegation of authority. He understood immediately that the scope and quantity of his tasks required that a great number of people be trusted to do their job without supervision. Therefore, he relied on his most senior advisors, generals, and admirals to know their people better than he and to select key staff members based on their own views of relative quality. He rarely, if ever, questioned a staff selection. But he was exceedingly diligent in selection of U.S. ground maneuver commanders down to and including regimental command. This was an area with which he had personal familiarity. These choices were always made with his immediate U.S. subordinate's input—primarily Lieutenant General Omar Bradley, who he trusted implicitly, and Lieutenant General Smith, who was responsible for the background homework.

Regarding other services—the Navy and Army Air Forces—he largely depended upon their internal selection systems. He also did this with the Allies, not knowing their internal personality history. He did make some exceptions based on exposure and personal preferences on his immediate staff. If he had an issue with a subordinate officer several levels down, he would have Smith engage the senior officer of the subject's nation and have a discussion. Never did he allow an officer of one nation to dress down an officer of another.

Key to Ike's success and a hallmark of his persona was a public attitude of humbleness. Having spent several years as MacArthur's aide, he could easily have slipped into a Napoleonic persona and developed a retinue of courtiers. He diligently avoided this. From the Italian campaign onward, he insisted that his residence and headquarters be relatively austere and simple. He worked to inculcate this approach with his subordinate generals with success (other than the general responsible for all supply and services, General John J. C. H. Lee, who consistently lived very well). Montgomery was a natural minimalist, always picking the simplest locations and this filtered down to his subordinate generals. Bradley, likewise, was very low key. The sum of this approach was that the subordinate soldiers saw that their seniors were not living a very different life than they, which provided a positive morale factor.

Ike had a healthy ego and a volcanic temper, but no one outside of his immediate staff knew this. In any public gathering or open forum, Ike was always quiet, attentive, and soft spoken. No matter how difficult or uncomfortable or bad a presentation or event might be, he kept his temper, was universally optimistic, and departed with a smile. It would be up to Lieutenant General Smith to make any necessary corrections in private.

Eisenhower truly believed that the job was bigger than the man, and that drove his leadership and management approach. As he told his son, Second Lieutenant John Eisenhower: "Always take your job seriously, never yourself."

This approach molded his own view of his job. He saw the whole undertaking as a team effort in which each person, from the lowly private to the prime minister, had a vital and indispensable role to play. His job was simply to fit the many disparate parts into one effective whole. It was a heavy job, but he did not feel it made him special. This underlines a very key aspect of Ike's management style—he always projected an air of humbleness, optimism, sincerity, and personal dedication to those that did the real heavy lifting. On visiting a unit, he did not give a speech from a podium to troops in formation. Rather, he just wandered into the troop mass, gathered them around and talked about them—their homes, sports, food, whatever would strike a familiar and common theme. And always as he left, he made a point regarding his complete optimism and success for the future tasks they would undertake. As he described his approach prior to D-Day, "I had to make them believe that everything was going to work."

Even with the most senior personalities, Churchill and Roosevelt, he spoke directly, impersonally, and with logic. If something was truly serious, such as Churchill's desire to accompany the navy on D-Day, he would impart great personal concerns, but would not issue edicts as others might in his position. He allowed reason to prevail—even to the point of great personal provocation such as he endured from Field Marshal Montgomery.

He never lost his perspective as to his responsibilities and his focus on those ultimately responsible for success: "It was 'GI Joe' who won the war", he said, not him.

Eisenhower delivered a victory on D-Day of the most complex operation ever undertaken by our civilization. He did this by molding himself, his organization, and his political leadership into a highly effective single-focus element. This was largely because he could rise above self-interest and inspire others to do, at their level, what he could not.

The extraordinary importance of the requirement for an invasion coupled with the aggregation of allies required management of an exemplary degree. Eisenhower, by emphasizing himself as a manager, coordinator, cheer leader and symbol of unshakeable confidence rather than as a personality, achieved what no other existing personality could have done—make the invasion a success.

Managing Charles de Gaulle

French General de Gaulle presented Eisenhower with a great challenge to his team building capability. His personality confounded everyone, but his cooperation was essential to ensure the French populace and Resistance supported the Allied invasion. De Gaulle represented himself as the symbol of a free France and its spirit of resistance. Roosevelt disliked him but Ike needed him.

Normandy demanded several aspects in terms of planning that only a credible French engagement could provide: in-country intelligence prior to the invasion; direct support of the invasion outside of the beach areas; control of the civilian population once freed from occupation; sustained security as the Allies moved across Europe; and additional forces to add to the Allied structure.

France, by nature, was a very complex confederation of people, parts, and agendas. The collapse of France in 1940 saw Brigadier General de Gaulle depart to North Africa where he established his Free French Army, consisting of colonials, expatriates, and others who fled the collapse. Initially supplied and managed by the British, these forces came increasingly under U.S. influence due to aid programs.

Roosevelt's key political advisor to the Allies, Robert Murphy, supported Eisenhower's desire to provide de Gaulle legitimacy in the equation, as did the British. Accordingly, in June of 1943, it was announced that both General Henri Giraud and de Gaulle would share authority in the High Commission/CFLN. Giraud would eventually fade into the background.

De Gaulle had an office in London to manage liaison as well as look out for French interests on the Continent. This was primarily for developing a strong political base within the occupied areas as well as building a military capability within the FFI/ Underground and Maquis. This office, in conjunction with de Gaulle's headquarters in North Africa, began extensive radio broadcasts to the French population, building the symbol of de Gaulle as the Spirit of France and the leader of the French nation.

Regardless of all the internal machinations and occasional obstinacy by de Gaulle, the French provided significant support and by D-Day, were a major factor in limiting German reinforcements. This is especially true of the movement of the 2d SS Panzer Division from the South of France to Normandy. FFI interdicted the trains in numerous locations and wore down significant German elements, stalling their arrival by almost a week.

CHAPTER 7

Force Selection and Controversies

General Morgan had identified Normandy as opposed to Pas De Calais as the suggested invasion area. In this, Eisenhower and Montgomery concurred when assuming command of the endeavor: Ike was to be Supreme Commander and Monty his ground forces commander.

Morgan had been limited in his force planning by original instructions that provided for no more than three divisions for the initial attack, all of which he placed against Sword, Juno, and Gold. Ike and Monty thought this was too small and that the draft did not provide for a deep-water port early in the campaign, thereby requiring an unproven across-the-beach supply and reinforcement concept.

The commanders identified Cherbourg as the key objective, which necessitated expansion of the area and the inclusion of at least five divisions in the initial waves and 10 just behind. Together, that made both Utah and Omaha essential. These requirements reflected the rapidly expanding U.S. presence in England as well as exposing shortfalls in sea lift that would have to be addressed.

This was not an anticipated issue, but took on crucial import regarding lifting the minimal force. Resolution could only be achieved at the highest level and exceeded anything the theatre of operations could satisfy.

Naval and logistic planners, given the five division requirement in March, quickly identified a shortfall in available LST, LSD, and LSI amphibious ships. Of the minimum requirement for 227 vessels, there were only 162 available. Ike took this as a personal priority issue and requested through General George Marshall, the U.S. Chief of Staff, priority for construction, crewing, and deployment in time to meet the initially projected 5 May invasion date. In this, he ran headlong into the Chief of Naval Operations, Admiral Ernest King, who opposed diversion of shipping from the Pacific.

General Marshall had several meetings with the War Production Board and settled on a compromise. Ship construction from March through May would be accelerated and prioritized for Europe. Ongoing production would continue in support of the

Pacific. In sum, more would be built to fill the void, but that came at a price: the initial May 5 date of the invasion.

More than 62 lift ships had to be added to the fleet to carry the assault forces, their reinforcements, and the follow-on elements from England. Immediate planning in the U.S. began with an expansion of the Ohio River amphibious ship production line and diversion of material as well as delays of other programs. Construction was done using the Henry J. Kaiser auto line assembly technique with expanded work forces. However, production capabilities were finite and could not assure completion until mid-May. The planned simultaneous invasion of southern France, *Anvil*, also provided a potential shipping inventory (see *Anvil* Controversy below). With a combination of production dates and a decision on *Anvil* dates, Ike shifted the invasion schedule from May to June. This, combined with new production, would provide for the minimum number of 227 LSTs.

This was only the first of several issues he had to resolve in force selection and management. The use of airborne forces consumed considerable planning and command attention while a strategic argument had to be concurrently resolved at the highest level.

The Anvil *Controversy*

Operation *Anvil*, the follow-on amphibious assault into southern France, was originally planned for early May. Churchill and the British Chiefs of Staff were lukewarm at best on the operation while the U.S. was strongly for it. This would be an exclusively U.S. force and would require considerable shipping, which would reduce available Normandy assets. Planning continued with the Combined Chiefs through Eisenhower's transfer from the Mediterranean to England.

Eisenhower sent a strong message to the Combined Chiefs that *Anvil* was essential for the success of *Overlord* and should be simultaneous in order to fix German forces and limit their reinforcement capability.

Once the SHAEF (Supreme Headquarters Allied Expeditionary Force) and Combined staffs examined a simultaneous operation, two things stood out: the Mediterranean fleet had a quantity of the crucial amphibious assault ships required for *Overlord*, and simultaneous *Overlord-Anvil* operations could occur but only at the cost of reducing Normandy forces.

After consultation with the Combined Chiefs, it was decided that *Anvil* would be postponed until late June at the earliest after *Overlord* requirements had been met and *Anvil* shipping would be temporarily transferred to support *Overlord* and later be released to the Mediterranean for *Anvil*.

This, plus projected construction, allowed for the minimum number of amphibious ships required for *Overlord* forces while still providing for a later occupation of southern France and linkup with those forces. *Anvil*, changed to Operation

Dragoon, was finally executed in August due to the intense demand for build-up shipping in France.

The Airborne Controversy

Airborne forces were a new force capability exploited by all sides during the war. The Russians and Germans were early pioneers in the 1920s and 1930s. Hitler had made them a significant element with their seizure of the Eban-Emael fortress in Belgium in 1940 and the seizure of Crete in 1941. Throughout the war, the German *Fallschirmjäger* forces remained a formidable force though they were never employed in an airborne role other than during the Battle of the Bulge and then in too small a number to be effective.

At the outset of the war, British and American armies developed and expanded this new capability, especially after the Americans saw the German successes. The British, who were more advanced, saw airborne elements as an extension of their well-developed commando forces and, under Churchill's relentless prodding, used them extensively against high value targets ranging from radar sites on the coast of France to bridges and key terrain in the Mediterranean.

General Marshall, Army Chief of Staff, was the major sponsor for airborne forces and pushed for rapid expansion, something the older, conventional leadership opposed. Their concern was that it would rob conventional forces of quality personnel. While in fact true, the clear need for the capability overrode objections. Quite quickly, between 1942 and 1943, two full Airborne divisions were created (the 82nd and 101st) to augment the 509th Airborne Regiment that had jumped into North Africa. Two additional divisions, the 13th and 17th Airborne, were earmarked for Europe, and the 11th Airborne assigned to the Pacific Theatre.

The vast fleet of C-46s and C-47s provided the ability to drop considerable forces. The relatively new inclusion of gliders, operating with the Airborne divisions, allowed significant artillery, resupply, and support elements to quickly reinforce the paratroopers. In combination, this became a major available asset and one in which all the senior ground commanders, from Ike on down, strongly supported.

The gliders brought a new and more potent asset to the equation. Three distinct types were built in significant quantities:

- The U.S. Waco glider was a steel-framed, canvas-covered glider that could carry 10 infantry or a jeep and trailer or a snub-nosed 105-mm howitzer. Its key value was that it existed in large quantities and due to its strong construction was less likely to break up on landing.
- The British Horsa glider was larger by a third and had a heavier payload. It was constructed of light plywood and usually broke up upon landing, not always to the occupants' benefit.

- The British Hamilcar was a huge glider that could carry a light tank. It was built in limited numbers and used exclusively by the British.

An Airborne army was created in England under U.S. Army Air Forces Lieutenant General Lew Brereton, with British Major General Frederick "Boy" Browning as the Airborne forces commander. The army included all the transport aircraft, gliders, and assault units. In practice, the divisions operated independently and would be passed to the appropriate ground maneuver commander for execution.

For Normandy, inclusion of airborne forces in the invasion was a major consideration for the planners, but carried significant controversy. Examination of the identified beaches combined with the necessary targets beyond the reach of the amphibious forces made it clear that airborne and glider forces would have to be included. In this, all the ground commanders concurred.

By April, they had identified the key Airborne/glider objectives. These were to be seized prior to the actual landing and act as security for overall force. These included the bridges over the Orne River and Caen Canal to be seized by Horsa gliders, and Ranville Ridge by the 6th Airborne Division to seize the high ground overlooking the Orne River and the last defensible terrain against German armored forces in the north and west. This would be the key target for the British 6th Airborne Division.

The Merville Battery had to be silenced prior to the landing and was assigned to the 9th Parachute Battalion, significantly reinforced.

The Saint-Côme-du-Mont/Sainte-Marie-du-Mont Ridge overlooking the causeway exits of Utah Beach was assigned to the 101st Airborne with the subsequent mission of seizing Carentan and allowing a juncture of the two U.S. beaches.

The locks at La Barquette that controlled the waters in the Carentan/Merderet flood plain were assigned to the 501st Parachute Infantry Regiment of the 101st.

The Cherbourg-Carentan ridge was assigned to the 82nd to block the road and pass through the Utah forces west to cut the Cotentin Peninsula.

The bridges at La Fière and Chef-du-Pont would be the primary passage points of the Utah forces cutting the peninsula and going to Cherbourg. The 82nd tasked the 505th and 508th Parachute Infantry Regiment with these structures.

There was considerable discussion regarding a potential drop behind Omaha to assist the landing. General Bradley was very engaged by this idea and directed the planners to develop options.

After considerable study, it was determined that there simply were not enough forces, both airborne and transport, to support the option. When presented with the numbers, Bradley dropped the option and focused on the land west of Utah Beach.

The C-47 could hold 20 jumpers and tow a glider. The lack of available C-47s argued against a full-up division drop if the minimum three divisions were to be dropped. Hence, each division was allocated 840 aircraft, which permitted the infantry from three Airborne regiments per division to jump. Additional forces and support would have to enter by glider after the aircraft returned to England.

Extensive aerial photography was available of the target areas and drop zone selection was made. Generals Bradley and Montgomery strongly supported the Airborne inclusion and believed the entire invasion might fail without their presence. In this there was considerable doubt on the part of Air Chief Marshal Sir Trafford Leigh-Mallory, commander of all air forces including the Airborne.

His concern, based on the significant casualties sustained on airborne operations in Sicily by both armies, was that Normandy would be a slaughter. He thought it better to land them immediately after the invasion and use them as a fast-moving commando-type force. On several occasions, he talked quite definitively to Eisenhower about this.

Eisenhower went to both Bradley and Montgomery with the issue in early May. Both strongly objected to any reduction or elimination and were adamant that airborne forces must be included prior to the landing for any hope of overall success. Bradley said:

> I talked to General Ridgway, General Taylor, and General Collins and they were adamant that the drops were necessary to ensure success at Utah and position the force to take Cherbourg. Consequently, I told Ike that the Airborne must go. He supported me on this and history proved it right.

Eisenhower asked Leigh-Mallory to put his objections in writing, which he did. Eisenhower's motivation, as he stated, was to have a record of the discussion and relative positions if the mission should fail with subsequent inquiries.

Leigh-Mallory accepted the decision with good grace. After the invasion, he sent Ike a very conciliatory note acknowledging his incorrect position and apologizing for adding an extra burden to him.

The 1st Division Issue

The next argument, although more muted, was the inclusion of the 1st Infantry Division in the initial assault at Omaha. The 1st Division had an excellent reputation in North Africa and Sicily and was sent to England under Eisenhower and Bradley's express wishes. They wanted a tested, reliable division on hand. All others, except the 82nd, were not combat tested.

Initially, they were to be a reinforcing as opposed to an assault element. Bradley felt that Omaha was so tough and so crucial that he assigned it to the landing. The 29th Division, a National Guard unit from Virginia, had originally been the lone force selected for H-Hour at Omaha. He chose not to risk failure and directed that the 1st land side by side with the 29th and assigned Major General Clarence Huebner, the newly installed Commanding General, to command the assault elements within the overall 5th Corps.

In April, the division troops were informed they would be part of the initial amphibious assault. There were widespread complaints and vociferous objections to the immediate leadership. They felt they had done their bit to date and deserved a break. This reached such proportions that General Huebner felt compelled to discuss it with Bradley, but only as a point of comment rather than a request.

Generals Eisenhower, Bradley, and Montgomery made a point of visiting the units, praising them and indicating the necessity for their inclusion. General Huebner, a strict disciplinarian but astute soldier, took a low-key approach, appealing to individual and organizational pride. By May, the issue had been reduced to soldier gripe levels. However, the resentment was carried throughout the war, but was also layered with the pride of the 1st's performance at Omaha.

Assault Force Size and Mix

By February, the available force in England was clear. The total British, Canadian, and Polish forces comprised 20 divisions. U.S. Divisions numbered 16 with two landing every month for the foreseeable future. While the British forces initially exceeded U.S. forces, it was a finite number while the Americans were prepared to ship in excess of 40 divisions, a fact that shifted the command authority from the British to the Americans on specific issues.

The Atlantic convoys were arriving regularly and the south of England was being hard pressed to find available grounds to hold it all: personnel, equipment, logistics supplies, and aviation. The critical issue that took much study was that of amphibious lift: how many elements could be landed at H-Hour, D-Day, and subsequently rapidly reinforced from offshore?

Montgomery, Bradley, and British General Miles Dempsey, the ground commanders, examined their respective beaches and determined that a minimum of one division must assault each beach with one immediately following followed by two more. Bradley determined that Omaha would require two divisions landing together.

The Navy took these units and divided them by available non-combatant lift and then amphibious assault craft. The desired forces could be lifted to the beach but follow-on forces would not exceed two divisions per beach without a return to England. Accordingly, the following forces were chosen per each beach:

Utah: The 4th Infantry Division would lead to be followed by the 90th and 30th Infantry Divisions. VII Corps under General J. Lawton Collins would command. The Corps would also be responsible for the 82nd and 101st.

Omaha: The 1st Infantry and 29th Infantry would assault abreast to be followed by the 2d Infantry Division. V Corps under Major General Len Gerow would command. The Corps would also be responsible for the Rangers.

Gold: British 50th Division would lead followed by 47 Commando and the British 3d Corps under Major General Gerard Bucknell.

Juno: This would be an exclusive Canadian beach with 3nd Canadian Infantry Division followed by the 2nd Armored Brigade and 7th Armored Division. This would be under the control of British I Corps that would also command Sword Beach.

Sword: The British 3rd Division and Lord Lovat's First Special Service brigade would be followed by the 4th Special Service brigade and the 27th Armored Brigade. I Corps would command it and the Juno elements until Canadian 1st Corps landed. The Corps would also be responsible for managing the British 6th Airborne Division.

The available amphibious lift allowed for more than 20,000 troops to be landed by D-Day with a projected 40,000 plus by D+5. This would be a turnaround by the lift ships on D+1, return to England, re-load, and arrive off the beaches by late D+3/early D+4. At that point, a continuous lift would land troops and materiel every day until Cherbourg could be opened around D+20.

As it happened, Cherbourg was never a factor as it was determined that over the beach re-supply was completely viable with the flat-bottomed ships and reduced transit to the battle area by more than 70 miles.

Support in several forms could now be planned to enhance the chances for success in what was known to be a high-risk operation. These ranged from cover and deception to isolation of the battlefield.

PART III
Preparation and Training

CHAPTER 8

The Work to Win

Preparing a million men and women of 27 nations on discrete land, sea, and air tasks as well as requisite support in relatively confined space and with a cramped time schedule was a management issue of the first order. All this had to occur while also fighting a war. How this was done was truly extraordinary by any standards. Delegation of authority and the strength of junior leaders were the outstanding tools in Eisenhower's box.

From the time troops landed in England, they began training for the ultimate invasion. Between 1942 and the spring of 1944, more than three million men and women arrived in England along with immense tonnages of supplies of all kinds. This friendly invasion taxed the British to the utmost, but in their way, they made accommodations and in a highly effective manner.

Most of the vast landed estates were converted to encampments and training grounds. The lord's golf course became a vast tent city and the formal buildings the housing of unit officers and staff. Areas were found for firing ranges and maneuver ground for everything from light infantry to armor.

The veritable river of aluminum airframes, fighters, bombers, transports, and reconnaissance found new homes in hastily constructed RAF bases or simply open, flat fields. Tents sprang up to be replaced by Quonset huts to be replaced by "temporary" wooden structures, many of which still exist and are used today.

The traditional fleet anchorages were greatly expanded with piers, jetties, and offshore buoys. Concurrently, the dozens of south coastal ports and prewar fishing and tourist spots, became home to hundreds of landing craft, their mother ships, and support vessels.

The crush of need became so powerful that the British government was forced to evict entire villages to make room. Salisbury Plain, previously a relatively small military training area, was doubled in size. This is but one of the more than 100 villages that became permanent training areas.

In the coastal ports, Churchill took an unprecedented move with Cabinet approval at the request of the British Chiefs of Staff by completely sequestering the port towns and villages along the south coast of England. These would be the ports of embarkation for the armada. The population was essential for the daily management and support of the ships as well as the minimal recreation and sustenance of the civilians living there. Transit in and out of these port areas was strictly controlled, making many villages a comfortable prison camp for the occupants.

However, this did have a positive side to it. The pubs and restaurants did a brisk business with troop influx and British women found a vast number of new suitors.

The incredible amount of logistics for the invasion buildup created unique problems and resolutions. Almost every stretch of southern English road with trees was pressed into service as a storage yard. Trees and camouflage netting covered thousands of vehicles, guns, and ammunition, creating even more narrow, already cramped roads by U.S. standards.

Barns and storage sheds were used to store communication gear, medical equipment, and navigational aids, displacing cattle, sheep, and hogs. The wonder is that the population generally acceded to this, supported it, and assisted in many ways. They knew the ultimate purpose of the material and were happy to "do their bit."

The sheer weight of logistics landing and then movement to a given destination brought the British labor and transport system to a break point. More than 100 ships a month were docking and requiring offloading in an expeditious manner. Labor unions objected to troop labor but were finally forced to relent in the face of an around-the-clock work day.

The U.S. Services of Supply, commanded by Lieutenant General John C. H. Lee, brought in dozens of Port Battalions to expedite shipping. The majority of these were segregated black units, as were the trucking and quartermaster elements. The vast military postal system was almost exclusively manned by black soldiers, with women doing the bulk of the sorting and delivering.

The road and rail networks, overwhelmed by movements, required huge augmentation. The U.S. brought in entire railroad units from rail construction workers to locomotives, and in several cases, created narrow gauge lines to accommodate the existing British rail systems.

Serious large-scale training, involving realistic invasion packages of regiments and divisions, complete with naval bombardment, armor, and air support, required large open beach areas and sufficient land inland to allow live fire maneuver. For this, two places were established, Slapton Sands and Croyde. Both were picked for their resemblance to likely invasion beaches and security from German discovery.

Croyde was on the northwest coast of England and Slapton in the extreme south near Plymouth. These became the 1st Army Assault Training Centers. Slapton Sands was acquired in December 1943 with 3,000 people cleared from an area of 30,000 acres. Croyde was acquired in November of 1943 with an equal displacement of civilians. Croyde had the additional advantage of having cliffs quite similar to those at Pointe du Hoc.

In both cases, mines had to be cleared that had been emplaced against a potential German invasion in 1940. Bunkers and fortifications were built to known German specifications and in accordance with imagery.

These became the primary training ground for the invasion rehearsals. Units from regiment through multiple divisions would rotate through, refining techniques ranging from on-loading Higgins landing craft to taking out concrete bunkers. By early spring 1944, the areas were in constant use. Likewise, other more specialized areas were employed, such as Achnacarry, Scotland, and Cornwall for the Rangers, and Salisbury Plain for armored forces.

As all invasion forces were moved into the embarkation ports, Slapton Sands became the training ground for all units. Major rehearsals were held that brought together the entire beach assault elements. This included all programmed live fire ranging from offshore naval bombardment to close-in small arms and rocket support. Casualties were fairly frequent and taken as regrettably necessary.

Key rehearsal exercises took place between 22 April 1944 and 5 May 1944.

The VII Corps (Force U), which had the mission to land on Utah Beach codenamed its rehearsal Exercise "Tiger," which took place between 22 and 30 April 1944. This is the exercise that was penetrated by German E-boats, resulting in three LSTs being sunk and the loss of more than 800 lives. The news of this tragedy was immediately suppressed so as not to alert the Germans to the Allies' intent.

The V Corps designated to land on Omaha (Force O) codenamed its rehearsal Exercise "Fabius 1" (Final Assault Before Invasion of the U.S. Army) from 2 to 5 May 1944.

The 2nd and 5th Rangers Battalion trained at nearby Blackpool Sands. The many types of climbing gear and devices were exercised against the cliffs. As in other places, troops were killed and injured throughout the training cycle.

The principal Airborne divisions, the British 6th and the American 82nd and 101st, required proximity to the air transport elements and generally open areas in which to jump. The general training grounds selected were in the south of England in the general locations of the many transport airfields. This was predominately in Wiltshire and Berkshire.

Due to the sheer size of the divisions, it was not possible to place any one together. Rather, they were placed in regimental base camps within walking or truck distance to training airfields. Key amongst them were Cottesmore, Spanhoe, Saltby, Up Ottery, North Windham, and Barkston Heath.

While in some cases, training and glider drops were done in small increments on or near the airfields, the larger exercises were simply held in the country farms and fields. Dropping amongst the general population, the troops went about their business in reasonably realistic settings.

All divisions participated in the major exercises at Slapton and elsewhere. Sometimes, they jumped and other times simulated jumps out of the back of a truck.

CHAPTER 9

Creating an Airborne Force

Pathfinders in the Beginning

The training and preparation of the Pathfinders, in support of the airborne operations for both the British and American divisions, was crucial for their success. As such, special attention was paid to that aspect even before training for Normandy began.

Both the British and Americans had suffered from mis-droppings and poor air-ground coordination as part of the Sicily invasion. Planes arrived at an intended drop zone based on navigational skills of individual pilots rather than a studied technologically supported system. The results were generally poor to disastrous. Winds, clouds, flak, and lack of experience resulted in only a small percentage of troops being dropped where intended.

The 509th Airborne, victimized by bad drops in North Africa, began an Airborne Pathfinder program using their scout elements. The 82nd, based in Oudja, observed this but did not use the concept for the Sicily drop, which was a disaster in terms of drop accuracy. Ridgway and Gavin vowed to change this immediately by creating a formal Pathfinder structure within the division. This group was the outcome of numerous meetings held in Comiso, Sicily between senior American and British commanders to critique the disappointing results of the Airborne landings there. General Gavin recalled:

> After Sicily, it was clear to all of us that we had to resolve the navigation problem and that a Joint Pathfinder capability and doctrine had to be developed and developed fast. The Comiso meetings, led by General Ridgway, became the basis for what we did in England as part of the train up.
> General Ridgway and I both agreed we needed to start a program and I volunteered Jack Norton with whom we had a high degree of confidence to run it. This had to be done in coordination with the troop carrier command which was fully engaged.

Accordingly, a Pathfinder training facility under the command of Major John Norton was created in Sicily. Emerging new navigational aids, Rebecca and Eureka gear, combined with early radio navigational aids called Gee, would be integrated. Major Norton said:

> Both Gavin and Ridgway were highly upset with Sicily and recognized we had to do a lot better. General Gavin came to me and gave me a classic mission order in the 82nd: Take some men and equipment, get with the troop carrier command and the regiments, and fix the problem.
>
> As it was, every day was a new adventure and experience. We had a big obvious field in Sicily initially and as we got better, moved our target locations and began night operations. We had a number of injuries but the task was so important that Gavin made sure I was always at full strength.
>
> The troop carrier guys were great. I had as many aircraft as I needed and the pilots were as interested in solving the problem as we were. It was an excellent relationship.
>
> In time, we had a high degree of confidence between the gear, the troops and the pilots. We did a couple of day and night demonstrations for Ridgway and Gavin and they went off well. At that point, General Ridgway told us to establish a formal school within the Division, which we did.
>
> We had our baptism of fire at Salerno, which went well, and took the concept with us when we deployed to Northern Ireland and later Leicester. I was always sorry the Pathfinders did not do better in Normandy but I think the problems were well beyond the men to solve.

Key to the program was the inclusion of the new Rebecca and Eureka navigational equipment. Eureka was a jump capable radio transponder that sent a coded signal to the airplane's Rebecca gear. Each code fixed a specific drop zone, theoretically allowing pin point drop accuracy. This would be augmented by holophane lights that were placed on the ground with a discrete pattern that confirmed a specific drop zone. Private First Class Murphy recalled this project:

> I was one of the first tasked with the Pathfinder program. I was "volunteered" by the Headquarters First Sergeant as were most of us. Regardless, we knew it was an important mission and Sicily had been a disaster.
>
> We were issued all this Eureka and holophane gear and had to figure out how to jump it. It was both bulky and delicate. None of it could be jumped with our gear. Apparently, Major Norton discussed this with the Brits and got a bunch of leg bags. These were basically heavy canvas laundry bags on a rope. You stuffed the gear with whatever padding you could find, attach the looped rope to your web gear and jumped.
>
> You were supposed to time dropping the gear so it fell straight down just prior to landing. That was the trick. Drop it too soon and it acted as a pendulum crashing you into the ground on landing. Drop it too late and everything was smashed. Daytime you could figure it out. Night was a lot more tricky.
>
> Salerno was sort of a graduation jump and worked fine probably because the drop zone was a sandy area. Regardless, we declared it a success.

The Salerno operation was the first test of the concept.

The team was composed of a team leader (a lieutenant), an assistant team leader, two operators of the Eureka equipment, two assistant operators, a holophane section head, seven men each equipped with two holophane lamps, and four to six men to protect the drop zone.

During a night jump, seven Pathfinders jumped with two holophane lamps, also called Aldis lamps. Seven of them were placed on the ground to form a T, the base of the T indicating the direction of the jump, and the crossbar the jump departure.

The lamps were lit when the hum of the engines of the lead aircraft was heard. They were placed on telescopic tripods so as to be easily visible from an airplane but almost invisible from the ground.

The last lamp was activated by an operator, who flashed the Morse letter of drop zone, which helped leaders identify their drop zones, which were also identified by lamps of different colors (green, red, and amber).

During the day, Pathfinders used phosphorescent orange panels that flattened on the ground to form a letter, smoke grenades, and a beacon.

The Pathfinder teams, approximately 20 men per regiment (one five-man team for each battalion and the regimental headquarters) would jump ahead of the main body, establish the drop zone and assembly areas, and guide the main body to their respective locations on the drop zone. They would then join their parent unit and perform their normal assigned tasks.

It was clear to both General Ridgway and Taylor that accurate Pathfinder operations would be essential for Normandy, the greatest planned airborne operation to date. Accordingly, when both airborne divisions began training in England, a consolidated Pathfinder training facility was established at RAF North Witham under the command of Captain Frank Lillyman of the 101st. This would expand on the experience in Salerno and would ensure a common doctrine between the airborne divisions and the troop carrier elements.

In full agreement and as part of the results of the Comiso meetings, the Army Air Forces gave Pathfinding a top priority. It created the IX Troop Carrier Command Pathfinder Group (Provisional) formed within the 52nd Troop Carrier Wing, under the command of Lieutenant Colonel Joel Crouch. This element would carry all U.S. Pathfinders to Normandy as the initial elements.

The pilots that would fly the mission would also fly the training missions. Each Pathfinder team was assigned a specific aircraft and pilots which worked with them throughout the train up period. Private First Class Murphy said:

> The air crews were great. We got friendly with the ground crew guys and they slipped us a lot of great food we didn't get, such as chocolate cocoa mix, whiskey, and fresh bread. The best we could do was buy them beer at the pub when we saw them. They also got papers from the States when the replacement birds and crews flew in.

The British 6th Airborne, already well experienced in the necessity for pathfinding, established a similar training facility. It did not work jointly with the U.S. elements but had the same equipment and air-ground training protocols. A mix of U.S. and British transport aircraft would be used, so all pilots had to have a common basis of operations. According to British Brigadier James Hill,

> General Gale was rightly concerned as were we all with accurate drops. Sicily had been a relative mess. We had good discussions with the American Airborne and shared much of our experience as well as issues with the new gear. In that we were somewhat differently organized and in more established bases, we trained separately. This worked out fine as we dropped quite far apart and didn't have to worry about mixing. We were quite jealous of the 82nd and 101st as they seemed to have training drop aircraft whenever they wished. We were generally starved except on special occasions.

Both the 82nd and 101st conducted Airborne drops throughout the training period in England. In all cases, the respective Pathfinders were used to a point. After several night drops, there were a number of jump injuries as well as broken equipment. Accordingly, toward the latter parts of April, the Pathfinders set up the drop zones by truck to preserve people and equipment. Only on the final major dress rehearsal with the 101st, Operation *Eagle*, did they jump as they would on D-Day.

General Ridgway recalled,

> We wanted to conduct as many night jumps as we could but it became too costly and I had to stop it. We were losing key leaders we couldn't afford to lose. Our training then was on night assembly and we simulated by dropping the men off the back of slow-moving trucks.
> The Pathfinders did as good as could be expected. With the exception of the 505th, most of the other teams were just mis-dropped on insertion. It certainly wasn't their fault there were so many scattered troops on D-Day.

The 82nd Airborne in Training

I have focused on the 82nd as that is where I gathered the most veteran input. My studies indicate that the experience of the 101st was very similar. Both divisions were located in south-central England on rolling farm land.

During the preparation for the 40th anniversary return, I talked and corresponded at some length with Generals Ridgway and Gavin. One of my questions was: what did you do for pre-invasion training and what did you feel was the most important part of that training? Both responded independently but consistently. To paraphrase:

We knew they could fight. Sicily and Italy proved that. We didn't need to spend too much time on basic tactics other than for the replacements. We needed to work on those issues that we saw as crucial—night Airborne operations, conditioning, and cohesion. And of course understanding the mission and tasks at all levels.

We had a lot of night jumps, road marches, and intramural athletics. Obstacle courses and baseball games and touch football were constant. Then we let them on the town at night and usually turned a blind eye when they got into fights. Like any team sport, it was great for morale and cohesion.

As the invasion got closer, we spent more time on briefings and unit rehearsals. We cut the jumps and long exercises as they got people hurt we couldn't afford to lose.

I questioned each on the rationale and received a similar consistent response:

We anticipated that the troops would be scattered and have to fight outside the usual organization. Sicily proved that and we prepared for a worst case. That meant the soldiers not only had to have confidence in themselves, but in their comrades. Sports and physical training provided that along with a lot of night jumps. Troops experienced isolation and being lost and having to make their way back with the help of unfamiliar faces.

Physical conditioning was key. We would be isolated for days before relief, fighting day and night and traversing a lot of difficult terrain. They had to have the stamina to do that and fight at the same time. They were used to hard work from jump school at Fort Benning, we just added new tasks within a unit framework such as road marches, night assaults, obstacle courses as unit competitions and athletics. It all served to discipline both minds and bodies and strengthen the chain of command. The faint fail; we were not going to fail.

The NCOs were key to our success. Sicily proved that. We had to make everyone understand everyone else's mission. The squad and platoon sergeants had to be able to exercise judgment, make decisions, and take on tasks usually reserved for seniors. We wanted to ensure that every squad clearly understood the company and battalion tasks and that of the division as a whole.

The bar fights were non-standard, but served a very similar purpose. Airborne troops stood up for each other regardless of unit, as they would have to do in France. A lot of non-Airborne infantry and support units suffered for our success.

A number of veterans recounted similar views. A standout comment was that both Gavin and Ridgway were seen everywhere. Ridgway particularly was fond of baseball but had problems with his knee that often kept him as a coach rather than player. Gavin was good at the obstacle course and often would surprise a soldier by assisting him through as he bypassed the field. Their physical presence had a marked positive effect on the soldiers.

Each was physically imposing, which was critically important in a unit such as the 82nd where physical aspects and personal leadership take on mythological importance and are crucial to developing soldier psyche. Ridgway, while austere and somewhat remote, was very physically engaged, and spoke to soldiers frequently, asking direct questions with his piercing hawk-like eyes and seemed always present if not participating. He had the utmost respect as their commanding general and everyone acknowledged he was commanding in the positive sense of the word.

Gavin, however, was universally viewed as "our commander." He was of their generation, was always up front, engaged at the hottest point, and had a friendly but professional intimacy with the soldiers that Ridgway did not. Gavin was the assault force commander at Sicily and Salerno and was indistinguishable on the battlefield from a private soldier. On that, I asked General Gavin why he always carried an M-1 (there is a famous picture of him during the Bulge moving through the snow with his rifle and a similar picture of him preparing for Operation *Market Garden* with an M-1). His reply was, "If I had a rifle there was less chance I would be recognized as an officer and if I needed to help out, I had the right weapon."

General Ridgway had a similar predilection for a rifle. He always carried a M-1903 Springfield in his jeep with AP (armor piercing) cartridges. During the Battle of the Bulge, then Corps Commander Ridgway took his rifle and worked his way down a trail seeking a unit command post. Observing a German covered vehicle, without hesitation (and suspect judgment), he fired three rapid fire shots into the vehicle, stopping it. His bodyguard counted three dead Germans. He and the General then continued their walk through the woods. Such were the commanders these soldiers were so fortunate to have.

On 14 February 1944, the 82nd moved from its camp in Northern Ireland to its invasion training area at Leicester, Camp Quorn, and the nearby countryside.

Unlike Ireland, the Leicester training facilities were primitive. Tent cities were built in the orchard and farm areas that became mud-choked in the routine English rain.

Each regiment was assigned estate land that the British government had confiscated during the war. These facilities provided excellent headquarters buildings and nearby flatland for the tent cities. The entire Airborne community was arranged with Leicester as its hub.

Leicester was also occupied by numerous logistics and signals units well before the Airborne arrival. The pubs, cinemas, cafes, dance halls, and other amenities were major attractions for GIs and led to countless fights between the Airborne and the "Legs," as well as between the black and white soldiers.

Rifle ranges and maneuver areas were established in the fields as well as baseball and volleyball fields. Basketball courts were rigged on the several paved parking areas near the division headquarters building at the primary estate house, Winstanley.

The division HQ was at Winstanley House, the 505th at Quorn (considered the nicest of the regimental locations), and the 507th and 508th in Nottinghamshire. The 504th from Italy was housed at Evington and the 325th Glider Infantry Regiment was at Scraptoft.

A major issue the division had to address in this period was exactly what units should constitute the 82nd for the invasion. The 504th Parachute Infantry Regiment was an integral part of the 82nd and had a superb fighting reputation. However, it had been held in Italy by General Mark Clark as an essential force for the Anzio/ Salerno operations. Finally, in April 1944, the regiment landed in the England and proceeded to its camp at Evington, near Quorn.

However, the regiment was at less than half strength and beat-up both physically and mentally. The replacement system was not able to provide sufficient replacements, and by May was of questionable status. This created a point of conflict between Gavin and Major General Ridgway. Ridgway had established that Gavin would lead the initial assault. But with what units?

Early on, the independent Airborne regiments, the 507th and 508th, were assigned to the division to strengthen it for the invasion. This would give both the 82nd and 101st three Parachute Infantry Regiments and one Glider Infantry Regiment, the 101st having been already organized with three Parachute Infantry Regiments, the 501st, the 502nd, and the 506th, when it arrived in England. The 501st and 502nd were separate Parachute Infantry Regiments assigned to the 101st upon landing to provide for three Parachute Infantry Regiment's per Airborne Division for the invasion. It was assumed by SHAEF that the 504th could not participate and accordingly assigned the 507th and 508th to the 82nd.

Neither of these units had any combat experience. Gavin argued that the battle-tested 504th ought to be filled out with replacements coming from the 507th and 508th. The tasks of the division required three relatively independent Parachute Infantry Regiment missions, which would require exceptional internal leadership. Gavin said,

> I observed these units in training and was not particularly impressed. The leadership seemed a bit hesitant and the troops were clearly inexperienced. The 504th, beat-up as it was, had a core of veteran dependable leaders and an exceptional commander in Reuben Tucker. I felt that a weak 504th was a better bet than a full up 07 or 08. This was the only time that General Ridgway and I had a serious disagreement.

General Ridgway's argument was,

> I had a serious decision to make regarding the final composition of the Division. I really wanted the 504 to participate, but I could see they were mentally and physically exhausted. The replacements were not arriving in quantity and time was running out. Gavin was quite adamant that we simply strip the 07 and 08 to fill the 04. I thought about this, but considered that both regiments had been training with us for some time and were becoming well integrated. The 04, even if filled, would need train up time we simply did not have. In the end, I told Jim we would stick with the original plan. Ultimately, we did use elements of the 504th in the Pathfinders as well as some fillers.

Quality training for anticipated combat presented several challenges for the leadership in terms of their immediate subordinates, Herb Batcheller of the 505th, George Millet of the 507th, and Roy Lindquist of the 508th. On the one hand, the 507th and 508th had no common training doctrine and not any with the 82nd. Gavin was charged by Ridgway to develop a common set of standard operating procedures based on the 82nd experience. These SOPs had to permeate from the top to the squad. It was here that major issues arose.

Lieutenant Colonel Herb Batcheller, commanding officer (CO) of the 505th Parachute Infantry Regiment, was a somewhat aberrant personality. He had been Gavin's executive officer in the Mediterranean and promoted to the 505th's CO when Gavin was promoted. He was an extremely "loose" commander, both organizationally and personally. This could be tolerated in combat but was a decided negative in training.

In Ireland, the 505th had major discipline problems, primarily AWOLs and bar fights. Batcheller was continuously disengaged with that due to his engagement elsewhere with local ladies, a situation most were aware of. Worst of all, he missed a lot of training that Gavin and Ridgway attended. This got worse when the division moved to Quorn. Gavin recalled,

> I was disappointed in Herb. I thought he would do better. He was OK in combat but pretty much a disaster as a commander in garrison. He allowed his personal desires to overcome his responsibilities. The troops were losing their spirit and discipline. Both General Ridgway and I noticed that. Later, when things did not get better in England, we had no choice but to relieve him.

Batcheller found a local widow who lived just outside the post gate. His car was frequently parked in front of her house and noted by the troops. Finally, due to the notoriety of his activities coupled with lack of participation in training, Ridgway made the decision to relieve him in early March and replace him with William Ekman. Gavin said,

> I had favored Mark Alexander as the replacement due to his proven experience in Sicily. He was highly reliable as a combat commander, but General Ridgway chose to go outside the Division, trying to deepen the quality of senior officers available. In the end, Ekman was a solid, dependable commander and did everything we wanted and did it well.

Rather than have Batcheller depart the division, Ridgway chose to soften the relief by making him commander of 1-508th, a highly unusual move. Ridgway said,

> We needed his experience in an untested unit. He was very happy for the opportunity and I was glad we added some experience to the 508th.

Ekman was new to the division but a strong character. He focused on regaining discipline by restricting passes and conducting grueling road marches, physical training, and night operations. He won the grudging respect of the 505th, which regained its Mediterranean élan and field competency. The other parachute regiments each had their own unique personality issues.

The 507th was commanded by Colonel George "Zip" Millett, a West Point classmate of Gavin's. He was very much a laid-back personality and not of the type the division had developed. However, he was a serious intramural athletics manager. He organized the regimental program and closely monitored daily events. However, he rarely went to night training and left tactical operations to his subordinates. Gavin said,

> Zip was a good friend from West Point, but he wasn't a tough commander as we needed. Both General Ridgway and I spent time with him, me especially due to the lack of combat experience within the unit. There wasn't a pool of senior leader material available so we made do.

Ridgway recalled,

> I had concerns about Millet's attention to training, especially the night phases. He was usually nowhere to be found. I had General Gavin talk to him and spend more time to get him in our mold. In the end, having just relieved Batcheller and the invasion looming, I didn't think it prudent to move him. We simply did not have a qualified candidate in the wings.

The 508th Commander, Colonel Roy Lindquist, presented a different set of issues. General Gavin noted that the regiment was always well dressed and disciplined but tactically soft. From Lindquist on down, the emphasis was on administration and administration done well. Coming from a notoriously sloppy administrative organization (the G1 [Personnel] had dumped a lot of personnel records in the Mediterranean), Gavin was impressed by the 508th's systems. He was not impressed by their tactical proficiency.

Lindquist commanded from a distance and did not lead as Gavin did when he commanded the 505th. Both Gavin and Ridgway found this unsettling, yet they were impressed by Lindquist as a person. Gavin hoped he could instill a tougher fighting quality through directed training and his presence. Gavin said,

> The 508th was the best administered unit in the Division, bar none. This was clearly due to Colonel Lindquist. His emphasis was not where we wanted it but we had to compensate for his strengths. His battalion commanders seemed pretty good so we hoped to mold the regiment. In time they became pretty good but we always had to backstop Lindquist with combat leadership which he just wasn't capable of providing.

It was clear in my many discussions with Gavin and several with Ridgway, that they knew they had to deal with the hand they were dealt in terms of parachute regiment assignments and the internal leadership. Beginning earnest training in March and understanding early June as the likely invasion date, they did not have the luxury of command reliefs and extended training. Accordingly, Gavin designed a continuous series of tough training exercises to establish SOPs and tough troopers, mentally and physically.

Training was conducted in the fields around their campsites, route marches took them to live firing ranges established in valleys or parkland requisitioned by the British government, and rehearsal parachute drops were conducted as and when they could be planned with the air force. Inevitably, fatalities took place, mainly on the parachute jumps but also in considerably violent circumstances. Two members of the division were stabbed to death in riots involving black soldiers in Leicester in which it is believed members of the 504th Parachute Infantry Regiment attempted to take over a pub reserved for use by black soldiers. These deaths led to more violence, but the impending invasion of Europe brought a welcome distraction and ended those hostilities.

Ridgway and Gavin designed a training regimen based on their experience coupled with their anticipated view of the coming invasion. The training model that developed had five components: Staff Planning and Intelligence Development; Intramural Athletics; Night Assemblies and Movements Off the drop zone; Small unit tactical operations; and Town recreation.

From the time the 82nd arrived in England in February, the planners and intelligence personnel were engaged in a constantly changing set of potential missions coupled with a daily deluge of photographs and intelligence data.

Insofar as possible, these would be digested, filtered, and passed to the appropriate units to train against. The HQ had a Bigot (the highest level of security clearance) room at Winstanley with a very small staff. They would take the input, filter out Bigot-specific data and pass it to the division staff, who would translate the new data into training and planning tasks. Ridgway said,

> I think we had three people in the headquarters cleared for Bigot at the time. The best we could do was develop generic items such as type obstacles, type building complexes, type drop zones etc. Later, we could get quite specific but that wasn't until almost the end of May.

General Gavin was temporarily assigned to SHAEF HQ as the head of airborne planning. He had to filter bright ideas with reality. His element studied drops on Cherbourg, drops on bridges, drops well away from the landing areas, and drops on Omaha. In the end, he coerced a relatively final plan for the 82nd to drop at Saint-Sauveur-le-Vicomte, about 20 miles west of Sainte-Mère-Église and the 101st at Saint-Côme-du-Mont. In this, General Bradley concurred which finalized the Bigot plan for the airborne phase. Gavin said,

> I had a difficult time at SHAEF. Leigh-Mallory was quite sure we couldn't do what we said we could do and would be lost. I did my best to convince him and left uncertain I had carried the day. We were constantly fielding some well-meaning idea from a senior officer in the headquarters or the States. In this, I had the strong backing of General Bradley who was an immense help in stopping bad ideas.

In the mid-May period, intelligence, primarily photography, began to pick up considerable anti-airborne defenses being constructed in the center of the planned drop area at Saint-Sauveur-le-Vicomte. This became a major planning crisis coming so late in the game.

On 26 May, with Ridgway, Gavin, and Bradley's acquiescence, the 82nd mission was changed from the Saint-Sauveur-le-Vicomte area to Sainte-Mère-Église.

General Ridgway discussed this point with me at his kitchen table and was quite animated:

> The overhead photos made it clear that our target area was heavily defended and getting more so every day. We looked at the ground available and could see a simple slippage east would be the best answer, and in fact, would improve the initial security.
>
> I went to General Bradley and he immediately agreed with the change. When I took it back, the staff, already very tired, were shocked. They envisioned a major planning exercise and then the briefings to the units which would undergo the same time-consuming process.
>
> After a few minutes of heated discussions, I just went to the map and unpinned the acetate with the drop zones and just slid it to the right placing Sainte-Mère-Église in the circle previously held by Saint-Sauveur-le-Vicomte. The other objective areas matched perfectly.

Shortly thereafter, the Bigot restriction was greatly reduced and the staff could share specific objectives with maps and photos. This was allowed down to company commander level and by 28 May to all personnel.

Intramural Athletics

General Ridgway and General Gavin were very athletic, pre-requisites for the Airborne. They were both West Point graduates and had a common experience with the highly programmed intramural athletics program. The events chosen for the train were baseball, touch football, volleyball, and obstacle course.

Ridgway added a twist with a purpose. All games were "pickup" with enforced mixing of units, e.g., two from 1-505th, three from 2-508th, one from 3-507th, one from divisional artillery, etc. Ridgway said,

> We did that as a means to get the men to work together very quickly from different units, exactly as would be expected for scattered drops which we assumed would happen. Everything was done with that in mind; getting men familiar with having to function together even if they hadn't normally trained together.
>
> We also made this a rankless exercise. The senior officer present would direct a trooper to "be in charge" and select his side from the assembled elements. Ditto for the other side. This would be exactly what would happen in combat. Someone had to take charge and it's not always an NCO who is present.

Both Ridgway and Gavin frequently participated, especially Ridgway, in baseball. He pitched (this was hardball) and played first base.

Both generals discussed the day's events at breakfast and ensured they were watching different elements every day and then comparing notes. Gavin was also given the specific task of working with the troop carrier command to ensure accurate drops and the integration of the Pathfinders. As such, the night Airborne operations became the focus of all training.

Night Assemblies on the Drop Zone

Initially, drops were made in company strength as airlift became available. It was much easier to get 10 C-47s for training than 100. Accordingly, drop zones were plotted throughout the greater Leicester area on reasonably open farm fields. The various RAF bases also became ad hoc drop zones, especially in the early phases. In that way, several companies in each regiment could drop in a night with turnarounds.

The night drop program gradually expanded into full battalion exercises as Gavin and the Troop Carrier Command became more and more focused and the pilots more proficient. This came with a price, specifically injuries. Initially, these were viewed as a tradeoff for operational proficiency. Regardless, from March to late April, troops dropped in increasing numbers.

Private First Class Bob Murphy said,

> I think we [505th] probably had some element jumping almost every night in the early phases. I had to be a Pathfinder for the battalion and an infantrymen so I got the double whammy.
>
> We jumped all over the country and a lot were mis-drops dumping us several miles off target. We had to figure out where we were and then get back. This usually took all night of walking so we didn't get a lot of tactical training.
>
> Toward the end, we stopped drops entirely. There were just too many people getting hurt and we were close to the invasion.

Private First Class Bill Sullivan added:

> Personally, I hated all the jumping. It took half a day of sitting around and then you put on the chute and your buddy had to make it really tight so you didn't come out with the opening shock.
>
> The drop zones were farm fields and we were always crashing into fences, trees and roadways. It took a good D-Day and more to recover physically. The pubs were great though for recovery.

The tactical problems after the jump and assembly usually had two components: a company approach march and separate platoon missions. These were designed by Gavin to replicate the anticipated issues in France. Battalion and company movements to contact followed by small unit tactical objectives. It was key that the junior leaders gain practice and confidence. Gavin recalled,

> I thought this model was extremely important to get the junior leadership proficient. We assumed there would be a lot of scattered drops and they would have to take charge. A lieutenant had to understand the battalion or regimental objectives and be capable of doing them in the absence of his seniors.
>
> I spent a lot of time with the 07th and 08th as we didn't know them and I needed to have an understanding as to what we could expect in ways of performance. Both had very tough missions and needed to be at the top of their game. I knew the 505th could fight, less so about the others.

Ridgway said,

> In my view, this training was crucial to our success. General Gavin and I went out almost every night to watch and evaluate. Each of us to different units unless it was a battalion drop.
>
> I would be on the drop zone when the jump was made and just watch. I didn't intervene unless it was an injury situation. I wanted to see how the unit handled itself and the leaders manage confusion.
>
> Jim and I would compare notes the next morning and then have an informal discussion with the leadership. We didn't want to make this a major event but simply learning points and non-threatening.

The follow-on tactical problems were usually road ambushes or raids on a building complex with the "enemy" from other elements.

On more than one occasion, civilian prisoners were taken that were "unprogrammed." Gavin said,

> The aggressiveness of the troopers sometimes resulted in them bringing in prisoners who were local farmers that had been tending their animals during a drop. As the men worked toward their assembly areas, they might capture a man and bring him in with them.
>
> We had the regimental commander go out to the farmer and mollify the situation which they usually did. The locals were very forgiving, but we had to finally issue a no-capture order to reduce local tensions.

Tactical Operations

General Gavin designed a series of grueling field problems to build unit and individual competency. These began with either a night drop or truck assembly and involved long cross-country movements or road marches with full equipment. Once at a location, the commander (battalion or company) would be given a hasty mission to execute. He would have to plan it, disseminate the plan, and then execute.

This would be followed by another long march and new orders. Gavin would intentionally push the unit to its limits with more orders, movements, and tactical objectives. This permitted him to evaluate commanders and units under stress while developing SOPs and standards.

Weapons ranges were established for each regiment in the back area of each estate. In some cases, prime farm land had to be acquired as the only land next to a hill that would be the ultimate bullet backstop.

Ranges were created for machine guns, mortars, and small arms. The artillery trained separately and used existing British ranges for live fire. Part of the range training was in the unpacking of the para-packs and getting the weapons in functioning order in quick time at night.

During that period, all machine guns, mortars and bazookas were brought in by para-pack. These were long containers underneath the C-47 that were jettisoned as the troops left the doors. Each type of para-pack had its own color coded parachute; red for weapons and ammo, yellow or white for medical, blue for signal, and green for general supplies.

The SOP was that troops would gather whatever para-pack landed and bring it into the assembly area. There the contents would be distributed to the appropriate personnel. Trucks would scatter para-packs and the troops would gather them, assemble the contents, and move out. All regiments practiced cross-training personnel so everyone was somewhat familiar with all the weapons.

Glider and 325th Glider Infantry Regiment (GIR) Training

The 325th GIR and gliders in particular created unique training challenges. The first was that training glider pilots required open ground, forgiving terrain, and transport aircraft. Early on, a decision had been made that glider pilots would be hybrid Army Air Forces (AAF) personnel: AAF pilots with some infantry training. On landing, they would become local security and eventually return to England. By necessity, this meant the pilots and the gliders were usually separate from the 325th.

The 325th GIR was housed on the Scraptoft Estate and was largely left alone by the 82nd. At this time the 325th was not emotionally integrated into the 82nd and were viewed as second class soldiers by the Airborne troops. The 325th was a non-volunteer draftee unit with no perquisites or pay enjoyed by the Airborne. It had not performed particularly well in Italy.

The commander, Harry Lewis, was older than any other regimental commander and somewhat austere. His battalion commanders were largely untested but seemingly solid. The troops did not show the spirit or aggressiveness shown by the airborne troops. Neither Gavin nor Ridgway expressed great confidence in or expectations of it.

Due to aircraft availability, the 325th was programmed as reinforcement on D+1 with no specific ground mission. Hence, they received minimal oversight from either Gavin or Ridgway. Gavin explained:

> I just didn't have the time to give the 325th what I felt necessary for the 07th and 08th. The unit had a reserve role. We were content to give them basic directives and visit as we could. I did make a point to go in on a glider once and would never do it again …
>
> I thought it important to see how the glider troops were doing and I had never ridden in a glider to that point [pre-D-Day]. I told General Ridgway of my plan and he looked at me a bit askance and wished me luck.
>
> The next day, I just looked at him and said: we don't pay these guys enough. It was one of the most sickening experiences I ever had and damn dangerous. My hat was off to them. We rectified the separateness issues after Normandy as well they [325th GIR] deserved.

The result of all this was that for the most part, the 325th GIR trained by itself as did the glider pilots. As March gave way to April and the pilots became more proficient, some integrated training was conducted. With few exceptions, these were daylight small unit operations with purposefully friendly fields.

By late April, the British Horsa glider was integrated with the Waco and 325th troops did static (ground training) with both as well as practice landings. By early May, the 325th conducted several night glider landings. There was great sensitivity to losing gliders and personnel, neither of which could be replaced, which limited operations as well as landing zone choices.

The troops noted that while the Horsa was spacious and could carry twice the load of a Waco, its light plywood construction frequently meant near instant disintegration upon landing. The Waco had a tubular steel frame that provided considerably more protection. The Horsa also required a two-plane tow, which meant considerable bucking, weaving, and diving as the tow birds struggled to stay abreast of each other.

Towns and Recreation

Both Gavin and Ridgway supported the troops using the local towns and Leicester for off-duty recreation. In fact, they both believed that the experiences would build greater spirit and cohesion. The anticipated bar fights between the Airborne and the "Legs" would have men from different units holding together in common cause. One thing they did not condone was the Airborne versus the black troops.

Earlier, before the main body of the division arrived, General Ridgway had toured Leicester after hours. He noted that black soldiers were accustomed to using the pubs and had a number of white girlfriends. They had been stationed in the area for more than a year, with new arrivals frequently. Quartermaster, truck, ammo, signal, barrage balloon, and construction units festooned the area.

Ridgway understood that a good portion of his men, raised in the South, would have immediate problems with this. Accordingly, he addressed it personally to the men upon arrival. He laid out the facts of the situation and made it clear that he would not tolerate racial confrontations. This was only partially successful as his men found many opportunities to get into fights. Sergeant Hill recalled,

> We had issues with black soldiers and white girls. It was quite a shock for our Southern boys and led to a lot of fights initially. Some of our guys got the worst of it one night and Colonel Lindquist got involved. Any unit that required an MP to get engaged was barred from passes for a week. From then on, we only fought when pressed.

The British pub owners, rather than risk relationships and endanger livelihood, posted signs, such as "This is a Black (Negro) Public House." In time, each pub had its own flavor: "Legs", Airborne, mixed, black, etc. This was only marginally helpful in maintaining the peace.

The issue of fights, drunkenness, and property damage became so acute that the military administrative authority in Leicester brought in an entire MP battalion to maintain order. The regional Commander of Military Police, a full colonel, visited Ridgway and Gavin to both complain and to ask for assistance. Gavin said,

> We had issues in town. We knew that but didn't want to shut it down. We worked the men hard and knew they needed some sort of relief. The fights were inevitable. General Ridgway and I listened politely and General Ridgway assured him we would do everything we could to fix the problem. He left, thanking us. We did nothing.

The normal training cycle was that a unit would undergo a long march and tactical problem(s). It would march back and then get a night off. Or it would conduct a jump, assembly, and tactical problem(s), then return to camp and get a night off.

This would usually be followed by two days of physical training, range work, intramural athletics, and cleanup. The night was free. With four infantry regiments and divisional support elements rotating through the cycles, that meant that Leicester and the surrounding towns had a healthy airborne population every evening.

The largest areas, Leicester and Nottingham, were most frequented due to their variety of options and larger population of unattached girls. Consequently, they were always crowded. Every night, trucks from each unit dropped off troops and later recovered them.

What made the pubs so attractive to the troops, other than beer and girls, was the simple nature of them. There, one felt like he was sitting in someone's home, a cross between a parlor and a dining room. The bar, to be sure, was there. A pull on the long arm of the faucet provided pressure for the beer to be brought up into the glass. A foaming head just barely running over the top of the glass and one was already wetting his lips in anticipation. Private First Class Sullivan said,

> I loved to just sit in a corner and watch. It was so different from our bars. When it got too smoky or out of hand, I just went elsewhere. I got to know the pub owner pretty well. He often had me back in the kitchen where I would fry up the sausages and onions which I loved. I snuck them sugar which was a treat for them.

Regardless of the town or pub, "glasses please" meant closing time. It was getting close to D-Day.

Final Preparation

A large room in the headquarters building was established as the Bigot briefing area. An elaborate sand table map—actually foam rubber and plaster of Paris—was built of the 82nd objective map area. This had annotated in blue paint the drop zones and operational areas and specific objectives for each regiment.

Initially, the regimental commanders and their operations officer were shown the map. They then had to determine battalion objectives and draw them in. As the access restrictions lessened in late May, company commanders then had to do likewise. Captain Bob Piper recalled:

> General Gavin established me as the Bigot control officer. I had to account for all people who had access to the room and who left, when. I also kept the notes when there were discussions. General Ridgway liked simple bullet points without detail. I did this all by hand initially and then had a typewriter for transcribing notes. I would make changes to the map locations and then give them a Bigot stamp and personally carry them to the regimental Bigot officer. I usually did this in the afternoon and they hated to see me coming because they knew it meant new work.

Each regiment, in turn, built its own Bigot room with sand tables, maps, and photographs. In this way, the chain of command from regimental commander down to platoon leader could meet and discuss their respective tasks. It wasn't until the men were at their departure "sausage" that everyone was made privy to the tasks and locations in detail. On the cusp of the buildup for the invasion, the troops and equipment needed for the first week plus of the invasion were moved to hundreds of debarkation ports and airfields in the south of England. These were called "sausages" and held the men who, now fully aware of their ultimate destinations, could plan in security. These ranged from tent cities to airfields and port buildings. This was 31 May.

All this was background to the daily training requirements and unit administration. By mid-May, the division staff was exhausted. Both Ridgway and Gavin were on a near 18 hour schedule. Critiquing airborne operations, providing follow-on tasks, participating in sports and physical training, as well as numerous discussions with other leaders away from Leicester consumed their time. Bob Piper said:

> We were exhausted and the pace never quit. We all stepped up and did each other's job and tried to anticipate Ridgway or Gavin's needs. Both were demanding yet understanding. Both made decisions that were very helpful. We could move on. The work really made us a family. Sleep was a luxury. We all looked forward to the invasion so we could get some rest.

Leading Not Sending

The Normandy invasion was perhaps the riskiest and most important military operation our civilization has ever undertaken. The leaders knew it and their troop commanders were exquisitely sensitive to the point that they could not fail. They had to succeed. One of those leaders understood the core of commanding in combat.

The youngest brigadier general in the Army, Jim Gavin, was the newly appointed assault force commander for the 82nd Airborne Division—one of the key spearhead airborne divisions to land in Normandy before the main force and to hold until relieved. Prior to this, he had joined the 505th Parachute Infantry Regiment at Fort Benning as a captain and followed it through to command the entire regiment in Sicily and Salerno.

On a cold, wet day in England, he demonstrated the essential necessary quality of any first tier combat commander. In so doing, he further gained respect from his soldiers and provided the indefinable will, purpose, and resolve that would see each through the coming conflict in one of the most confused and risky battlefields they ever would fight.

General Gavin had been appointed by the division commander, Major General Ridgway, a formidable soldier in his own right, as the assault force commander for the entire division. General Ridgway would follow in the morning, approximately six hours after the initial parachute insertion. To this point, the actual objective area was withheld from the general troop body.

The troops knew they were going to France. But where, when, and how remained a mystery and subject of scuttlebutt. That day it changed—less than two weeks before the assault.

It was important to both Gavin and Ridgway that the troops hear directly from their leadership what their fate would be; it would not be passed by paper, mimeographs, and telegrams.

Gavin's plan was simple and borne by his previous experience. Soldiers want to see the man who will control their lives. He had spent his time in combat up front at the toughest places at the toughest times. To his soldiers, he was a force of nature and one of them. Where he led, they would assuredly follow. He would talk to them—face to face—just as he had done at Biazza Ridge, across the many hot and dusty roads and villages of the grinding combat of Sicily, and the tense beachhead at Salerno with German armor staring them down. He was one of them and would communicate as he had always done when it truly counted—face to face and close.

Each regiment, on schedule, assembled in an open area. Treated to the cool and misty English weather, the battalions stood close together in parade formation. He arrived in his jeep and parked close to the troop center of mass. He mounted the hood of the jeep and commanded all to gather around him.

In a minute, 1,000-plus airborne soldiers were gathered around as closely packed as humans could be. They had the studied anxiety and interest of veterans and knew now, with this man, the answers to their key questions. All else would follow. Those that were there described it as a moment as quiet as a thousand held breaths could bring.

Looking at the sea of faces, he said in a clear parade ground voice that easily carried to the furthest ranks, "I am not sending you to Normandy. I am taking you there."

With this simple yet most eloquent statement, each of his soldiers knew they wanted to go, who they wanted to go with and that they would win. That is a gift beyond price for any leader and for his men. The many would be one and we would win.

CHAPTER 10

The Rangers

I have chosen to explain the experience of each of the three Ranger task forces on D-Day rather than attempt to lump them together as is often done. Each had very different experiences and effects on the mission. As I was able, over time, to talk to veterans of each, I thought it most valuable to describe each independently, which is how they were initially.

War has a tendency to produce the law of unintended consequences and the Rangers on D-Day are an excellent example. The Rangers' entire focus was on Pointe du Hoc with no emphasis on Omaha Beach other than moving off of it as plan B.

However, as the gods of war dictate, the presence of the 5th Rangers and Task Force C on Omaha arguably saved the day. The Rangers were able to clear the cliff bunkers that had stopped the 29th Division on the beach, allowing success. Concurrently, their presence as the only viable infantry element in that sector provided sufficient force to repel German counter-attacks until the bulk of the 29th Division could get ashore. This merits a description of each Ranger element that day.

Despite the separate missions, the entire Ranger force trained the same way and usually together. Lieutenant Colonel Earl Rudder and Major Max Schneider traded ideas as well as solutions to issues.

Of all the U.S. units that landed on D-Day, the Rangers had the most complex organization due to the difficult tasks assigned. All focus was on neutralizing the large guns at Pointe du Hoc. These guns could range both Omaha and Utah and had to be neutralized on or before the main landings. Understanding both the challenge and necessity of the tasks, General Bradley personally chose the Rangers for the mission.

After forming in the U.S. in 1943, the 2nd and 5th Ranger battalions deployed to England, arriving in late October 1943 to be stationed in Cornwall for training and whatever invasion task was to be assigned. Lieutenant Colonel Earl Rudder was the 2nd battalion commander and the most senior. Hence, he was made head of a Provisional Ranger Group, as yet unassigned to a specific element. This changed in February when the Rangers were assigned to V Corps.

Both Ranger battalions had been training with Combined Operations personnel in standard Commando tactics and techniques, including cliff climbing.

On 4 January 1944, the Operations Officer of Combined Operations and the Commanding General of V Corps, Major General Gerow, called in Lieutenant Colonel Rudder and briefed him on the Pointe du Hoc task, presenting him with several options. These ranged from overland assaults from Omaha to airborne operations to cliff assaults. Gerow rejected the airborne option and left it to Rudder to make a final call. Rudder was tasked with three missions: secure the guns at Pointe de la Percée that overlooked Omaha; secure the guns at Pointe du Hoc; and block the road paralleling the beach from Grand-Camp to Omaha

Very quickly, Rudder and the 5th Battalion Commander, Major Max Schneider, the only Rangers allowed to know the real objectives, settled on a plan to satisfy all near simultaneous requirements:

Task Force A, 250 men consisting of 2nd Battalion Companies D, E, and F, would land at the base of the cliffs, climb and secure the guns, and then block the road.

Task Force B, 59 men of 2nd Battalion, Company B, would land on Charlie Beach, Omaha, and conduct a ground assault from the landward side to clear Pointe de la Percée.

Task Force C, 665 men of the 5th Rangers, would either land at Pointe du Hoc to reinforce the 2nd or divert to Omaha and come overland to reinforce or attack German defenses in support of 2nd Battalion.

2nd Battalion Companies A and B would land on Charlie Beach and either move independently overland to reinforce 2nd Battalion or join 5th Battalion if it landed at Omaha and move with them to join 2nd Battalion.

2d Battalion Companies A, B, and C would load together and initially assault independently of 5th Battalion, as it might not land at Omaha, but an overland assault capability was deemed essential.

In the case of all but Task Force A, it was assumed that fighting on landing would be minimal to non-existent. The Rangers would be landing behind the 116th Regiment, which was tasked to take the draw at Vierville, permitting a quick exit to overland routes above the beach.

Though not yet allowed to provide specific locations to the Rangers, both commanders were able to develop like scenarios in terms of tasks and difficulties. The cliffs of Cornwall were excellent stand-ins for Pointe du Hoc and multiple capabilities were developed within the Rangers, helped in large measure by Commandos from Combined Operations, which lent Lieutenant Colonel Trevor full time to Lieutenant Colonel Rudder.

Between February and May, the Rangers underwent extensive hard training, including live fire and demolitions, resulting in a number of injuries and some fatalities. Both Rudder and Schneider embraced this training and experimented with various devices for cliff climbing.

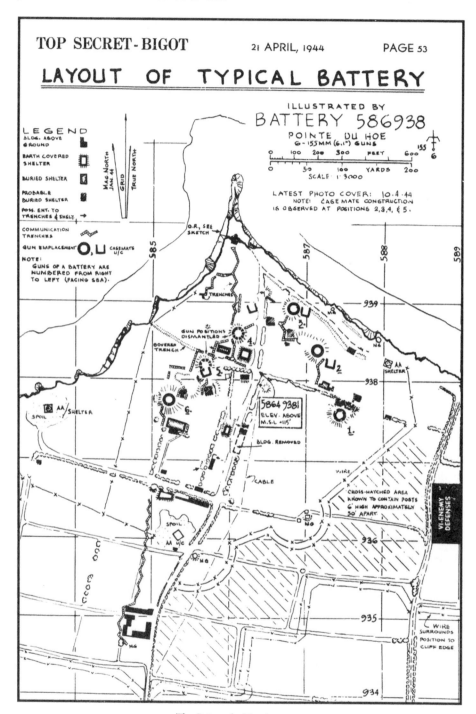

The Pointe du Hoc battery.

The Commandos jury-rigged several grapple systems that could be mounted on Higgins boats. These had toggle ropes, ladders, and plain ropes, three systems for each craft. Rudder chose the newly arriving DUKWs for the London fire ladder systems, and after much wrangling got three assigned.

Almost every day saw some Ranger element using these devices until everyone was familiar with everything. Fear of heights weeded out some and the rest took the task as a requirement where experience eventually overcame anxiety.

Bud Lomell, reflected on this part of the training:

> This was a very tough period. We had a lot of injuries and lost people because of either accidents or just being scared of heights. A lot of the stuff we used was experimental. Some worked and others didn't. When you are 100 feet up a cliff with nothing to hold, it weeds the men from the boys.[1]

In early May, Rudder briefed the Omaha assault force commander, Major General Huebner, Commanding General, 29th Division. Huebner and Gerow approved the plan and assigned the Provisional Ranger Group (PRG) force to the 116th Infantry regiment of the 29th Division for the assault phase. On paper, Rudder reported to the regimental commander, Colonel Charles Canham, but in fact worked directly for Huebner due to geographical distance from Omaha.

On 19 May, the PRG moved to RAF Warmwell, their assigned sausage. This was within 5 miles of their embarkation port, Weymouth. For the first time, all the Rangers could see their assigned targets and the full array of intelligence, sand tables, and models.

For the remainder of the month, the Rangers studied their targets, worked on alternative actions and tested the cliff equipment, although with no cliffs, they used building walls and hangar roofs as objectives. Both commanders traveled frequently to General Huebner's headquarters for updates, intelligence, and shifting plans. On one of the last visits, it was briefed that a French source reported the guns at Pointe du Hoc as having been removed. Rudder chose to say nothing to his men as it was unconfirmed by other sources, including aerial photography.[2]

On a wet 1 June, the Rangers trucked to Weymouth, walked through the streets and loaded their lighters to board the five ships that would carry them. The ships rode at anchor until 4 June where they departed for a 5 June landing (which was called off while the Rangers were at sea).

---

1   Many Ranger vets said the same thing. There was heavy emphasis on live fire and demolitions and firing while climbing and providing suppressive fire while others climbed. Accidents were frequent, which added to attrition.

2   Many of the veterans talked about the great food they had in the sausage, which was offset by almost continuous rain, forcing them to spend a lot of time in the very crowded tents.

Upon returning to Weymouth, a change of Ranger command was necessitated. The Task Force A assault was planned to be under command of the 2nd Battalion executive officer, Major Cleveland Lytle, with Rudder remaining offshore to manage both battalions. A promotion party for Lytle took place aboard ship which quickly got out of hand.

Lytle became abusive, assaulting the Ranger doctor as well as shouting about the hopelessness of the operation. Rudder conducted an investigation that corroborated Lytle's conduct. He immediately relieved Lytle and sent him to a hospital ashore under armed guard. Rudder was very concerned that Lytle might expose the invasion, as no one ashore other than the most senior knew the time or place. Bud Lomell recalled:

> We had a promotion party early in the afternoon and being a British ship, there was a lot of beer and whiskey available. People started to get out of hand by dark and we had to break it up. Lytle was getting very loud and saying a lot of stuff about disaster and failed mission, etc. It finally got so bad several of us grabbed him and chained him to his bunk. That's where he was when we brought Colonel Rudder to see for himself. Lytle was passed out.

Previously, Rudder had been ordered by Huebner not to land at Pointe du Hoc until it was secured. Now, he sent a short message to Huebner saying that he was going in with the force as a necessity or else it might fail. He did not ask for permission. Huebner sent no response.

On nightfall, approximately 2230 5 June, the Ranger force departed for France with the more than 4,500 ships for the invasion.

CHAPTER 11

British Airborne

The 6th Airborne had the most crucial tasks of all elements on D-Day. Blocking the known panzer divisions from the west would prevent a wholesale slaughter on the beaches and imperil the entire operation. Further complicating matters was that it had to hold intact the same bridges the Germans would need, rather than destroy them, all with very light infantry. As masters of planning, the leadership expertly ate the elephant one bite at a time.

The British 6th Airborne Division was given a number of very hard tasks, specifically, take and hold Pegasus Bridge, take Merville Battery, hold Ranville Ridge, and link up with forces emerging from Sword Beach.

Of all the tasks, the last, linking up, was the least difficult, but the other three required separate distinct planning actions and very resolute commanders as well as the maximum in innovative thinking. I was very fortunate to be able to have extensive discussions with three key commanders: James Hill at Ranville, John Howard at Pegasus, and Terence Otway at Merville. I also had separate discussions and correspondence with Napier Crookenden, later a lieutenant general. At this time, he was the brigade major in 6th Brigade and responsible for much of the planning. It is their recount that I focus on rather than the bulk of the 6th Airborne Division.

Unlike the American Airborne task, which was essentially generic and common for all the Parachute Infantry Regiments, the 6th was required to identify specific elements and assign them discrete Bigot tasks separate from all others. In the case of Pegasus and Merville, the respective brigade commanders were "Bigoted" as to their objectives very early in the training cycle. Hill said,

> General Gale called myself, Brigadier Poett and Brigadier Kindersley into his office in early February. He showed us a covered map of Merville and Pegasus. Initially, I got Merville for planning, later getting Howard's men from Kindersley to execute. Then they were later passed to Poett for the operation and I got Pegasus. He further went on to explain how extraordinarily important Merville was and that he would put the entire division to our disposal once we determined what was needed.

Without making specific assignments yet, he left us alone to study this along with a bit of photos and intelligence. We quickly determined that gliders were the only thing that could take the bridges and not many of them due to restricted space.

Merville was a bloody tough task and would require at least a battalion with reinforcements. We discussed this with Windy and he approved our approaches and in briefing our respective commanders. I picked 9 Para because I thought it had both the command drive to do it and was the most open to ideas on the matter.

The discrete nature and specific details of the tasks required each task commander to manage the issue in isolation of others. While they were part of the division, they quickly became quite separate in terms of training, priorities, and authorities. For a time, Lieutenant Colonel Otway and Major Howard probably had more influence and priority than most generals. Crookenden said:

We knew in time that Otway and Howard had the initial key objectives. General Gale made it clear that we were to support in most whatever they wished. There were some grumbles, but Gale was quite firm on the point.

For the most part, their senior generals provided what was needed, often to the detriment of the larger elements, and supported their approaches. Too much supervision was never an issue; trust was everything. Prior to the command decisions, General Gale assessed what elements would best accomplish the tasks. Crookenden said,

When we got the Bigot tasks, we had no idea as to who would do what. I sketched out a plan after examining the intelligence and briefed the brigadiers with Gale present. There was some shifting of locations and units but the key items, Pegasus, Merville, and Ranville were clear. It was up to the commanders to assign forces. I made no attempt to do so.

As we found out, task assignments went under some flux and the commanders did some horse trading until we got settled. They made my job easy as they filled in the blanks.

Pegasus Bridge

Pegasus Bridge, the complex of two bridges spanning the Caen Canal and the Orne River, required a reinforced company only as a specific glider mission. But it was considered the single most important task of the entire division. General Gale decided that it was necessary to assign generic type tasks to several elements to determine which unit performed best and should get the assignment.

In time, after a major exercise in March, called Bizz, and the debriefing on 15 April, it was determined that the best suited unit for the Pegasus task was Company D, Oxfordshire and Buckinghamshire Light Infantry, commanded by Major John Howard. His battalion commander, Mike Roberts, called him into his office. Howard recalled:

Colonel Roberts faced me across the desk and, holding my eye, told me that D Company, plus two platoons of B Company and 30 sappers under command, were to have a very important task to carry out when the invasion started. The colonel went on to tell me that our task would be to capture two bridges intact.

A parachute assault, the primary capability within 5 Brigade, was judged too slow and inappropriate for such a small target complex. Brigadier General Poett says in his book *Pure Poett: The Autobiography of General Sir Nigel Poett*:

> that only a glider-borne force could be landed sufficiently concentrated and close enough to the bridges to enable them to be rushed before the Germans could destroy them. The General accordingly placed under my command a glider-borne Company of the Oxford and Buckinghamshire. My 5th Parachute Brigade was given the task of seizing the bridges and securing the bridgehead in depth... General Gale, in giving me my orders, specified that, in seizing the bridges, reliance should be placed on speed and surprise and that the assault should take the form of a coup de main. The bridges and their defenses must be rushed before the bridges could be destroyed. The General, in studying my 5th Para Brigade problem, had concluded Light Infantry...
>
> Possible landing grounds close to the bridges were very restricted in size and only three gliders could land at each bridge. It was felt, however, that provided the bulk of Howard's six platoons were landed accurately, they could hold out until relief came from a parachute battalion landing in the area north of Ranville. I selected Lieutenant Colonel Pine-Coffin's 7th Para Battalion to be responsible for relieving Howard's force at the bridges... The speed with which the 7th Battalion could reach the bridges would depend on the accuracy with which they were dropped. The river bridge was some 1200 yards from the centre of the dropping zone and the canal bridge 400 yards further.
>
> There was a considerable element of risk in the coup de main operation and a contingency plan was necessary in case it miscarried. The contingency plan included an assault crossing of the two waterways by the 7th Para Battalion.
>
> Detailed orders were issued to the Battalion for this operation. They carried thirty inflatable dinghies and twelve recce boats in large kit bags attached to the legs of the paratroopers and released on a cord before landing. I decided to drop with a small command post at the same time as the Pathfinders, so that, if the coup de main did miscarry, I could control the contingency plan and adjust the deployment of the Brigade.

The Pegasus task force, reinforced by three infantry platoons and engineer elements, organized itself as a separate entity near Exeter in Devon. Howard planned on a simultaneous assault on the bridges. His executive officer, Captain Brian Priday, would take half the force to seize the Orne River bridge and Howard and an equal number would take the Caen Canal.

However, at this point, mid-April, Howard could not tell his men of the specific location as he did not know, only the type of target. They laid out engineer tape for the dimensions and dug defenses as Howard directed. Howard also found a pair of bridges in town that reasonably resembled the target. Against these, he would arrange periods of traffic stops and isolation and attack with various scenarios. Howard said,

> I learned that, above all, my plans must be flexible. It was made clear to me in that exercise that events would take place incredibly fast, but in what order and who would carry out the task,

was entirely in the lap of the gods. I realized that the chances of us all getting to our destination in the order we wanted was remote."

Howard mixed and matched his forces every day to ensure that every man could do every other man's job. He conducted exercises day and night and used live fire frequently. Howard said:

> We were totally dependent upon the gliders landing us where we needed to be. I assumed that would not happen and trained accordingly. I wanted to be confident that whatever was landed could do the job.

Finally, on 2 May, Brigadier General Poett called in Howard and briefed him on the precise mission and targets. He was formally "Bigoted." He had access to all the intelligence and an excellent model of the area. He was denied the ability to brief his executive officer. Only he could have the precise information and he could take nothing out of the briefing room other than geographical distances which he wrote on a piece of paper. Howard recalled,

> I finally got the targets and was very impressed with the intelligence. I made mental notes but was warned I could take nothing back with me. I did write the distances so I could develop a training plan on the ground. I wanted to brief my Executive Officer Brian Priday, but was told I could not. I confess I fudged a bit on that one.

On 16 May, Howard was shown a pair of bridges in Exminster. They crossed the river Exe and were almost a match in terms of distance. The city fathers and police were informed and Howard immediately moved his force to the area and conducted D-Day and night rehearsals against the bridges to include live fire.

This caused some consternation in town as the bridges were crucial to normal movement near the center of the city. Regardless, the priority of invasion training and the unique priority of Howard's mission prevailed.

Howard conducted five exercises, four at night, with live fire. Howard explained:

> I worked them hard but I was fully confident that we could do the job under any circumstance. Exminster was our graduation exercise.

While Howard was training his men, the glider pilots were also training separately at RAF Tarrant Rushton. Fourteen men were selected by the RAF, all NCOs or junior enlisted, and began intensive training on the Horsa.

Target dimensions were laid out in open fields and pilots trained against the targets, initially in daylight, later at night. Several gliders were destroyed during this phase but were rapidly replaced. Between April and May, training had progressed to the point that full force night landings could be conducted.

The pilots conducted a total of 43 training flights using both instrument and visual flight techniques. Various courses were designed, with navigational legs requiring the pilots to use compass and stop watch to determine course navigation accuracies.

> Your task is to seize intact the bridges over the Canal at Benouville and the River Orne at Ranville and hold them until relieved by the 7th Parachute Battalion.

The Bigot building with its precise model and supporting photos was now open to Howard as he wished. He took considerable notes as to specific objectives he could see and transferred them to the men for planning and rehearsals. He was not allowed to indicate any location to the unit, generic only. This was the basis for the earlier exercises at Exeter.

On 26 May, Major Howard and his men, 181 strong, moved to Tarrant Rushton to join their glider force. Here, on 27 May, Howard was able to finally brief his men on the actual targets. Here, he was also able to develop further training. Howard said,

> The men finally saw what they were going against. The photos proved the value of the training and we had a high sense of confidence. Regardless, now that we had the gliders, I wanted to make a real team.

Howard arranged for gliders to be towed by truck to the target area he created in a field. He had the men load the gliders, trucked to the targets, and then conduct an attack as planned. He again mixed loads and switched targets so the men did not know where they were until they got out and had to adjust.

His plan was quite simple, seize whatever bridge you are near and hold it.

As a sidebar, he asked his engineer element to conduct a "full kit" weigh in to see if the individual weights assumed for each man were correct. This was a crucial issue for the gliders as the weight determined how fast they would land and when the pilot would have to touch down on a very narrow piece of land.

The engineers were grossly overweight. Howard then had his infantry weigh in with similar results. They then had to drop equipment and ultimately cut one man per glider to stay within reasonable weight for the glider. As it was, the pilots told Howard they would be approximately 1,500 pounds overweight but that it was manageable.

In the early evening hours of 5 June, they loaded their Horsas to be the first Allied force on the ground.

Merville Battery

As part of the 40th anniversary, we met Otway, Hill, and Crookenden at Merville where they gave us an on-site lecture of the preparation and execution of the Merville assault. Later, they held a smaller officer call-in in one of the bunkers, expanded a bit on the initial discussions, and then took questions. The discussion was led by Crookenden but the dominate personality was Hill. I can assure you that for that period, he was every bit the commander in charge of us troops. The Grenadier Guards would have been proud. Age was not a limiting factor that afternoon.

In late April, the 9 Para Battalion commander, Lieutenant Colonel Martin Lindsay, was shown the battery complex by Brigadier General Hill, but not told where it exactly was. Very little in terms of details were provided. His 2IC (Executive Officer) was Major Terence Otway. Otway was an exceptional planner and very detail conscious. But he was also extremely ambitious, cold and, while respected, was not particularly well liked. It was up to Otway to develop the assault plan and do the necessary support work to allow meaningful training.

As part of the local training, a number of airborne operations were conducted. Numerous troops were injured, ranging from minor to significant. Lieutenant Colonel Lindsay, on his own initiative, arranged for a local doctor to assist in managing the casualties. During his service, Lindsay allegedly revealed that France would be their target. This was a major breach of security and was reported, allegedly by Otway, to Generals Gale and Hill on 18 March. Lindsay was immediately relieved, arrested, and shipped to London. Otway was placed as interim commander. Crookenden (in his private correspondence), wrote,

> Lindsay was a very popular and competent commander. The friction between Otway and Lindsay was apparent. However, Otway was a very skilled planner unlike Lindsay who was a first-rate troop leader. They balanced each other. The relief was a major struggle within the command, but had to be done. Lindsay was done in by his well-meaning intentions. Otway was the obvious choice and we were well along in planning, too long to have a new face introduced.

On 1 April, Otway was informed he had been promoted to lieutenant colonel and would be the commander of 9 Para. At that point, Brigadier General Hill took Otway to the Bigot room and showed him the battery in detail, something Lindsay had never seen. Otway was left to plan with a comment from Hill to plan with whatever resources you need without restriction.

Otway spent an entire day planning and then returned to the battalion where he engaged his 2IC for further planning. Otway showed details regarding the target but not its location. A complex plan began to emerge.

A major bombing strike would hit the battery prior to assault. This would destroy much of the minefield and concertina fencing.

A reconnaissance party with engineers would arrive early at the rear of the battery area, a covered wood north of Ranville Ridge. They would confirm the defenses and the engineers would begin clearing seven lanes through the minefield and barbed wire perimeter.

Assembling after airborne insertion, the main body, including more engineers, medical, and weapons elements would move to the objective to link with the recce/engineer force. Machine guns would be placed on the flanks and mortars in position.

The assault force would move into the cleared lanes and proceed to the last belt of concertina wire just inside the main defenses.

The assault would be initiated by three gliders landing in a coup de main on top of the battery. This would be the signal for the main body to assault with the covering fire of the machine guns in support.

After securing the casemates, engineers would destroy the guns and the force would return to their final linkup point a kilometer to the south. The mortars would fire several yellow signal flares to notify the Navy the battery had been taken and not to fire.

There were many moving parts and delicate timing. After several planning sessions with his company commanders and 2IC, Otway determined his final force structure of infantry, engineers, medical, signal, and support. It would total 733 men, almost 10 percent of the total 6th Airborne assault force and twice the battalion's normal complement. Lieutenant Colonel Otway said,

> I had some concern when I first presented our plan and requirements to Hill but we had thought it out and were satisfied that what we asked for to do the job we needed. I presented the case and he agreed immediately.

Brigadier General Hill added:

> When Colonel Otway presented his requirements, I agreed. The battery was the key to the entire beach assault and we couldn't afford to shave. His plan was quite compelling and thought out. General Gale agreed and directed full support.

Crookenden explained:

> The plan was very complicated, but Otway made it clear there really were no options. He had the deepest knowledge of the objective and masterfully handled all the questions and rationale. We all had the greatest confidence that he could manage this task if anyone could.

Otway assembled his force with its various pieces and proceeded to make it a cohesive unit. They did physical training, road marches, live fire exercises, and specific tactical tasks without regard for the battery mission per se. This was an exercise in developing unity, teamwork, and honing element-specific tasks.

While this was going on, Otway searched the countryside for land that could accommodate the force with a realistic battery layout, to include live fire. He found it near a place called Inkpen near West Woodhay. Acquisition was rapid but not easy. Seven different ministries were required to concur. But with the priority the division enjoyed, approval was granted within 48 hours.

Otway immediately deployed his engineers and began to construct a like battery between two large hill masses. Engineer tape was replaced by barbed wire, and plywood and sandbag casemates constructed. Insofar as possible as could be derived from the photos and analysis, the interior bunkers and weapons systems were also replicated.

This aerial photograph shows the Merville Battery. The main gate is on the northern side, it is surrounded by several lines of barbed wire with an anti-tank ditch protecting the northwestern approach, there are four casemates, and a number of other buildings. The main 9th Battalion assault approach from the southeast, with a diversionary attach approaching the main gate along the curved road heading in from the east.

To the side, away from the target battery, ranges were setup for demolitions, small arms, and mine clearance. Otway said,

> I insisted that the battery be as absolutely accurate as possible down to the meter. I intended to work the place hard and we needed every man to know every job. I didn't know when we would go but I knew it wasn't long. Hence, I wanted to get on with it as soon as possible.

While construction was taking place, Otway was driving the main force hard at Bulford. He insisted on a rotation between day and night exercises and emphasized road marches with full equipment as the core.

The specialized elements such as weapons, medical, demolitions, and mine clearing had specific training areas for their skills but would regroup for the road marches. Otway remembered,

> I was determined we would be a solid team. No special care or separateness would help. We were all going to go to Merville as a unit so we would march around Bulford as a unit.

Otway took the task force from Bulford to the Inkpen mock battery on 8 May. He did this by way of a near 30-mile road march to their field encampment. They would not return until 24 May.

These 16 days were spent in continuous training on the model, ending up with five daylight and four night rehearsals of the whole assault, each with ball ammunition. Otway, like Howard, changed up the forces so they could do each other's job if necessary.

Otway was also mindful of not wearing the troops down mentally. As such, he permitted troops going downtown to the pubs. Security was a major issue in his mind and he lectured constantly as to the need to say nothing to anyone as to what they were doing.

He went to the unusual length of recruiting more than 20 of the best looking Women's Auxiliary Air Force (WAAF) personnel from the nearby RAF facility. They were to be scattered amongst the pubs and be friendly toward the troops. In time, they would press the troops for information as to what they were doing.

The WAAFs were to report back to Otway the following morning with the names of those who succeeded or failed. Any failures would have their post-training leave canceled. Much to his surprise, there were no violations. Otway recalled,

> I was extremely concerned about loose tongues and my decision to allow the men downtown. The WAAF idea came to me as the best means to determine how disciplined the men were. Much to my surprise, no violations were reported. I always wondered if some of the WAAFs became real girlfriends.

Training took on a clear pattern. Each team would conduct internal briefings and discussions in camp, usually with a sand table or drawing. They would then conduct a rehearsal on their own near camp.

This would be followed by a full up force daylight rehearsal and then a night rehearsal. Each full dress would begin with an overland march of varying distances and culminate in a live fire execution on the battery.

Otway was very concerned as to obstacles and minefields and spent considerable time and cross-training on breaching, clearing, and crossing techniques. By the end of the training on 24 May, Otway was satisfied that the men knew the tasks well and could succeed even with significant issues. This would be the last day at Bulford Barracks.

By this time, and after viewing each rehearsal, Otway finalized the assault plan. It was quite complex, required a number of moving parts, and had a strict time table. It is best described using the 6th Airborne After Action Report (AAR):

Preliminary Organization

(a) In order to disorganize the defenses, damage obstacles, and possibly clear a route through the minefields it was decided to drop an Oboe (bomb drop plan) of 4,000 lbs bombs each from 100 Lancasters on the battery position between 0030 and 0400 hrs.

(b) One aircraft to drop a party of parachutists at 0020 hrs consisting of:

    (i) A battalion RV [rendezvous point] Organization Party to organize the Battalion RV on the drop zone.

    (ii) A Recce [reconnaissance] Party to recce route forward and defenses.

(c) A first glider element of 5 glider loads [Ranville Ridge drop zone] containing special heavy equipment; this included two 6-pounder anti-tank guns and three jeeps and trailers containing ammunition, special stores, etc. Special stores included:

    (i) 24 lengths of scaling ladder for anti-tank ditch.

    (ii) 60 lengths of lightweight Bangalore torpedo.

    (iii) 12 specially constructed duralumin foot bridges to be used if possible to cross the anti-tank ditch, thereby avoiding mines in it.

Note. A further 120 lengths of Bangalore torpedo, and 48 lengths of scaling ladder to drop with parachutists. This glider element to land as close as possible to the Battalion RV at 0035 hrs.

(d) The battalion was to drop at 0050 hrs, re-organize at the RV, which had to be cleared by NO LATER than 0235 hrs.

(e) A taping party of 1 officer and 8 ORs [Other Ranks/Enlisted] to travel with CO in first aircraft, and also duplicate RV organization and battery recce parties in case the original parties had gone astray.

Taping party to proceed immediately to battery position and to lay tapes as directed by recce party to most suitable points for gapping the inner wire defenses. This party was equipped with Polish mine detectors.

(f) Recce party to meet CO during approach march, to confirm or otherwise layout of enemy defenses, and to lead the battalion to their final assembly area.

(g) The assault party was to go in from the southeast. The assault plan was based upon blowing three gaps through the inner wire defenses. A "Firm Base" to be established about 300 yards outside the perimeter from which the taping party was to clear lanes 4 feet wide through the minefields to each intended gap.

(h) The battalion to be organized as follows:

    (i) Breaching Company: One platoon to each gap.

    (ii) Assault Company.

    (iii) Glider Assault Party—3 Officers and 47 Infantry, 1 Officer and 7 Engineers [RE].

    (iv) Reserve—One Company [less glider assault party]

    (v) 2 sniping parties [each 3 Bren guns, 3 snipers, 3 anti-tank rifles].

(vi) Diversion Group [5 PIATS and 2 Bren guns—including 2 German speakers].

(vii) "Firm Base" party [rest of battalion under second in command].

(viii) Mortars in position 500 yards behind "Firm Base."

3. Organization on arrival.

(a) Head of battalion to reach "Firm Base" between 0410 and 0420 hrs.

(b) Breaching Party to divide into three Breaching platoons and move to wire on orders of CO and lay Bangalore torpedoes.

(c) Assault Company to move to first cross tape behind Breaching Company.

(d) Reserve to move to second cross tape behind Assault Company.

(e) Sniping Parties 150 yards to each flank.

(f) Two 6-pounder guns to position 150 yards west of battery.

(g) Diversion Party to Main Gate north of battery.

4. Assault Plan.

Movement of Breaching Coy silent if possible; if surprise lost bugle to sound "CHARGE" on which fire to be opened by all supporting arms.

0424 hrs—Glider Assault Detachment released by tugs at 6,000 feet—three gliders. To land in the battery position. Armed with Sten guns, grenades, and General Wade charges [a shaped charge demolition] for blowing casemates.

0424½ hrs—tug aircraft to signal letter 'M' to battalion HQ after releasing.

0425½ hrs—"Reveille" sounded on bugle—one mortar to switch to star shells to give glider pilots their targets. No smoke to be used until gliders landed.

0428 hrs—"Fall-in" on bugle—all fire to cease except for Diversionary Party to enable gliders to land.

0430 hrs—1st glider to touch down. "Lights Out" on bugle—star shells cease.

As soon as dark Bangalore Torpedoes to be blown, and successful gaps indicated by light signals.

Assault Company pass through gaps—re-organize inside into four parties and immediately rush to four gun positions followed by engineers.

Battalion Command Post move behind Assault Company and establish inside wire. Reserve Party move up under hand of battalion commander. Sniping parties join reserve.

Note.

(a) Gliders on landing to rush the two center gun positions and destroy.

(b) Diversionary party to break through at Main Gate as Assault Company goes in.

(c) Recognition signals arranged between all parties involved.

Otway briefed the plan to Brigadier General Hill, who appreciated the complexity. Both understood that parts might not happen and that should be anticipated. Otway assured him that his plan had great flexibility and that the men had trained for all contingencies. Both also understood that this was a no fail event. Hill said,

> The battery was a bloody hard task and Otway had planned to the nth degree. I saw no other real option other than what he had planned. I was sure this was the best we could do and had to do.

Otway recalled,

> We had worked the battery as hard as possible. We had gone through every possible contingency. It was now up to the gods of fortune. We just wanted to get on with it.

On 25 May, the task force moved into its sausage at RAF Broadwell. Broadwell would also be the deployment airfield for the glider coup de main force as well as the airborne assault element.

The next day, Otway held his first "O" group (Orders) meeting. Here, he revealed for the first time exactly where the battery was and what it was. A very intricate model of the battery had been made by the RAF. This was placed inside a wooden hut as well as dozens of photographs of the battery and its specific defenses.

For the first time, the men could see how their action meshed with the larger operations and exactly how crucial success was to the overall mission. Otway said:

> I could sense a feeling of pride as the men could see how important their task was and how they were a part of it. This provided a sense of dedication and purpose. I believe every man had a great sense of confidence and will to succeed.

The first briefed were the company commanders. The next day, they briefed their platoon leaders who, in turn, briefed their men. Time was then provided for every team to spend time with the model and go over all details.

On 3 June, Otway ordered full rest, believing that 5 June would be D-Day and that 4 June would be the day all the teams moved to their respective airfields and hangars.

Ranville Ridge

Ranville Ridge was key to the entire eastern portion of the invasion area. It would act as a solid block preventing German armor from counter-attacking as well as act as the jump off point for the subsequent breakout. This geographical feature was Montgomery's "Solid Hinged Door." It was the last defensible ground against armor flanking the British beaches from the considerable panzer forces held by Field Marshals Gerd Von Rundstedt and Erwin Rommel. The feature also encompassed both Merville and Pegasus on its eastern edge. The mass was very hilly and forested with rivers and streams bounding it. Brigadier General Hill would be responsible for holding it.

When the key 6th Airborne objectives of Pegasus and Merville were assigned, that left less than 85 percent of strength for the rest of the task, which was considerable. It had to seize and hold Ranville Ridge, isolate the bridges over the river Dives, and ensure that Pegasus was held. All this against what would be vigorous German armor attacks.

Brigadier Hill's 3 Para Brigade would have the task of holding the forward ground between Ranville and the Bois de Bavent. In that he had "lost" the 9th battalion, he would initially have only 8 Para Battalion and the 1 Canadian Para Battalion to occupy ground best covered by a full brigade and supporting forces. Despite the fact that the brigade was likely to bear the brunt of an armored counter-attack, the brigade had only the man-portable PIAT gun (a spring-launched shell with a range of about 50 yards) and the 57mm anti-tank gun. The 57mm would be available on 7 June after a major glider reinforcement.

Hill had been "Bigoted" in February along with his fellow brigade commanders. As such he was able to develop training and tactics for targets, but he was not free to address in terms of location. Foremost in his mind was the necessity to be fit. Hill recalled:

> One thing I was sure of was that the unit must be exceptionally fit. We would be isolated, have to move far and fast and live by our wits. I greatly believed that fit bodies make fit minds. I chose road marches and physical training as the key to this.

Hill quickly established long road marches as the core event. They ranged anywhere from 12 miles under speed to extended marches of 150 miles. These became the most hated entrance and graduation exercises for all the training. And Hill led. A veteran trooper recollected to me about Hill's training:

> Hill was a son of a bitch and we hated the marches and hated him. But he made us what we were and for that, I believe we were all most grateful. But not until much later.

Having studied his tasks, it was clear that he would be unable to hold the ground in a traditional defensive sense. Rather, it would be a series of outposts on key terrain with minimal reserves. He would have minimal artillery or armor support and was therefore having to rely on mortars and small unit ingenuity. Hill said,

> I knew we would be well stretched from D-Day on and worsening as the Germans overcame the initial surprise. I required the units to develop confidence in fighting in small units not necessarily attached to each other. This meant a great deal of night operations and live fire, which was limited only by ingenuity and stocks of ammunition.
>
> I left Otway to work his problem and spent the bulk of my time looking after the rest. By April, there was a lot of mixing up of men and plans between the several brigades due to the complexity of the tasks and our minimal resources.
>
> General Gale was superb in bringing us [brigade commanders] routinely to discuss issues in light of new intelligence and to share or trade assets. I give him very high marks in this regard. We could have had a lot of jealous angry brigadiers but we were always solid friends and very supportive of each other.

From April to late May, Hill distributed his men to several training sites in the general Nottingham area. He made a point of switching companies and platoons from one battalion to another as a matter of course. This was because he anticipated mis-drops and scattered drops and that whoever showed up was going to have to do the job.

Several live parachute operations were conducted that upheld his assumption. Due to both the unavailability of aircraft as well as injuries, trucks became the means of insertion. This provided an opportunity to switch loads and locations without the troops knowing it until they arrived at the drop off point. Hill recalled,

> When the trucks for an insertion were loaded, I would have drop-off locations for each truck given to the drivers. In this way, we could reasonably simulate mis-dropped or no dropped units. In retrospect, it was a bloody good idea.

On 28 May, having satisfied himself that Merville was in hand and that all that could be done had been done, he sent his forces to their various departure airfields. It was here that the majority would finally learn of their specific target locations. Hill said:

> I spent most of my time talking to the officers as to their requirements and the men as to the importance of the work. I wanted to ensure that everyone had the utmost confidence in their missions.
>
> I much preferred walking amongst them rather than having assemblies. It was more casual and didn't disrupt them more than necessary. I was often asked if there would be a road march. I responded "Only if you are taken prisoner."
>
> I had separate discussions with the battalion commanders where we discussed what might go wrong and how to manage it. The rest of my time was getting daily briefings of the latest intelligence and then commander's casual conversation as to anticipated events. Even then, we only had a basic appreciation of the actual D-Day. Finally on 1 June, we were told to plan on 5 June.

CHAPTER 12

The Decision

The Briefing at St Paul's School

Prior to the decision to go, the ground forces commander, General Montgomery, convened a unique briefing and presentation to outline the entire plan to virtually all the key players of that event: military, political, and royal. All who attended and wrote about it later regarded it as a seminal event.

St. Paul's School, London, has a long history. In 1944, it hosted perhaps the most significant meeting in our civilization—the gathering of the primary leaders of the European theatre. They were there to explain, for the first time to all, the plan to invade France in less than three weeks' time.

The attendees were well aware of the scope and mass involved and their own part in detail, but they had never seen or conceptualized the entire enterprise until this moment. For every person there who later related his impression, it was a stunning moment in their life. It is one thing to see a plan on paper, it is quite another to have it presented by the principal commanders for each and every part.

St. Paul's School was the school Bernard Montgomery had attended as a boy; the 21st Army Group, the operational headquarters for the invasion, now occupied the ground. The ancient assembly hall, a large two-story room in an opera house configuration with center stage, was chosen by Montgomery for this event.

Attendance was strictly controlled by MPs with lists of the permitted august personages ranking from King George VI to division commanders of all Allied forces; there were no lesser lights. The dark narrow oak and walnut benches curved around the room in tiered step backs to near the ceiling. The seating protocol was rigidly but politely enforced, with those with fewer stars on their shoulders seated furthest back.

Division commanders were in the topmost rows with ground corps commanders and senior air and naval personages scattered between them and the first two rows at center stage. General George Patton was on the second row with General Bradley to indicate the ranked array.

Montgomery had created a huge map of the invasion area on the facing wall in addition to a large three-dimensional model on the floor. There was a small walking space on the sides of the model for presenters to use.

On the edge of the stage, seated in leather chairs, were the king, Churchill, Eisenhower, Montgomery, and the most senior air and naval commanders along with General Alan Brooke, the British Chief of Staff. Most of the attendees were intently smoking but barely speaking. They intuitively understood the gravity and quality of the moment to which they were now a part. The tension was palpable.

Eisenhower rose from his chair, walked to center stage, hesitated for a moment and began to speak. He did not have to wait for silence and attention. On his facing the audience, there was a sudden collective hush of anticipation. The invasion had begun.

He spoke for 10 minutes and his confidence and certitude as to the mission transmitted the strength of 10 divisions. A feeling of true confidence went through the audience as sunshine for their troubled souls. He said,

> We can and will do this. I am absolutely confident in the outcome.

Montgomery then rose and briefed the major points of the overall effort with focus on the ground plans. He was very much the teacher to the pupils. Never raising his voice, pointing to the map and slicing the most complex into the simplest for the students at hand. It was masterly and put the glue to the puzzle parts.

He was followed by the air and naval commanders providing their portions of the enterprise with varying quality. Regardless, to those attending, it placed great clarity on the seemingly opaque. Lunch was called.

Reconvening, the two army commanders, Bradley and Dempsey, and the several corps commanders, U.S., British, and Canadian presented their parts. Most effective was the VII Corps Commander, General Lawton Collins, responsible for Utah Beach and the capture of Cherbourg, the jewel in the invasion crown.

He was highly energetic, animated, and concise. The perfect antidote for a post-lunch presentation in exceptionally hard seating with a smoky atmosphere. He moved deftly across the stage with pointer and perfect Fort Benning styling. Everyone knew he would succeed as would they all.

At the conclusion, there was a moment of silence as the stage was empty. The king arose and faced the audience. He began to speak and it was clear he was fighting to retain lucidity from his innate stammer. His words were precise, measured, and utterly sincere. He understood the gravity of this moment with the background of a thousand years' familial history, a burden and role he played well. He was William the Conqueror in reverse and all appreciated that. The crown glowed.

Last to speak and the master of the moment, was Churchill. With serious expression, he took a square stance, pulled at his black lapels and began to speak. The tone was melodic and the phrasing poetic. All the strength and sinew of his verbiage—the only tool the English had in the beginning—was sonorous and cut to the inner being of all who heard his words.

> We will invade with all our might and will. We will defeat the Nazi beast and expunge it from the earth.

He paused, as only Churchill could, magically, magnetically holding all in thrall and concluded,

> I am hardening to this enterprise.

In 1941, soon after becoming prime minister at the absolute nadir of the British war effort, he had made a speech in response to President Roosevelt's offer to assist. At its conclusion his voice dropped an octave and took on a hard firmness:

> We shall not fail or falter; we shall not weaken or tire. Neither the sudden shock of battle, nor the long-drawn trials of vigilance and exertion will wear us down. Give us the tools, and we will finish the job.

At St. Paul's that misty British day was the toolbox from which our civilization finally drew. A day which confirmed and affirmed the distilled essence of that spirit, which is the hallmark of our civilization.

The Sausages Are Stuffed

The vast majority of the troops earmarked for the invasion of Normandy made their final pre-deployment movement into the sausages. They would reside within them until called to mount their transport aircraft or board their ships. Here, they would mentally prepare themselves for what lay ahead. It was not particularly pretty, but the program was singularly effective.

More than a year prior, the British government, in coordination with General Eisenhower's staff planners, began to establish the sausages. These were tracts of land on the south and east coast areas of England to house the half-a-million-plus assault troops. They were in woodlands, fallow farms, and the rugged coasts that marked this part of England. Here, they would be closer to the ports and airfields designated for the invasion embarkations.

The sausages had a commonality of design that only an organization of this magnitude and a preference for engineered uniformity could create. There were entrance and exit control points in echelon from the most distant gates to those closest to the troops themselves. Vast quantities of tentage were established—generally parallel to the coast to take advantage of what land and vegetation allowed. These invariably were elliptical in shape, hence the name sausages.

They contained the necessary sleeping areas for the troops, as well as mess, medical, and staff tentage. Within each unit area, the most important tent or facility was further secured as a Bigot area. Here, from regiment to squad, unit targets would be shown as sand tables, maps, models, and photographs. Within these sausages, they would figure out what to do when they got there.

In many cases, when the sausages were created the British government forcibly removed the civilian population. Such an action was impossible in the major port areas, and the population was simply sequestered, unable to leave the outer secured ring. People rarely complained (the government had a covert pulse feeling system in place) as they knew why this was all happening.

More than 500 airfields had been constructed or expanded in the area to handle the 2,000 C-47 and glider transport aircraft for the airborne elements and the 4,450 bombers, 3,950 fighters, and support aircraft protecting them. In the ports, more than 4,500 ships held anchorage. These included the major capital ships—the two dozen battleships, four monitors, and 25 cruisers, and more than 100 destroyers, minesweepers, and escorts. Sheltering within that mass would be more than 3,000 transport and supply ships encompassing everything from large bulk freighters to channel ferries to Rhino ferries—simple open platforms holding vehicles—initially towed and then moved by outboard motor to the beach.

Within these sausages, now jammed with the requirements for the initial beach and airborne assault elements, serious planning began. On narrow company streets, the specialized equipment of each element was laid out and utilized. Firing ranges were established for small arms, and the final assault supplies broken down from unit to individual soldier.

Within the Bigot tents, elements shuttled in and out to discuss the "how to's" necessary to subdue a bunker or a beach depending upon size. Special tasks such as major cable cutting or crucial demolition tasks were assigned and practiced. Intelligence from the French Resistance, aerial analysis, and radio intercepts was disseminated. Each entrance and exit was managed by a roster held by the MPs and approved by a unit officer. No outsiders were allowed.

The airborne forces had an additional facility to hold the flight routes. These were black and white ground images of the exact route each unit would fly. The jumpmasters were to study this for key landmarks, so they could gauge their positions along the route and know with some precision when they had to stand up the troops for the "green light." Postwar, a number of veterans indicated how crucial this was when the flights became disorganized due to flak and clouds.

The messes were a highlight of an otherwise dull situation. The armies went to some length to bring in the best food available. In fact, General George Marshall,

U.S. Army Chief of Staff, made a point of this for planners a full year ahead of need. Accordingly, pork, ham, chicken, turkey, steak, and fresh vegetables were routinely issued—"Fattening up for the kill" many said. In most areas, coffee, tea, donuts, and biscuits were usually available 24 hours a day. This was crucial for the airborne elements as they did considerable night training against mockup targets and assembly exercises.

Movies and music were common staples. Mini-USOs—run by internal unit personnel—provided an emotional relief. In many cases, due to size and schedule complexities, movies ran on a 24-hour basis. Emergency supplies of bulbs and cameras were a common request.

Mail usually came and went twice a day and significant supplies of writing material, tobacco, gum, and candies were provided. Medical support was also provided in unusual quantity and timeliness. The organizational medical staffs, augmented by division and corps personnel, established continuous screening and treatment. Where before a troop might see a doctor only under unusual circumstances and time, here the visits were instantaneous.

In those locations adjacent to an embarkation port, the beach assault and support elements were mixed. Each had to board ships on an exact schedule as there were insufficient wharves to accommodate simultaneous loading. First serviced were the supply and logistical support ships. Their loading began very early in the process so they could be moved out and space made available for the immediate assault support equipment—artillery, tanks, field hospitals, immediate follow-on ammo, food and water, communications, and high level command/control elements. Last would be the troops themselves embarking on a wide array of ships. These ranged from previous channel and inter-island ferries to combat assault support ships (LSIs) to troop ships. From East Anglia to the Isles of Scilly and to Bath, the coast was jammed with ships from horizon to horizon.

On the fantail of most transport vessels, barrage balloons were fixed. These were manned by all-black elements very recently shipped from the U.S. specifically for this event. Each balloon had a five-man crew managing the inflation and control cables. Their quarters were dependent upon the attitude of the ship's captain and ranged from the best available to huddling on the deck.

In the segregated army of the time, black soldiers were usually assigned to quartermaster and logistical support elements rather than combat elements. The barrage balloon units were part of this structure. Once the shore was secured, the balloons and their management would follow. For now, they would arrive in the stern, much as they did in the Dixie busses of their recent training camps.

The loading went on non-stop, supported by the sequestered civilian longshore-men, dock hands, and tug crews. In most cases, the Higgins boats for the assaults would be used to ferry troops to their ships, but this would not begin until 1 June. Long lines of vehicles of all shapes and classes lined the cobbled streets awaiting their turn to load. The slate roofs and window glass continuously vibrated with their passage. The locals knew that when the vibrations ceased, the invasion would begin.

To support this endeavor, the government lifted the pub closure hours to accommodate the extended schedule. Maintaining high morale among the locals was a key requirement.

The weather over the Channel that May was not cooperative. Often, rain and fog descended for days on end. The tents and living quarters were jammed with men and their soaked clothing and gear. Most smoked and sweated with the pores of active youth. Troops ran through the rain with full mess kits to eat in the shelter of their tents quickly adding the smell of freshly forming garbage to the dense blue air. Fans were mostly non-existent and stoves roared.

Wet fingers penned moist pages. The Home Front recipients would only understand the unusual smearing when they read the papers or heard the news on 6 June. In some cases, mail was intentionally held within the sausages for the last week to ensure no leakage of dates or locations had slipped by an errant censor. This resulted in some next of kin receiving a death notice telegram prior to the loved one's letter.

This was a highly organized enterprise that reflected the best managerial aspects of Allied civilization. It had to be as it focused the very best of our humanity on the most important task it would ever undertake.

The kraken was now in the cave.

Ike's Longest Mile

The woods near Portsmouth, England in the early morning hours of 4 June 1944 were rent with near hurricane winds and pelting rain. It came in a near horizontal stream as so many bullets stinging and exploding against any surface, man or timber.

Into this maelstrom, a hunched-over man walked purposefully toward a waiting Packard. It was General Dwight Eisenhower en route to perhaps his most significant decision of the war—to go ahead with or postpone D-Day. The decision was his alone to make.

It was unusual that his naval aide, family friend, and constant companion, Commander Harry Butcher, did not accompany him. Instead, knowing his presence would be irrelevant, he remained in the small cottage and busied himself with replenishing Ike's cigarette supply, cleaning the coffee cups, and re-arranging the checkers set.

The road, more a mud track than solid pavement, wound through the encroaching forest for the mile to his headquarters at Portsmouth House. Like a Disney movie, the deep black fir branches waved at the car and the rain, now in torrents, smashed against the windshield, overwhelming the feeble attempts of the wipers to retain clarity.

The headlights streaked and shimmered through the multiple prisms the water offered. The rain crashed against the car with a single streaming cacophony the entire journey. Ike, silent, sat somewhat hunched over in the passenger seat pulling on his always-present Camel cigarette. His driver, Kay Summersby, somewhat of a confidant and diversion, sensed the moment and said nothing other than a hesitant hello. In silence, the two wound their way to the large portico at the front of the house.

Out of the car, he paused for a moment to light a new Camel with the butt of the old, which he casually flipped into the maelstrom. The guard opened the large wooden door.

Shaking himself off, he strode purposefully into the large reception area. The supreme commander was prepared to make a supreme decision.

It was this one mile that set the tone and backdrop for the last gathering of the men charged with civilization's greatest roll of the dice.

The Decision to Go

I have written this as a "best guess" based on readings as well as extensive discussions with Susan Eisenhower, who had access to both discussions within the Eisenhower family as well as some documentation. I would surmise it is a reasonably correct description of one of the most historic decisions within our civilization today.

Perhaps the most well-known and most-described action for D-Day was Eisenhower's decision to go on 6 June. It was very much a collaborative discussion, but it was his decision alone.

In the pounding rain, Southwick House, a Georgian cum Greek edifice, stood ghostly and brooding, taking the wind and water pelting like bullets across its marble colonnades. The tall ground floor windows echoed the storm for those inside, the sound only partially dampened by the thick blackout curtains.

Arrayed in old English club chairs and oak tables around the reception room were the most august of Allied military bodies subordinate to Ike's direction. Montgomery quietly chatted with his Chief of Staff, Lieutenant General Freddie DeGuingand. Also present were Admiral Bertram Ramsay, commander of all sea forces; Air Chief Marshal Tedder, the Deputy Supreme Commander; Air Chief Marshal Trafford Leigh-Mallory, commander of all air forces; Major General Kenneth Strong, SHAEF G2; and Lieutenant General Bedell Smith, SHAEF Chief of Staff. Only Monty was not smoking—a habit he found loathsome but was unable to extinguish due to his subordinate position.

No others were physically present as they knew they would be both irrelevant and excluded for this discussion. It was approximately 0415, 5 June 1944.

Just beyond the reception area, the large high-ceilinged map room could be seen. There was a heavy, rectangular oak table facing the wall of maps with chairs and a sofa arrayed on the opposite side. Notepads were in front of each place, as well as ashtrays. Only eight chairs would be needed this morning.

As soon as Eisenhower's presence was felt at the main entrance, all rose as one and moved inside to the table. There was little discussion. The import of the moment hung heavy like a velvet cape.

Making small talk in greeting, Ike took his customary position at the center, sat down, and took a pull on his cigarette. As if on cue, Group Captain James Stagg, the tall Scots weather chief, walked in quickly, gathered himself, grasped a long pointer, and stood before Ike. The room was dead silent save for the constant rhapsody of the rain. Needing no introduction and awaiting Ike's head nod, he began.

His first comment was a rather pointed recount of the decision to postpone operations the previous day. Pointing to the smaller weather maps to the side, dazzling with their millibar lines and whorls of barometric measurement, he clearly stated that as predicted, the invasion would have been an utter weather disaster.

> Gale force winds would have destroyed the Airborne assault, Force 6 & 7 waves would have done equal damage to the seaborne assault, and the bombers would have been unable to see any targets—an unmitigated disaster had it gone as originally scheduled.

With this sobering introduction, his voice changed to a somewhat higher octave, almost indiscernible in his brogue.

> We have detected a small break in the weather, and I can reasonably predict a decent window of approximately 36 hours beginning approximately Noon our time. We have studied the patterns and discovered a new High over Greenland that will traverse toward us to calm the present storm and provide decent cloud clearance, and lessening of water actions.
> While all our stations are not unanimous in that feeling, I believe it to be true.

The room had a collective intake of breath at these words. Fingers drummed the table and eyes followed him around the room. All wanted to say something but held comment pending Eisenhower's response.

Ike asked, "Are you confident of this break?"

"I am reasonably confident that it will occur," he replied.

All of this discourse happened with the constant beating rain less than a dozen feet from them.

"What do we think?"

Ike turned to his left and looked at Ramsay, awaiting response.

"If we postpone, we will again have to recall the Utah fleet almost immediately," replied Ramsay. "We can work with this sea state."

Next was Leigh-Mallory. He was clearly ambivalent and conflicted and found it difficult to be definitive. Instead, he commented that cloud cover might make it difficult for pilots to see the drop zones or bombers their targets. It just depended on conditions of the moment. A pass.

Next was Montgomery. He looked up with bright eyes and without hesitation. "We must go. I say go."

With that, Ike turned to Smith. Smith, knowing his role, carefully summarized the situation and the options and subsequent consequences. This took less than a minute and silence, save the rain, descended.

Hanging over the back of this discussion, as a Sword of Damocles, was Operation *Fortitude*, the deception operation designed to trick the Germans into believing Pas De Calais was the invasion area, not Normandy. Should the Germans discern *Fortitude* was a myth, it could be utterly disastrous for Normandy.

Fortitude was built on air, rubber, and controlled publicity. Its success depended upon the Germans believing what their logic dictated. Patton would lead the assault, and it would be at Pas De Calais—less than 15 miles across the Channel.

Elaborate programs had been established to ensure this mindset was viewed as the answer as to where the invasion would occur. All German spies in the England had been captured, flipped, and were sending contrived messages to the Abwehr—half-truths and half fiction—to ensure the continuity of the ruse.

Patton had made appearances and pronouncements in East Anglia as the Commanding General, First Army Group. The land and ports of the area had emanated false radio traffic indicating the major invasion force buildup—a ruse that worked, as the Germans wished to believe their logic would be the Allies logic.

Constant air and sea patrols had kept the German attempts at penetration away from the coast. Had they penetrated the coast, they would have seen the masses of shipping and personnel in the south—the way to Normandy—and the absence of forces in Anglia. *Fortitude* would be destroyed.

The room knew that continuous integrity of the deception was tenuous and that a single German E-Boat or aircraft penetrating the screen would compromise all. The disaster at Slapton Sands with its E-boat penetration was a precursor. It was just a matter of time.

Postponement meant another month before tide and moon were best aligned. A month for the Germans to get lucky. Decent weather of 36 hours for the Allies was also 36 hours of decent flying weather for the Axis.

Ike sat silent for a few moments, the smoke from his ever-present Camel spiraling from his hand. The others gazed down at the table or fixed on him. All besides him were irrelevant at this point. The rain continued in its thunderous percussion.

Ike arose from his chair and began to pace back and forth looking at the dark blue carpet. He paused and looked up. "Well. There it is. The question is just how long can you keep this operation on the end of a limb and let it hang there."

"OK."

"We'll go."

There was a collective exhalation, and all immediately arose to their tasks. Now, Ike was irrelevant. He sat for a moment, lit another cigarette, and then moved purposefully toward the door and the continuously pounding rain.

Bob Murphy and 140,000 of his companions began to move toward their "rendezvous with destiny." By daylight, a mighty weight had been lifted across the land. For the first time in a week, the cloud ceiling began to rise, and the torrential rain finally began to ease.

PART IV
Execution

CHAPTER 13

Good Vibrations

The Normandy invasion is usually depicted with great crashes, bangs, and volcanic energy combined with broad scenes of masses of materiel and manpower. But we should remember and reflect that the invasion began with subtle sounds and vibrations and brought the message of liberation to Europe on cat's paws, growing to crescendo. We remember and depict the climax but forget the subtlety of sounds that brought it all together.

It began on the late evening of 4 June in several of the western ports of England. These held the derelict hulks designated to be the breakwaters for the Mulberry harbors at Omaha and Sword beaches. They were pulled by ex-commercial tugs manned almost exclusively by civilians, as were the wooden minesweepers—more than 250—exceeding today's total surface combatants of the U.S. Navy. As the slowest of all vessels, these had to precede the vast armada restlessly waiting in more than 150 English ports. It was a quiet throbbing vibration of engines lost in the Force 3 and Force 4 winds and waves of the moment. But it was the first and the baseline for the rest.

By the morning of the 5th, many of the slower transports, attack transports, larger landing craft, and Rhino ferries began their slog to sea. They had just returned to ports on the initial postponement and in less than 24 hours returned to their original routing. Steam turbines, diesel engines, and a vast array of more than 4,000 ships and craft now began to inch out of the many coastal ports filled to capacity into the penetrating wind. They covered the design gamut from huge square concrete caissons for Mulberry to the sleekest of capital ships. Their vibrations, now so collectively blown across the ports, were not lost on the population. These small sounds, by their diversity and number, signaled something special was occurring. Within the buildings, the occupants felt more than heard the motions, stopped their drinking and conversations, and looked out the windows. Despite the spitting rain and driving winds, they collectively understood what those vibrations and dull sounds meant. Many went home and, with their families, lined the streets and the quays, and waved a forced cheery goodbye to the last loading soldiers.

Somewhat later, the larger surface combatants and fast destroyers and escorts began to add to the atmospheric acoustics. Huge chains rattled through their lockers and anchors clanged against steel hulls. They slowly turned into the Channel and began their choreographed and tightly disciplined movements toward the distant French shore—still indiscernible in the daylight. These sounds were generally lost on the civilian population as most of the ships were stationed beyond seawalls in the several major naval roadsteads in the south of England. But they added depth and strength to the growing steel stream as the morning light dwindled with the mist and spume.

In those instances where a capital ship visibly departed a fixed position in port, the observers understood this as a significant moment in their history. The large guns, the fast ships, and the preceding soldier-laden cargos meant that the greatly anticipated event was underway. People thought more than spoke and knew this was an important moment in their lives as it was for those at sea.

In all, more than 150 ports felt the subtle noises and vibrations as their departing guests churned in concert to obscure but crucial points more than a hundred miles away. Collectively, the throbbing vibrations of more than 4,000 vessels began to merge and roll across the water as the host coalesced into minutely detailed and efficient streams led by slow and crucial minesweepers and their mostly civilian crews. The ancient ancestral sea-going skills of the British population were leading the way as much as did Drake and Nelson.

A bit later, on the land, beginning around 2100 in the still light-brightened green of a June English evening, the vibrations began again. These were of a different timbre. From more than a hundred airfields scattered throughout the southern and eastern portions of England, aircraft coughed, sputtered, and began to come to life.

The 40 airfields supporting the airborne assault awakened in clouds of blue exhaust. C-47s, Lancaster, Stirling, and Halifax bombers, loaded with their human cargos, began to wind their way along taxiways. Stretched behind many were tow ropes attached to hundreds of gliders—Hamilcars, Wacos, and Horsas equally loaded to capacity with people and materiel. On several hundred other ancillary airfields, the support structure also came to life. Fighters, bombers, spotter aircraft, and ground support aircraft churned to life in clouds of blue smoke and self-generated fuel-laden density heat currents and moved to the edge of runways. Slowly, but with increasing frequency, all these engines churned the air, bit for lift, and waned into the ebbing light. Together, more than 4,000 aircraft filled the air—all pointing east and south toward France.

The vibrations of this armada could first be sensed, then felt, and then seen. The sky was thick with columns of moving aluminum and wood—once fully formed, the column was more than 50 miles wide and 100 miles deep. For those in the aircraft looking out, it was impossible to see an unobstructed sky. The mass became an overwhelming noise for those below on the land. Windows rattled and shook. Tiles slipped off of ancient buildings. People stopped, looked up, and realized what was happening. Many went straight to churches. Others gathered their children on the stoops and gardens and silently watched the aerial procession pass from view.

Below, in the thousands of ships coalescing in this moment, the vibrations and movements from every direction began to have a telling effect. On the all-important LSTs (Landing Ship, Tank) with their flat bottoms, the people within suffered with each yaw and pitch in the rough Channel water. Many soldiers were assigned deck space only and endured both the cutting rain and wind and the occasional breaking wave in addition to violent seasickness. Some hoped for reaching the land. Others knew better. Each wave and its continuous accompaniments hit the large flat sides and shook these ships and soldiers to their core as they slipped and shifted toward the distant coast as rocks skipping on water.

On the stern of virtually all the transports, there arose a barrage balloon dangling long steel cables intended to ensnare low-flying German fighters. These were manned and secured by five-man all-black crews who upon initial anchorage, would be part of the first 10 waves ashore. The anchor cables hummed and shivered in the wind and set a low but discernible tune for their owners who so recently had enjoyed the warmth of Georgia, Mississippi, and Alabama. Strangers to this environment, they covered themselves in ponchos and sat huddled on the steel stern deck trying to protect themselves against the constantly chilling blow of spume and spitting rain.

A number of these crucial vessels had been commissioned less than 30 days ago on the banks of the Ohio River. Now crewed by teenagers and commanded by twenty-somethings, the residue of hastily finished naval schools, these ships were at the apogee of their purpose. If they survived or if they sank, they would have served their purpose for this moment and been cheap at the price.

On the smaller craft, the minesweepers and DEs (Destroyer Escorts), the passage point for the waves was less than the length of the keel. As the propellers suddenly found only air where water had been, their shafts dramatically increased RPM, slamming against the protective steel shaft cover and rending the ship with constant banging and shuddering bulkheads and frames. The process was reversed when the props hit water again, sending the shaft against the cover as the blades ate into the sea, repeating the endless crossing process.

Below decks, the soldiers quietly endured what they could not control. The constant thumping and vibration of their ship went through their bodies. Their stomachs rebelled and the decks were covered in vomit as waves washed it through the flooded scuppers. The heat, humidity, and collective smells could not be dissipated as the rough seas forced the crew to seal the ventilators. For many, these vibrations and impacts felt far worse than anything they could envision that might occur on dry land. But they didn't really know.

By now, more than 5,000 ships and craft of all classes added their subtle individual sounds to the growing host. Under the sea, this collective energy had a coincidental effect. Well after the invasion, the French noticed that fishing in the Channel was less productive but that they enjoyed a banner year for oysters and mussels. The vibrations had an unexpected effect.

Above this winding metal river rode the Airborne assault force—more than 850 aircraft for each of three divisions, two American and one British. Virtually all flew with open doors. This had several effects. The open door allowed the rushing air to fill the interior with a cold rush alerting the senses. The act of lighting a cigarette took some effort. The skin of the aircraft assumed a hum and transmitted the harmonic vibrations to the aluminum benches on which the grossly overladen soldiers sat. Outside, but within view of most of the passengers, was a never to be forgotten scene which would be recounted in great detail for the rest of their lives.

Below were the small white trails of the thousands of ships wending their way east. The last light glanced off the barrage balloons and added to the impression of the mass below. Horizontally, the paratroopers could see nothing but sister aircraft. The aircraft were virtually wing to wing, close enough to discern the faces of their friends. Darting above and below and catching the glimmering light were the hundreds of fighter escorts. Together, these sights and sounds coalesced to give each member of the initial airborne assault force a huge feeling of confidence and inner strength. Each participant had trained and worked for months within a microcosm. For the first time, everyone could see the immensity of the whole—above, below, and alongside. It was unstoppable. A feeling of great confidence surged within each spectator from the commanding generals to the junior teenaged soldier.

At about the same time the airborne assault began, the seaborne forces started arriving at their designated initial assault positions. For more than 150 linear miles, thousands of ships found their spot in the intermittently dark and moonlit night. The minesweepers closed to within 4 miles of the shore, did a 180-degree turn and vanished in the dark toward their home ports and welcoming pubs. The remainder echeloned in proximity to the Normandy coast by their assigned tasks. The largest bombardment ships were 10 to 12 miles offshore. Then came the assault forces and closest in, the smaller patrol craft and the more than 100 destroyers and escorts—the nearest to the still unseen and unfelt enemy. Interspersed were the command ships, staffed by the leaders responsible for the events of the coming dawn. Each awaited their moment of duty as prescribed by the plan titled *Neptune*. This was an apt name for the force about to erupt from the sea.

The vibrations and sounds for each ship and craft were relatively uniform but with the intensity and tone dictated by size, from the huge anchor links of the battleships rattling through the guides sending continuous shivers through the hull to the simple tension of a steel cable singing out the mud anchor on the light assault craft. The passengers and crews felt the engines slowly cease, the anchor chains grow silent, and only the lapping of the waves and wind interrupted the night. Along the length of the Norman coast, the thousands of previous sounds dissipated and a quiet settled, broken only by the whistling wind and internal noises of on-board preparation for this moment.

For the airborne soldiers, the noises and vibrations grew with fearsome intensity as they crossed the coast of France. Antiaircraft units below began to wake and fire. Clouds impeded the vision within tight formations and pilots fought to control their aircraft, maintain formation, and avoid the flak. Aircraft RPMs were increased to maximum throttle. Planes dipped, slid, and skidded to avoid collisions and ground fire. Within the aircraft, the skins of the fuselage began to strain and shake in response to pilot actions. The collective noise blotted out most senses. German fire resounded clearly to the soldiers inside over the din of everything else, like gravel on a tin roof. Sudden explosions exposed moonlight through the skin and outside the door, flames, flares, and burning aircraft could be clearly discerned. Noise, flames, and visual clues overrode everything else. It was about 0115 on 6 June.

Through shouts and signals, the troopers gained a footing, felt and held the anchor lines, and staggered toward the door. The closing snap of the static line snap hook could be both felt and heard. The last feelings before exit into the maelstrom were of a rush of air, a sudden body shock, loss of senses, and then the silence of descent.

In the momentarily quiet sea, beginning about 0300, orders were issued to lower the assault craft and assemble the initial waves for debarkation. Cables and ropes slid through pulleys and momentarily shook ship sides as the small boats bounced their way along the sides and finally settled into the bucking sea below. Most were Higgins boats, designed and primarily built in New Orleans. Unarmored except for the British version, they were made mostly of plywood and had about 2 feet of freeboard in a calm sea. This was not a calm sea.

Joining them were several dozen Rhino ferries—essentially large rafts with outboard motors. Laden with wheeled and tracked vehicles, they bucked and buckled their shelterless crews, plowing through the deep waves as they joined the assembling forces. Largest of the initial assault craft were the Landing Craft, Tanks (LCTs) carrying the experimental duplex drive swimmer tanks. The tank engines sprang to life with clouds of blue exhaust sending individual shivers throughout the craft. Just behind them were the large assault ships, the Landing Ship, Infantry (LSI). Their forces huddled on the deck and hoped for warmth within the mass much like penguins in a storm.

From Sword Beach in the south to Utah in the east, by 0430, more than 140,000 men were afloat and moving toward the Norman beaches. The Bay of the Seine quietly resonated and shook with the collective energy of this force. From the initial engine starts in single ports of England and the isolated whining motors from inland grass strips, the largest single purpose force ever assembled had come together in the quiet of this June night and begun to exercise its purpose. It began with the smallest of sounds, much not initially discernible, and grew to an overwhelming, focused chorus.

These vibrations coalesced in a small part of our planet and grew to the point where they became noise. The noise we see depicted today in all replications of that event. But it began with small but growing vibrations—perhaps the manifestation of Eisenhower's comment that there is no force to equal the fury of an aroused democracy. These were vibrations of energy we will never hear or feel again. Immersed in today's issues and emotions, we may forget what he wrote to his brother as a colonel—yet to conceive of his future role as the Allied master of his point for all his command—"It is a grievous error to forget for one second the might and power of this great republic." On 6 June 1944 this was demonstrated and the world was forever changed.

CHAPTER 14

Omaha Beach

Support Plan

The support plan for Omaha Beach was both impressive and irrelevant. The virtual 100 percent failure of the various aspects of the support plan combined with the unusual tenacity of the Germans in well-sited defensive positions made the quality of the event much like Admiral Nimitz's comments regarding the Marines at Iwo Jima—uncommon valor was a common virtue. Of all the places and experiences of our men on D-Day, this, above all others, demonstrates ordinary people doing extraordinary things.

The nature of the Omaha defenses became abundantly clear to the Allied planners by late winter of 1943–44. The daily photographs, coupled with intelligence from the resistance, allowed a very precise picture to emerge as to what the invaders would have to defeat. In this, an elaborate and, what was believed to be, extremely thorough support plan was developed. This would have several components: strategic bombing; naval gunfire; amphibious tanks; artillery afloat and accompanying; and engineer demolition teams. In fact, the planners were so confident that the developing wall of explosive technology would be effective, that they believed infantry would be a secondary requirement, a fact the load tables reflected. John L. Hall said:

> Christ, when we saw all that stuff planned against our sector, we thought it would be a cakewalk.

Hall continued:

> The battalion commander briefed us on the support plan and our job with a very elaborate sand table and photographs. They really had it down to a gnats eyebrow. We would be coming in behind this huge mass of ordnance and just behind the Ducks with the 105s. It was really a Wild West movie.
>
> All we had to do was offload from the LCTs, form up on the beach and go up the cliff exit to our battery position. We did not see much of a problem. Impossible with all that stuff thrown at the Germans.

Strategic Bombing

Much against the judgment of the strategic bomber leadership, Lieutenant General Tooey Spaatz and British Air Marshal Arthur "Bomber" Harris, the B-17s would be used as the initial softening up of the Omaha defenses. There would be in excess of 1,300 B-17s, B-26s, and B-24s dropping tons of bombs between the morning of 4 June and 0630 6 June.

Beginning in April, these aircraft would continuously interdict transport points in the Omaha area. This would culminate in a massive strike between H-30 to H-5 striking the close-in beach defenses. Bombs would range from 100 pounders to blast the barbed wire and surface obstacles and 500 pounders to attack the stronger positions. Both would have super quick fuses so craters would not impede rapid progress off the beach.

The B-17s would cruise at 20,000 feet, requiring relatively clear cloud cover to be effective. The others could operate between 5,000 and 10,000 feet. If clouds were an issue by 0600, the bombers would hold past the safety line to insure troops afloat were not hit.

Naval Gunfire

The bombardment forces afloat consisted of two U.S. battleships, the USS *Texas* and USS *Arkansas*, together mounting a total of 10 14-inch, 12 12-inch, and 12 5-inch guns, four British and French cruisers each with nine 6-inch guns, 10 U.S. destroyers with 5-inch guns, and three British destroyers with 3-inch guns. These would all commence firing at 0550 and cease at 0625 with 0630 as with the Ramps Down command. The destroyers would be available for close-in support throughout the day. Naval gunfire control parties were assigned to every battalion and would accompany them in.

In addition to these ships, a large number of specially designed fire-support craft were employed. Five Landing Craft Guns (LCGs) with two 40mm Bofors guns each, accompanying the leading assault wave, were scheduled to fire on selected strongpoints beginning at H-20 minutes.

Beginning at H-Hour naval fire would shift to inland targets such as possible assembly areas, or wait for direction by naval shore fire control parties. There were 24 of these, permitting an allotment of one to each battalion (including the Ranger battalions) in the two assault divisions, excepting the regiment in corps reserve.

Floating Tanks

Sixteen LCTs would carry 32 amphibious tanks to land in the first wave; each ship was fitted so that two leading M-4 tanks could fire over the ramp, beginning from a range of 3,000 yards at about H-15 minutes. These were a British design and one of the products of General Percy Hobart's "Funnies." His inventions included flail tanks, road mat laying tanks, bridging tanks, and engineer demolition tanks in addition to the floating design. These were demonstrated to the Americans who were reluctant to incorporate any due to the lack of training time. Bradley explained:

> We saw them operate in a major demonstration and were impressed. However, it was so late in the game [April], that after discussion with the Corps commanders, we used only the amphibious tank design. We had some hesitation as to the reliability but they worked fine at Slapton and a couple of lakes. The idea of them emerging out of the water to support the troops was a well worth the risk.

Second Lieutenant Vincent E. Baker recalled:

> I was a spare officer and on a dry landing tank which I thought was great. We watched the amphibious tanks at Slapton and a local ocean area. It was all pretty delicate and we had to make stronger struts for the skirt. The battalion commander did a scrub so only the smallest and lightest were in those tanks so they could get out the hatches if need be. I weighed almost 200 pounds so I got a pass for which I am eternally grateful. I can't say anyone had a high degree of confidence in it, but the Brit instructors were very enthusiastic so we thought it a great idea at the time.

Floating Artillery

Another surprise package developed was the addition of 10 LCTs carrying 36 105mm howitzers on self-propelled halftracks of the 58th and 62d Armored Field Artillery Battalions. These would land in the Third Wave for direct beach support. Meanwhile, they would act as floating batteries firing overhead, supporting the first two waves. From a range of 8,000 yards at H-30 to closing at a range of 3,700 yards by H-5 minutes, they would fire at targets throughout the beach area. Each LCT had a small fire direction center and assigned targets. John L. Hall said:

> I was the gun chief of a halftrack 105 Howitzer. We had never fired from a floating platform. We were told this would be open sight, direct lay, maximum charge. We were given photographs of likely targets based on where we were in relationship to the beach. Seemed simple until we tried.
> We had several training events at Slapton and near there. It was very hard to pick out specific targets even on relatively clear days what with the craft moving up and down, mist and smoke and all. There was a lot of guesses in the firing computations. The BC [battery commander] just told us that everything we shot would be German so don't worry.

An additional punch would be supplied by nine specially configured LCT(Rocket)s. These vessels had racks of a launch tubes that would fire 130mm rockets in a barrage just in front of the first wave, obliterating any obstacles at the water line and beyond.

Analysis of the combined plans shows that the great weight of air and naval bombardment would fall on the immediate beach defenses in the Omaha area, including positions which could put flanking fire on the beach. All the main enemy strongpoints, and the Pointe du Hoc coastal battery, were targets for attack both from air and sea.

What Actually Happened

The bombers, flying at 17,000 feet were unable to see the targets due to cloud cover. Ensuring that they didn't kill the troops afloat, the bombardiers held the drop for 30 seconds, which placed the bombs harmlessly in apple orchards well past the defenses.

The naval bombardment was forced to fire blind and spent most of its shells past the cliff tops, missing the beach defenses entirely.

Of the 32 programmed swim tanks, 27 sank upon launch. The remainder were held from launch and were dry landed despite orders to the LCT commanders (two Lieutenant JGs) not to do so. Only two of these were able to provide fire support and one of them was actually disabled in the surf and fired with the turret partially submerged. Of the total 51 dry landed at Omaha in the first six waves, 21 were knocked out. Vincent E. Baker recounted:

> It was horrible. As soon as we landed, it seemed we were smothered by AT [anti-tank] fire. We were being blown up as fast as we could get out of the landing craft.
>
> My tank was lucky, we landed near Dog Red and just ran straight to the cliffs where we had some defilade protection. I guarantee you we didn't roam up and down the beach.

Of the 18 artillery DUKWs, 12 were swamped and the remainder spent most of the morning bailing and trying to stay afloat in the relatively rough waves. The addition of an artillery piece and its ammo proved too much for the boat's bilge pumps as waves constantly broke over the low freeboard.

The 10 LCTs with artillery were unable to provide effective supporting fire to the landing waves due to a combination of wave action and obscurity. The beach was both cloud covered and blanketed in smoke from the German and U.S. fire. Gunners could not hit pre-programmed targets due to wave actions. Direct fire was impossible due to concern regarding hitting troops they could not see through the smoke. For the better part of the morning they were forced to cease fire or fire well inland.

All 9 LCT(R)s failed to hit the landing tideline. Instead, for reasons still unknown, their blanketing rounds landed more than 100 yards short of the intended target.

Of the 16 lanes to be cleared of obstacles by high tide, only three were somewhat clear. The intense fire killed the beach parties, but the men hiding behind the obstacles avoided their deaths.

In sum, the intricate fire support plan for Omaha failed completely. The troops, landing in the acknowledged toughest beach, did so totally deprived of assistance. This would be a highly personal battle between the individual soldier, his psyche, and the best the Germans could do. Fully alert, the defenders crouched in their well-constructed positions and executed their well-rehearsed defensive plan.

The Scene

If you were assaulting Omaha, this is what you would face.

Unlike the other four invasion beaches, Omaha presented significant advantages to the defender. The Germans, being reasonable map readers and professional military students, saw Omaha as an essential part of any invasion of France with Normandy as the focus.

Accordingly, beginning in early 1943, they began an aggressive construction program, the majority of which was completed by the time Rommel arrived to provide even more support. The basic plan called for an interconnected defensive belt along the cliff tops as the key. These would be hard concrete bunkers connected by deep protected trenches from one end to the other, a distance of approximately 3 miles.

Key to these were the 14 large *widerstandsnestern* (strongpoints) scattered at key terrain locations along the bluffs and covering the three primary exit points of Viervielle, Les Moulins, and Saint-Laurent-sur-Mer. These were built to support a full infantry company complete with protected mortar, machine gun, grenade launcher, and anti-tank gun apertures.

Those on the cliff top were connected by the partially covered trench that also had smaller bunkers and protected fighting positions. From end to end, the beach was designed to occupy a full infantry regiment of two large battalions. German planners dedicated a battalion for the actual manned defense, initially an Ost (eastern) fortress battalion of dubious value, replaced by a quality battalion from the 352nd Infantry Division, a first line division recovering from the Russian front. This replacement was not picked up by Allied intelligence planners.

To add depth to the position, the German planners took note of available space for exploitation. At low tide, almost a kilometer of relatively flat, hard sand beach was exposed. This expanse was to be covered with a variety of obstacles that would destroy landing craft as well as canalize assault infantry into preplanned fire zones.

Following the direction an assaulting force would take, initially near undefended infantry, a variety of problems would be encountered.

Part of the tidal beach obstacles included Belgium gates. These were vertical railroad rails welded together creating impassable wide fences. They were placed so as to put massed infantry on a course directly in front of enfilading machine-gun fire and pre-planned mortar kill zones.

Once passed and near the high-tide line a seawall extended in a crescent the entire length of the beach. This was an old French wall designed to keep the sand from shifting. It was between 3 and 5 feet in height and constructed of both planks and concrete with stone.

Assaulting infantry would bunch behind it seeking shelter before advancing. Anticipating that, mortar and artillery fire was pre-set to fall just on the tide side of the wall. Along the bulk to the wall, the tide side would also be exposed to the full effect of the enfilading machine-gun fire. Ballistics being what they are, a machine gun firing from either far edge of the beach would effectively engage targets in the center, an event pre-programmed to occur.

In some portions of the beach, wooden groins had been built by the French earlier to keep the beach sand from shifting. These were perpendicular to the sea wall and ranged from 1 to 3 feet in height. They were predominately in the center of the beach and hindered any cross movement.

Past the sea wall was a rough shingle beach between 6 and 30 feet in width before reaching the actual cliff edge road that paralleled the beach. This was packed with triple apron concertina wire and heavily mined. The shingle itself was composed of baseball sized rocks a foot or more in depth, greatly hindering foot movement.

Reaching the cliff road, infantry then had to contend with the first key defensive belt. This was a series of concrete bunkers designed to bring enfilade fire along the beach and be well protected from naval gunfire due to low profile and extremely hard construction. These would be manned with anti-tank guns as well as machine guns.[1]

Once past this, the cliff side of the road presented additional problems. A major barbed wire obstacle stretched from one end of the beach to the other. This was usually a single or double apron concertina face heavily mined before, inside, and after the fencing itself.

Beyond that, depending upon location, more problems would be encountered before gaining the cliff tops. The bulk of the center was open space leading from the road to the base of the cliffs. A large moat had been created along the base of the cliff which was filled with water, wired, and mined. In the shallower areas near the edge of the beaches, the cliff faces were heavily mined with numerous barbed wire obstacles.

The Germans paid particular attention to the three exits, as they understood that any success required passage to the open ground beyond the beach itself. Each of these had one *widerstandsnestern* and supporting bunker complexes. Each had a large concrete anti-tank barrier built across the road with extensive approach mine fields. These were the toughest of all areas to assault as experience proved.

Unfortunately, the exits were planned to be the primary focus of the assault force which was trained to key on them. Elements that by chance or design moved to the flanks or periphery usually experienced success and/or salvation. The 5th Ranger battalion landing is an excellent example of this.

---

1   The 29th Division monument is the best example of this. The concrete protective shields have been removed for convenience of the tourists.

Upon gaining the top, infantry would have to drop inside the defensive connecting systems. These were designed to be cramped, impeding any buildup of forces. Concurrently, the many side trenches and covered saps allowed defending infantry to pop up in the rear, shoot, disappear, and re-appear elsewhere. Task Force Bravo of the 2d Ranger battalion experienced such a situation.

Behind the entire defense, deeper in the high ground farm fields, six artillery batteries supported the defenders. This was about twice the usual array for a German defensive sector.

Due to the steep drop between the cliffs and the beach, the guns were pre-registered for three fire belts:

- Maximum range out to sea for interdiction of approaching assault craft. The guns at Pointe du Hoc were to concentrate on deeper targets of shipping beyond the reach of standard artillery.
- Within the defensive belt of obstacles on the beach at low tide line.
- On top of the cliff defensive positions in support of covered defenders.

Indicative of the time and thought the Germans had dedicated to Omaha was the allotment of machine guns. These were the MG-42, probably the best infantry machine gun of WWII. It fired 1,200 rounds per minute compared to the U.S. M-1917A1, which could muster 650 rounds per minute before overheating, which was frequent.

The span of distribution on notional defensive ground per German doctrine was about 450 machine guns. At Omaha, there were more than 1,000. These were in protected bunkers with extended supplies of ammunition.

In sum, this was a very tough nut to crack. Between the enfilading cliff defenses, defense in depth and dense weapons allocations, this was the hardest of all beaches to be taken. Yet its occupation was crucial to the overall success of the invasion.

It stitched together the U.S. beaches, with the British beaches providing a continuous front denying the Germans the option to defeat the invasion in detail by placing forces on the flanks of Utah and Gold. Carentan, Bayeux, and Isigny were major German force locations and a secure Omaha would greatly limit their interdiction potential. Bradley stated,

> We knew Omaha would be a very tough piece of work, but we had no choice. It was essential to keep German forces off of the Utah forces so they could cut the peninsula and take Cherbourg which was the key objective. We couldn't afford to have German forces roaming between them and the British beaches.
>
> When we knew we would have to take it, I talked to Ike and insisted on using the 1st Infantry. I knew it would not be well received, but I just had to have a dependable proven division on that beach. The beach required two divisions and it took every bit of them we could land.

Omaha Beach by Time

This is an overview combining many of the facts and some of the voices and faces gleaned from over 50 years of talking to those that landed on Omaha Beach.

0300

They were awakened in the more than 100 transport ships that carried them from England to this point and place in time—perhaps the most significant moment most would ever have or recall. The ships ranged from the larger attack transports carrying more than 1,000 troops to the LSIs with more than 200 men aboard. The men, with a high degree of anxiety and a mostly sleepless night, dressed, went to the latrines, and then shuffled off to the messes for a final breakfast.

In that the transport shipping was both U.S. and British, the meals were different, but overwhelming in quantity, for this was the potential last meal. The British ships featured eggs, sausage, bacon, baked beans, cold tomatoes, toast, jam, butter, and tea. The universal comment from U.S. troops was that the British simply did not know how to make a decent cup of coffee.

The U.S. ships had a decidedly larger variety. For that day, the Navy pulled out all the stops. Troops were faced with options for steaks, pork chops, eggs, bacon, mashed potatoes, gravy, sausages, toast, fruits (canned apricots, peaches, and strawberries were noted), ice cream, cocoa, tea, and hot coffee. Some even had cold Coke on the line.

Most ate only halfheartedly, a combination of anxiety and caution. Others ate to the point of stupefaction, a condemned man's last meal. Most took some fruit, apples or oranges, to take ashore. The vast majority were packed inside the waterproof gas mask cover along with as many cigarettes as the container would hold. Silvio Marcucci recalled:

> I didn't eat much. Too many nerves. I grabbed some apples and went back to my bunk. I just wanted to get it over with. I saw several just stuff themselves. I am sure they later regretted it. The navy really went all out, but I just didn't have the appetite.

0400

Whistles, bells, and bosun's pipes sounded throughout followed by the general order: "Report to boarding stations."

The troops, now well or somewhat fed, had taken on their complete gear (life belt, equipment harness, musette bag, gas mask, weapon, ammo, and grenades as a minimum. Then the specialty equipment, wire harnesses, demolitions, machine gun spare barrels, mortar baseplates, telephone wire, typewriters, radios, bazookas, etc.) and shuffled up the narrow companionways to their boat deck. Marcucci said:

> I could barely stand up with all my equipment. We were helping each other up the steep and slippery companionways to the deck. I think everyone alternately pulled and pushed each other

to the top. The sea air was cold and bracing. Woke me up immediately. I couldn't see much as it was still dark and we were pressed close together.

The deck railings were conveniently dropped by half height during breakfast and the crew had draped the cargo nets over the hull to the now circling empty Higgins boats. Several would come along side, bang sideways, secure the net from the sea, and await cargo.

The command, "Load the landing craft" rent the air. Naval and Army guides with clipboards would announce the load sequence as troops appeared on deck and lined up parallel to the rails.

"Landing Craft 22A, 22B, 22C, face the ship. Load."

Loading was an artful skill. Hands on the vertical rope, feet on the horizontal. Time the drop so the craft met your release as it achieved its apogee. Not a moment after. Too soon or too slow and ankles could break on impact. Or worse, a troop on the edge would miss entirely and be slammed between the craft and the hull, usually a fatal occurrence. Hall said,

> I didn't have half the stuff the infantry had on but I just hated this part. Scared me to death.

Vincent E. Baker remembered:

> As an officer and with the tanks, I just loaded on deck first with our LCT and then lowered into the sea. We then went to the other side to get our tanks which were lowered one by one with cranes. This part was OK.

0435

The now-loaded assault craft moved away from their respective mother ships and coalesced into the appropriate circles depending upon location and wave increment. Guiding them were dozens of small patrol craft, each with colored pennants displaying numbers for the bosun's to cue upon—White DG1 (Dog Green First Wave), Yellow ER5 (Easy Red Fifth Wave), etc. With a combination of signals and bull horns, the circles found their space as sheep herded by dogs. They were between 10 and 12 miles from shore, protected by the bombardment group of battleships, cruisers, and destroyers.

The sea was rough, fluctuating between Force Three and Force Five waves and wind. The men were quickly drenched by the cold water constantly breaking over the sides and chilled by the biting, scudding wind piercing their thin, soaked fatigues and the constant pitching of the flat bottomed craft. For most, seasickness struck within minutes of boarding and was manifested by the constant vomiting and choking of the packed mass. The men had to stand for the most part or sit on closely jammed bench seats. The result was that everyone was covered in vomit and spume for the entirety of the voyage. Marcucci said:

> I've never been so sick in my entire life. I am a devout Catholic and usually do not swear, but God damn I was sick.

Twelve of the 18 floating 105mm guns, mounted on DUKWs, begin to take on water. The bilge pumps were increasingly overloaded, to the point of failure. They fought the flood until at approximately 0530, they began to founder. Only six survived to shoot.

The 16 LCTs carrying 32 of the engineer bulldozers also began to take on excess water. Only two made the beach, landing four dozers, two of which were immediately knocked out.

0500

The run-in began. As horses at the gate, the circling craft for Waves One through Three began to pass the protective hulls of the combatant vessels arrayed parallel to the beach. They crossed in between the vintage battleships USS *Texas* and USS *Arkansas*, arrayed at each flank, with four British and French cruisers in between, with a seeding of eight U.S. and British destroyers between them. Eight other U.S. destroyers, well forward, provided close-in protective hulls. The sky was now brightening and the men could see better than a mile in all directions. Marcucci recalled:

> I could see where we were for the first time. It was amazing. I could finally see all this. I didn't know we had so many ships. Sick as I was, I understood the moment.

Hall said:

> I was sitting up front holding onto the barrel trying to stay above the waves. I suddenly looked around and it took my breath away. It seemed like the entire ocean was covered with ships.

Baker said:

> I vividly recall sitting in the turret when I saw the immensity of what we were doing. It was really quite stunning. A scene in my memory I will never forget.

0550

The USS *Texas* and USS *Arkansas* and their fellow ships commenced the bombardment. For all those afloat, it was a stunning moment. The relatively flat trajectory and high velocity of the main guns sent rapid shock waves and created vacuum cells as they passed. Craft would be lifted from the water and then slammed down. A brown smoke soon obscured the low sky as round after round screamed overhead. While it gave the infantry a sense of strength and confidence, the effect on the Germans was virtually nil.

Now, the assault craft passed their guides and crossed the forwardmost line of ships, the eight destroyers tasked with close support. They were silent as even as close as 2 miles from shore, they could not discern targets. Now in front of all others, the assault craft arrayed in a line toward the obscured shore.

0600

The 36 M-7 Priest self-propelled howitzers and 34 tanks that were approaching the beach on LCTs began to supplement the naval guns. They were joined by fire from 10 landing craft-mounted 4.7-inch guns and the rockets of nine LCT(R)s, the latter planning to fire as the assault craft were just 300 yards from the beach. The rough seas combined an inability to see specific targets, and made most of the fire useless.

German fire began to have effect. Artillery, firing pre-determined zones, began to fall among the assault craft. Hits were achieved and holes punched in the close-packed craft. Bullets from firm firing positions began to hit water and craft, inflicting casualties among the tightly packed troops. None of the German positions were identified by the Navy and they remain unsuppressed.

The last craft moved into line. The obvious fire forced the men to lower themselves as much as possible even when doing necessary bailing to keep their craft afloat. The guide boats, once so numerous and searching amongst them, now departed, their duties fulfilled.

The 448 bombers began their traverse of the beach line. Intending to destroy the bulk of the beach and cliff obstacles, the bombardiers could not see any of the targeted area. Cloud cover negated any ability to discern beach from sea. Following safety protocols, they held the bombs for an assured distance, cratering the ground more than 5 miles inland with zero effect on German defenses.

0632

The four LCT(R)s rippled their 1,000 130mm rocket rounds just in front of the first wave. Every round landed well short of the intended destination, creating neither craters nor destroying the now exposed beach obstacles more than 600 yards from the beach edge road.

The 32 duplex drive tanks were launched in rough seas. All but five were immediately swamped. Eight more were held back from launch and later landed dry at a critical moment in direct disobedience of the naval commander.

Ramps dropped as the sand dictated along the 5-mile stretch of Omaha. Due to the heavy cross current, the sea had etched deep runnels parallel to the beach. These were anywhere from a foot to more than 10 feet in depth. The boats would beach against the leading edge, ramps would drop, and troops would pour out, the unfortunate dropping into the deeper channel to drown. Then there was between 800 to 500 meters of obstacle strewn open beach to cross. Marcucci explained:

> I ran off amidst a hail of fire and immediately went under. I had on all that commo gear I went down like a rock. I pulled the string on my life belt and dumped my gear.

The Germans then initiated the heart of their defensive plan. Mortars and artillery fired dense concentrations at pre-planned targets. The areas behind and astride the seawall and the low tide mark were most effective. The enfilade positions poured fire across the entire length of the beach. The troops, massed behind obstacles, the Belgium gates, and dead tanks and landing craft were constantly hit, the fire coming from the flanks as opposed to the front. With no suppressive fire, the Germans had near 100 percent quality participation.

On Dog Green, A Company, 116th Infantry ceased to exist. Assaulting with 200 men at 0632, they mustered 18 at 1800. Similar events were happening across the beach.

0700

Along the entire beach, the first two waves huddled behind whatever protection was available. There was no attempt to cross the beach and assault the cliffs. More than 20 percent of the assault craft were hit and sunk, making it more difficult to land the successive waves. Most of the swim tanks were sunk as were the floating artillery platforms. Success at Omaha Beach was in doubt.

The sweeping enfilade fire and pre-set indirect fire destroyed most of the initial assault leadership. The troops, leaderless and greatly affected by the ferocity of fire, simply focused on survival.

0710

Elements of the Third Wave landed, bringing in a fortunate combination of command personalities: Brigadier General Norm Cota and Colonel Charles Canham of the 29th Infantry Division and Brigadier General Willard Wyman and Colonel George Taylor of the 1st Infantry Division. These four uniformly provided the spark of leadership to convert a disaster into a victory. The statement of Colonel Taylor would demonstrate what all four brought to the moment:

> There are two kinds of people who are staying on this beach: those who are dead and those who are going to die. Now let's get the hell out of here.

Each disregarded the German fire and exhorted the men to move forward, off the beach and up the cliffs. They had no troop units to command at this moment. Instead, they had clusters of frightened, psychologically exhausted men in desperate need of a purpose other than survival. These four provided that.

Canham was wounded in both the head and arm. He cradled a Browning Automatic Rifle (BAR) and moved from obstacle to obstacle urging the troops to move forward. Cota personally led a soldier to the top of the cliff. Wyman and Taylor performed similar acts. The men began to respond with individuals and small groups moving forward.

0830

The admiral in charge of the amphibious assault studied the immediate conditions. Swamped tanks and artillery were being reported. Returning assault craft reported horror stories of the initial landings as well as evacuating considerable wounded from the run-in. A study of the beach showed much of it blocked with dead landing craft and tanks.

He ordered the beach closed, stopping the landings of the subsequent waves. This leaves the first three waves alone at a moment when they most needed reinforcements.

Lieutenant General Bradley, on the command ship *Augusta*, had no communication with the beach elements. He sent in the captain's gig with some of his staff to assess conditions. They got within 800 meters of the beach and reported a disastrous situation with no visible movement off the beach. Bradley began to study the possibility of stopping the subsequent waves and landing them on the British beach, Juno, about 5 miles further west.

The 5th Ranger Battalion was intact on Dog White Beach and began to move toward the cliffs under General Cota's direction. Concurrently, the remnants of Ranger Task Force Bravo, decimated on Charlie beach, gained the cliff top and noted they had flanked the defenses. Disobeying initial instructions, they began to clear the trenches and bunkers on the extreme right of Omaha, silencing a major enfilade bunker and markedly relieving pressure on the 29th Division troops.

0930

The captain of the destroyer USS *Frankford* was increasingly frustrated by his inability to support the troops. He saw the wreckage of the initial assault and the reports of the returning craft hiding behind his hull. Without authority, he immediately ordered the ship to move closer and began to fire on the cliff tops without waiting to see clearer targets. The other seven ships also began to move in the rising tide and rake the cliffs.

With less than 3 feet beneath the keel, the *Frankford* and fellow destroyer, the *McCook*, shifted broadside to the beach and raked the cliffs with 5-inch guns. The other six destroyers, seeing this maneuver, shifted positions and followed.

In totality, this placed the fire of 35 5-inch guns against the cliffs. This was the first effective support the troops had and it makes all the difference.

By 1200, the destroyers would have exhausted their ammo lockers.

1000

High tide. The waterline laps the beach road. Of the 16 planned cleared lanes, the assault engineers managed to clear four. Follow-on landings would trigger many of the Teller mines, now underwater.

Two lieutenant JGs, each commanding an LCT with four DD (duplex-drive) tanks made independent and congruent decisions. They circled just in front of the destroyer screen looking for opportunities to beach land despite the admiral's order of a closed beach. Without communication other than visual, each spotted an opportunity, swung their prows to the beach and went ahead with full power, firing their machine guns as they went. They slammed into the surf line, now well past half tide, dropped ramp and discharged their loads. Of the eight tanks landed, only two survived past the first five minutes.

Off-shore, the admiral saw this act of disobedience and announced a commencement of reinforcements to the beach. Waves Seven, Eight, and Nine began to move past the bombardment line of ships and pick their way through the destroyer line.

1100

The massive destroyer barrage began to have telling effect on German fire, which markedly lessened. Subsequent waves included infantry, armor, and self-propelled artillery. Intact leadership shifted focus from the exit defenses to the less defended flanks, gained the cliff top, and began reducing German resistance. This was unknown to Bradley, who was developing an alternate landing plan.

Both Ranger elements met at the Vierville-sur-Mer exit, effectively eliminating immediate German defenses of the beach in the 29th Infantry Division sector.

1200

Major General Gerow, V Corps commander, radioed Bradley that troops could be seen on the cliff tops and moving inland.

1230

18,772 men were landed and began to provide some depth to the battlefield.

1721

Omaha Beach was declared open, though intermittent German artillery continued to fall. A POW camp was established near center sector cliff top as well as two large field hospitals. Bulldozers began digging a large mass grave under the cliffs in center sector. The Quartermaster Graves Registration units gathered the corpses littering the area. It would take more than five days to collect the dead.

Approximately 4,500 Allied soldiers were killed on the five beaches. Of that count, approximately 2,725 came from Omaha.

Combat, Orders, and Judgment

Combat is decidedly fatal to the participants. Leaders, officers, and enlisted are charged with execution of orders and the strict adherence to a commander's intent as the responsible agents for the men they serve—both above and below them. Failure to do so in peacetime can be professionally suicidal. Failure to do so in combat may be either suicidal or the key to success. The difference is called judgment. And good judgment is the holy grail of any combat unit.

On rare occasions in our history, the leader on the ground, at the crux of a fleeting moment on the battlefield, has decided to disobey his instructions for what he judges as the greater good of the unit and the larger task at hand.

A point often forgotten is that the enemy gets to vote. Conditions may be assumed by the chain of command when orders are developed, but they cannot rigidly be assumed at the sound of the first hostile round. We pay our leaders, at all levels, to exercise judgment rather than rote mindless adherence when the enemy votes. Judicious leadership, combined with the changed nature of the environment and the immediate necessary actions, lead to success. Failure to recognize significant changed conditions leads to defeat. D-Day is replete with positive examples of this and should serve as a guide for future combat leadership.

At approximately 0830, 6 June 1944, Omaha Beach was virtually lost to the Americans. Disaster stretched across the 3-plus miles of beach. Bodies piled from horizon to horizon. None of the extensive fire support was effective or even applied due to weather and smoke. Units ceased to exist as the ramps dropped on the hundreds of landing craft. Not a single command radio functioned on the beach, robbing the commanders afloat of the ability to render sound decisions. Lieutenant General Omar Bradley, the overall commander, began to formulate plans to withdraw from the beach and land behind the British at Juno. He and the remainder of the force were saved by several junior officers and NCOs who disobeyed orders with studied judgment. They realized that disobeying clear orders was a necessity for success where adherence would underwrite defeat.

Part of the initial assault plan was that 32 DD tanks would be launched approximately 5 kilometers off the beach. They would swim in and provide surprise armor support to the troops on the beaches. Their ability was proven in the calm training waters of Britain. Normandy was not a calm sea. Waves, surging erratically with 5-to-8-foot swells, swamped 100 percent of the DDs launched.

Two navy lieutenant JGs, equivalent to an army first lieutenant, each in charge of an LCT with four tanks aboard, saw the failure of launches left and right and refused to drop the ramps, keeping their tanks on board. They did not ask permission. They independently saw the folly of the act and judged that better opportunities might exist. They did not report this. They simply continued toward the shore with their loads intact.

As the morning wore on, they each independently maneuvered closer to the shore looking for opportunities to land the tanks that were desperately needed. All this with no communications between them or their higher command.

Noting the disaster ashore and the accumulating debris in the water, the beachmasters responsible for the landing closed the beaches and ordered all ships to stand offshore—effectively isolating the already decimated First through Third waves. The lieutenants each heard the order to close the beach.

This was a decision made by the assault force landing admiral who had no communications with the beach and could not see the close-in situation. Some troops had already made it to the top, but could only see the huge piles of burning debris, overturned and broached assault craft, as well as the total failure of the demolition elements to clear obstacles.

At virtually the same time, the lieutenants made the decision to crash through everything and land the tanks. They were immediately opposite Dog Red and Easy Green.

They saw each other and acted in tandem, aligning about a mile out and surging full speed ahead firing their 20mm guns and .50-calibers as they went forward. Each crashed their loads on the beach and disgorged their tanks. Six were immediately hit and burned. One retreated to the deeper water with the turret above water and began firing. The eighth surged across the beach and made it to a protected defile against the cliff face and began to engage targets on the bluff. There was no functioning radio on board. The two surviving tanks began to snatch victory from disaster.

Seeing the two craft successfully land, the admiral ordered the beach re-opened and reinforcements to move past their destroyer shield. The Fourth through Sixth waves, follow-on reinforcements, were considerably reduced by the loss of assault craft in the first three waves. Regardless, they were reinforcements, intact units and badly needed.

The Rangers also practiced selective disobedience. Previously, at approximately 0700, companies A, B, and C of 2nd Battalion landed on Charlie Beach—the extreme west flank beach. They were immediately decimated as A/1-116th had experienced. Of the 64 that landed with A, 34 of the 64 were killed outright. B Company had a similar experience. C Company had 19 killed and 18 wounded out of the 68 that landed.

The surviving officers and NCOs, two lieutenants and two platoon sergeants, dragged their remnants to the cliff face out of sight and began to recover. Their location was a deep V inverted into the cliffs that gave excellent protection from German sight and fire.

Quickly, the leadership took out their bayonets and climbing ropes and began climbing, back-to-back, up the narrowest portion of the V, using the bayonets to secure handholds. Atop the crest, they found that they had flanked the German defenses. The Rangers dropped their ropes and brought up the rest of the survivors. Though their orders were to go to Pointe du Hoc as soon as possible, in the words of several veterans I interviewed: "We were pissed and mad as hell. We were going to kill some Germans and do it now." They did. Pointe du Hoc would have to wait.

Their first objective, and a crucial part of the German defense built on the enfilade aspects of the beach, was the deep concrete flank bunker facing along the entire beach just above Charlie Beach, easily visible today from the National Guard monument. It held both an anti-tank gun and a 20mm gun with a MG-42 machine gun above. The Rangers immediately cleared the machine gun from the rear and roped down above the bunker, destroying it with a white phosphorous grenade. This markedly diminished the fire against the Dog beaches and ceased a great deal of the enfilade fire that was halting movement. The beach forces could now begin to move forward and up the cliffs.

Disobedience that day began to be a shared virtue. About 5 kilometers off shore was the destroyer line. Their job was to protect the landing craft from interference by German E-Boats—which never showed—and to assist in shore bombardment. As the assault progressed—or in some areas did not—they became a shield to returning craft as well as the last safety zone for the inbound assault craft. To this point, they held their fire on the beach due to lack of a clear view.

The captain of the USS *Frankford*, a lieutenant commander, was closest to the shore and grew increasingly frustrated by events. The many failures were constantly passing by his ship with wounded and dire tales. He went to the gunnery officer's position and began to examine the beach with the best telescope on the ship. What he saw through all the chaos was the lone tank that made it to the cliffs as well as the broached tank in the water. He could see those engaging targets. He immediately moved his ship, without authority, closer—less than 800 meters from the beach and a rising tide. There was less than 3 feet under the keel.

Immediately, he began firing at the targets the tanks were engaging. The tanker near the cliff quickly figured out what was happening, and a sergeant rose out of the turret with a signal flag and waved at the ship. The two in tandem then began a methodical bombardment of the cliff bunkers. The tank would fire a round indicating target and the *Frankford* would mass fire at the same spot with positive results. Several bunkers were undercut and literally rolled down the cliff face. One such undermining is clearly visible today above Dog Green as a deep "V" incised in the crest.

Very quickly, the other destroyers, also without authority, began to support. They moved in much closer to where their observers could physically see the cliffs and bunkers and began to engage. The shore bombardment admiral, seeing and sensing, then ordered what was already occurring. All eight destroyers were ordered to commence firing and support the beach with direct fire.

The eight destroyers echeloned themselves across the entire beach area so each had a clear view, with the *Frankford* closest to shore. As they fired, they methodically, at Dead Slow, began to move from west to east firing as they went. At the extreme eastern end, the deeper water ships executed a 180 degree turn and continued to fire as they moved west. The *Frankford* and two others, too shallow to execute a turn, simply shifted into Reverse Dead Slow and moved west, stern first firing as they went. This was the moment for the troops ashore. They saw this, took heart, and for the first time, began to coalesce and move forward.

This was the pivotal watershed moment of D-Day—three Navy officers and four Rangers, who disobeyed orders and created the decisive acts of disobedience that saved the beach. As a major in Frederick the Great's German army admonished a lieutenant during a battle: "The King gave you a commission because he assumed you knew when to disobey an order."

There is a lesson here. Flexibility exercised with good judgment is a pearl without price if it resides within the mind of the man on the spot.

The Song of Silvio's Sleep

As best I could, I have tried to synthesize the extended discussion I had with Silvio Marcucci, 1st Infantry Division, First Wave on Omaha Beach. It is as accurate as I can remember. At best, it paraphrases his description. At worst, it is a reasonable approximation of his experience that morning.

The USNS *Henrico* lifted anchor in broad daylight with dozens of other ships in Portland Bay as it joined the mass migration to the south and Normandy. Silvio could see nothing but grey steel hulls from horizon to horizon. Many were festooned with barrage balloons on the stern, which glinted and glowed with the passing rays of the sun. It was a stunning and invigorating sight. So many ships with such purpose.

Like all his companions, Silvio Marcucci was moving toward the most important event in his life, one they clearly understood as such. He had survived North Africa and Sicily and hoped he would not fall prey to the inexorable math of time at war: death or injury.

Enjoying the fresh air as a contrast to the fetid cloud in the berthing spaces, he and his companions jammed all available deck space to watch history unfold, the ships kicking up bow and stern waves in the sparkling blue-black sea.

Fast patrol craft darted between ships with escort destroyers arrayed at all points of the compass. The immensity of the site was overwhelming for all as they looked on in silence at the passing scene, deep in personal thoughts.

As dark finally descended, about 2300 British Double Summer Time, he descended to his space to get some sleep before a very early wakeup call. He found this a wasted effort. The combination of the sight of streaming steel as well as the knowledge of what was to come made sleep impossible. He closed his eyes to the constant drumming of the ship's propellers as the slamming vibrations of a ship's life clouded his mind. Silvio was twenty years old and already more experienced than most adults.

He was loudly alerted by the bosun's pipe about 0300 on 6 June and began his journey. He and hundreds of others slowly made their way through an immense chow line, preparing for loading into the assault craft for Omaha. Today, unlike the two previous skimpy breakfasts, they could have a huge array of choices.

Most everyone took as much as their steel mess trays could hold, some even using canteen cups to hold the largesse—an act they would all later regret. Silvio sat on the deck by the stacked bunks with his buddies and wolfed the food down. NCOs went through the spaces warning them of load time and hustling the feeding process.

Soon, he looked at the load card he had been given. As a communications technician, he drew a roll of assault telephone wire to be attached to his web gear, a heavy wooden frame with his SCR 300 radio attached, weighing more than 30 pounds, and two waterproof bags. One would hold the spare batteries and the other the spare tubes and necessary tools. This, all before his basic combat gear of rifle, ammunition, grenades, rations, shaving kit, rain jacket, ground cloth, and signal smoke and flares. Very quickly, the load almost equaled Silvio's weight—140 pounds soaking wet.

He ditched the issued rations in favor of several apples and cigarettes that he stowed in his rubber gas mask bag just under his chin. With all this, and on the announcement for loading, he stood in line and staggered to the deck. It was about 0400.

Fresh sea air hit him as he emerged on deck to a forbidding weather and sea state. There was a constant gusting wind with mixed rain coursing over him. Even in the dim, somewhat moonlit dark he could discern a rough sea beaten with spume and rolling waves. This would not be a fun ride.

He was lined up by petty officers per his boat number and jammed against the railing, now lowered by half. The heavy boarding netting was attached to the rail top. The Higgins boat, less than 50 feet below, bucked and slammed into the side of the ship and finally settled into a roughly parallel position alongside the hull. Crews, barely discernible in the dark, positioned the end of the netting into the boat.

He took a position along the rail per shouted instructions, did a reverse to face the ship and in line with five others, grasped the rough hemp and began his descent. As soon as he cleared the railing, his position was filled with a seemingly endless line of replacements stacked in the companionways, awaiting their turn.

By the time Silvio reached the bottom, his knuckles were bleeding and he was exhausted. With practiced eye, he timed the drop perfectly and found himself jammed in the fourth row from the front. The excessive gear ensured that most would have to stand for the ride into shore. The Higgins, now fully loaded eight lines deep with 30 laden troops, freed itself from the netting and moved through the pre-dawn light to meet its companions.

The sea was in an ugly state and waves broke constantly over the front, soaking the troops in less than a minute. Constant droning wind whipped spume. It was 0430 and landing was scheduled for 0630. This would be a very long day.

The craft joined dozens of others, now discernible in all directions, as it bucked and slid, attempting to hold direction against the coursing waves. The freeboard was less than 4 feet under decent seas and this morning, the waves were breaking over less than 2 feet of plywood protection. Very soon, the copious breakfasts arose simultaneously amongst the men with most impacting on the man to the front. Save for the wind, the stench of vomit wafted constantly over the packed men, now somewhat stupefied by the experience. It was approximately 0445.

Water steadily rose within the hull and alarmed the crew. Quickly, they yelled at the men to use their helmets as bailing buckets to forestall sinking. Silvio could see several of his traveling companions broaching with the waves and going under. Despite his incredible seasickness and vomit covered clothes, he bent to the task. Bailing and barfing. Bailing and barfing.

The outboard file of troops on each side, having the favorable locations, took on the primary bailing tasks. In time, a reasonable compromise had been reached between the flooding water and the efforts of the personnel to save the craft. This constant process became a rhythmic habit for the voyage. Troops would alternate by the hull, bail, and then shift to a replacement. The work was exhausting, but necessarily rewarding in that the boat did not sink. They still were more than 2 miles from shore. It was about 0500 and dawn was clearly present.

Due to the low freeboard, it was extremely hard to discern shore from sea as both were a dark blue-black with only a hint of horizon. What Silvio could see was an endless line of his assault companions passing through the larger steel-clad hulls of the escort and support vessels. He saw them clearly between swings of his helmet which had provided some relief from the agonies of the sea.

The first line he crossed from his transport, about 12 miles out, was the bombardment line. Here, the cruisers, monitors, and battleships stood at anchor, parallel to the unseen shore. They would begin firing at 0600, judged to be when light was best for target selection—an ephemeral thing with the clouds and fog obscuring any definition of terrain.

Dramatically floating just to his left as he passed was the battleship *Texas*, a mountain surrounded by the smaller shapes of other craft. In the distance, less than a mile away, reposed the battleship *Arkansas*, a solid shape against the scudding clouds.

Altogether, Omaha, somewhat less than 5 miles in width, was to be saturated with the fire of two battleships, four cruisers, and 12 destroyers. Their effectiveness was to be determined, but it gave Silvio and his companions a great sense of confidence as well as the knowledge that they were participating in a truly historic moment. After a moment of reflection, it was back to the bailing and barfing.

Closer in, less than 5 miles out, was the destroyer line. Unlike the larger bombardment ships, they roamed slowly parallel and echeloned to the beach. Once beyond their screen, the Higgins boats all came on line to the blaring guidance and flags of the control craft. It was approximately 0545.

For the remaining run in, protection was provided by darting patrol craft, guide boats, and the obscuring waves. German shot was beginning to fall randomly among the horde now racing toward the beach. Silvio noted that he was suddenly unable to see the vast array of shipping as it passed to his rear. He was utterly alone with 140,000 of his companions. The outline of the bluffs of Omaha could be dimly seen in the distance and fog. It was 0600.

Suddenly, the men in the boat were physically lifted up and slammed back down. A broadside from the *Texas'* 14-inch guns had just screamed overhead, creating a vacuum as it passed.

The sky suddenly filled with arching shots from dozens of vessels ranging from the battleships to the rocket firing landing craft. Silvio passed through a line of DUKWs carrying 105mm artillery for direct support on the initial landing and the several LCTs with the floating DD tanks yet to be determined as something other than experimental. The immensity of effort was largely lost on the boat's members as they focused on their impending arrival.

The bombardment had begun, its effectiveness to be noted by Silvio at a slightly later time. It was 30 minutes to touchdown and the churning lines pointed in continuous waves of streaking white wakes toward the shore.

NCOs prompted the men to recover their helmets, buckle up, check their weapons and gear, and stand by for ramp drop. The waves and wind constantly swept across, obscuring any ability to note landmarks save the rapidly growing masses that were the cliffs and shore.

By now, less than 2 miles from shore, the Germans were clearly fully awake and responding. The artillery intensified, dropping amongst the packed craft and impacting with increased frequency. Higgins boats were turned into flaming wrecks. Men could be seen struggling in the unforgiving sea, largely ignored by the escort craft, ordered to proceed without halting. This was the run in. It was 0615.

Bullets began to lash the water and the steel ramp of the Higgins boat. Some shrapnel could be felt and heard beating against the wooden sides. This was getting in close. The men instinctively lowered themselves, jammed forward in anticipation, and awaited the drop of the ramp. At the front, an officer, marked by the vertical white stripe on his helmet, peered carefully through the small slit in the ramp to judge touchdown. It was 0632.

The boat suddenly came to an abrupt halt throwing everyone forward simultaneously with the ramp drop. The first three rows were scattered across the open ramp and deck and struggled under all the gear to gain footing and move forward.

Machine gun rounds began to search the mass and Silvio could clearly hear and see the impact on his companions. Most did not make the sand.

As the fourth row, Silvio was blocked from falling by the mass of men in front of him. He stumbled and pushed his way over the bodies, jumped off the ramp, and promptly sank. His boat had grounded into one of the undiscovered deep runnels created by the tide as it crossed parallel to the beach, dredging a channel from several feet to more than 10. It was into the greater depth that Silvio descended.

Weighed down by his exceptional load, he sank promptly to the bottom despite his fully inflated life belt. Regaining his senses and reacting to training, he reached down and uncoupled his quick release, dropping the gear. The sudden loss of weight coupled with the life belt shot him to the surface. But the surface was not what he expected.

In the short time it took from descending to arising, the Higgins boat had broached and overturned, jammed broadside against the sandbar. It was in the small gap between the prop and the hull that he emerged. The craft was stern to the beach. Silvio gasped, now helmetless, and grasped the large bronze prop and attempted to regain his composure. He was in the front and almost fully exposed.

What he saw in the thin daylight before him shocked him. The beach stretched more than 500 yards from his position to the cliffs. He could see no one moving in the massive tangle of steel tetrahedrons, Belgian gates, and telephone poles scattered along the beach. The tide was rushing in and pushed the bow across the channel to the next bar. Silvio couldn't move to the more protected bow as a combination of bullets, shrapnel, and the sandy bottom prevented any movement. In essence, he was trapped to ride the tide to shore. He held tightly behind the blades and began to note the overriding sounds.

He was jammed between the rail protecting the propeller from the beach, the hull bottom, and a severely bent rudder. The hull, thoroughly holed and flooded, was slowly grinding its way forward with the rapidly rising tide carrying him toward the cliffs.

Silvio's precarious position required constant adjustment and a tight grip. The water was dirty and cold, but that was largely lost on him as he struggled for survival. The sounds against the prop quickly gained his attention.

Mortar and artillery rounds were landing all around him. He was swamped with waves as well as the whistle of shrapnel, some making clear impact with his hull. He could see bullets sweeping the water, bodies floating at the more distant tide line, flaming vehicles, and landing craft to his front.

He quickly became conscious of a more constant ubiquitous sound, that of bullets impacting the bronze props less than a half inch from his face. Ping. Ping. Ping. Alternating, pausing, and then rapidly, Ping. Ping. Ping. It was approximately 0645.

From time to time as the tide carried all before it, Silvio would release the blade and hold the connecting shaft for a moment of physical relief. He heard above all other sounds, Ping, Ping, Ping.

He searched the scene in front of him through salt burned eyes, seeking any form of companionship—a wish not granted. In time, by 0730, he saw some elements hunkered behind the beach obstacles and random movements obscured by the flotsam filling his sight line. Still, he didn't think he could emerge to join as the fire was a continuous song. Ping. Ping. Ping.

As he progressed toward the cliffside road, the tide increased with intensity, surging his precarious foxhole forward. It was 0800.

To his immediate left, several Higgins boats surged past, breaching the shallower bar. He could see them and a number of companions beach less than 50 yards away. This was the reinforcing wave, but it still provided him no relief. Ping. Ping. Ping.

A third wave passed him by at 0830 and he could, for the first time, sense some degree of order and suppressed fire. The flipped craft finally came to rest breached against a steel obstacle less than 50 yards from the seawall that lined the entire beach. Sensing no further forward movement, Silvio peered over the tips of the blades, saw some men to his front and, crawling toward them, sank into the sand.

Two men half-crawled toward him, grabbed him by his shirt and dragged him to shelter behind a dead DD. He propped himself up against the torn tread, took a deep drink of water from his rescuers' canteen, and slumped in exhaustion. He quickly woke to the sound of bullets glancing off the hull. Ping. Ping. Ping.

It was approximately 0900.

Years later, in the banquet room of the Sainte-Mère-Église Hotel De Ville, Silvio Marcucci had described his day to an intensely interested major. Clearly both exhilarated and exhausted by his lengthy exposition, he fell for a moment into silence.

Not wanting to break the moment, I let him recover.

He looked up, tapped my knee and said with a firm husky voice: "Ever since then, when I go to bed, I always hear Ping. Ping. Ping."

He always would.

Walking the Beach with Ernie Pyle

I have always been a fan of war correspondent Ernie Pyle. As a soldier, I appreciate his deep insight into what soldiers actually do, what they think, and how they exist in the temporary world required of them. Though never a soldier, he understood them from the depths of his soul. His writing put those images into words and the audience was educated as it never had been before. I read all that he wrote that I could find and found inspiration with every posting.

He landed shortly after the serious killing was concluded and walked Omaha Beach. He put his fingers to his portable typewriter and wrote of the profoundly moving morning walk that had spoken to him. I took his words to heart as I made a similar walk many years later. He spoke to me as I speak to you.

I Walked Omaha
(with homage to Ernie Pyle)

The beach today is broad, clean, and filled with the life that liberty bestowed 75 years ago. As I walk, I reflect on what I read and what I heard from those that were here on that day of days. An obscure and unremarkable beach stretches in a long, light umber crescent. It is bisected by several draws that allow penetration up the steep cliffside—now occupied by vacation homes and gardens. Regardless, the sheer physical aspects of what the scene was then are easy to imagine now despite the dust of time.

As I walk the sand and close my eyes, weaving into the filing cabinets of my mind, images of June 6 emerge that meld the past events with the present place.

Today is a lovely day for strolling along the seashore. Men are sleeping on the sand, some of them sleeping forever. Men are floating in the water, but they do not know that as they are beyond introspection or enjoyment.

Gulls dip and swirl, and the sun sparkles off the receding foam. Only an occasional craft passes across the scene, and it is clear to the horizon. But my mind sees the two thousand-plus bodies and the hundreds of wrecked craft piled together along the shore—still too soon for the niceties of the Graves Registration and naval salvage units to take effect. And much too soon for my mind's eye.

The wreckage is vast and startling. Both the material and human waste of war is a common denominator of conflict. But, here, in the compressed spaces of sea and cliff, those words—waste and junk—are most pronounced and supremely evident.

This one great human endeavor proves that in such catastrophic and important human events, everything is expendable in the pursuit of a larger objective. They are just people and things and the price we pay for what we undertake. Here on Omaha, that is a distilled and obvious fact.

Hidden by the cold, dark bay lies continuing evidence of both the waste and cost of war. Scores of craft, some ships, and more than 30 duplex drive tanks rest in the same repose where they died on 6 June 1944. Salvers occasionally dredge one up to decorate a museum or to turn into scrap, but on the whole, they remain in their original repose. A tragically heavy price to pay, but it was for a greater cause.

The bones of their crews have long since been recovered or recycled into the sea, but their names reside forever in cemeteries and minds throughout our land. The sea obscures the facts, but the memories remain.

Erasing the vestiges of time, we can visualize the trucks tipped half over and swamped. Partly sunken barges, and the angled-up corners of jeeps and small landing craft appearing half submerged. As the tide recedes, the vast array of tetrahedrons, Belgian gates, concertina wire, and Teller mine log barriers become visible—at least if one closes his eyes and allows the mind to conjure what history relates.

Where I walk, on firm, dry sand, there are all kinds of wrecked vehicles. Tanks that had only just made the beach before their demise—victims of a great imaginative thought, lost in execution. Jeeps are burned to a dull gray, their tireless rims resting half buried in the sand. Bulldozers, cranes, and flatbed trucks are askew across the scene as in some huge modernistic sculpture garden.

Scattered amongst this are wrecked halftrack personnel carriers and deuce-and-a-half trucks. Aid bags, typewriters, ordnance tools, bedding, stacks of weapons, telephones, switchboards, and cases of grenades lie strewn around them and are visible through gaping shell holes. Maps and papers flutter and dive with the wind. When the light hits at a specific angle, viscera, body parts, and a reflective shine of iron red ochre shows. Battle is decidedly messy, and this is a supremely messy place.

Everywhere are discarded life belts, gas mask containers, telephone wire, helmets, and weapons. They all lie on the sand and roll with the whims of the tide. Now valueless from their expenditure.

Interspersed along the tide line are the parts, pieces, and possessions of the previous occupants—an orange, a photograph, ration boxes, a half-rent shirt, a letter soaked beyond comprehension. Between them all are spent field dressings, the occasional bandanna, and parts and pieces of fatigues—the detritus of the effort.

Between exposed obstacles, bodies and parts emerge. Some skeletonized by a sudden blast of flame. Others separated into many parts. A gaitered leg rolls and swims with the tide, the rest of the body no longer extant. Only the living have the ability to depart this place where order and process are yet to be introduced.

This place, if resurrected, could arm a reasonable nation. Yet, we spent it without question as a trivial part of the bill to buy what we are and what we hoped others would be. The people are forever lost, but their spirit and purpose remain—they were and are us and what we are all about.

A few hundred yards from the shoreline is a near continuous high bluff. Against its face, grass grows in thick clumps, interspersed with climbing white roses wending their way to the top. These trace the white tape of trail markings through the minefields bought at a great cost in limbs and lives, driven by the necessity to get off this beach and onto the high ground. The remnants of the initial surge lay in repose—some pointing the way for those more mobile and some beyond effort.

Above, where the roses now end, on the first flat ground obtained, are a myriad of tent hospitals, filled to capacity. Nearby are hastily constructed prisoner of war compounds, casually guarded in the time before organized law and order arrives. The occupants are the dazed, dumbfounded, and scared remnants of their lost cause. From here, you can see the vast panoply of the effort, lost to most in the mass of the endeavor.

Further inland but still close is a patchwork of rough new airfields. Light spotter planes, fighters, and the occasional Dakota medical evacuation plane continuously enter and exit, providing a symphonic counterpoint to the constantly rumbling artillery, both friendly and unfriendly. This is a crowded and confused place, but it has a sinew of purpose that glues the greater effort. It is the first sense of organization and structure out of the chaos welded to a purpose, something we do very well.

Beyond the horizon, the huge industrial juggernaut of fixed purpose and production begins to wend its way through the docks and airfields of England, soon to place more than a million men and their materiel at the disposal of General Eisenhower. At home and at the places of production, workers stop, listen to the radios and church bells, and bend harder to their tasks.

The prisoners, leaning on the hasty wire enclosure, look out to the largest single-purpose armada ever assembled. This vista that was for so long empty is now occupied. They look and wonder—once it was "When will they come?" Now they have and each reflects inwardly—"How could we have thought what we did?"

Perhaps if their superiors had the ability to conjure what they now see, the beach would have been unspoiled and our pool of humanity markedly increased. But it was not so then and not so now.

The walk concludes with the sun and surf disappearing from view, as do the older images I hold. But the memories and purpose do not fade. This place is a sandy sepulcher of the noblest aspects of the human spirit. Its memory hopefully ensures that its images may never again have to be repeated.

Facts Emerge Not Written

Over the course of almost 50 years, I have talked to dozens of veterans of Omaha Beach. They ranged from senior officers such as the tank battalion commander to myriad lower-ranking enlisted and junior officers. Overarching all was the description provided by General Bradley on a cold windswept day overlooking Pointe du Hoc.

Each recounted their story of the moments of that terrible trial for their souls in multiple ways. Some halting, others clear and concisely narrative, and others in between. It was always intensely personal and delivered with some force and passion that transcended the years. I found four themes emerging that were almost universally consistent over time and it is these comments I think the worthiest of mention of any narrative of Omaha and its effect on the soldiers that were there.

Movement off the Beach

You see all these movies with people charging around and bounding around. Never happened. We were as close to the sand as we could get. There weren't any charging heroics. If you got up, you were shot. We crawled slowly forward and found every bit of cover we could.

The Sense

The sensory deprivation was overwhelming. There was constant drumming of the artillery and mortars, the whipping steel of the multiple enfilading bullets and the constant pinging of steel off of the devastated hulks that dotted the beach. It forced one's view narrowly, barely inches to the left and right and to the immediate front. An impression 10 feet left or right is lost to memory. The very slight images were burned forever, but they were not broad.

The noise was overwhelming to the point it drowned out all else. Normally discernible sounds, voices, engine coughs, and explosions were lost in a huge auditory mix that saturated the brain and provided a degree of comfort from the realities of sight and sound.

Only when other troops coalesced around a person or created a womb of togetherness was the sensory blanket lifted.

Seeing, hearing, and comprehending on Omaha was a daunting task.

The Destroyers

Everyone I talked to or heard described the emergence of the destroyers as a highly emotional and important event that allowed them to collect themselves, believe there could be progress, and emerge as part of unit rather than as individuals. In sum, the destroyers gave life to the battered units and collective associations and were the catalyst that allowed the many parts of the whole to move forward up the cliffs.

Without the intervention of the destroyers, the success of the invasion at this location would be very much in doubt. With it, success was assured and provided the necessary shot of adrenalin and confidence to restore success from disaster.

The View from the Cliffs

The ultimate comment was consistent with all. At some point during the course of the day between 0900 and noon, the veteran managed to progress either individually or as part of a small element up the cliff face to the top. Either during the transit or at the top, he would stop to catch his breath and look back. This is what he saw.

For the first time, the scope of the beach events was revealed. He could see the vast burning and broached wreckage from one end of the crescent to the other. Most striking was the water's edge.

As far as the eye could see on the tideline, soldiers were shoulder to shoulder, aligned with the water's advance.

Behind them, from edge to edge of Omaha, there coursed a long pink streak, clearly discernible against the now sparkling blue sea.

CHAPTER 15

Utah Beach

Of the five invasion beaches, Utah was arguably the most important at that moment as it was the only beach that led directly to the key strategic objective of the port of Cherbourg. It also held a significant secondary advantage in that its position allowed forces to immediately begin sealing off the entire Cotentin Peninsula and create a sanctuary against expected German mechanized and armored attacks.

Utah is dramatically different from the other four beaches, providing a distinct advantage for the attackers, unlike Omaha which was the most formidable. For more than a year, the Germans had flooded the low ground between the beach defenses and the high ground to the west. Only by using six of the narrow causeways connecting the land with the beach could the Germans either retreat or reinforce.

As a result of the flooding, the actual beach defenses were very narrow—in some cases less than 200 meters between the beach and the western edge of positions. The Germans had built extensive interconnected concrete defenses along the entire beach area as well as mining and barbed wire obstacles. The bunkers are still visible today—the museum is built on one as is the Teddy Roosevelt restaurant nearby. Rommel personally visited this area and was toured by the responsible officer, Leutnant Arthur Jahnke, who was later wounded and captured on 6 June.

Unlike Omaha, everything planned for the assault on Utah beach worked, including the swim tanks and air support. The air assault was assigned to B-25 Mitchell bombers that specialized in low-level attacks. Flying south to north with formations of three in a V, they were able to saturate the defenses with great effect. Here, the winds blew a steady east to west keeping the targets clear for both bombers and naval gunfire.

Offshore, the bombardment fleet—four battleships, six cruisers and more than 20 destroyers—began their work with a high degree of accuracy. One destroyer was hit by a mine and sunk. One significant problem arose when the large German battery just inland to the northwest at Crisbeq maintained steady but essentially unobserved fire on the fleet. This battery created considerable difficulties among the fleet.

The battery remained in action for more than a week and finally required an infantry regiment with tanks and engineers to be neutralized.

Beginning at 0630, the assault force approached the beach accompanied by the swimmer tanks. Here as at Omaha, the combination of current (north to south) and bombardment smoke obscured the few navigation aids on the very low land, causing the first waves to land considerably south of their objectives. This was a fortuitous accident—one of the few for that day.

Landing in the first wave of 4th Division forces, Brigadier Teddy Roosevelt, Jr. and the regimental commander, Colonel James Van Fleet (later four-star commander in Korea), did a quick recon and agreed they had been landed more than a mile south of the intended beach.[1]

The flexibility and agility demonstrated was highly successful. By noon, defenses had been cleared for several miles north, the entire division was ashore, linkup had been established with elements of the 101st on the high ground and the bulk of reinforcements were moving ashore. Key to this was the sea tail of the 82nd Airborne under Colonel Edson Raff. Reinforced by tanks and engineers, he began movement toward Sainte-Mère-Église to provide badly needed supplies and medical support. It would be 48 more hours before he could close on the 82nd due to enemy defenses en route inland.

The 4th Division established its initial command post in the German bunker that is now the Teddy Roosevelt Restaurant. Soon, due to the narrow dry land and limited causeways, vehicle jams became a huge control issue. Regardless, with a total killed in action count of 197 and a firm foot ashore, Utah Beach was a huge and crucial success. Cutting off the Cotentin and seizing Cherbourg were within the grasp of the Allies.

---

1   If you look south of the museum, you will see a copse of fir trees, which is the approximate landing area for Roosevelt. The result of this error in navigation was that the force had landed on the flank of the primary defenses rather than in front. Roosevelt saw the opportunity and ordered that the succeeding waves land on him. They would then swing forces north like a door on a hinge and roll up the defenses in flank south to north.

CHAPTER 16

The American Airborne

U.S. Airborne Insertion

The following is a depiction of a variety of experiences of the Airborne troops on D-Day. In some cases, the flight and drop were exactly as planned and without issues. This was an exception, because for the majority of the 2,500 jump aircraft and the nine Airborne regiments, it was chaos, confusion, and casualties.

Planning for the airstream management of thousands of aircraft at night was a monumental feat. The Airborne insertion was more than 2,500 aircraft to take approximately 6,300 troopers for each division to be delivered to nine discrete locations. This required six Troop Carrier Wings with augmentation and 15 troop carrier groups with augmentation.

Few of these troop carriers had combat experience, but all had trained extensively with airborne forces in England. Correct planning would be a masterpiece in backward planning with the Pathfinder drops and the main body jump by drop zone being the anchor point. From a field in England to a spot in France, computations had to be accurate within five minutes, which was the norm. Take-off speed, altitude, positioning, and the vagaries of wind and engines all had to be considered. And, as always, the enemy gets to vote.

A plan was developed. Whether it could be executed was another issue.

A precise series of navigation check points was established to keep this aluminum stream, more than 20 miles wide and 100 miles deep, in order. These consisted of marker ships at sea, guide planes aloft, and timing by the individual navigators.

Whereas the British flights would go direct from the Channel to the drop zones, the Americans would fly "back door" from the Brittany side, seeking surprise. The U.S. flights enjoyed the permanent navigational aids of the islands of Jersey and Guernsey, but also loitered overland more than the British.

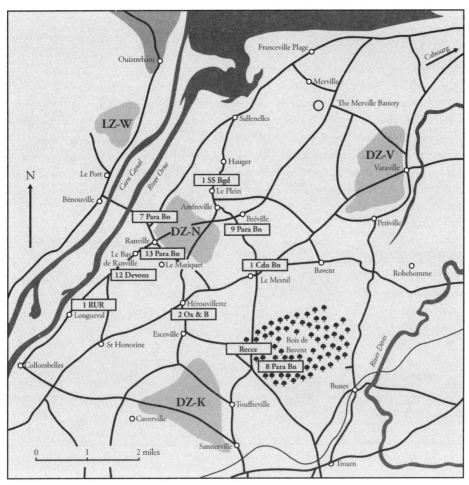

British effort.

The British effort was in a relatively confined space compared to the Americans. The entire 6th Airborne would be fitted between the Orne/Caen bridges and Ranville Ridge. The plan was not followed due to operational issues.

The U.S. Airborne area was significantly wider than the British, spanning from almost Utah Beach in the east to Picauville in the west and Carentan in the south. Unlike the British drop zones that were in essentially a long valley, the U.S. drop zones were across two north–south ridgelines and low ground to the west. This presented some navigational challenges as the 101st locations were visibly undistinguishable from the air as were two of the three 82nd objectives. These would be hit with only very accurate timing.

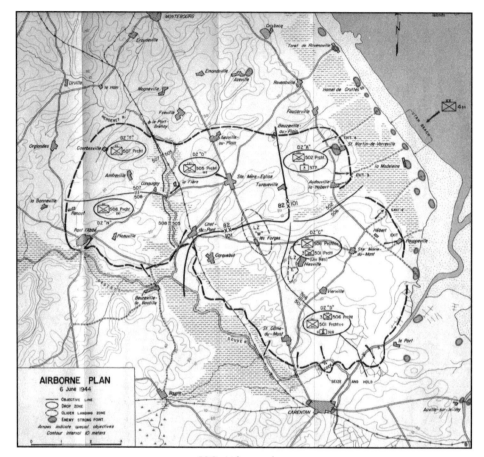

U.S. Airborne plan.

The British Airborne forces were distributed to nine departure airfields and the U.S. to thirteen. Regardless of distribution, the experience was virtually identical on the afternoon of 5 June. Each trooper was assigned a specific aircraft and moved to it with his brothers.

Each runway, wherever it was, was a maze of tightly packed aircraft as far as the eye could see. This was even more so in the British fields as the gliders were parked adjacent to their tow planes with the long tug lines rolled behind the tails.

In between, jeeps and trucks worked their way along the massed planes to administer last minute orders and supplies or add and subtract personnel. Finding the correct plane in the maze required detailed listings of tail numbers, runways, and parking slot. Typewritten pages of this information were distributed to each leader.

The paper indicated the precise aircraft location, the para-pack contents, and the number of jumpers by unit as well as planned drop time and drop zone. Considering that there were more than 2,500 aircraft, creation was somewhat of a miracle in itself.

Some aircraft were cross-loaded, which meant that elements of several squads or companies would be inter-mixed. Others were straight loaded with an integral unit such as a squad with the platoon headquarters or weapons elements. Regardless, the troopers coalesced around their aircraft and waited for the order to "'Chute up."[1]

Deposited under the wing and by the fuselage was the equipment to be worn or dropped. Piles of ammunition, grenades, and other materiel were positioned near the runway for easy access. The contents of the para-pack containers were under the wings either loaded or awaiting a final inventory.

Each trooper had his own personal parachute that he would have carried from the sausage or hangar location. This, as well as his personal web gear, weapons, and Mae West life jacket, was carried to the aircraft.

Ammunition distribution took several forms. In some cases, the men would be issued ammunition, grenades, anti-tank mines, Bangalore torpedoes, etc., in a buffet style table at the departure area. In other cases, trucks would roll by each aircraft issuing materiel as requested.

The troops were not dictated to as to what weapon to carry. There were a great deal of independent choices. Some liked the Thompson or Sten submachine guns. Others desired the reliability of the M-1. Many chose several and virtually all desired some form of sidearm. Hanging under a parachute was the most vulnerable period and a pistol could be used if needed whereas a rifle was inconvenient.

In time, the order to 'chute up would be given and the process begun. First came the basic web gear with ammo, medical pouch, grenades, and bayonet. A second bayonet or knife was always placed on the right boot for cutting the suspicion lines.[2]

Then came the parachute and the Mae West. Attached to the parachute would be a Griswold paratrooper drop bag for the M-1 and the leg bag if used. At this point, the soldier was loaded with about 50 to 75 pounds of gear and tightly bent over, the 'chutes of that period requiring a very tight harness.

Once loaded, depending upon time, the troops would lie on the ground under the wings or load onto the aircraft. There were small stairs leading into the fuselage. The weight and bulk of the trooper required one or more personnel to push him

---

1   On the 40th anniversary of D-Day, there were more than fifty 82nd and Para Regiment veterans visiting us planeside. Their account is depicted in the above passages.

2   The British had the quick release mechanism on their parachutes that allowed them to release themselves with a twist and fist bump. The U.S. did not, requiring a slower process to jettison the 'chute. Usually this meant a trooper simply cut the lines. After Normandy, all parachutes had quick releases.

from the rear and another to pull him through the door. He would then stagger to his assigned seat to await takeoff.

As adrenalin, time, and anxiety coursed through the veins, the requirement for relief became a dominate theme. Men would stagger to the edge of the runway and with considerable diligence, empty their bladder on the coping or grass. Getting out of the aircraft was always considerably easier than getting back in.[3]

In time, a Very flare would course across the sky and engines would cough awake. The sky quickly became blotted with blue exhaust from several hundred aircraft close together, the sound of the engines inhibiting all conversation. The troops gripped the aluminum benches, inhaled the air, and awaited their destiny.

Between 2100 and 2300, the thousands of transport aircraft broke the ground of England and moved in an inexorable stream toward France.

The Pathfinders

This is a narrative of one man's journey on D-Day, what he saw and what it meant. He was Private Bob Murphy, Pathfinder Team, 1-505th Parachute Infantry Regiment. He was not unique; he was just a friend who educated me on Normandy and took me under his arm from 1977 until his death. He was both a tour guide and an educator into the heart and soul of the youth of that moment. He would be the first to say he was not special, but it is not true. His presence and his character drew everyone who knew him to Normandy, from his Boston friends to the troops that stood at La Fière every year and heard from the "Original" what occurred. In sum, Bob was a symbolic representative heart of all of those more than 150,000 men that arrived in Normandy beginning 6 June 1944.

The Pathfinders had been created after the disastrous airborne drops in Sicily in 1943. Their job was to jump ahead of the main body and mark the drop zones to ensure accuracy. They were volunteers, but as Bob said, "They were usually volunteered by a senior NCO." Bob was part of this initial training and marked the drop zones at Salerno for his unit. Upon transfer to England, the Pathfinders—both U.S. and British—began experimenting with the Eureka-Rebecca navigation gear. This gear was a major technical improvement over eyeballs and guessing.

The "Eureka" transceivers, carried by the Pathfinders, sent pulses picked up by the "Rebecca" transceivers installed under the fuselage of the C-47s. In theory, they provided each pilot with a specific fix on the ground location and a "read" on specific units based on the colored signals on his display.

---

3   My troops did exactly this on the 40th and the vets all recounted very similar circumstances. A good laugh for all. History repeating itself.

The Pathfinders were also equipped for day drops as they would be shepherding full daylight reinforcement drops later in the day. Normandy in June was light at 0430 and not dark until almost 2230.

The daylight system consisted of yellow-colored panels aligned to form the letter "T" as well as smoke. These smokes were green in color to indicate a "clear" drop zone or landing zone and red in color to account for the presence of enemy. For follow-on night drops, the Pathfinders were equipped with holophane lamps.

Bob was responsible for jumping with a Eureka set in addition to the daylight equipment. This device weighed almost 40 pounds and was carried in a British designed leg bag—essentially a heavy canvas laundry bag on a rope. This was in addition to the more than 40 pounds of weapon, ammo, food, and material he also had to jump with. In sum, his equipment and parachute almost exceeded his own weight at the age of 18.

Bob's team was to mark Drop Zone O. This drop would be about a half mile west of Sainte-Mère-Église on the high ground between the town proper and La Fière Bridge—both crucial targets for the 82nd Airborne. With good fortune, Drop Zone O would collect the entire 505th Parachute Infantry Regiment, as well as the Division Commander, Major General Matthew Ridgway.

In the language of the operational plan named *Neptune*, Bob was part of 29 total aircraft dedicated to the Pathfinder mission—nine each to the U.S. 82nd and British 6th Airborne and 11 to the 101st Airborne. Bob was assigned Stick 1, Serial 4, Plane 10.

The 82nd Pathfinders would all depart from RAF North Witham in the rolling fields of Lincolnshire. The men had originally moved from their encampments to the airfield in the early hours of 4 June in pelting rain for a 5 June D-Day. The postponement until 6 June meant they traveled back and forth, getting little sleep.

Bob and his compatriots loaded themselves with parachutes and gear beginning around 1900 on the 5th. By 2100, they had been pushed and pulled onto their aircraft and sat jammed on the small aluminum benches that lined the interior fuselage. The door had been removed, and the men sat in a torpor, exhausted. Some smoked while others were lost in thought or having quiet conversations. It was broad daylight and each point of view was covered with fuselages, tail fins, and running vehicles. The war was about to begin.

Beginning at 2130, the aircraft started their engines. A loud blast of rotating propellers and clouds of blue exhaust permeated the cramped interior space. For 30 minutes, the planes revved engines and began a slow movement to the takeoff runway. Conversation was impossible. Bob said he could almost reach out and touch the other aircraft.

Quickly, the noise and vibration increased as his aircraft lurched down the runway and gradually became airborne. Through the door, the troops could see the grass and trees blur by and then a bright blue and grey patchwork of sky. Quickly, it became cooler, a bit quieter, and calmer. They turned mostly inward and were lost in thought. Some fitfully lit cigarettes, cupping their hands around lighters to shield the butt from the constantly moving air.

Very soon, the Channel came into view. Here, Bob and his companions had a remarkable epiphany unanimously similar to that of all the veterans that rode in the more than 2,500 jump aircraft of that day.

Under them, the entire armada of ships steaming south came into view—those which were not lost on the horizon. Four thousand ships of all classes ploughed through the chop, each trailing a long white wake marking passage. This was easily seen by those above and caused a universal shock and realization of what was occurring and of what they were a part. Barrage balloons, shining in the last of the light, marked the transports. Smaller curling and twisting wakes revealed the escorts. On separate fast lanes, the major capital ships were transiting to their bombardment points. In front of them all were the squat wooden minesweepers marked by their widely sprouting drag arms. Bob and his companions could clearly see and discern these shapes. They were not formless blobs, but distinct individual entities and they stretched for as far as they could see. The scene was both immense and overwhelming.

Above and below them, swarms of escorts darted and swooped. Fighters flew by, wagging their wings and boxing the transport aircraft in a cocoon of armed aluminum.

Bob noted that for the very first time, he understood the whole. He and his companions had seen small parts and pieces and heard of the whole, but to this moment it was ephemeral and theoretical—this was decidedly real. The other fliers, the generals, and colonels later recounted this same sight from their level. It was one thing to see and hear of the force in briefings and symbology; it was quite another to see it in reality. For all that flew that night, the sight had a huge reward.

Bob and his companions knew and understood for the first time what they were truly a part of and palpably recognized the mass and strength of the effort. They, most importantly, had a sudden sense of great confidence—both in their participation and the greater endeavor. It was a sight never to be forgotten by those first in.

The Run In

Regardless of location or unit, the troopers inside the more than 2,500 C-47s had a similar experience. Only the most fortunate, less than 1 percent of the total, went exactly where they were supposed to without incident. This describes the experience of the majority.

The invasion aircraft began to take off in almost broad daylight—around 2100 British Double Summer Time and blended into huge circles until all were airborne and then began to fly in a V of Vs south and east. Virtually all the veterans I spoke to described a similar experience.

They could see almost no sky for the sea of black with white-striped fuselages headed toward France. To paraphrase them:

> I looked out at the sea below and could only see the immense armada of ships below steaming for France—an unbroken line of black streaks with tiny white wakes to both horizons occasionally broken by a glimpse of the actual sea.
>
> Looking level through the door all I could see were aircraft literally blocking out the sky. I knew then that we would win. There was no power on earth that could stop this force. I gained a strong sense of self confidence at that site. It immensely helped our morale.

Depending upon leadership position, officer by the open door, troops next to a window, they saw and marveled at the sight.

Lieutenant Colonel Vandervoort, Commander, 2-505th, looked out from his position by the open door as the plane reached altitude and leveled off.

> I looked out and as far as I could see in front of me, in back of me and off to each side, the sky was filled with aircraft. The V of Vs went to the horizons at all points of the compass. I could see the slight tracing of contrails of the following jump aircraft in the receding rear as well as hundreds of fighters escorting us all on the flanks. I had never seen so many aircraft at any one time and hardly realized so many existed.
>
> I looked below as we flew the Channel. All I could see was an immense trail of white wakes of the ships pointing toward France, the last light of the sun glinting off the barrage balloons tethered to them. I felt I could have walked to France and never gotten my feet wet. I knew then we were going to win this war.

General Gavin added,

> I saw the immensity of the power we had concentrated for this moment, the focus of all our resources and preparation, and thought to myself there wasn't a force on earth that could stop us. I had always thought that of the invasion but now I knew it.

General Taylor remembered:

> I looked out and was startled at the vastness of the air and sea force all moving steadily to France. It's one thing to see it presented in a briefing and on paper but quite another to actually see it arrayed. I turned to my aide and told him to look at it and remember the sight—he would never see it's like again. I then went to the middle of the aircraft and slept on the floor for a brief time.

Private First Class Murphy said:

> I looked out and said to my buddies, the Germans are in for a hell of a night.

Paraphrasing further many of the veterans:

> I looked out and saw all those planes and ships and I realized for the first time what I was part of and what was about to happen. I had never seen so many ships and planes before. We were always training by ourselves and never saw all the parts, only our part. From that moment, I was absolutely sure we were going to win. I had never felt so good about anything or had such a sense of pride and confidence. We were going to beat the Germans and I was going to be part of it.

The crossing of land from the English Channel would test that new-found resolve.

The British air stream, a mixed flotilla of C-47s, bombers, and gliders moved directly toward the drop zones. The cloud cover was mixed between 1,000 and 2,000 feet. The U.S. contingent, two separate streams of C-47s, took the backdoor crossing near Brittany and Jersey/Guernsey to landfall. The pilot experience was roughly the same with the same effect on the jumpers they carried.

The cloud cover required pilots to independently seek an opening to the ground within acceptable jump altitudes—somewhere between 500 and 1,500 feet. German antiaircraft artillery began to open up very shortly after the first aircraft appeared overhead. This further forced pilots to adopt a survival mode to the detriment of accuracy and safety of jumpers.

Planes dove up and down to escape the fire as well as to seek some sight of obscured navigational aids. Engines were full throttled to well past safe jump speed of 140 knots. The red and green jump lights became an afterthought to pilots anxious to return safely to England.

Many of the Pathfinders either failed to land correctly, experienced broken Eureka gear, or were killed. For many pilots, correctly spotting the drop zone was not a priority.

O. B. Hill described his experience:

> We could see flak tracers all over the place. The plane began to veer around and do dips. We had to hang on for dear life. We could hear the flak as it hit the skin of the plane. Just like gravel on a tin roof. I saw a couple of aircraft hit that were flaming out.
>
> The red light came on and we tried to hook up. We were being thrown all around and had to hold on to each other. Our jumpmaster yells out real quick, "Stand up! Hook up! Sound off for equipment check!" It was that fast. We did our best as we were holding on for dear life. Then the jumpmaster screams out "STAND IN THE DOOR." We jammed up tight. I couldn't see the light for the back of the man in front of me.
>
> The green light went on and we all squirted out the door. I had this tremendous opening shock and my lines were all twisted. I tried to catch my breath for a moment and saw in the moonlight I was going to land in water. What the hell! There isn't supposed to be any water. Before I could fully process it all, I hit the drink, went under and couldn't get up. My parachute had floated on top of me. My feet were on the bottom but I couldn't get my head above water. I felt this tugging and came out. The wind had inflated the chute and was pulling me against the bank. Thank God. I felt the bank and just held on for a minute.

All across the peninsula, similar events were being acted out.

Each aircraft carried nine para-packs, six under the wings and three under the belly. Many had an additional door bundle inside the aircraft. By the exit door, there were three toggle switches, one for each wing load of three and one for the fuselage of three. Depending upon stick position, a jumper would be designated to "Hit the switch" when he exited. The idea was that the para-packs would then land where the unit landed. A door bundle added more but also complicated the jump.

508 Parachute Infantry Regiment troops 'chuting up in the UK for a training jump. (US Army Signal Corps)

Pathfinders on 5 June 1944. Bob Murphy is third from the right, back row. (US Army Signal Corps)

Troops move in chalk formation to their aircraft. (US Air Force Number A51875AC)

Packed aircraft and gliders typical of the more than 20 RAF D-Day departure fields. (US Army Signal Corps)

Water near Merderet meadow today. Peaceful now, on 6 June the deep waters of the flooded Merderet meadow drowned many paratroopers burdened with heavy equipment. (Author's photo)

Ranger training in Cornwall prior to D-Day. (US Army Signal Corps)

The cliff face that the Rangers ascended at Pointe du Hoc. Rudder's CP is visible center top. The rubble at the base made climbing much easier. (US Army Signal Corps)

The casemates at Pointe du Hoc today. (Author's photo)

Lomell and Kuhn sit astride one of the guns located around three kilometers north of Pointe du Hoc, on probably 8 June. (US Army Signal Corps)

Ben Berger points to himself with Rudder's HQ on Pointe du Hoc. (Author's photo)

Dog Red today, where the Rangers landed, looking toward Vierville. The remains of the wooden groins, so important to the Rangers as protection from enfilade fire, are visible. (Author's photo)

Lieutenant Colonel Terence Otway. (US Army Signal Corps)

Brigadier James Hill talking to his commanders just prior to D-Day. (US Army Signal Corps)

Hill at Merville in 1984. (Author's photo)

Reinforcements move across Pegasus. (US Army Signal Corps)

Major John Howard at Pegasus Bridge in 1984. (Author's photo)

Omaha Beach: note the long crescent the Germans used to extreme advantage. (Author's photo)

The German view of Omaha Beach. (German photograph from the US Army)

Probably the fifth or sixth wave near the center sector of Omaha. Note the dead DD tanks and troops hiding behind the obstacles and the men against the seawall. Tide is about three-quarters in. (US Army Signal Corps)

View at high tide from extreme right of Omaha Beach, probably taken soon after the war—note submerged assault craft remain on the beach. (US Army Signal Corps)

Active-duty troops with the author at the 29th Div monument, extreme right of Omaha Beach and where the 29th Div took more than 75 percent casualties in the first three waves. (Author's photo)

The farmyard at Neuville looking north. Niland's position is the wall to the right of the fence. Turnbull's CP is the barn to the left of the road. (US Army/SME Museum)

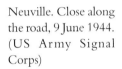

Neuville. Close along the road, 9 June 1944. (US Army Signal Corps)

The farm at Neuville now. Note the location of the main road and the positions that Turnbull took relative to it. (Author's photo)

The lead Jagdpanzer at Neuville. Note the two 57mm holes on the armor. (US Army Signal Corps)

Lt Turnbull's grave at Omaha Beach. (Author's photo)

Lt Turnbull. (Courtesy of Colonel Ben Vandervoort from the US Army)

La Fière Bridge and Cauquigny Church, taken around 10 June. (US Army Signal Corps)

The Causeway today, looking west. The 1-505 positions were aligned with the nearest hedgerow, and water came to that point. (Author's photo)

The manor at La Fière, July 1944—note the damage to the buildings. (US Army)

La Fière Manor today. The door on the left of the umbrella leads to the 507th medical clearing station in the three-foot crawl space underneath. (Author's photo)

Colonel Lewis on right, Gavin in center, at La Fière Bridge on 14 June 1944. (US Army)

Iron Mike statue at La Fière Bridge. (Author's photo)

Brécourt Manor. Winters took us to the triangle where he stuck his head out on the battery side. We were standing on the gun position looking at Winters standing by the fence post at the extreme left of the picture. (Author's photo)

Aerial view of Brécourt—note the triangle shape of the field as well as the two woodlines Winters used to his advantage. (Author's photo)

General Gavin leads the staff ride at La Fière Bridge, 0730 6 June 1984. (Author's photo)

General Gavin at La Fière. (Author's photo)

Local children honoring the dead at the Sainte-Mère-Église cemetery. (Renaud family collection)

The church of Sainte-Mère-Église on 6 June 1944. (US Army Signal Corps)

The stained-glass window in the church depicting St Michael, patron saint of paratroopers, and dedicated to those who sacrificed their lives to liberate the town. (Author's photo)

Children and veterans at the cemetery at Omaha Beach on the 75th anniversary of D-Day. (Author's photo)

French children at the cemetery at Omaha Beach.

Paratroopers jumping into Sainte-Mère-Église, 1984. (Author's photo)

Lieutenant Colonel Nightingale leads his men through the streets of Sainte-Mère-Église, June 1984. (Author's photo)

The 82nd Airborne *fourragère*. (Author's photo)

Veterans at the Sainte-Mère-Église hôtel de ville: Ray Fary, Duke Boswell, Fred Morgan, Bill Sullivan, Duaine "Pinky" Pinkston, and John Perozzi. (Author's photo)

Veterans visiting Isle St Marie beyond the Causeway near La Fière on 4 June 2004: from left, a 101st veteran, Emil Lecroix (not a veteran), Ray Fary, Bob Piper, Bill Tucker, Zane Schlemmer, Bob Murphy, Bill Sullivan, and a 101st veteran. (Author's photo)

Seven Originals at Iron Mike, La Fière, for the 60th anniversary of D-Day. (Author's photo)

Bob Murphy talking to active-duty troops at La Fière. (Author's photo)

Vets Bob Murphy and Howard Manoian at the STOP bar, visiting for the 65th anniversary. (Author's photo)

Sully, Bob Murphy and the author at Mont Saint-Michel, 4 June, 2008. (Author's photo)

Zane Schlemmer in Normandy. (Courtesy of Zane Schlemmer)

Zane walking to the Sainte-Mère-Église Church in 2016. He knew he would not be back. (Author's photo)

The door bundle would be placed next to the open door. The jumpmaster or next man in the stick would be designated as the "door bundle jumper." His job was to push the bundle out the door and immediately follow it. The concept was that he would land next to it and put it to use. Unfortunately, wind and physics created problems that night.

If the bundle was not pushed out with great force, it often jammed itself in the door blocking further use until extracted. A plane would cross the drop zone and not drop anyone. In some cases within the 82nd, two or more passes would be required to drop the bundle and the troops. In many of those cases, the pilot just kept going and dropped the troops wherever he was when the bundle finally cleared. Corporal Dave Jones explained:

> We learned in England the best way with the door bundle was to prop it up on end and lean it against the forward door frame. With a good push, it would exit and the wind would carry it away. If it was too big or too heavy, we would have the jumpmaster and one other guy do a two-man push. We hated them because it always slowed the exit.

All across the Cotentin Peninsula and the Orne Valley, similar events were playing out. The German anti-aircraft artillery was fully awake. Fingers of tracers coursed across the sky at the hundreds of aircraft veering out of formation as they tried to avoid the most effective fire. Occasionally, a plane would be hard hit, begin burning, and make a fiery descent.

The fires, combined with clouds, created issues for the jumpmasters attempting to track the ground landmarks to ensure the plane was where it was supposed to be. Often, this was not the case. Vandervoort recalled,

> I had studied the route very carefully. In England, I laid out the path I would see with photos. I studied that route until I had it memorized and could track it in my sleep.
>
> When we crossed the Guernsey Isles, I began to pick up the trace. The red light came on but we were nowhere near where we should have been for it. Then the green light came on. I told the crew chief to tell the pilot to turn it off. We were still miles from the drop zone. Finally, it went off.
>
> When we did get the red light a second time, he was right on course. We finally jumped and were exactly where we were supposed to be. I hate to think of what would have happened if we had jumped earlier.

The drop zone for the 505th Parachute Infantry Regiment was on a long, flat farm plain stretching between the west side of Sainte-Mère-Église and the eastern side of Le Manoir, the farm complex that overlooked a key objective, La Fière Bridge, and the connecting causeway to Picauville and the land beyond.

This route would be the primary conduit between Utah Beach and the neck of the Cotentin. From here, VII Corps would cut the peninsula and shift north to Cherbourg, the grand prize of the invasion strategy.

The regiment landed largely intact and by 0230, its three battalions were beginning to move to their respective objectives: 1-505 to the bridge and causeway, 2-505 to seize Neuville-au-Plain and block the road to Sainte-Mère-Église from the north, and 3-505 to clear the town and block the road from the south.

The 82nd generals had their own issues.

The Airborne LGOPs

The concept and ethos behind the term LGOP (Little Groups of Paratroops) is the heart of the American Airborne culture. It is the idea that wherever a trooper is dropped, regardless of error, they do whatever they can to wreak havoc on the enemy. Rank and structure are not needed. Only to be there and functioning. Normandy was the birth of the concept, a concept that today is the heart and soul of whomever wears jump wings.

Of the nine parachute infantry regiments inserted on D-Day morning, only one, the 82nd's 505th Parachute Infantry Regiment, landed where planned. All the others were badly scattered throughout the peninsula. From the 82nd, the 507th and 508th Parachute Infantry Regiments assembled less than 30 percent of their troops. Gavin recalled:

> The railroad was a magnet. I started a collection station by the bridge and assembled several hundred men over time. We formed them into units based on their affiliation, but at a decidedly smaller strength. Regardless, their presence was a Godsend.
> I had the 508th commander, Lindquist, and Ed Ostberg and Art Maloney, both great commanders. All fortunately mis-dropped. They were a great strength and major help. I tapped Lindquist and his men to be the reserve behind La Fière—we had to hold it. The others I took to Chef-du-Pont with Ostberg and Maloney or placed them where they could do the most good.
> The 507th was even worse. We recovered a good bit of the men but very few leaders. When Raff came up from the beach on the 8th, we installed him from the sea tail as commander but he didn't have many troops.

As examples, the regimental commander of the 507th landed within 10 miles of Cherbourg, more than 30 air miles from his intended drop zone. One of his battalions landed at Graignes, south and west of Carentan, more than 20 air miles from where he was intended. Lieutenant Colonel Charles Timmes commanded the 2-507th:

> I landed pretty much where I was supposed to, just east of Amfreville with my back to the Merderet. But I had only about 150 men. The rest were dropped somewhere else. You mentioned General Gavin landing quite close. The fog of war. We never knew of his presence or of his men.
> I just had to pick up and go with what I had. I was determined to get to Amfreville to link up with the rest of the regiment. While still dark, we approached the outskirts and met very heavy fire. The Germans were fully awake and very aggressive. I had to give the order to fall back as we were getting hard pressed, about to be flanked, and had a lot of casualties. We returned to the orchard area and dug in with our backs to the river. The Germans pretty much locked us in and we fought there until 9 June.

We were reinforced by Teddy Sanford and his battalion, but we were collectively held in check and stayed that way until 9 June. I believe we tied down a lot of Germans who otherwise would have been defending the causeway.

Elements of 3-508th landed well to the west and took more than three days to finally unite with the 82nd. The 508th Parachute Infantry Regiment HQ landed relatively intact but was well away from its programmed location but fortunately mis-dropped amongst the 505th. It also found two of its battalion commanders, less their troops, also on the wrong side of the Merderet River but on dry land. Hill explained:

> I landed nowhere near what we had planned. It was in a swamp and I nearly drowned. When myself and Davey Jones finally figured it out, we were about 5 miles from where we were supposed to be. Near Beuzeville-au-Plain and along the main road. There were Germans everywhere.
>
> During the night, we picked up about 25 men, all mis-drops. We had men from several battalions including the 101st. We finally found Sergeant Hummel who had about the same amount with lots of mis-drops. No officers or medics and only what we had. It was obvious to us that the road net and houses we occupied by chance were astride the primary German road net. We talked a minute and decided to fight here, as much by chance as anything. I called this Hell's Half Acre and it was. We had half the men wounded and no resupply. We fought until 9 June when we finally met some troops coming up from Chef-du-Pont. I was really proud of what we had done holding off armor and infantry with a bunch of men who had never worked together until that moment. I would like to think we made a difference.

The 101st had similar experiences dropping men from Cherbourg to south of Carentan. Four were dropped at Omaha Beach and fought with the Rangers at Pointe du Hoc.

The British experience was somewhat the same with 3 and 5 Para brigades. Neither assembled with 50 percent, with many landing in swamps and rivers. However, due to the nature of the restricted drop area, many troops managed to find their way back after a day or so.

Regardless of affiliation, these mis-dropped became what today is known as the LGOP, or Little Group of Paratroops.

Everywhere they dropped, individually, or if fortunate, collectively, they went about their business. They got out of their parachutes, unlimbered their weapons, and went about finding their brethren.

In some cases, this was one or two individuals who joined in the dark or groups of 10 or more. The unit affiliations were invariably mixed as was the rank. General Taylor (commenting on his command group with a majority of senior officers and few junior enlisted) said: "Never have so few been led by so many."

Regardless of association or rank structure, they amalgamated in common cause, moved to the sound of the guns, and were extremely disruptive. They cut phone lines, ambushed passing vehicles and messengers, attacked anti-aircraft guns exposed in open fields, and left a much larger impression on the German high command than numbers or plans warranted.

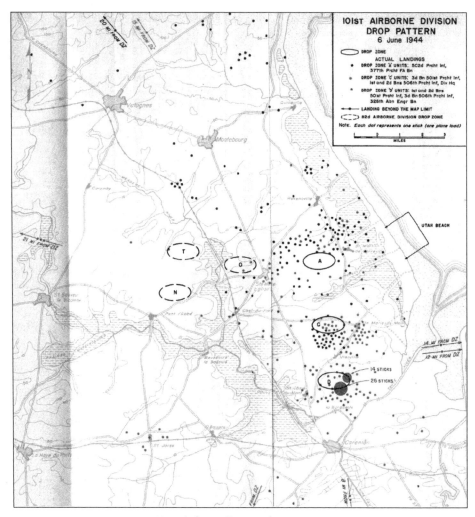

101st Airborne Division drop pattern.

Lieutenant Malcolm Brannen and his band is an excellent example of the LGOP phenomenon.

Earlier, on 15 May 1944, Field Marshal Rommel visited the key defending division for the Cotentin Peninsula, the 91st Airlanding Division at Chateau Bernaville at Picauville. He met the commanding general, Wilhelm Falley, and had a lunch. He departed believing that Falley could ably manage any invasion. The dessert served on 6 June greatly altered the plan.

Barely making it out the door due to the constant gyrations of his C-47, Lieutenant Malcolm Brannen, 508th Parachute Infantry Regiment, rode the turbulence and

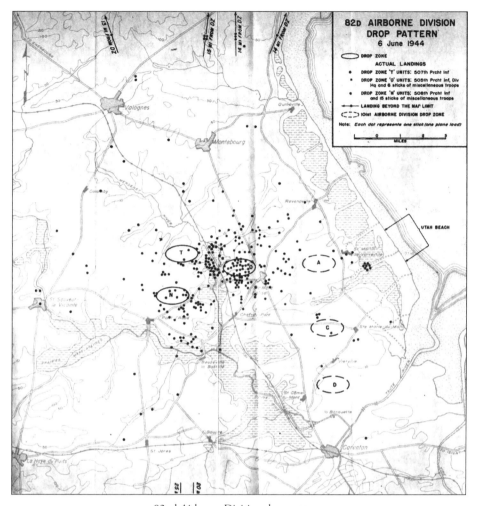

82nd Airborne Division drop pattern.

felt the extreme opening shock. His parachute was severely twisted and he slammed through a large apple tree and came to an abrupt halt, his feet more than 4 feet from the ground.

As his breath returned and he gained a consciousness of the place, he perceived he was on the edge of a large orchard and tall hedgerow border. He could see patches of pavement on the other side as the moon shone intermittently between the clouds.

He thought for a moment and decided to hold in the tree until he could get his bearings and determine if any of his unit were around. Soon, a group of soldiers rapidly tramped by him on the road but he could not identify them.

After less than an hour, he cut himself loose, dropped down, and waited in silence. He soon heard noises of movement to his right and strained to make out the figures. Quickly the shapes revealed jump fatigues and the distinctive silhouette of the American helmet with leather chinstrap dangling.

He quickly moved to intercept with the challenge Flash and was greeted with a Thunder. It was another mis-dropped lieutenant and two enlisted men. The group paused to collect themselves. They could see flashes and explosions to the east and occasional gunfire and tracers. Brannen indicated that east was where they should go to find the rest of the 82nd Airborne.

Decision made, they paralleled the hedgerow, but did not use the road as they were uncertain who was on it. Over the course of the movement, they collected individuals and small elements until by 0600, the force numbered 13 with mixed weaponry including a bazooka, a BAR, and several Thompsons in addition to M-1s. Well-armed for the circumstances.

The terrain had changed from open farms and orchards to more forested land with stone walls lacing the several converging road intersections they observed. A reading of the signs showed they were literally miles from their intended assembly areas well to the east.

Unbeknownst to him, Chateau Bernaville and the entire array of the German 91st Airlanding Division was less than a hundred yards away. The walls and trees shielded both adversaries from knowledge of each other.

Brannen chose to continue his circuitous march to avoid German patrols and vehicles, a number of which had been spotted nearby. The group found itself in a deep wooded roadstead covered with tall trees. He slowly emerged from the hedgerow and collected his men in a file on the narrow trace.

The northern side was bounded by woods that came up to the road and hung over, providing a deep shade despite the rising sun. The south side was marked by a large stone wall of loose rock, accumulated organic manner, and the tips of overhanging trees. The overall effect was that while the road was relatively visible, the rest of the scene was totally shrouded.

Very quickly, the road opened and a large two-story concrete and stone building was observed to their left. Brannen decided it was time to determine with some specificity where they were and reckoned the occupants would be French and friendly. He signaled the rear to post a road guard and with a sweep of his hand indicated his men to stand against the southern wall rubble.

He and his brother lieutenant stood on the small portico and knocked loudly on the door. Quickly, a head appeared above them through a window with a querying gaze.

As quickly, the road guard gave a shout that a car was approaching. Brannen could hear the loud chuffing of the engine as it blew through the shrouded archway to his rear. He took out his pistol in haste and stepped partway into the road raising his hand as a policeman might.

The car, now clearly seen as German with flags and plates, continued to roar along not making any attempt to comply. As if on common signal, but in pure animal reaction, everyone simultaneously opened fire, riddling the vehicle.

Brannen had shot the driver, he thought. The car turned slightly off the road and crashed into the portico. The impact threw open the passenger door and a body fell across the threshold as a hat and pistol skimmed across the road. Brannen, with adrenalin pumping, quickly moved toward the slumped body, still very much alive but clearly incapacitated. The person kept repeating in a whispered voice, "*Nicht schiessen, nicht schiessen!*" (Don't shoot).

But he also kept crawling toward the pistol. Brannen instinctively fired at the man's head, killing him. Turning toward the pistol and hat, he recovered both. Looking into the hat, he saw in red block thread "Falley."

With a fusillade of bullets from a little group of mis-dropped paratroops at 0635 on D-Day morning, all the plans and programs that Rommel expected from the 91st Airlanding Division evaporated with their commander's life blood.

Graignes, Okefenokee, and the Alamo

This is truly an action lost to all but the most diligent students of the events. It is also one of the ultimate displays of the LGOP ethos.

There is a small town in the southern swamps of the Cotentin peninsula called Graignes. It holds a story unknown to all but the most industrious historian or that rare World War II veteran of the 507th Parachute Infantry Regiment still alive. Graignes is a living symbol of the best of the Norman French and their unceasing affection for those young soldier-liberators that joined them on the 6th of June 1944 by chance not choice. The history is of two peoples that came together and found common cause. No better example exists for why the invasion took place.

South and slightly west of Carentan, a key objective of the Normandy invasion, is a large swampy area akin to Georgia's Okefenokee Swamp and only slightly smaller. To the French, it is simply known as Le Marais—the wet lowland residue of the passage to the north by the Douve and Merderet Rivers and their interconnecting offspring. It is a boggy land, cut with many canals and creeks with small standing plots of relatively firm ground that has been farmed for centuries by people who enjoyed and prospered in the fetid and protective isolation. The air is heavier than the rest of the peninsula, the humidity fed by the copious quantities of open and near-stagnant water. On a warm day, the air hangs heavy.

The trees tend to blot out the horizon. The light as it filters through the woods casts an amber hue on whatever it strikes. The ground is a bit soft, bereft of rocks, and the surface dries quickly into powder. The roads trace darkly through the woods and are quickly lost to view. There is a distinct feeling of loneliness and isolation. The small villages and farm communities are not visible except to the immediate entrance a visitor may make in a chance encounter. To the unknowing visitor, it would be virtually impossible to visualize the significance this place holds for American history.

Approximately in the center, on the largest and firmest ground, lies the small village of Graignes. Inhabited probably since the time of Vikings, it offered safe haven off the path of surrounding and competing forces and civilization. At the very highest point, less than 15 feet above sea level, rests the church. Constructed over time since the medieval period, its present structure rises on the foundation of the original as soldiers found it on 6 June 1944. Why and how it is a new building is the story.

Attached to the 82nd Airborne for the D-Day invasion, the 507th Parachute Infantry Regiment was the last regiment to be dropped. Its troop carrier elements had no previous drop experience and flew into the peninsula under a disastrous combination of bad weather, low ceiling, and a fully aroused German anti-aircraft force. Elements of the 507th were scattered from the tip of the peninsula near Cherbourg to Omaha Beach and the English Channel. Those few sticks that dropped where they were supposed to discovered their drop zone to be in the middle of the Merderet swamp. The majority of the 507th that survived the night did so because they were mis-dropped on or near the 505th drop zone near Sainte-Mère-Église. Part of this regiment had an unusual experience and created their own Alamo at Graignes with the fervent support of a people they had never previously met.

At approximately 0200 on 6 June 1944, 12 sticks (20–23 paratroopers per stick) of 3-507th Parachute Infantry Regiment landed relatively close together in the swampy land well south of Carentan. In the early morning light, small groups of soldiers were able to see the steeple of the Graignes church and moved toward it as if drawn by a magnet. By 1000, 25 soldiers led by Captain Leroy Brummitt emerged on the edge of town. With them were an unusually large quantity of weapons and ammunition bundles—the residue of a regiment—machine guns, mortars, and ammunition for both.

By 1200, Major Charles Johnston, also from the 3-507th, arrived with more soldiers. The officers had a short debate. Brummitt thought it best to move immediately north toward Carentan and link up with elements of the 101st. Major Johnston thought that too risky and believed it best to hold until relieved. Besides, Graignes was at the confluence of the few road networks that laced the area, all of which ended at Carentan, the headquarters of German defenses between Omaha and Utah beaches.

Graignes quickly became an Alamo position with outposts guarding each road, machine gun positions and mortar pits dug, and forward observers placed in the church tower. Over the rest of the day and night, small groups of soldiers emerged from the swamps and coalesced on the position. By nightfall of 6 June, 182 soldiers including 12 officers manned the perimeter. Some were equally mis-dropped soldiers from the 101st.

Early in the morning of 7 June, Captain Brummitt met with the mayor, Monsieur Alphonse Voydie, and the two attendant priests. He asked for the support of the village in retrieving supply bundles from the swamp and assistance in collecting food for the soldiers. He also asked permission, albeit a bit belatedly, to use the church for his headquarters and medical collection point. The mayor and priests readily agreed but Voydie tempered his decision by saying it needed a vote of all the town because of the potential consequences of a German re-occupation.

Quickly, the town assembled in the church, virtually the entire population from the documented reports. The mayor described the issue and recommended support to the Americans. The parish by show of hands unanimously agreed and the die was cast. This was despite the certain knowledge of intermittent Gestapo presence and strict wartime occupation rationing and monitoring at

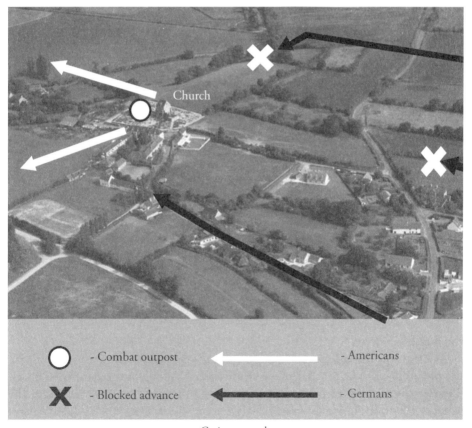

Graignes stand.

the outlying village markets. Known or suspect support to the invaders would result in instant death.

Madame Germaine Boursier, owner of the only café, assumed the task of food collection and distribution. The men and boys deployed throughout the area to collect supply bundles in the swamps. A considerable quantity of material was recovered—medical supplies, food, ammo, commo wire, telephones, and weapons—but no radios.

Madam Boursier organized two food deliveries each day, personally taking it around to each position to ensure equal rationing. The wives each added a little bit to the whole by buying just enough extra so as not to arouse suspicions. Throughout 8 and 9 June, this pattern was repeated without any contact with German forces. On 10 June, things changed abruptly.

At mid-morning on 10 June, the forward observer in the church steeple saw a German column approach in administrative order, clearly not expecting resistance. The observer immediately notified the defending road block, which laid a perfect linear ambush that virtually wiped out the column. As darkness fell, around 2300, Germans began probing Graignes on all the road networks but made no significant entry. Ominously, one of the Germans killed in the ambush had papers indicating he was from a recon element of the 17th SS Panzergrenadier Division "Götz von Berlichingen."

At 1000 on the 11th, the town, augmented by many Catholic soldiers, entered the church—now an active aid station and command center—for Sunday mass. Partway through the service, a villager burst through the door shouting that the Germans were attacking. The soldiers raced to the rear of the church, grabbed their weapons, and bolted through the door to their positions. Mortar and artillery fire began to land in the village and small arms ricochets rattled off of the stones and slate roofs. The villagers, at the suggestion of the mayor, decided to remain inside the church and wait out the attack.

By 1400, the Germans were spotted in a distant field establishing a battery of 88mm guns. At the same time, a determined infantry attack hit several points. The Germans combined mortar and artillery attacks throughout the village but were unable to break the defensive lines. However, U.S. casualties began to mount and they were collected by villagers and soldiers and deposited inside the church, now a fully engaged casualty collection point. The two village priests, augmented by their aged housekeepers, assisted the few medics and 3-507th doctor in treating the increasing flow.

As night fell, the villagers dissipated back to their farms or chose to remain with friends inside the village. Defenders clearly heard sounds of mechanized vehicles. The German artillery and mortar elements began to heavily engage the village. The primary target of the artillery was the church steeple, which they hit on successive occasions, killing the observer party and Major Johnston, thereby destroying the most effective observation point for the defenders. The successive barrages also materially reduced the mortar crews who were dug in within the church cemetery. The loss of the previously very effective indirect fire materially reduced the ability of the 3-507th to defend its out posted positions.

Regardless of the loss of mortar support, the defenders still exacted a very heavy price from the attackers. The narrow roads and limited dry ground forced the Germans to attack on restricted terrain, making them very vulnerable to the paratroopers. Hundreds of German bodies littered each lane as the afternoon wore on. However, the sheer weight of arms began to take a toll. One by one, each roadblock began to disintegrate under a combination of casualty attrition, very effective German indirect fire, and masses of German infantry. By 1700, much of the village had been captured. Captain Brummitt, now in command, ordered the survivors to escape and evade into the swamps and move north to Carentan where it was assumed the 101st would be.

At 2200, life in Graignes changed dramatically with the arrival of the headquarters of the 17th SS Panzer Division. The unit had suffered a very embarrassing near defeat from a force of less than 200 paratroopers. It counted more than 500 killed in the approaches to the town and were treating more than 700 wounded. The commanding general arrived at the church in a very ugly and vengeful mood.

Quickly, Germans took the wounded, the medics, and the doctor to the edge of the swamp and executed them in two groups. Separately, they marched the two priests into the rectory and summarily executed them. They then burned the remainder of the church and rectory, but not before shooting the two housekeepers in their beds. Sweeping through the town, they rounded up 44 villagers.

They were herded into the remains of the church and the SS began individual interrogations to determine who were the village leaders. In particular they wanted the name of the mayor and those that supported the U.S. soldiers. They knew full well that the Americans had to have had significant local support to be as supported as long as they were. Despite a night's worth of threats and beatings, not a single one of the 44 villagers gave up a name.

Frustrated at the lack of cooperation, the commander ordered the village to be ransacked. Houses were broken into, windows, furniture, and possessions were destroyed or appropriated. Any food was taken and clothes burned or torn apart. On the 13th, the village was put to the torch. The villagers were prohibited from attempting to stop the flames.

The fire consumed 66 homes, the village school, Madam Boursier's café, and the furniture, pews, and remains of the church. More houses were scorched or intentionally damaged. By the end of the day, only two of 200 houses remained unscathed. The now homeless villages gathered what possessions they had and moved to outlying farms to shelter with friends for an uncertain future.

On the 13th, at an outlying farm, the most distant from the village but still less than a mile away, the Rigault family began its morning routine. The two daughters, Marthe and Odette, moved from the house to tend the livestock and the barn. Odette noticed several furtively moving paratroopers on the edge of the farm where the land fell off into the swamp. On her own initiative, a girl of 13, she ran to the soldiers and led them into the barn. Pointing to the hay loft, she motioned them up the ladder and raced to the house to inform her parents. Over the course of the day, she and her sister walked the swamp edge and recovered more soldiers, always pointing them toward the barn. By late afternoon, 21 soldiers were in the hayloft. Madame Rigault began to feed them what little food the family possessed. Always mindful of possible German observation, she distributed the food in small hidden quantities on the girls who disguised their movements as part of the daily farming routine. On several occasions, Germans came through checking for Americans but the family always appeared to be isolated and alone.

The soldiers had hoped that the 101st would eventually move through the area. By the 15th, the troops agreed this was probably a forlorn hope. One of the soldiers was a Louisiana Cajun who was enlisted to talk to Monsieur Rigault about the best route through the swamp to Carentan. Monsieur Rigault went to several of his outlying neighbors to develop a plan. He engaged a 15-year-old boy, Joe Folliot, who was very familiar with the confusing maze of canals, creeks, and outlets that characterized the ancient swampland.

At 2200, Joe appeared at the edge of the farm with a punt boat that could hold five soldiers. He began the long process of poling through the swamp, landing the troops on a spot past the German outposts and pointing them in the direction of Carentan. This process continued throughout the night. Several times soldiers tried to give Joe money or a small gift and he consistently refused with a whispered "*Merci, Américain.*" By 16 June, 150 3-507th troops had gained the front lines of the 101st, all those remaining from the 182 that assembled at Graignes on 6 June.

The troopers of the 101st might have provided the Graignes survivors a warmer reception had they known how important the stand of the mis-dropped 3-507th troopers were to their own survival. The 17th SS Panzer Division had been ordered to reinforce the German headquarters at Carentan. It never got there before the 101st was able to capture the city on 12 June. The chance encounter at Graignes, the intense combat, and inordinate casualties kept the SS division from reinforcing the city. Had it passed through Graignes without incident, the 101st would have had a much more difficult outcome.

The Night of the Airborne Generals

Over time, I got to know both Generals Ridgway and Gavin. Even with the passage of time, they exuded all the leadership qualities and force of personality that made them such revered figures. In my mind, the true underpinning to that were the accolades the veterans provided. Combat develops opinions and their opinions of their generals was both positive and sincere. I could see that years later in my interviews and visits. A lot of meals, drinks, and talk convinced me the troops got it right.

General Ridgway, a late entrant to the jump having been programmed as a glider insertion for 0430, landed just west of the town and designated a farm house near the road on high ground as the division command post:

> It was an uneventful flight. I rode in with a stick from the 505. I only had one bodyguard, a tough pirate looking guy from the 504th that Colonel Tucker had insisted I take. I never saw him again.
>
> I jumped second and landed on a grassy field. I could see the fires in St Mère and hear our men all around. I got out of my parachute, said a prayer in thanks and moved to where I could see men in the light. That's where I met Piper. My thought now was to get established and see what was going on. Remember, those were the days before we had the radios of today [1984].

The headquarters commander, Captain Bob Piper, set out several white reserve parachutes as a designator:

> I landed and rolled up my stick. We assembled just a bit to the north of the high ground on a slight dip. I got everybody together and we moved toward the fires we could see in St Mère. We hadn't gone a hundred yards when General Ridgway appeared with one other troop. He stopped us and we talked.
>
> He wanted his command post to be where it was visible to everyone and close to the roads so he could intercept traffic. We saw this farm house on the high ground and it was all by itself. No outside walls or barns. We both agreed that was perfect. It was less than a hundred yards from the main La Fière road.
>
> I sent out several guys to get our door bundles with the radios. They came back with some weapons, ammo, and medical supplies, but no functioning radios. The two radios we did have, one for internal communications and one between the division and corps, were badly damaged in the drop. Several of the tubes had broken as well as the spares. I designated a couple of men as messengers. I saw General Ridgway move toward the main road to talk to troops as they passed.

General Ridgway was now in the position of being in command of an organization on its most important mission to date, but with minimal ability to exercise that command. He recalled:

> I was extremely frustrated and had to really control myself. Without radios, I had no idea what was going on. I only knew what I could see or what I was told. I could see that the 505 had things pretty much in hand. Krause sent a runner very early to tell me they had cut the cable at the town hall. I knew nothing about how the 507th and 508th were doing and of course I had no radio to Gavin who had jumped with the 507th.
>
> This didn't change as the night and later day wore on. I finally met with General Gavin [probably around 0900] and we talked things over. He had a very bad night and it was clear we had a lot of mis-drops. He was sorting it out with what he could get from mis-drops on our side of the river.
>
> We could hear the rumble of fire from the beaches but didn't know how things were going. The Germans were attacking from both north and south and I was increasingly concerned. He

> [Gavin] and I agreed we would do an Alamo position in the town if we had to and just fight as long as we could.

Jim Gavin had a considerably worse experience than Ridgway, but in his style, went about sorting it out. He had made the decision to jump with the 507th Parachute Infantry Regiment rather than the 505th Parachute Infantry Regiment, his favorite.

> I had decided early on to jump with the 507th. They were untested and had a very tough mission—to take and hold the road net at Amfreville west of the Merderet. I thought by my going with them, I could lend a bit of experience and prod where necessary.
>
> My aide, Hugo Olson, and I, loaded out with part of the 507th HQ elements at RAF Cottesmore. The ride in was fine until we were about 30 minutes out. As was my practice, I had everyone stand up and hook up just in case we had an issue en route. We ran into clouds and a lot of ack-ack and the pilots, green to combat, began to do a lot of jinking around. I saw the red light and made a mental note we were not where we were supposed to be. Too much water below. Regardless, I gave a "Let's Go" and went out on the green amidst a lot of tracer fire.
>
> My chute opened up fine and I could see we were near a large body of water which didn't register. I landed in an orchard area with cows. I got loose, found Olson and followed a dirt trace to the east. I came out quickly and saw a huge body of water. I saw a C-47 cutting in low across the water all aflame. I thought to myself we were in for a hell of a night.
>
> We began to pick up other jumpers, a number from planes other than ours. I tried to get the men organized and recovering the para-packs, which would be essential. The 507th men were fairly unresponsive and acted very tired.

Gavin and his party had landed on a small spit of dry land on the edge of the flooded Merderet. He had about 150 men around him, which he quickly assembled with the officers and NCOs. Unbeknownst to him, he was less than 300 meters from Lieutenant Colonel Timmes and 150 men from 2-507th Parachute Infantry Regiment. Neither party ever knew of the other's presence.

Gavin had two priorities on his mind: determining where they were and recovering weapons, particularly anti-tank weapons. He set his men out to clear the swamp of para-pack containers and sent Olson out to scout. It was about 0300.

Olson came back shortly to report that he believed they were just across from the Merderet. He had seen the glimmer of railroad tracks in the moonlight across the water and knew the only railroad was parallel to the river and on the side of Sainte-Mère-Église. He also reported he had found a possible sunken road across the flood to the other side. Olson said:

> As I went along the bank toward the south, I found this farm track leading from the orchard into the water. I stepped out on it and followed it. I went almost half way across and my waist never got wet.

Concurrently, troops had come back to report they found a glider in the swamp with a jeep and 57mm anti-tank gun. Gavin ordered two things: Olson was to cross the swamp and determine locations and situation and the men were to attempt to extract the gun. Gavin explained:

I was very anxious to be somewhere I could manage the action. My aide gave me potentially the best answer if he could find a way across. I also needed that anti-tank gun as I knew it would be needed.

Lieutenant Olson's Sunken Road has taken on a mythology as to its origin, as a secret road created by the Germans or another mystery element. The locals knew the road had been there for more than a century.

Every year before the war and with the intentional flooding, the Merderet had flooded in the winter, creating a shallow lake that went more than 30 miles upstream from its confluence with the Douve near Carentan.

As a consequence, for the farmers to move their grazing cattle from one side to the other, they had, during the dry season, erected several narrow, raised roads across the flood. They lined these with rocks and marked the track with stakes driven into the ground. It was one of these tracks that Olson providentially found and would be so important as the battle wore on. Olson said:

> When the general sent me back. I took two troops with me as the Germans were now plinking at us as it got lighter. I grabbed a long pole I found and used it to probe the edge as we went across. Fire was getting uncomfortably close and we went across hunkered down and as fast as we could.
>
> I got to the other side and pulled myself up to the railroad. We were pretty much where I thought. Just a bit above La Fière. We gathered ourselves and went south. We were soon joined by others. Mis-drops from the 07 and 08 as well as a few from the 05. I found the road bridge over the rails and knew exactly where we were at.
>
> I found an NCO from 1-505 and queried him as to status. He reported all was in hand. I told him to put up a collection point there and sort the troops out by regiment and that we would return shortly. I immediately went back to report to Gavin. I guess it was about 0630.

While Lieutenant Olson was crossing the flood, Gavin was organizing his men, now numbering nearly 200. He had them scour the swamp and land for para-packs and sent a dozen out to recover the jeep and 57mm that was in the swamp.

Earlier, Timmes and his 150 men of 2-507th had assaulted Amfreville and been thrown back to an apple orchard less than 200 meters from Gavin. Timmes said:

> I had no idea that General Gavin was that close. I was completely focused on gathering what men I could and going to Amfreville, the regimental objective. I had an extremely hard exit and lost all my equipment due to opening shock. We were obviously mis-dropped, but I had to go with what I had. There was firing and explosions continuously, which probably accounts for why General Gavin and I were never aware of each other.
>
> After our attack into Amfreville, the Germans pressed us all the way to the apple orchard where we were able to establish a defense. We had a machine gun covering the road into the orchard and the Germans held back.

On Olson's return, Gavin ordered a cease work to all and prepared to go to the other side of the Merderet:

Olson's news was great. I was extremely anxious to get to the other side and ensure we had a firm hold on La Fière and Chef-du-Pont. By then, it was light and the Germans were aware of our presence and engaging any of us that were near the flood.

Gavin and his men followed Olson across the water to the other side on the Sunken Road. This was later used by elements of the 325 GIR to assist Timmes. The force reached the railroad embankment and went south to the bridge. There, Gavin reinforced the collection point, established his headquarters, and set up a straggler collection.

Already, elements of the 507th and 508th were collected, the 508th being the greatest with over 200 men including the regimental commander, Colonel Lindquist. The 507th had less than a 100 but included two battalion commanders, Edwin Ostberg and Arthur Maloney. Gavin moved toward the bridge at La Fière.

Lieutenant Turnbull at Neuville

Lieutenant Turner Turnbull's actions at Neuville-au-Plain are largely lost to history. Yet what he did was so exceptionally important to the 82nd on D-Day that his battalion commander, Lieutenant Colonel Benjamin Vandervoort, believed he fully deserved the Medal of Honor. This section largely describes the events and personalities that Ben Vandervoort related to us on site at the 40th anniversary as well as numerous discussions with him on his porch at Hilton Head enjoying a very cold gin and tonic. It displays the nature and qualities of the men that jumped that night.

The 2-505th, composed of approximately 640 men, exited their aircraft at 0141. By 0400, Ben Vandervoort had more than 90 percent of the 2-505 in the assembly area, the northernmost portion of Drop Zone O. He had spent the initial part of the evening sending out parties to recover the many para-packs dropped in the area.

These contained the machine guns, mortars, ammunition, and medical supplies for the companies. Most had been found by 0430 and he directed movement to the east and then north.

His mission was to block the main Cherbourg–Carentan Road at a small farm complex about a mile north of Sainte-Mère-Église called Neuville-au-Plain. The primary buildings were astride the road with a chateau and farm on the high ground. With three near full-strength rifle companies, this was a reasonable mission.

The battalion was to pass through the northern portion of St Mère, clearing it of any Germans in concert with 3-505th, tasked with seizing the town itself. As the battalion began its movement, Vandervoort received a written message from the regimental commander, Colonel Ekman, to halt in place and be prepared to assist the 3-505th.

Ekman came to the 2-505th, halted mid-way into the town and found Vandervoort. The 3-505th had problems clearing the town itself and defend against a very aggressive German counter-attack force coming from the south at Les Forges. The 2-505th was to hold the northern edge of town with a screening force and send the rest to relieve the 3-505th in town so it could concentrate on the attacking force. Vandervoort was instructed not to go to Neuville. Vandervoort recalled:

> We were pretty quickly assembled. My ankle was killing me but a couple of troops wrapped it tight and found me a cart for movement. I had a long stick but it was pretty useless in the soft earth. The cart was embarrassing but effective. By morning, a nice old lady gave me some crutches she had. These are the ones in several pictures.
>
> My plan was to simply sweep east along the edge of town and then go north keying on the road until we got to Neuville. It was readily identifiable on the map and everyone knew where to go. We had studied it to death in the hangers.
>
> We had barely made the main road when a messenger told me to stop, and that Colonel Ekman wanted a change of plan. I stopped the movement and very quickly Ekman joined me. He was not aware of General Ridgway's prior approval of going north.
>
> I told him about my discussion with Ridgway but he said things had changed and that Major Edward Krause (commander, 3-505th) had a major German counter-attack in the south and we were needed to hold the northern piece of St Mère.
>
> The place [Sainte-Mère-Église] was only marginally cleared. In that it was key to the whole division, Ekman told us to clear the town and allow Krause to defend the south in full strength.
>
> I brought up the company commanders and briefed them. Krause and I met at the square and divided the city like a pie with my battalion command post at the church. I thought a moment and told D Company to drop off its 3rd platoon and have Lieutenant Turnbull report to me.

By now, it was 0630 and in full daylight. The companies, less Turnbull's platoon, moved out to clear Sainte-Mère-Église while Vandervoort briefed Turnbull. He was to take his platoon and move directly to Neuville and block the road. He was to hold out as long as possible. Vandervoort continued:

> I took some liberty by extracting Turnbull's platoon. I needed a screening element to the north to alert us of any German activity so I could swing our elements around to meet it. While this was contrary to Ekman's guidance, I felt it necessary though I did not inform Ekman.

At this point in our discussion, he paused and began to discuss the necessity for hard basic small unit training. This then brought him back to addressing Turnbull.

> I made a conscious decision to give Turnbull what I knew was a very tough task. He had been with me since North Africa and had a reputation as a hard-ass lieutenant. When other units were taking a break, he was constantly pushing his men, battle drills, movements, hand and arm signals. You name it, he was doing it.
>
> He was half Cherokee so of course he was called Chief, but I recognized him as a superb platoon leader that could handle a very tough independent mission that I gave him. He was the best I had and proved it.

Turnbull had a total of 42 men including a spare lieutenant, two machine guns, two BARs, and one bazooka. Turnbull sent his men straight up the road to the juncture of the Neuville farm house and the main road, the highest ground looking north.

He did a quick assessment of a simple yet effective plan. One squad with the spare lieutenant, a machine gun, and a bazooka would occupy the large farmhouse on the west side of the road. It had the best view looking north and would provide protection in flank for the rest of the platoon.

A second squad would deploy to the Duchemin chateau and church crossroads to the east. It would block any movement from that direction and provide flank security for Turnbull and the remaining squad.

This squad would deploy just forward of the farm house which was Turnbull's command post. It had a machine gun which was placed between the two eastern squads, providing enfilade fire for both. It was about 0930.

While Turnbull was disposing his men, Vandervoort was busy managing two concerns—Turnbull in the north in a very precarious position and his own situation attempting to clear most of Sainte-Mère-Église as well as provide some form of security element close to the north end of town.

Earlier, at 0400, the first glider reinforcement began to land on Drop Zone O where the 505th Parachute Infantry Regiment had previously jumped. It was dawn and the gliders made near perfect landings.

These contained the anti-tank elements with the 57mm guns, some of the snub-nosed 105mm guns, medical and signal elements, and several jeeps laden with ammo. Vandervoort grabbed one jeep for himself to provide some mobility and two others with the 57mms and headed north to Turnbull.

He met Turnbull at the edge of the road. Turnbull placed one gun directly against the barn where they stood looking straight down the road. The second was placed on the road midway between Turnbull and Sainte-Mère-Église on a high dip in the road. It was about 1000.

They were standing on the road when a Frenchman on a bicycle came down the road. He stopped and in halting English said a group of Americans were coming down the road with German POWs. He then pedaled off toward Sainte-Mère-Église.

Turnbull and Vandervoort went to the west side of the road, closest to the chateau, for a better look. The initial impression was as the Frenchman indicated, but something seemed not quite right to Vandervoort. He spotted two tracked assault guns in the rear.

He told Turnbull to have the machine-gun fire across the road to halt the unit, hoping for a recognition signal from the Americans. The gun fired and the column immediately hit the ditches and began returning fire. The assault guns began moving directly down the road. The war had begun.

The 57mm crew was initially hesitant, but Vandervoort "persuaded" them to return and start firing. This they did, disabling both assault guns and turning the morning into a basic infantry contest. Vandervoort returned to Sainte-Mère-Église with Turnbull managing the northern war.

Assaulting Turnbull was a regiment of the 91st Airlanding Division. Though handicapped initially by the death of its commander, Wilhelm Falley, it was beginning to react. It sent out elements to reinforce Hill 20 south of Sainte-Mère-Église, another to defend the causeway at Cauquigny and attempt to re-capture La Fière, and a third force to probe from the north. To this point, 1030, the German command was still very unsure as to exactly how many Americans were where and in what numbers. Accordingly, they began to develop probing attacks until they could determine a better picture.

After the gun crews disabled the two tracked vehicles, Turnbull's infantry began to display why Vandervoort had such confidence in them.

The machine guns and BARs tore holes in the jammed ranks. The Germans got off the road and began to probe across the fields toward Neuville. As they did, the three squads acted as independent arms of the same beast. Using the intuitive instincts of seasoned soldiers combined with the relentless battle drills they had undergone, the squads picked, probed, and ambushed at the attacking Germans.

The infantry focused fire on the road ditches and then in supporting enfilade fire across the front. Germans attempting to move forward were cut down by flanking fire. This forced the Germans to retreat to reorganize and determine what size force they were actually facing.

The American squads sent out two- or three-man patrols, armed with BARs and Thompsons, several hedgerows past the defensive positions. They would lie in wait while the Germans crossed the fields, assuming distance from the main position equaled security.

Initially, the Germans moved en masse with 20 or 30 men in a loose group, not yet believing they had to deploy. They were quickly cut down from the rear and the attackers would retreat before they could recover. In this way, from approximately 1000 to noon, the battle was fought.

Perplexed, the Germans assumed a much larger force than actually existed was present. They brought up a number of mortars, 81mm and 120mm, which began to traverse and search Turnbull's line with increasingly telling effect. By 1500, all three elements had significant casualties, more than half the total force. These were collected in the barn Turnbull was using as his command post.

The Germans, sensing less pressure and under cover of the mortar fire, began to seep around the Airborne positions. The far-right squad, now reduced to four men on the chateau roof with a machine gun, had to send two men to the church crossroads to prevent infiltration in the rear.

The squad across the street was heavily engaged and had to retreat from the chateau and hold a bow shaped position in the apple orchard to the rear.

The center squad was holding position but close to being flanked on both sides. The time was approximately 1545.

What follows is derived from Vandervoort's debrief of Turnbull later that day.

Turnbull signaled the remainder of the right-hand squad to close on him. His intention was to hold a quick discussion as to stand and die or surrender. In the farmyard shelter holding the casualties, Turnbull's radio operator, sans radio, told him there was a chance they could escape to the immediate rear but they had to do it immediately.

Turnbull looked at the casualties and winced. The medics immediately said they would remain with the casualties. Simultaneously, Staff Sergeant Bob Niland, the machine gunner, said he would remain and provide covering fire. With that, Turnbull turned to his radio operator and said "Go!" The entire discussion had taken less than 15 seconds by Turnbull's account.[4]

Meanwhile, Vandervoort had been monitoring the sound of the conflict all day and understood the position was about to be lost. He took an element of the 507th that had been sent to him and told them to advance to the hedgerow north of town to provide covering fire if Turnbull's men came across the open field along the main road.

He sent part of E Company to the forward edge of the western side of the main road overlooking Neuville. There, the mortar ace of the 2-505th, Otis Sampson, set up to shoot. Vandervoort explained:

> I had become pretty good at differentiating between our weapons sounds and that of the Germans. I needed to in this case as we had no radios. My intent was to send reinforcements to Turnbull if I could, but we were fully engaged.
>
> For most of the morning, it was predominately our weapons, but then it was increasingly German. By 1500, it was clear that Turnbull was about done in. I grabbed what I could with the 507th guys and sent them forward and shifted a portion of E Company to overwatch. Just as soon as E Company was in position, Turnbull's guys emerged from Neuville running up the edge of the big open field.

Turnbull was oblivious to these actions and totally intent on a covered retreat. Rather than cross the open field near the main road leading to Sainte-Mère-Église, he led his men further to the east along a tree line marking a farm road. He halted everyone, now exhausted, at a small stone barn alongside the larger open field.

---

4   Staff Sergeant Bob Niland was one of the four Niland brothers, the family on which the movie *Saving Private Ryan* was loosely based. Niland was killed at the barn. Vandervoort returned the next day and recovered his body, slumped in the courtyard, his position full of spent brass and cotton ammo belts. On the 40th anniversary of D-Day, he showed us the bullet marks on the stone wall which remain there today.

The Germans attempted to move up the field, but were cut down by Sampson's very effective 60mm mortar fire and plunging machine-gun fire. However, the Germans who had stayed well east began to have effect on the stone barn.[5]

The 507th element emerged from the hedgerow, less than a hundred meters from the barn, and yelled and waved at Turnbull. He picked up the remainder of his men and ran across the field to join them and disappeared into the edge, leaving the Germans with an empty bag.

Turnbull joined Vandervoort at the edge of town near the geriatric hospice. It was approximately 1630.

Of the 42 men that made up Turnbull's platoon, 16 returned. Two medics and eight wounded were captured, and the rest were killed in action.

The next day, Turnbull was killed by German artillery as the battalion moved north toward Neuville-au-Plain.

Lieutenant Waverly Wray

This account was given to me by Ben Vandervoort, many years later. Ben spent the last 20 years of his life battling the bureaucracy to recognize Waverly Wray as worthy of the Medal of Honor. He never succeeded but he never quit trying. His love of Waverly and what he did was always center focus. This is what he said.

Lieutenant Waverly Wray, platoon leader, Company D, 2-505th Infantry, was trying to catch his breath on a small wooded outcropping north of the main Carentan–Cherbourg highway. It was about 1000 on 7 June 1944.

As usual, he took the most exposed position—"Better to see 'em" as he told the battalion commander, Lieutenant Colonel Ben Vandervoort. Waverly had a practiced eye from his rural Mississippi hunting background and was a crack shot. As with most 82nd officers, he led from the front. With a studied sweep of the ground to the north, he spotted the German positions and was assessing the best way for the company to counter-attack.

Throughout the early morning, the Germans had steadily attacked attempting to re-take Sainte-Mère-Église. They had attacked with armor as well as infantry and it took everything the 2-505th had to hold its ground. Ammunition was running low, the company commander had been wounded, and casualties were mounting. Waverly knew they had to seize the initiative or lose the ground and he wasn't going to let that happen.

The company command post was about 50 yards to his rear behind a large oak tree. The supplies had been placed there earlier, but the constant assaults and indirect fire had prevented replenishment of the line. Waverly grabbed a number of machine

---

5   A panzerfaust impact crater exists on the edge of the barn today.

gun belts and draped them across his shoulders, several bandoliers of M-1 ammo, stuffed his pockets with grenades, and moved forward, seemingly oblivious to the impacting rounds.

The German fire was reaching a crescendo, signaling another assault. The defenders had hunkered down in their positions and held fire, saving ammo for when a clear target presented itself. Waverly moved from position to position, dropping a belt here, grenades there, a couple of BAR magazines and cardboard boxes of medical supplies as bandoliers. He would return to the command post dragging wounded he managed to extricate from their position. This was done more than half a dozen times and always under intense fire.

The wounded company commander provided emotional support, but could do little else. Waverly was the acting company commander. The phone rang against the tree and the company commander answered. He turned to Waverly and told him to go to the battalion command post for an operations order. This Waverly did.

He was met by Lieutenant Colonel Vandervoort. Vandervoort ordered D Company to mount a counter-attack to seize the initiative and clear the road to the north. Wray said nothing as to the condition of the company commander or the precariousness of the position and returned to the command post. There, he told the company commander that they had been ordered to attack and he, Wray, would do a recon first. Plan approved.

What the company commander and Vandervoort did not know was that Waverly planned not to employ the rest of the company.

Waverly unslung his M-1 from his back, stuffed his pockets with grenades and took bandoliers of M-1 clips. Utilizing all his hunting skills, he slowly zig-zagged his way forward from his own lines until he actually was behind the main German lines, undetected.

He noticed a deep ditch paralleling the farm road hidden within the trees. Something clicked inside and he began another very careful move to a position from where he could scan the ditch.

His hunch was rewarded, because lined inside were more than 10 Germans, clearly the command group and staff. At a range of approximately 50 yards, he rose out of protective cover and took a standing position. He quickly worked off all eight rounds, knelt down, re-loaded, stood again and fired two more rounds. He had killed the entire command group and staff in less than 30 seconds.

To his rear, a pair of Germans heard the firing, swung around, and fired at Waverly, a round hitting him in his ear, leaving him bloody. This irritated more than hurt him as he pivoted, found the targets, and fired two killing shots. Knowing his time was limited, Wray quickly re-traced his steps back to his lines and reported to Vandervoort what he had done.

Vandervoort smiled, laughed a bit, and commented, "Looks like they got pretty close to you, Waverly."

Waverly retorted in his deep drawl, "Not as close as I got to them."

Wray was awarded a Distinguished Service Cross for this action although Vandervoort put him in for the Medal of Honor. He had, in less than a minute, destroyed a battalion command group and any hope it had for a serious attack on the 2-505th. All this because he had a lot of training in the forests and fields of his home as well as a seemingly bottomless pool of combat competency.

Prior to the invasion, a gentleman's agreement by the division and corps commanders was made that only one Medal of Honor would be awarded per division for the Normandy period. This was done in the belief it would remove any organizational competitiveness.

With one exception, imposed by General Eisenhower, the agreement held. In subsequent years, General Gavin, long retired, told me that he strongly approved Wray's nomination as well as that for Sergeant Owens at La Fière Bridge, but could never force a change despite repeated attempts to do so.

Waverly Wray died in Holland leading his men from Hunnerpark, Nijmegen, in a hail of fire to seize the north end of the crucial Nijmegen Bridge. He reached the leading German positions despite being completely exposed and was cut down.

Ben Vandervoort said it was one of the saddest days in his life and hung a pall over the entire battalion. Wray had a special grace and spirit that imbued those ordinary people that find it within themselves to do extraordinary things on behalf of others.

The Taking of La Fière Bridge

The La Fière battleground is the Gettysburg of the 82nd Airborne Division. It is the sepulcher of spirit, sacrifice, and service that is the ethos and soul of the division and always will be. What the division means to itself and to the nation was created on this ground.

I consider the taking of La Fière Bridge the ultimate moment of glory for the 82nd Airborne Division. It is the distillation of the spirit and sacrifice that epitomized Normandy for all of the participants. I walked it with General Gavin and dozens of veterans of that conflict. It was the utmost personal privilege to be able to relate their story. If you go nowhere else in Normandy, come here. You will be struck by the seemingly inconsequential small bridge and narrow causeway and may have doubts regarding its importance. Then read the plaque on the Iron Mike paratrooper statue and you will understand. Walk this with me on that day. This description is a composite of the many discussions I had with veterans who were there.

The 82nd Airborne Division (of which then-Brigadier General Gavin was Assistant Division Commander at the time) had three key missions on D-Day: seize and hold Sainte-Mère-Église, seize and hold the bridge and bridgehead at Chef-du-Pont, and seize and hold the bridge and bridgehead at La Fière. The bridgehead was considered to be sufficient land on the far side of the bridge to expand forces. Seizing the bridges at Chef-du-Pont and La Fière were strategically crucial tasks in order to cut the Cotentin Peninsula, stop German reinforcements, and seize Cherbourg. These two apparently insignificant bridges and road networks had to be taken to provide passage for the major forces coming from Utah Beach. The division took Chef-du-Pont on D-Day but battled to take the La Fière Bridge, which it still did not hold by 9 June.

The morning of 9 June, Major General J. Lawton Collins, the VII Corps Commander (of which the 82nd and 101st were a part for the battle), arrived in Sainte-Mère-Église, surveyed the battlefield and troops, and met Major General Matthew B. Ridgway, the 82nd Airborne Division Commander, approximately where the railroad tracks cross under the road to La Fière. Note that the field next to the location was the major medical dressing area and casualty collection point. In Collins' words, he saw the troops were extremely tired, seriously weakened by losses, and, in his view, marginally effective as a major fighting unit. He went to Ridgway, an old friend, and said, "Matt, your troops are tired and beat up and fought themselves to a standstill. Why don't I pass the 90th [Infantry Division] through and have them clear the causeway and move west?"

In 1983, in General Ridgway's kitchen, I asked him about this. Then 91, he looked at me with his sharp hawk-like eyes and said with all the youth and vigor of 9 June 1944, "This is the only mission this division has not accomplished and we will complete it. This was our task." I am fairly certain that this is almost verbatim what he told Collins, as when I corresponded with Collins this is almost exactly what he wrote regarding the meeting.

Also present was Major General Raymond O. Barton, the 4th Infantry Division commander, who was also very close to Ridgway. He turned to Ridgway and with intensity said: "What do you need, Matt? It's yours. Trucks, guns, ammunition? Whatever you need I will get you." Gavin and Captain Bob Piper of the 505th Parachute Infantry Regiment said this had an electrifying effect on the 82nd command group. Eyes lifted, they suddenly felt infused with positive energy. Ridgway turned to Gavin and said, "You are in charge. We attack at 0930."

That was about two hours later.

Then-Lieutenant Colonel Frank Norris, the commander of the 90th Division's 345th Field Artillery Battalion (155mm), was on the scene as well. He told Ridgway and Gavin he was moving his unit off the beach, but it wouldn't be ready to fire until around 1030. Ridgway looked at Norris and said, "Can you do this by then? It's imperative that you can do what you say you can do."

Norris thought a moment and said, "Yes sir. We can do it, but not until 1030."

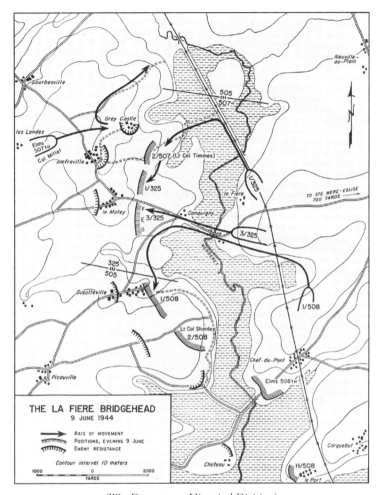

THE LA FIERE BRIDGEHEAD
9 JUNE 1944

AXIS OF MOVEMENT
POSITIONS, EVENING 9 JUNE
ENEMY RESISTANCE

Contour interval 10 meters

(War Department Historical Division)

Ridgway turned to Gavin, "The attack is postponed until 1030."

As an aside, Frank Norris, later a major general, was my next-door neighbor for many years and in his book, *The 90th Division*, he related how terror-struck he was when Ridgway asked him that question with those cold, brown eyes less than 3 feet from his face. This was a moment he could not fail for he knew how crucial this attack was. Virtually every veteran I have met that described Ridgway, highlighted those eyes and their laser-like abilities to penetrate the soul of the recipient. I saw that in his kitchen and the force had not diminished in 40 years.

Bob Piper described this gathering as one of the best examples of leadership at the higher levels he saw in the war. They were standing in a circle with a map

Aerial view of the La Fière Bridge battlefield. In this photo, west is up. Sainte-Mère-Église is east/down off the photo. Gavin's foxhole is near where the causeway road clearly emerges at bottom of picture near the orchard. The Manoir complex is just east/down from the river, running under La Fière Bridge near the bottom of the frame. The Iron Mike statue now stands to the northeast/down-right of the bridge. The Cauquigny church is just to the right of this split. (U.S. National Archives)

on a C-ration box in the center. Ridgway was tired, haggard, and full of nervous adrenalin-charged intensity. Gavin was tall and somewhat stooped with a uniform in tatters, dirt and sweat on his face like a basic infantryman, and was intent on the map. Collins, immaculate, holding his helmet in hand with a shock of white hair around a pink face, feet spread equally apart, was looking at Ridgway. Barton, shorter than the rest with a prominent stomach (hence his nickname Tubby), exuded physical energy. Norris, the tallest of the group as well as the youngest, nervously moved his feet side to side and looked back and forth to the others as a cat eyes a group of dogs. The respective staffs were equally circled outside the ring of principals. Within 30 yards and well within view, were the wounded and dead of the 505th and other units—a constant reminder to the commanders of the cost and consequences of their deliberations.

Gavin mentally went over the division force list available and immediately selected the 325th Glider Infantry Regiment as the assault force. Despite its bad experiences on landing—approximately 30 percent casualties—it was intact, rested, and uncommitted. He ordered them to move immediately from their position in Sainte-Mère-Église and Chef-du-Pont to La Fière where he intended to brief them. His intent was to force a crossing over the causeway, place one battalion on the left/south of the bridgehead after relieving Lieutenant Colonel Thomas Shanley and his force (2-508th Parachute Infantry Regiment) on Hill 30, place one battalion on the right/north after relieving Lieutenant Colonel Charles Timmes and his force (2-507th Parachute Infantry Regiment) from the orchard along the Merderet, and place the third battalion in the center in the approximate position of Le Motey. The 325 Parachute Infantry Regiment would then assume control of the bridgehead and pass the 90th Division through. Who would actually lead the initial assault was entirely dependent upon who led the march column from Sainte-Mère-Église.

At approximately 0900 on 9 June, G Company, 3-325th led the regimental column on the road from Sainte-Mère-Église, crossed the railroad overpass, and turned the down-sloping corner toward the bridge. The column stopped at the large protective cut in the road just before it turns into the bridge/causeway. This could not have been a pleasant traverse on a warm June day.

The cut was the final protected ground from the ongoing raging battles continuously engaging the bridge and its defenders. Casualties had been so high in the 1-505th Parachute Infantry Regiment that Gavin relieved the remnants with a scratch company of 1-507th soldiers and odd pickups organized as A/1-507 under the command of Captain Robert Rae. They now occupied the La Fière/Manoir area (a complex of stone farm buildings) and the ground where the Iron Mike statue stands today.

Only briefly described in historical narratives, but vivid in the mind of participants on site, was the incredible din, smoke, shrapnel, dust, dirt, and materiel continuously assailing the defenders and now the march column. The Germans were engaging the whole area with mortars, artillery, and small arms from the other side of the Merderet. Gavin believed, and it must have felt so to the defenders, that the Germans were giving much better than they got. Lieutenant Colonel Norris noted that from his position on the high ground looking to the bend in the road where today's "General Gavin foxhole" is marked, the pavement was continuously dancing with bullet and shrapnel impact. That piece of road, which the 325th had to cross, would surely be Purple Heart alley. The effect of all this was overwhelming to the senses but especially so to the unblooded G Company.

To add to the psychological impact was the physical and visual nature of the cut. The arriving soldiers were standing on a narrow farm road subjected to the worst noise and realities of a true combat engagement; and this after an extremely bad experience landing into Normandy. The right side of the road cut (west) was stacked with the poncho covered bodies of dead troopers. To the right (east) was the immediate aid station. Wounded troopers were laying on every inch of available space, legs and boots on the road, and medics were going from patient to patient administering aid, inserting IVs, and moving the dead to the other side of the road between the standing rows of soldiers. For G Company, there could have been no better reality check on the true nature of combat than their immersion in the road cut.

Just before the bend in the road, General Gavin and Colonel Harry L. Lewis (325th Regiment commander) met the column. Lieutenant Colonel Charles Carrell, 3-325th battalion commander, and Captain John Sauls, G Company commander, approached the pair. In General Gavin's description to me, he said the noise and distractions were so great that they had to be almost face to face to effectively converse. Gavin assumed that Carrell was already aware of the task and was going to brief him on the plan. Carrell wavered a bit and told Gavin he felt ill and wasn't sure he could physically lead the assault. He also made a comment regarding the plan itself that Gavin interpreted as showing a distinct lack of confidence. He immediately informed Carrell that he was relieved and asked for the battalion executive officer. While this was going on, he turned to Sauls and told him to get ready.

In Sauls' later narrative, he told Gavin, "I think there is a better way to do this rather than down this road. Give me some time to make a recon." Gavin said, "OK. You have 30 minutes. At 1030 you go." It was now about 0945 and Lieutenant Colonel Norris, above them on the high ground, was beginning to adjust his artillery.

Sauls passed through Norris' position and went down behind the stone Manoir and followed the defense line established by Captain Rae's soldiers and crept along the stone wall that reached almost to the bridge road. Satisfied that he had a covered and concealed position as close as possible to the causeway, he returned to the column and briefed his soldiers and began moving them to their assault positions.

Meanwhile, the respective generals were performing their tasks. Ridgway went through all the troop positions and picked up a number of strays, unattached field grade officers, most of whom had lost their units on the jump, but were reliable soldiers such as Lieutenant Colonel Arthur Maloney and Lieutenant Colonel Edwin Ostberg of the 507th. These and several senior NCOs he assembled in the courtyard of the Manoir. His intent, as he explained, was to insert them in whatever critical situation arose to ensure his conglomerate force did what it must to carry the causeway. He positioned himself in what is now the garage of the Manoir, less than 50 feet from the front line.

Collins and Barton, now joined by a colonel from the 90th Division, sat behind Norris' position on the high ground where they were relatively safe from incoming fire but could still see the objective, brilliant in the morning sunshine but largely obscured by the smoke, haze, and fire of the opposing exchanges. Portions of the church and stone buildings at Cauquigny would be exposed as the smoke ebbed and flowed. Just to the rear of the cut, a number of Sherman tanks from the 4th Infantry Division had arrived as well as two 57mm anti-tank guns. They were deployed in

THE AMERICAN AIRBORNE • 179

a line on the high ground overlooking the causeway and began to seek and engage targets with their main guns.

Gavin, after seeing Sauls off, went to Captain Rae and pulled him aside. The precise location of this conversation is where the Manoir stone barn abuts the wall leading to the main road. According to Gavin's description at the bridge in 1984, he told Rae, "I don't think these guys can take the causeway. At some point they will falter. I need your people to be prepared to carry it. When I give you the sign, move out, and take over. We must take this causeway." Rae said he understood completely and began to brief his soldiers. This was all done under the heavy backdrop of a continuous rain of artillery, mortars, and machine-gun fire.

The causeway presented a number of issues for Sauls and his assault. The road itself was narrow with a high crown in the center. It was lined with old sycamore and willow trees anywhere from 2 to 4 feet in girth. Over the course of the battle, they had been shattered and shaved to where nothing remained of the trees but 3 or 4 feet of trunk connected by brush and debris. The Germans had dug fighting positions between the trees on both sides of the road and many were still actively occupied. There was less than 20 feet of ground between the lapping waters of the flooded Merderet on both sides. Maneuver space would be at a premium.

Immediately in front of the bridge was an overturned French truck placed earlier by Company A of the 1-505th as a roadblock. They had also scattered a number of anti-tank mines on both sides. The width of the road on the bridge preceding this obstacle, the first thing to be crossed by Sauls, was about 12 feet. Farther along the road were four Renault tanks killed by bazooka teams on 6–7 June. One was less than 50 feet from the truck, partially skewed on the south side of the road. The second was another 50 yards farther along the causeway on the north side astride the road. The third was another 50 yards back on the south side of the road, tilting against the tree stumps. The fourth was flipped on the side of the road less than 50 yards from the Cauquigny church. Remaining along the road, both on the pavement and between the trees were innumerable bodies, mostly German, from previous engagements. Sauls and his soldiers would have to assault what was in effect a bowling alley lane with obstacles throughout, as well as dug in and fully engaged Germans.

The Germans were mindful of the significance of this causeway and were sensitive to any penetration to their side of the bank. They had reacted strongly to Shanley and Timmes' elements and had ensured they were bottled up and could not assist the units on the other side of the lake. Earlier in the week on 7 June, 1st Battalion of the 325th under Lieutenant Colonel Terry Sanford had attempted to relieve Timmes and secure Cauquigny but had been strongly counter-attacked and had to join Timmes' force to keep from being annihilated.

The primary force Sauls was asked to overcome was approximately a regiment-sized element from the German 91st Airlanding Division. At this point, the true size was unknown by the 82nd. It was well-disposed along the flooded bank on both sides of the lake and with plentiful artillery and mortars to its rear. The German command post was established in the stone barns and outbuildings behind the church and was impenetrable to all but heavy artillery, of which there was very little. The front line, with many MG-42 medium machine guns, was forward of the church cemetery and almost at the water's edge. Both German and U.S. troops were continuously engaging each other across the water, creating a torrent of fire in both directions. Both sides could interdict the causeway with ease. Sauls recounted later that as he observed the causeway and mapped his assault in his mind, he was distinctly aware of the constant falling rain of leaves, twigs, bark, and pavement along his restricted course as both sides engaged each other.

At this time, neither Gavin nor Ridgway were aware of the true defensive strength holding the bridgehead. Intelligence indicated portions of a battalion reinforced with some heavy weapons. In Gavin's mind, he had now assembled sufficient force and reinforcement to carry the position with relative ease. At 1030, he would find out.

While Sauls was maneuvering his force into position, Norris initiated the artillery barrage. Sauls brought his company around the rear of the Manoir and using the protection of the stone wall ringing the property he slid his unit along its length. He and his lead platoon squeezed tightly into the last 30 feet of wall before it ended at the road. He estimated that this got his force closest to the bridge, minimizing their exposure before actually clearing the causeway. The other two platoons massed just behind a hole in the protective wall to Sauls' rear that had been created by earlier German fire.

Erroneously, Sauls was informed that he was to assault as soon as he saw smoke rounds, which would be the final rounds fired. Much later, Norris said that he never addressed smoke and if it had been raised he would have informed them that no smoke was available. The bulk of his ammunition was still on trucks moving from Utah.

At approximately 1035, the barrage ceased and there was a stunning silence as the smoke slowly drifted away from the targets. Some Germans began appearing on the road and around Cauquigny, dazed and bloody from the barrage. Gavin looked at Sauls and shouted "Go! Go!" Sauls looked back and then led the way to the road and the near side of the bridge followed by his lead platoon, a total of 31 people on the most significant journey the 82nd Airborne had taken to that point.

By the time Sauls exposed himself, the Germans began to recover from the artillery and resumed firing. Immediately behind the lead platoon, the first man in the second platoon began to cross the hole in the wall. He was virtually decapitated by a stream of machine gun rounds, fell in a heap, and everyone behind him froze. Unbeknownst to Sauls, he and 30 soldiers were on their own for this journey.

How did they survive? The disabled truck on the other end of the bridge forced the unit to split in half, Sauls leading one column and an NCO the other. Both elements sought the relative protection of the tree stumps lining the road and the dead tanks as they moved down the road. As either would come across an occupied

German position they would grenade it and clear with Thompson submachine guns—the paratroopers' favorite close-in weapon.

By this time, both sides were fully engaged, with a hail of fire going both ways. In fact, the assaulting force was already flanked by enemy elements lining the banks perpendicular to the causeway. They only had to fire into the causeway to engage Sauls, which they did. The 1-507th troops, the Sherman tanks, and elements of 1-505 from forward reserve positions were firing across the entire front in support of the assault.

About a third of the way down the road, the terrain makes a subtle but significant change. The bridge can no longer be seen and the friendly support forces can no longer see the assault force. Friendly supporting fire from other elements necessarily slackened and diverted to the positions on the far bank. Any supporting fire on the causeway would have to come from Sauls and his small group.

Slightly less than halfway along the causeway, as the assault moved forward, it came upon the second knocked out German tank on the left of the road. Immediately, the road took a straight line to the edge of Cauquigny. In front of the church wall and aimed straight down the narrow road was an MG-42 position fully engaging the assault force. The two split elements received unexpected cover from the third and fourth dead tanks protecting them from the withering machine-gun fire but not from flanking fire.

Sauls and his platoon were moving at a trot as the enemy and the debris permitted. German mortar and artillery fire now began to fall along the causeway. American mortar and artillery also began to renew their fire on German positions. At this point, Sauls and his two elements reached the point where the causeway meets dry ground. They had made it, but with significantly less personnel than they began. The force had shrunk to less than 25 but this was all unknown to Sauls who assumed the rest of the company and the regiment were following just behind. He was totally focused on what was forward and could discern nothing toward the rear due to the smoke and flying debris.

At the Manoir, the leadership were equally ignorant of events beyond their view. Both Gavin and Ridgway saw the collapse of the G Company elements and began to take action. Gavin and the senior leadership Ridgway had assembled began to hastily push the soldiers down the road. Ridgway waved a Sherman forward and personally pulled the tow cable out and tried to attach it to the overturned truck to get it out of the way so tanks could support Sauls.

Frank Norris would later recount this scene as a major general lecturing at the Joint War College in Norfolk, Virginia. Ridgway with stars on his shoulder trying to tie a cable to the truck. Gavin pushing soldiers down the road. Lewis leading a tank around the curve. Officers and NCOs moving back and forth trying to get the frightened and wary soldiers moving forward. It was a stunning example of the very best in combat leadership under the most trying conditions.

As soon as the G Company troops were pushed down the road, they began coalescing in anxious leaderless groups. Ridgway sent Lieutenant Colonel Maloney to the first bunch. Maloney was a big man with a nasty head wound, face and neck covered with blood. He literally threw soldiers down the road and began to get them moving, but they lost momentum again as they collected behind the first knocked-out tank. Gavin sent more leaders to that location to repeat what Maloney had done. It was imperative that the division get as many people as possible to the other side if it was to succeed.

Gavin could see nothing to his front but confusion, fear, and failure. Smoke and fire obscured any vision past the bridge itself. Just as Ridgway waved a tank past the truck, it hit one of the earlier Airborne-emplaced mines and lost its track, effectively blocking the road except for a small opening to the right of the truck, sufficient only for a single person to pass. At this moment, enduring increasingly heavy German incoming fire and assuming Sauls had failed, Gavin grabbed Captain Rae at the point where the stone wall meets the road and said, "You have to go. You have to do this. Go. Go."

Rae waved at his troops, now assembled behind the wall, shouted "Let's go" and ran straight for the bridge, his soldiers close behind. Once past the truck and Sherman, Rae's men spread out and ran as best they could through the smoke, haze, and fire at the enemy beyond, which they could not yet see. Rae assumed he was now the point of the assault and all depended on his success.

Meanwhile, Sauls and his now-reduced force were quickly reacting to fortune and fire. Somehow, the machine gun on the road had been silenced. It was either hit by a mortar or the crew had withdrawn. Sauls' force momentarily slowed their progress as they met the dry ground. They had effectively flanked the German positions on the left and were receiving withering fire from the church area on the right. Sauls took one element and went down the flank positions, clearing Germans as it went. The second element raced up the small rise and hedgerow left of the road, which gave them protection from the church positions and also provided a flank opportunity.

In Sauls' interview in England after withdrawal, he noted that his mission was to clear to Hill 30 (south). This, plus the very heavy fire from the church area, convinced him to continue on the left and south, ignoring the right. After all, he thought he had the rest of his company and battalion immediately behind.

Rae and his soldiers arrived at the church positions and were immediately taken under heavy fire from their right and saw no sign of Sauls or his people. Rae immediately began clearing the buildings and was heavily engaged. The time was now about 1115. Between both Sauls and Rae, in the apple orchard between the road splits astride the Cauquigny complex, was a very active MG-42. Both commanders made an independent decision to take it out, each ignorant of the existence of the other. Rae's soldiers began directing suppressive fire at the gun while Sauls' radio operator crawled behind the position, using a hedgerow for cover, and killed the crew with his M-1. With that issue settled, both returned to their seemingly independent tasks.

Nervous and with increased tension and frustration, Gavin decided to go to the other side. Eyes focused straight ahead and seemingly oblivious to his surroundings—the constant fire, explosions, ricochets, quickly moving soldiers, the wounded and dead, and the huge detritus of battle littering the now-conquered roadway—he reached Cauquigny, spotted the intersection just ahead, and found Rae clearing the orchard and barns. He, like Rae, assumed Sauls and his element were dead on the causeway and that Rae had taken the prize. Gavin ordered Rae to clear the complex and as soon as relieved by the remainder of 325th Regiment, to move forward to Le Motey and hold. This would be the most advanced element of the division and the route the relieving 90th Division would take.

Oblivious to all this were Sauls and his small band. They continued clearing the southern area, their actions muffled by all the other battlefield noises. Only when he sent out a team to bring up the rest of the unit did he realize he was utterly alone: just he and his surviving 12 soldiers. But, in truth, he had carried the position with 12 on a mission that should have been conducted by 140. Historically, he and his soldiers received little credit while Rae received a great deal. Such is the fog and confusion of war.

In July 1944, the Army historian, Brigadier General S. L. A. Marshall and his team, assembled elements of the division and debriefed them at the small-unit level to gain insight into what actually happened. Only then did the facts come together in an indisputable manner. For whatever reason, General Gavin was always reluctant to award Sauls and his men full credit. In his heart, I believe he thought that it was really Rae and Company A of the 1-507th that truly saved the day. In several interviews with him, he would acknowledge Sauls' actions, albeit with some hesitation. Of note is that Rae was awarded a Distinguished Service Cross for his actions whereas Sauls, later in England, was awarded a Silver Star.[6]

---

6   The fighting in and around La Fière was the most intense the 82nd experienced in the entire war. This is reflected in the casualty figures.

   A/1-505: 147 men assembled on the drop zone under Lieutenant Dolan. By 10 June there were 46 killed and 81 wounded. The killed included two battalion commanders.
   A/1-507: Assembled 90 men under Captain Rae. By 10 June they had 20 killed and 35 WIA.
   G/3-325: In march column on 9 June, Captain Sauls had 148 men. By 10 June, there were 35 killed and 102 wounded. Within that total, of the 32 men, including himself, who reached the other side of the causeway on the assault, 12 remained.
   2-507 under Lieutenant Colonel Timmes at the orchard: initial headcount was 142 men. On 10 June there were 65 killed and 45 wounded.
   2-508 under Lieutenant Colonel Shanley at Hill 30: Shanley assembled 206 men. On 10 June there were 58 killed and 82 wounded.

On the terrain walk in 1984, General Gavin led us all on the route of Sauls and Rae, stopping and explaining actions and issues much as this narrative repeats. He halted us all at the intersection of the split where Sauls and Rae's elements divided. He was looking back to the causeway as we faced him in a crowded semi-circle. His voice dropped several octaves and he looked at us and said,

> When I came to this point and met Rae, I had no idea as to how hard this fight was. I looked back down the causeway. It was covered from the church to as far as I could see with bodies. I could have walked back to the bridge and never stepped on pavement. I just had no idea as to the strength of the position. It took Airborne soldiers to do this.

He then looked up at us and the sea of red berets, swept his eyes over everyone and said, "Don't you ever forget what you have to do. Our nation depends on you like it depends on no others."

La Fière was the bloodiest action per square foot in the European theatre. The 82nd won the ground and passed through elements of two divisions. In so doing, the residue of four days' combat on constricted ground created the chalice of purpose that is the soul of the 82nd Airborne. Every trooper then, now, and in the future will sip from that chalice and understand what being a member of the 82nd is all about. For troopers in the 82nd Airborne, there was no better place to die.

Somewhat later in life, as the honored guest, Gavin attended a small, insignificant dinner at the invitation of another division veteran. The flight and travel had taken a toll, combined with his advancing Parkinson's. Before the dinner began, he turned to his host and said, "Do you know why I came here?"

The veteran, taken somewhat aback, said, "No."

The general turned to him with a shake of the head but firm voice, "I can never say 'No' to someone who crossed the causeway."

The Work Site

Sometimes it is not the edifice that designates a cathedral, but the labor done in that place that makes it sacred. For four days in June of 1944, the manor at La Fière was one of the most contested, punished, and sacred sanctuaries of the Normandy invasion. Near Sainte-Mère-Église, the manor connected the Allies to the critical causeway that would permit the U.S. forces to sever the German defenses of the Cotentin Peninsula. The seemingly insignificant small place and rude bridge had become a strategic aspect of the entire invasion effort.

During this period, every numbered element of the 82nd Airborne attempted to clear the causeway of German defenders and their reinforced elements of infantry, armor, and artillery. The Germans, a first-class fighting element of the 91st Airlanding Division, fought with increased tenacity against the lightly armed American forces.

The buildings and ground were held by the 82nd in only the most tenuous manner. The action ebbed and flowed across the little available land—the constrictions designed to prevent just such an attack as was ongoing. The overall effect was that the narrow road connecting both sides of the flooded land had become a narrow course of death and destruction for any elements attempting a crossing. For this area, less than 300 yards of road and four acres of land, the casualties amounted to the point where Brigadier General S. L. A. Marshall, Chief U.S. Army Historian, called the land the bloodiest battleground per square foot in the European theatre in his book *Night Drop*.

The nature of the ground mitigated against evacuation of the wounded as that required exposure up the clear high ground to the rear and safety. The Germans, less than 300 yards on the other side of the causeway, maintained constant fire superiority denying any exposed movement. Both rifle fire as well as indirect mortars and artillery continuously rained down on the participants and the steadily accumulating combat wounded. Desperate for some reasonably safe site to administer first aid, a frontline medic with the 1-505th, selected the only reasonable clearing station for the immediate combatants—the crawl space beneath the main house.

The house today is reconstructed from its state following the fighting. Observe the black and white image of the manor taken just a few days after the conflict. The walls are collapsed, the roof holed in numerous places, and no floor or room remained untouched by the four-day rain of steel. In the necessities of the moment, the crawl space was the immediate version of acceptable. The partially collapsed foundation was cleared, permitting a small opening sufficient for a man on hands and knees with a litter to enter.

There was less than 4 feet between the dirt and the floor foundations but that was sufficient for the pressing needs. The available medics and walking wounded pulled the mounting casualties under the shelter of the floor boards and began to do what could be done, which was minimal under the circumstances.

Lacking light, flashlights were rigged to provide illumination. Medics labored eye to arm to find a useable vein for the plasma or to sense the entrance and exit wound trail. Morphine was jabbed into exposed skin and a device pinned to the collar to prevent overdosing. In some cases, a medic would make a compassionate judgment and administer a sufficient amount to cease both pain and life. In time, this became impossible as syrettes were expended far faster than resupply could accommodate. Tourniquets were tied and battle triage done by feel.

A lighter would be held to a face to determine dilation of the eye. Movement demanded whatever care could be provided. The state of breathing would be ascertained as the heaving body bubbled air through a damaged mouth or nose. In some cases, parts of bodies were removed due to the severity of the wounds, the remains stacked in a corner of the foundation. German mortars and artillery constantly pummeled the building and its grounds as the human detritus of the conflict mounted. The sounds, dust, and vibrations were often overwhelming and the medics simply had to stop and lay across the closest patient to the crash and jar of the moment as dirt and ground-up masonry filtered through the now exposed floor above. Sanitation was a word unknown in this place.

During World War II, liquid blood plasma was created by passing distilled water from one bottle to another containing dry plasma. Shaken, this was then injected into the wounded soldier. The process required some height for gravity flow to be achieved, with two bottles working for every casualty. But there was little height. The normal solution of an upended rifle with a bayonet in the ground was impossible in this space; there was simply no room for the rifle to be placed vertically. Nails were picked from rubble, collected from the stable and barn, and hammered into the floor joists with rocks, rifle butts, or any steel implement that could be found.

The space quickly became an accumulation of death, dying, and salvation—all in constant conflict with the realities of the situation. Flickering lights, constant dust clouds from impacts above, and the low cries and whimpers of the wounded were mixed with hasty comments and expletives from the medics as they struggled to salvage lives from the jaws of death. Some troops just quietly bled to death in the dusty, dark, flickering shadows. Others, quieted by morphine and their inner strength, waited for the night to descend where they could, somewhat safely, be transported outside to a clearing stationed to their rear manned by the few doctors present.

Very quickly, this small, dank space became a complex mass of parts. Glass bottles were suspended on the floor beams. Tubes, tourniquets, litters, sections of parachute strips, spent bandages, boots, pants, and equipment littered the small work space. Medics simply ploughed through the detritus to find a space for a new arrival as they worked the requirements of combat triage, playing God's messenger. In the dark corners lay their failures and the increasing accumulation of body parts.

On 9 June, a little after noon, the impacts ceased and a blessed silence descended, The medics, now assisted by other soldiers in the new tranquility, stood straight for the first time in several days, and removed those left living from the small cell and joined their clearing station on the hill just 200 yards to the rear, a distance which had seemed impossible in the days previous.

In time, the owner of the manor returned to reconstruct and return the farm to its previous habitable state. He did make one important concession. He repaired the entrance door to the crawlspace and locked it. He chose to leave the waste and detritus exactly where it was on 9 June as a personal memorial to what had been an exceptional display of dedication, will, and responsibility.

In later years, guiding soldiers to this place, I would assemble them in the driveway facing the manor. I would ask for a show of hands for any medics or doctors, requesting they gather by the door. I would then ask them to go inside and examine their work station. For each year I did that, I would see the same response. They would come out of the door in a stunned silence and could say nothing but shake their heads. Tears were sometimes present.

This was not a cathedral but unarguably a sanctuary. Sometimes, nobility arises from the worst of circumstances and the strength of spirit of the participants spreads a great light where only darkness should reign.

The 101st on D-Day

I interviewed General Taylor in the Pentagon in 1981. He was ravaged by time and could barely walk. Yet his mind was crystal clear and he became very animated as he described D-Day from his experiences. He spoke with very concise and clear descriptives. He was extremely proud of the division and was particularly proud of how his badly scattered 101st was still able to accomplish its mission. He was very unhappy with the transport pilots and wanted to ensure that I understood the 101st performed as well or better than the 82nd under the circumstances.

The mission of the 101st Airborne was to seize the causeways leading off of Utah Beach; pass the Utah Beach elements to the 82nd; seize the locks at La Barquette; destroy the bridge over the Douve connecting Carentan; seize the towns of Saint-Côme-du-Mont and Sainte-Marie-du-Mont; and silence all artillery elements within the objective area.

To accomplish this, the division had the following plan:

502nd Parachute Infantry Regiment would seize the northern exits and silence the battery at Brécourt.

The 506th Parachute Infantry Regiment would seize the center and southern causeways, Sainte-Marie-du-Mont, and assist the 501st in the defense of the southern boundary.

The 501st would seize the locks at La Barquette, the Douve bridges, and provide a division reserve.

Defending the area were battalion-sized units of the German 91st Airlanding Division, the 709th Infantry Division, and the 6th *Fallschirmjäger* (Parachute) Regiment. Lieutenant Colonel Von Der Heydte was the primary area commander/coordinator.

General Max Taylor was programmed to land at Drop Zone C near the center portion of his operational area with the 1-501st. Instead, his stick landed just to the south of Sainte-Mère-Église, more than 3 air miles from where he was expecting to land. Taylor recalled:

> I landed just south of Sainte-Mère-Église. I knew that almost immediately as there was a road sign nearby. We gathered about 15 people, mostly officers, and moved directly east. I was very anxious to get to our main body and ensure the causeways were clear.

They moved cross country, gathering more troops along the way. There was considerable firing from Sainte-Marie-du-Mont, which indicated a major encounter. Not wishing to get involved, and fixed on the overall mission, Taylor and his forces skirted south and moved toward the beach. Along the way, they collected several dozen men from the 3rd battalion, 501st Infantry, the division reserve force.

These elements integrated with the junior members of Taylor's scratch force and became the clearing force for Exit Two.

By 0600, they arrived in broad daylight at the small complex of Pouppeville, just below Exit Two. A fierce fight broke out and house-to-house fighting ensued. An increasingly frustrated Taylor had to wait between Pouppeville and Sainte-Marie-du-Mont until the town was cleared around 1200. Taylor moved immediately to Causeway 2.

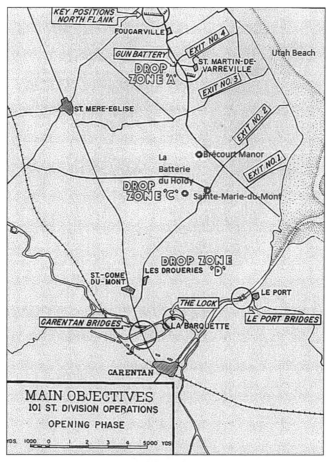

Drop plan for the 101st.

I finally saw the sea and heard all the firing and explosions to our north. I ordered a halt at the farm complex we came across and sent out several patrols to make a linkup and establish exactly where our forces were. We suddenly had a major fight at Pouppeville which lasted several hours.

One patrol from the west returned to say they had linked up with elements of the 506th which had things in hand. I was finally clear to go to the Causeway where I met a captain from the 4th. I finally had a sense of confidence we had done our job.

There, on Causeway 2 a bit after 1200, Taylor was introduced to Captain George Mabry of the 4th Infantry. The linkup had been achieved.

General Taylor's division had a very tough slog. There were considerable mis-drops, quite similar to the experience of the 82nd. Of the three Parachute Infantry Regiments, only the 506th was able to constitute as a viable regiment—the 501st and 502nd were scattered into packets. However, these packets went about their larger missions and generally succeeded. Taylor explained to me in the Pentagon in 1981:

> I knew the jump had not gone as planned but I also knew we could sort it out since the 4th Infantry was getting inland. That meant we had done our job. I did not yet have a radio so I couldn't know what was happening overall. I heard a lot of firing everywhere and decided to move to Sainte-Marie-du-Mont with its distinctive tower, my intended location for the division command post.
>
> We moved along the high ground hoping to get to the north of the town. There was very heavy fighting so I couldn't go there. Instead, I had our command post just sit astride a road intersection east of the town. The 4th Division was already coming up so I wasn't too worried about security. I needed a jeep to get around and sent my aide down to the beach to get one.

Further north, the 502nd was initially almost non-existent due to mis-drops. Ironically, the three battalion commanders—Steve Chappuis, Patrick Cassidy, and Robert Cole—began to pick up small packets of men and then proceeded to their objectives, but with much smaller forces than intended.

These small elements began to accomplish quite a bit. They cleared German security units overlooking Exits Three and Four and took the battery at Brécourt.

The 506th was the most intact of the three regiments, assembling about 60 percent of the unit just west of Sainte-Marie-du-Mont. Colonel Robert Sink, the regimental commander, sent elements to seize Sainte-Marie-du-Mont as well as the central causeways exiting Utah.

Sainte-Marie-du-Mont was occupied by a German artillery unit and numbered about 200 men. While not infantry, they had the advantage of the stone buildings that composed the village and controlled access into the town.

The area commander responsible for defense, Lieutenant Colonel Baron Von Der Heydte, commander of the 6th *Fallschirmjäger* Regiment, arrived in Sainte-Marie-du-Mont about 0700 on 6 June, before the 101st began to probe.

Von Der Heydte mounted the stairs of the Baroque-steepled church to the bell tower. There, he could see in the morning light the vast array of shipping at Utah Beach and see naval gunfire exploding inland. He is alleged to have turned to his driver and said: "We have lost the war." He ran back down to his car and drove off to Carentan to gather his forces and strengthen the key towns of Saint-Côme-du-Mont and Sainte-Marie-du-Mont to the south. He would almost be too late in both cases.

Elements of 3-501st, the designated 101st Reserve, had a scattered drop. Some elements, less than a full strength battalion led by the battalion commander Julian Ewell, proceeded to probe Saint-Côme-du-Mont from the south. Concurrently, elements of the 1-506th began to enter the town from the north. Colonel Sink intended to occupy it as his headquarters, but first he had to clear it. By 0800, both units of the 101st were engaged in uncoordinated fire-fights. The German artillerymen-cum-infantry were putting up a credible fight and causing meaningful casualties.

The Americans, unused to the stone buildings, windy streets, and elevated stories, took casualties as they moved through the streets. Quickly, they learned to go building to building and to seek cover via second stories and roof crossings.

The battle raged through the morning as the 101st learned under fire how to clear a Norman village.

To the south, mis-dropped troops of the 3-506th under Captain Charles Shettle were able to capture the foot bridges at Le Port while Colonel Howard Johnson, regimental commander of the 501st Regiment, plus a scratch force, seized the locks at 0430. The locks controlled the Douve Valley with the confluence of the Douve and Merderet Rivers.

A similar mixed group from the 506th regimental headquarters, led by the executive officer, Major R. J. Allen, seized the Douve River Bridge over the main road between Carentan and the north. The bridge was a key German reinforcement route from Carentan and one Von Der Heydte needed. There were less than 200 men defending at each location and they were under constant pressure to hold.

Colonel Johnson, holding the locks, made several trips back to the assembly area to feed additional 501st and 506th troops to Le Port, the Douve bridge, and La Barquette. Despite the reinforcements, by mid-afternoon Allen was forced to withdraw from the bridge to more defensible ground and Shettle had less than 75 effectives left to hold a reinforced German force. Von Der Heydte had been very busy.

The 6th *Fallschirmjäger* Regiment was headquartered in Carentan with two light infantry battalions of less than 600 men. However, they were elite troops and

Aerial photo of Saint-Côme-du-Mont showing the church in the center and the clear laterals into the village. The Germans held the central part of town and defended in concert.

well-armed with small arms but with no artillery. One of the battalions was bicycle mounted and the other barely transportable on old captured vehicles.

After seeing the forces at Utah, Von Der Heydte rushed back and made several decisions. He would attempt to clear the U.S. troops from La Barquette and hold Sainte-Marie-du-Mont and Saint-Côme-du-Mont. He would succeed only in holding Saint-Côme-du-Mont and that for only two days.

The German paratroopers were able to barricade Saint-Côme-du-Mont and hold out until 8 June, a very credible performance. Troops reinforcing Sainte-Marie-du-Mont were assaulted from all sides as they attempted to cross the Douve swamps and could only reinforce Saint-Côme-du-Mont. The Germans attempting to clear La Barquette and Le Port were repeatedly repulsed with everything from hand grenades to 8-inch naval gunfire.

The 101st had done extraordinary work through small unit initiative and exceedingly high leadership at all levels.

Off and on between 1984 and recently, I attended a number of the veteran 101st reunions held in Sainte-Marie-du-Mont. These usually included veterans of the German 6th Fallschirmjägers. There initially was great hesitancy from the local leadership to receive the Germans. However, the mayor, Michel de Vallavieille, also the owner of Brécourt, convinced them after talking to both elements that a mix would not create issues. In fact, the opposite was the case.

I observed groups of both sides together at the several bars and restaurants telling war stories, laughing, and displaying that special camaraderie unique to men who have been seriously shot at together. Baron Von Der Heydte made several visits and was well-received by the 101st veterans.

At these gatherings, I also noted some distinct differences between the 82nd and 101st veterans in terms of their internal social culture. The 101st veterans were very "corporate." Most wore ties and adhered to the WWII rank structure in terms of social settings. The men were generally reserved, respectful, and rarely intoxicated.

The 82nd was much more casual with almost no ties except for those attending a formal dinner. Rank structure was not in evidence. The groupings were by choice and involved considerable drinking, loud banter, and occasional arguments. It was clear that this group had an extraordinary cohesiveness and that their bonds had not only lasted, but strengthened over time.

Virtually all are gone now and their laughter is sorely missed.

Brécourt Manor

On the 60th anniversary of D-Day, I was privileged to meet Lieutenant Dick Winters and the members of his company, several of whom participated in the taking of Brécourt Manor. We met in a huge tent erected for the premier of Band of Brothers *with Steven Spielberg and Tom Hanks, the key producers.*

Lieutenant General John Vines, then commanding General of XVIII Airborne Corps and a good friend, sat at a large dinner table with me, Winters, and others. We were close enough to easily chat and at the conclusion, he invited us for a private tour of the manor fight with his men; there were no others save for a couple of handlers. We gladly accepted and about 0900 the next morning, met him at the intersection leading to the manor farm. This was their first return since 6 June 1944.

He led the tour and as he did so, the elements of his charm and command style clearly emerged. He would lead us, stop, and point, addressing an issue. He would then invite his men to comment on the point. They readily did so, somewhat revealing their own personalities; Don Malarkey, William Guarnere, Carwood Lipton, and Robert Wynn on crutches. Collectively, they provided a history and insights lost to the traditional historian. Much of what they discussed differs from what was depicted in the television series. It was if the sight of all this brought back a flood of memories hidden for so long in the wellsprings of their minds. Winters would wait until all had finished and then gently summarize and move on. For John and I, it was both a treasure and an epiphany.

The land was virtually as it was then, save the guns and the defending Germans. What he and his men accomplished is one of the greatest examples of what happened at Normandy that day—ordinary people doing extraordinary things.

Lieutenant Dick Winters and Company E, 2nd Battalion, 506th Parachute Infantry Regiment, were scheduled to drop at 0114 on Drop Zone C, just south and west of Sainte-Marie-du-Mont, the planned headquarters for both the regiment and the 101st Airborne Division. He and his stick of 20 jumpers landed approximately on time, but more than 6 miles west of Sainte-Mère-Église. Winters told me:

> We had a very rough ride once we crossed onto land. German AA fire was terrific and the cloud bank was continuous. The pilot swerved around a lot, went up and down, and went full throttle. It was all we could do to hang on.
>
> I was the jumpmaster and we got the red light about on time and just wanted to get out of that plane. It was tough standing up and guys were continuously falling down. The green light came on and out we went.
>
> I had a huge opening shock due to the airspeed. When I became aware, I saw the fires in town, didn't know then what it was, and a lot of white German tracer going up all around. I landed with a heavy impact and took a moment to catch my breath.
>
> I got up and out of my chute and began to collect people. That's when I learned where we were. One of the men reported he read a road sign for Sainte-Mère-Église. Well, I had about 25 men. I took a compass reading to the east and we moved out.

Malarkey added:

> I just wanted to get out of that damn airplane. I could see flak everywhere, burning planes, and then nothing with the clouds. We were being thrown around like nuts in a can.

By 0630, and after several encounters with German elements, the group, now about 150 gathered along the way, found itself at the intersection of two farm roads near Le Grand Chemin, the assembly area and headquarters for his battalion. Not knowing exactly the status of security, he deployed his men, crossed the road, and approached the complex from the hedgerowed farm field. Winters saw other paratroopers there casually moving about.

Winters arrived and found the battalion commander, Lieutenant Colonel Robert Strayer, with less than 20 men. Winters' men collected themselves in the farm courtyard and helped themselves to the rations that had been collected from para-packs. Malarkey recalled:

> We were beat. We had been moving all night and had been fighting most of the way. Our adrenalin had pretty much given out and all we wanted to do was eat some chow and get a nap.

Winters reported to Strayer, who informed him he would be acting company commander. Along with Lieutenant Nixon, the S2, he took Winters to the road overlooking the field to the west. Nixon told Winters a German battery was there that had to be taken out and Winters was to do it.

Winters pointed out that he had only 13 men and they were exhausted. Strayer told him he had to do it as he was the only force available. The rest of the men were needed for other missions. Strayer had less than 200 men now from a jump strength of 650. Winters explained:

> I got the mission and was about to protest but didn't. I could tell he [the battalion commander] was very tired and as exhausted as we were. We had the mission and went about it.

Winters asked exactly where the battery was. Strayer pointed toward the west, across the field, "Out there." Without further clarification, Winters returned to his men who were eagerly eating their rations. He told them they were going to pick up and move out to take an artillery battery nearby. This created a small shock among the troops. Guarnere remembered:

> I was hungry and tired. I wanted to take a break but I wolfed down the rations and grabbed my Thompson.

Malarkey added:

> I wanted to get some sleep. I was smoking a cigarette when Lieutenant Winters came out and gave us our orders. I wasn't happy but we grabbed whatever spare ammo we could find and got ready.

Winters explained:

> I had 13 men including myself. I decided to take two machine guns and leave the bazooka and mortar. I told Buck [Compton] and Lipton to get the men organized and that we would figure out what to do once we got a look at the battery.

At approximately 0730, Winters put his men in file, crossed the farm road and proceeded along a tree line toward where Lieutenant Colonel Strayer had indicated the battery might be. Winters recounted:

> I had no idea where the battery was. I heard no firing. My intent was to simply keep moving until we found it and then develop a plan to take it.

Winters moved his men in a file formation across the farm road and in the direction that Lieutenant Colonel Strayer had indicated. Winters was at the point and moved the force along a tall tree line that shrouded them from casual observation.

They had moved no more than five hundred yards when Winters and the men immediately following saw artillery barrels projecting through a perpendicular wood line. Winters immediately stopped the unit and brought it up to create a small perimeter under the trees. He decided he would conduct a one-man patrol to determine exactly the battery location and its disposition.

> We suddenly saw the barrels through the trees. I halted us immediately and told them to get down. I needed to get a fix on the battery and then develop a plan.

Sergeant Carwood Lipton recalled:

> I saw the gun barrels as we moved along the trees. Holy shit! And then Winters stopped us and we went to ground. There it was, less than a mile from the battalion command post.

Winters went forward at a half crouch, burying himself in the wood line to avoid detection. He arrived at the juncture of the two hedgerows where the three barrels were clearly visible protruding from the hedgerow facing Utah Beach. He could see no Germans.

He low crawled approximately twenty yards to the juncture of the hedgerows. He pushed quietly through to where he was looking at the battery position. His head, next to a fence post, was less than 10 yards from a German MG-42 position.

Winters told me:

> I stuck my head and whoa, I was staring at a MG-42. Fortunately, there wasn't anyone near it. I looked around and saw the basic layout. One gun was to my right pointed north and the others were all lined up about 20 yards apart in pits. Connecting them all was a trench that varied from deep to shallow. I could see Germans across the field and they looked like *Fallschirmjägers*. The guns had crews in them but none were firing.

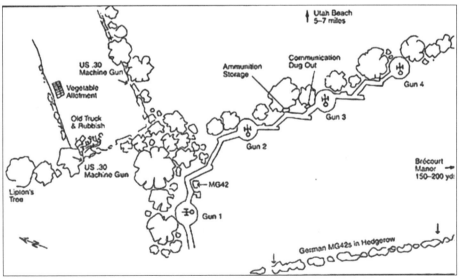

Winters' plan and battery layout

I thought the only way we could take this position was a surprise attack on the machine gun position, take it and get low and then go for the north facing gun and then the others as we could get organized. Any other way would disperse us too much.

He continued:

In my mind, I tried to develop a plan that was simple and could take advantage of what we had which wasn't much. I focused on the machine gun position making that the center effort with a diversion to hold the Germans from getting into the trench line before us. If they got to the machine gun, we were dead ducks.

I had two machine guns which would fire blind. There was a wrecked truck and a tall tree we could use for covering fire. We would have a diversionary attack with grenades on the first artillery piece in line and I would assault directly into the machine gun position. Once we were in, we would all rush forward and get into it. It was the deepest part of the trench line and could hold us all making the assault.

Winters, using classic patrol organization, divided his men to each task as he briefed them by drawing on the ground. He described his impressions to us.

We crawled up that creek [center-east] and I had a chance to see the layout for the first time. It looked tough and was fully occupied. The guns were hidden in the woodline with one pointing north and the others east toward Utah. There was a zigzag trench connecting all the guns and a MG-42 at the corner where the woodline connected.

I could see immediately that there was no way we could take the whole thing at once. I concluded the key spot was the machine gun and if we could take it and the northern gun, we could work our way to the rest of the battery.

We weren't really a unit in the sense of the word so I tried to keep the parts as simple as possible with an officer or trusted NCO in charge of each part. It looked like Lipton and his group could engage the machine gun and first gun from the northern running creek and that a second attack could be mounted through the eastern creek toward the number 2 gun. I would take a group and assault the machine gun directly. Once we got into the trench line, we were protected from the bulk of the German defenders which appeared to be in the western rear portion of the field.

I tried to keep it as simple as possible. We had never been in combat and faced such a situation but we had to do it. There were a couple of things we could guide upon, the old truck, the gun barrel and the junction of the wood lines. My greatest concern was that the machine guns would hit us going in so I was going to place them myself and control the firing.

Donald Malarkey explained:

When Dick came back to us and outlined the position on the ground. I was really nervous. I had confidence in Lieutenant Compton and Guarnere was my squad leader so I thought that this was what combat was all about.

William Guarnere added:

I was definitely nervous when he came back, especially with what we had been encountering all night. The plan seemed pretty simple and I was in no position other than to get with Buck and get it on.

Carwood Lipton commented:

> I didn't know enough to object. We had a plan and it was my responsibility to do what I was told. I was young and fully confident of anything and probably thought myself sort of invincible. I did things that day I would never do later on.

After briefing his men, no more than 10 minutes total, Winters led the men, single file, to the juncture of the tree lines. He pointed Compton to the gun barrel and Lipton to the rusting truck. He then moved each machine gun to less than 5 feet from the brush line and pointed the barrels, instructing the first gunner not to move the barrel to the right and the second to not move it to the left. He created a small tunnel of fire for himself and two other men to take the position.

Once he had his men in place, he retreated to where he could see Compton and gave a thumbs up. Compton responded likewise as Winters returned quickly to his position by the field fence post.

Lipton explained:

> I got over to the truck but I couldn't see anything. There was a large tree shadowing everything and I just went for it, motioning for Ranney to watch for me and fire at the direction I did. I climbed up the tree and could see the first gun real well and the people in it as well as a bunch of German infantry on the other side. I aimed for the gun and waited for the grenades that would signal the assault.

Guarnere said:

> I crawled along the brush with Buck and Malarkey and we got just to the right of the gun. Buck gave us the two thumbs up and we waited. Each of us pulled pins. When Buck let it go, so did we and we began to fire. I just sprayed with my Thompson. The grenades went off, the machine guns fired, and we all rushed through the brush and into the ditch. Man. I was still alive.

It was approximately 0830. In less than two minutes, Winters and his men had succeeded in carrying the position. The violence of the attack carried several into the northern gun, which was captured and the crew killed outright. They then settled in. Winters recounted:

> We had the ditch. I needed to see who we had left and tend to a couple of the wounded. Popeye [Wynn] needed help and we laid him out in the bottom of the ditch and bandaged his rear end. The Germans started opening up from across the field pretty strongly. I put our two machine guns on the top of the ditch and told them to fire short bursts. We didn't have a lot of ammo and still had the other three guns to take.

At this point, unlike the *Band of Brothers* depiction, the men settled down and took their time before taking the second gun. Ammunition was redistributed and most, hungry for more than 24 hours, started to eat their rations. Virtually everyone was smoking. The German infantry across the field was beginning to rake the top of the trench. Perhaps 20 minutes passed when Winters, intuitively, moved along the trench toward the second gun.

> I don't know why but I went down the trench to where we had thrown up some boxes as a barricade. I saw two Germans coming up. One had a machine gun. Instinctively, I rose over the boxes and began firing and moving forward.

The men, at a combat pitch, dropped their rations and immediately charged down the trench. They carried Winters into the position, killing several of the gun crew. They erected a barrier in the trench connecting to the third gun.

The same plan prevailed as before. The men sat down, regrouped with ammo distribution, got out their cigarettes, and ate the chow they had left behind. The gun pit was more than a foot lower than the ditch so it provided additional protection against the now searching German machine guns.

While clearing out the position, Winters found a large map under acetate. It had all the German positions in the area and the units occupying them. Winters knew this was important. He pulled the map from the board, rolled it up, and sent three men with it back to the battalion along with Robert Wynn and several prisoners. They were to return with more ammo and any men they could find.

The issue was how to destroy the guns. Lipton mentioned that he had left the thermite grenades in a bag under the tree he climbed. Winters told him to go back and get them. Lipton recalled:

> The fire from across the field was fierce and I wasn't anxious to go back and get the bag but I didn't have much choice. Our grenades and Comp B didn't do much. I low crawled back to the tree, got the grenades, and slid back in the ditch.

Winters had both guns rendered inoperable and saved the rest for the last two guns.

Around 0930, Captain Clarence Hester, the battalion S3, appeared with one other man as well as ammo and grenades. Winters said:

> Captain Hester showed up with another troop and some ammo. He was eager to help and we were trying to figure out how to take the next gun. The fire from across the field was fierce so we had to stay in the trench line. I thought we could take the gun the same way Buck had assaulted the number 2 gun.
>
> I told Hester and his guy to low crawl to the front of gun number 3, throw the grenades, and we would assault down the trench. He agreed and moved out. I gathered the men just behind me in the trench and waited for the explosion of the grenades.

Malarkey added:

> I had one of the machine guns as the original gunner got hit in the neck. I was working bursts across the field at the other machine guns. By this time, it was lawn mowing. Nothing moved between us.

The plan worked. Hester threw the grenades, which landed inside the gun pit as Winters' men fired into it as well. They charged down the trench and secured the gun, taking more prisoners and killing several others. The remaining Germans retreated to the fourth gun. It was about 1030.

The same process ensued. The men barricaded the connecting trench and collected themselves around the gun. Winters placed two men in the trench overlooking the last gun. The men redistributed ammo, smoked, and ate what rations were left.

During the lull, Lieutenant Colonel Strayer, knowing Winters was short people and ammunition, sent Lieutenant Ronald Speirs and two men, loaded with ammunition and grenades, to the battery. Winters said:

> We had the last gun and it was jammed with men, many of whom were engaging us. The bullets rattled off of the gun forcing us all on the other side of it [gun number 3]. Speirs arrived anxious to assist. I didn't have a better idea so I outlined the same concept. Speirs and his two men would get on the other side of the tree line and toss grenades into the gun tub and assault through. We would provide covering fire and move down the trench.

Again, the plan worked, but with casualties. The numerous compacted Germans in the gun pit fired continuously and some hit their mark. One of Speirs' men was killed outright and the other wounded. However, Winters' assault through the trench line cleared the position. They now had 12 prisoners, with the rest killed or wounded. It was approximately 1100. Winters noted:

> We had done what we came for and I didn't want to risk anything else. The farm complex with a lot of Germans was across an open field and I didn't see the point. I was concerned they would flank us along the tree line as we had done to them. I decided we needed to go back.

Winters gathered his group, now with two wounded and three killed. The plan was to go back the way they came—through the trench line and back by the fence post.

The prisoners were tied together—right arm and right boot with commo wire—and were pulled out of the position. The American wounded were placed in the rear and the dead were assigned to a trooper who used a looped commo wire under the armpits to pull them along.

The German wounded were treated as best as could be done and left in the gun and trench line.

Guarnere was assigned as POW guard. He placed himself at the rear of them and ensured they understood he would kill them if they tried to escape. The unit, as a snake, moved through the trench line and low crawled to the entrance point. The Germans continued to fire but, in a miracle, never tried to flank the force. Winters added:

> I never understood why they didn't try and flank us from the manor. I put a man to our rear to keep lookout but it never happened. Had they done so, I think our goose would have been cooked.

The unit moved back to Le Grand Chemin. Exhausted, they gathered in the courtyard to rest. It is unclear if Winters then went to the beach to get tanks or the S2, Lieutenant Nixon, had already acquired them. Regardless, Winters, upon returning, left the men and gathered three tanks. He explained:

I was damned mad. They had killed and wounded my men. I mounted my men on the tanks and went back. This time down the road next to the battery leading to the manor. When we got to the battery position, we dismounted and left the tanks to go to work. They cleaned house and I felt a lot better.

Malarkey added:

We were beat. When Dick told us to gather our stuff and mount the tanks, I was not happy, but we did what we were told. The tanks were just up from Utah and loaded for bear. As soon as we saw Germans, we dismounted and the tanks just started firing everything they had. It was beautiful. Took maybe five minutes and the place was ours.

It was approximately 1200. Winters and 13 men had taken a fortified position with more than 150 Germans. This action is considered one of the finest small unit actions in the history of the U.S. Army.

A review of the awards and decorations for this fight indicate the nature of the conflict:

Distinguished Service Cross—First Lieutenant (later Major) Richard Winters

Silver Star	Second Lieutenant (later First Lieutenant) Lynn "Buck" Compton
	Sergeant (later Staff Sergeant) William "Wild Bill" Guarnere
	Private First Class (later Technician Fifth Class) Gerald Lorraine

Bronze Star	Sergeant (later First Lieutenant) Carwood Lipton
	Private (later Sergeant) Robert "Popeye" Wynn (WIA)
	Private Cleveland Petty
	Private (later Sergeant) Walter Hendrix
	Private (later Technical Sergeant) Donald Malarkey
	Private (later Sergeant) Myron N. Ranney

Purple Heart	Private (later Sergeant) Robert "Popeye" Wynn (WIA)
	Private First Class John D. Halls (KIA)
	Sergeant Julius "Rusty" Houck (KIA)
	Lieutenant Ronald Speirs

Walking back across the meadow after the discussion, I was toward the rear with Malarkey. I asked what was it about Winters that made him so effective and the men so revere him. Malarkey thought for a moment as we avoided the cow pies and then said: "First, he never did anything stupid. Second, he was always part of us but never lost his position. By this I mean Winters never lost his distance as an officer, but was always considered the core part of the unit. Third, we knew if he planned something and led it, we had a good chance to do it and return with minimal casualties."

With the 101st

Congressman Sam Gibbons, as a captain with the 501st Parachute Infantry Regiment, 101st Airborne Division, jumped into Normandy, the only later-serving member of either the House or Senate to do so. He wrote an extensive narrative of that time and his personal experiences, which were typical of most mis-dropped troopers. It is included, in part, here as a more than adequate descriptive of the event from a soldier's eye. It is unique in that he has an eye for detail unique to most narratives. His words cover the range of issues from his personal feelings to the nature of the immediate combat and the quality of the rations. His description as to the importance of a can of Schlitz beer gives an insight into the mentality of those that jumped that night.

I have excised certain portions of his narrative to focus solely on the immediate D-Day period as typical of most members of the 101st.

Congressman Gibbons never forgot this experience and it molded much of his life and manner of dealing with issues on the Hill. He was always a man of clarity in speaking and vision. One might quibble with his position, but there was no doubt as to what it was.

It was dark—slight ground fog—body arched forward, feet together—head tilted forward...

My parachute snapped open with a loud crack—reflecting the added weight of combat equipment—and as I had been taught to do, I looked up to check the parachute canopy—it was functioning perfectly—then looked around to make sure I was clear of other jumpers—couldn't see anyone. Did see and hear rifle and machine-gun fire coming up from below me about 75 yards to my right—guess about 15 weapons in action. Could see muzzle blast and occasional tracers—apparently aimed at the waves of planes flying on toward the southeast. Got brief glimpses of small, blacked-out town six or seven hundred yards in front of me. Guessed it to be Sainte-Mère-Église. Guess later proved to be correct. Prepared to land—focused eyes on ground—looking 50 yards ahead of me (looking straight down might cause a broken leg). Knees slightly bent and feet together so that bone and muscle in both legs would absorb the force of landing. Feet hit—knees give—roll forward—end lying flat on my back. Lie quietly, after a noisy landing, my camouflaged parachute settles to ground right above my head. Germans 50 to 70 yards to the southeast would have heard that landing had they not been so noisy shooting at low-flying planes.

Instantly I knew I was in the wrong place—at least 6 miles from my planned drop zone and far deeper in German territory than planned. The time was 1:26 a.m., June 6, 1944. D-Day was to begin on the beaches at 6:30 a.m. The parachute jump from plane to ground in Normandy, France had taken 35–40 seconds, maybe less.

I was 24 years old—a captain—in the 501st Parachute Infantry, a part of the 101st Airborne Division which, together with the 82nd Airborne Division, landed a total of 12,000 parachutists that night. We were the spearhead of the invasion of Europe. I realize that 12,000 sounds like a large force, but when you consider that we had been told there were 70,000 Germans there, you can see what the situation looked like to us. I jumped from plane number 42 in a total of nearly 1,000 planes used in that assault. There were 17 of us who jumped from that plane, all from Regimental Headquarters, 501st. The 501st jumped about 2,000 officers and men. All of us were volunteers and received extra hazard pay for our line of work... Of the 18 in plane number 42, I can only tell you what happened to a very few of us.

Shortly after 1:26 a.m. while still on my back, I wiggled my feet and legs to make sure they were okay. Then unfastened my reserve chute and chest straps came off, but I couldn't get the leg straps unbuckled because the harness was tight, so I cut those straps with my switchblade knife. Next off came the life preserver and my personal equipment bag that had been hanging below my reserve chute. I took my folding stock rifle out of the holster, checked the safety, and finally rolled over on my stomach.

All this probably took less than a minute, but it seemed like an hour. No one had seen me, and I had seen no one else, but there was plenty of shooting by those Germans about 70 yards from me. Their shooting was a blessing because it drowned out any noise I might make and because they were paying more attention to the sky than they were to the ground.

I was in a grassy field or pasture, which seemed to be about 200 yards long in a north–south direction, and 150 yards wide east to west. I couldn't tell if there was anyone else in the field except those Germans near the southeast corner and they seemed to be just outside that corner. The nearest edge of the field was south of me about 30 yards. So I crawled or really slid on my stomach until I reached the boundary hedgerow, then got up on my knees looking and listening. Finally I moved to a crouched position. Nothing moved in the field. Then I crawled up to the side of the earthen hedgerow and looked on the other side. Nothing moved. No sound except the shooting at the southeast corner of the field.

Now I could hear new firing behind me but because of its distance I knew it was no immediate danger. Occasionally another plane or two would come over. They seemed to be on an erratic course and their engines seemed to be wide open, apparently trying to dodge the fire coming up from the ground. They certainly were not at any flight altitude to be jumping parachutists.

I slid back down the hedgerow and turned again to examine the field in which I had just landed. There was just enough moonlight coming through the clouds to allow me to determine that no other Americans had landed or were landing in my field. I could not hear any American weapons being fired. The German weapons sounded distinctly different from ours; the principal difference being the rate of fire for their automatic weapons. Theirs fired much faster and did not seem to sound as deep in resonance as ours. This made it easier to determine who was friend or foe in the dark.

The Germans to my southeast—about 70 yards away—were manning a roadblock and the new firing about 1,000 yards to the north appeared to be near Sainte-Mère-Église.

I turned west and began crawling along the edge of the hedgerow rather slowly, trying to be as quiet as possible. The firing continued behind me at the crossroads. I must have crawled slowly for 5 or 10 minutes. Then I halted and again crawled up on the hedgerow and looked across. I could not see or hear anyone. Occasionally a plane would come over; all generally headed southeast, confirming my suspicion that I was too far north and too far to the west— away from my designated drop zone and assembly area. I had other thoughts. I began to doubt that I knew exactly where I was. Maybe I was closer to the beach than I thought and the planes had already dropped their parachutists. Then I began to wonder whether the whole mission had been aborted and I just hadn't gotten the signal. I resumed moving again, still trying to get away from that crossroads fire without being detected. This time I was crouched over and moving a little faster. I finally came to the southwest end of the field. To my left were a cattle gate and other things that cows leave around when they are in a field, but at least I knew the field probably wasn't mined if there were cows around. We had been told that there was a good possibility that our landing fields would be mined and booby-trapped. I eased the gate open because, like most gates, it squeaked, and found myself in a narrow, paved road with hedges on each side. The tall trees in the hedges gave the place a spooky look, but still no signs of anyone except those people back at the crossroads. By this time I was sure that they didn't hear me and couldn't see me so I began walking in an upright position, my rifle in both hands ready for action and my cricket between my left thumb and forefinger. I must have walked along for about 10 minutes keeping to the right side of the road near the edge where there was a shallow ditch. Then about 25 feet in front of me I thought I saw a helmet silhouetted against the sky. It looked like an American helmet, but in the dark I couldn't tell, so I kneeled down in the ditch and "cricked" my cricket one time. Instantly the response came back with two cricks. I felt a thousand years younger and both of us moved forward so we could touch each other. I whispered my name and he whispered his. To my surprise, he was not from my plane. In fact, he was not even from my headquarters group. He was a sergeant and lost, too. He also had been heading away from the firing at the roadblock that was now about 200 to 300 yards behind us. This meeting happened about 45 minutes after my landing.

We kept going down the road for about 50 or 100 yards when we suddenly ran into some more cricks and picked up three more people, none of whom were from my plane. But they seemed to know each other and they were from the 501st. By that time we were beginning to feel pretty good and our confidence was coming back. We got out the maps, pulled out the flashlight, and covered it as best we could and began to figure out exactly where we were. We concluded rapidly that it was impossible to get to our designated assembly area and that we had best try to accomplish the 501st's mission of securing the Douve River line as that seemed to be the most practical thing to do because of distance and time. We then decided that moving along the road, while it might be productive in finding other friends, also might be extremely dangerous. So we decided to take off across the field to our left and head for the Douve River line. As we entered the field, we found some more 501st parachutists. Still no one from my plane and no coherent pattern to the people we were finding. They were from different groups and it seemed that the scattering had included far more people than I had first imagined. I learned later that our scattered pattern had covered a distance of about 15 or 20 miles in a north–south direction and at least 15 miles in an east–west direction.

Some people in the division had actually landed in the ocean east of the beaches and some in the Douve River to our west and some even further west than that—almost to the west coast of the peninsula we were attempting to capture. But at this moment all I knew was that we had about 12 or 14 people, some of whom knew each other, most from different units, so we began to move out more rapidly. I don't mean we were walking at a normal pace. We crouched down low, we would move a while, stop, and listen; then continue to move and all the time keeping within visual distance of each other. I took a position in the middle of the column of twos and prescribed its general direction. This certainly wasn't the way I had thought the invasion would go nor had we ever rehearsed it in this manner. We had always rehearsed with rapid assemblies in a drop area with quick, personal identification and would move out in organized units. Here I was, an officer who had been doing staff duty for a year and a half, leading a patrol of men, none of whom I knew personally and probably few of whom had ever heard of me, but we worked together surprisingly well. The sergeants took command of the corporals and privates and quickly organized them into small units. I thought how unusual this patrol leader job was for me, but I learned later that this was the way it was on that early morning. Instead of a highly organized landing and assault that we had planned, most of the first day 12,000 invading parachutists fought as very small units and sometimes as individuals. The only thing that saved our plan was that we all knew the overall mission and most of us tried to perform it in the best way that we thought was available.

It was about three o'clock a.m. when we hit the next road. It was a paved road and generally ran east–west. It was a little larger than the first road I had been on, and we seemed to be getting closer to the river line because the land was flatter; the hedges not quite so high. In fact, as you looked ahead you didn't see so many of those spooky, eerie trees that had surrounded the field where I had first landed. We moved out vigorously on this road, with not quite a carefree manner, but our spirits were rising. We walked in a generally westerly direction when the lead man signaled a halt, and I went forward to see what the trouble was. He said he could see a small town ahead—or at least some buildings that he thought was a town—so we halted for a minute or so and listened. No sound came from the town.

About that time we heard noise toward the rear of the column and a couple of shots were fired by my patrol. There was a clatter of someone falling to the pavement. I ran back and found that they had shot at a German who had been riding a bicycle. He apparently was a messenger of some sort. He was more injured from the fall and the scare he had gotten than anything else. We disarmed and searched him, and tried to figure out what we would do with him. His bicycle was a wreck, and he was skinned up from his tumble. The men took off his belt and tied his hands behind him, and we decided then that with that noise if there were many more Germans in town they had had heard us, so we moved in rapidly. It was a short dash into town. It was a very small town, completely dark. At the head of the column there were a few more shots fired and the word came back that they had killed some Germans—probably two who were apparently trying to run from one of the houses in town when we ran in. By this time we were making so much noise that if there were anyone else there, they certainly would have heard us. The noise of the shooting seemed to raise our spirits even more. Still we didn't know where we were. Those little towns had no signs in them and there was nobody out there to greet us. I began to pound on doors and shout for people to come out, but, of course, none of the doors opened and no one moved. I was shouting in English and if there was anyone in that town that understood English, we never found them. Finally, after two or three minutes, one man about 50–55 years old came to the door of one of the houses. He was a short man, about 5' 6", and had on farmer-type clothing—a light shirt and dark trousers. He had apparently been dressed for some time—most of the night—because his shoes were tied and he had on a sweater. In English I began to ask him where we were, what was the name of his town, and he just stared back and began to speak in French. He was excited and eventually some other people in the house came forward—none of whom could speak English. Some of my men had gotten responses at doors and windows, and were running into the same trouble. Finally I went into the dark house, pulled out my map and flashlight, and began to make gestures, hoping he would point to where we were. But he was either afraid or was determined not to get involved—even though I recited with my best French accent the names of some towns that I thought he would know and would point to, I got no response. Finally one of the sergeants came up and said he had found out the name of the town was Carquebut. At last we knew where we were!

During all this exchange with my first Frenchman, I tried out some of my high school Spanish on him but he looked at me with even greater puzzlement when I tried Spanish. I'm afraid that even if he had known Spanish, he wouldn't have known what I was saying. But when I said "Sainte-Mère-Église," he responded "église, église" and began to point down the street. I got my first French lesson. "Église" means church. He hadn't understood my "Sainte-Mère-Église," but he did know where the church was in town and he started to point to it. On checking my map, I confirmed that we were in Carquebut, because there was a little church by the street where he had pointed and the pattern of the buildings in the town seemed to be the same as the pattern shown on my map of Carquebut. We continued our search of Carquebut and found no Germans. There was some more shooting at the end of town by some of my group, and the word came to me that the two Germans who had been seen running from the house were dead. We still had one prisoner with whom we didn't know what to do. We took off his shoes and threw them away, figuring that he couldn't run very far without shoes. We tried to turn our prisoner over to the small group of Frenchmen who were now appearing near the center of the town but they didn't want him. Most of this was through hand gestures and through some broken French and English that somehow spontaneously came out of the group of American soldiers and Frenchmen.

We tried to find out from the French people gathered there if there were any more Germans in the area. To that question they usually stared back with blank expressions on their faces. I believe they thought we were a raiding party and they were afraid to commit themselves, thinking that with the coming of light we would be gone and they would still be left there with the German occupation forces. No one wanted to cooperate.

The action in Carquebut had taken about 20–25 minutes. It was now approaching 3:30 a.m. We knew that Carquebut was outside of the sector of the 101st Airborne Division—our parent unit—and was in the sector of the 82nd Division, who had a different responsibility than we did that first day. After a quick conference with some of the sergeants, I decided that we should move to the south toward Saint-Côme-du-Mont, which was about 5 miles from where we were. Saint-Côme-du-Mont had been a part of the 501st objective. It was on the Douve River line and it was not far from the bridges across the Douve that we had been assigned to seize and destroy.

We had three approaches to Saint-Côme-du-Mont. We could attempt to go across country, but some marshes showed on the map and no one was anxious to tackle them. Or we could follow a railroad track slightly to our west that crossed some of the marshes and crossed the Douve River just west of Saint-Côme-du-Mont—or we could follow the roads to Saint-Côme-du-Mont. While the road route was slightly longer—perhaps adding a mile or so to our distance, we opted for the road because we figured the railroad track would be guarded at its bridges and trestles and that there would be some long open areas that we would have to cross that could be pretty dangerous. The route across the field we figured would be too slow and time-consuming, so the road was the best bet. When we left Carquebut we were heading east, dawn was just beginning; it was at least 45 minutes to sunrise but it was already lighter. The firing of our weapons had been heard by other parachutists who were in the area and when we hit the road to move east we found them coming out of the fields to join us.

We were still using a basic column of twos, with a single file on each side of the road and me giving commands from the forward center part of the column. We still were close enough together to maintain eye contact but we began to move more aggressively. We passed through a town that we figured was Eturville, hardly much of a town—one farmhouse on the left of the road and two or three on the right. The doors and windows were all closed and if there were any Germans there they didn't bother us.

In about 30 minutes we hit the main two-lane, north–south road between Sainte-Mère-Église and Carentan. At a little town called Les Forges, as soon as we got in sight of town, we could see two or three American soldiers near the crossroads and we moved more rapidly to meet them. Here for the first time I ran into someone I knew.

As dawn came it was possible to see scattered parachutes lying around in the fields. Some hanging in trees; some lying partly in the road. It was obvious that we were coming closer to a place where more men had been dropped. Lieutenant Poze reported that the road to the north of him seemed to be clear—at least there was no firing from that direction so apparently the roadblock that I had spotted earlier had either been moved northward toward Sainte-Mère-Église or else those German soldiers manning the roadblock were holding their fire. But our mission was to the south so we moved out as rapidly as possible along the highway.

Just a short distance along we ran into the town of Blosville. We encountered some fighting from our left but it did not appear to be well aimed and when we returned the fire the hostile firing would die out, so we chose to ignore it and to move more rapidly toward Saint-Côme-du-Mont. I was now approaching 7:30 or 8:00 a.m. We had gathered strength as we had moved along and we now had approximately 50 men, including Lieutenant Poze and myself.

By the time we got to the end of Blosville, a Captain MacNeilly, also with the 501st, moved out on the road and we had a reunion! I had known and worked with MacNeilly. He was from San Francisco and a genial fellow and a good man. But his experience in leading a combat patrol was even more limited than mine so I remained in control and gave Poze control of the men on the right-hand or west side of the road and MacNeilly control of the men on the east side of the road. Since it was now daylight and we could see and be seen at greater distances, we changed our patrol formation to a diamond-shaped wedge with a point to the front and rear and a flanking point to the right and left of the center.

Upon signal we moved out toward the south. Here again it struck me how peculiar this was. I had never envisioned myself leading a combat patrol. The skills I was using were ones I had first learned at Plant High School in junior ROTC in 1936, and were skills that I had taught during basic training instructions in 1941 and 1942.

While our confidence had returned, we all still felt very isolated. There was firing going on to the east of us, but it was so faint that it was hard to distinguish what we heard. There was one sound though that I will never forget. That is the sound of a gun that we learned to call the "burp gun." It was a German weapon that could be fired either automatically or semi-automatically. I had never seen one before and had never heard one.

The flankers to the east and west and all of the riflemen were walking in the fields and having to cross hedgerows and some of these hedgerows were 6 feet high and were a solid combination of stone, dirt and bushes, vines and trees. And, of course, before each hedgerow was crossed it was necessary to make sure no one was ready to surprise you on the other side. So while daylight had its advantages, one of them was not speed.

We continued to move. After about an hour, I called a halt, brought in Poze and MacNeilly and the one flanker from both the east and west and held a council. At the end of this council I brought out my two cans of beer which we shared. I estimate we had moved about a mile and a half south from Blosville. When the cans were empty we decided to leave them in the middle of the road as a monument to the first cans of Schlitz consumed in France and moved on.

In about five minutes the point man signaled with his hand and beckoned me forward, and I discovered what he had found. In the west ditch was a wounded German soldier. I moved the patrol on up. The German had been hit in the stomach area and was in bad shape. He had already turned rather gray-looking and seemed to be rather incoherent. There were some parachutes lying in the fields nearby and I assumed the parachutists had gotten him. We searched the area but found no one. The German was moaning, his eyes closed. We disarmed him and then had to decide what to do with him. We finally decided just to leave him where he was. He was a pitiful sight, so all alone, so badly injured and so near death, with us standing over him. We didn't waste much time. We just went on. He was no danger to us. As I recall, one of the men did give him some water and someone propped his head up a little and he quit moaning, but his breathing was laborious. Down the road a point man spotted a sign post on a little concrete marker on the right-hand side of the road: Carentan—6km, Paris—250km. We joked about being in Paris that night or maybe it was just the fact that it was broad open daylight and that our luck seemed to be going well.

The road was now straight and well-paved with shallow ditches on each side; hedgerows out from the fields and occasionally a shallow stream. To our left were more parachutes and to our right were a few. We were now running into our equipment bundles, some of which had been opened but were still connected to their parachutes. We could tell from the markings what they had contained, but since we had no need for any of the materials we left them alone. If we could only have found a bundle with some radios or some machine guns in it, we would have been in great shape. Our rifles were fine but a few automatic weapons and some radios would have improved our capabilities.

We had moved a short distance when the flanker on the left to the east signaled for a halt and word came that he had found a dead American parachutist. No one knew what to do. We just went on and left him there. By this time we were picking up occasional hits to our patrol, usually from the left-hand, east, side of the road where the greatest concentration of parachutes could be seen.

Around La Croix-Pan we came to the low point between two shallow hills. There was a marsh of the Douve River on the west side and some low marshy land on the east. Here also was another road intersection but we continued straight ahead. We were picking up more dead and injured American parachutists. We were also picking up more fire from our left flank, most of that was not particularly serious—a single shot or so or perhaps a burst from a burp gun. And then after we returned the fire there would be no further exchange.

The hedges were so thick that it was impossible to tell whether you were firing in the right direction. You had to hope, and if there was no further enemy fire, you had to assume it was safe to proceed. This we did until about 10:30 or 11:00 in the morning. By that time we had crossed another crossroad that I vaguely remember the road to the right led to Houesville, and on the east, the road let to Angoville-au-Plain. We kept moving straight south to Saint-Côme-du-Mont. It was obvious that the flankers in our diamond formation were getting tired. They had covered about 3 miles in fields with rows of hedges to get over. All of us were tired because we hadn't had a chance to eat or sleep since leaving our airfield in England. We had been awake and moving for 30 hours. Our last meal had been 17 hours earlier. We halted for a minute and I called Poze to me and told him to go up and take the forward point position because we needed to make better time.

Saint-Côme-du-Mont was near—perhaps 400 yards away.

According to the regimental plan, Saint-Côme-du-Mont should already be in the 501st's hands. In fact, it should have been in the 501st's hands for about six hours. Unfortunately, I was wrong.

Poze took over the point position on the right hand side of the road and one of the sergeants followed him on the left side of the road about 15 yards behind. The flankers were now about 100 yards out to the east and west with a rifleman filling in between and the bottom or rear part of the diamond was still covered by two glider pilots and our prisoner. I'd pulled the patrol into a tighter formation because the hedgerows seemed more ominous and our visibility was limited to about 100 yards in each direction from the road. In this formation we continued our advance toward Saint-Côme-du-Mont.

Just as we moved out, we cleared a handsome looking farmhouse, set back from the right hand side of the road. A hedgerow divided the house from the field to the south and at the corner of the hedgerow and the road we came upon an empty foxhole that we knew had been there from our intelligence briefing and aerial photographs. The foxhole was empty but appeared to have been recently used so we continued on. Now we were about 200 yards from Saint-Côme-du-Mont. I was in the middle of the road controlling our diamond-shaped formation patrol with hand signals. MacNeilly was behind me on the left-hand side about 15 yards and Poze was about 30 yards to my right front.

I moved over toward the edge of the road to the right. I was now at the bottom of a very small hill with Saint-Côme-du-Mont sitting at the crest. We found the main body of forces, but it wasn't the 501st. In fact, it wasn't even a friendly force. Shortly after I had given the signal to Poze to continue forward I heard a gun bolt move just on the other side of the hedge on my right-hand side. I looked toward the sound and there was a gun muzzle pointed in my direction. As I dove for the ditch, all hell broke loose! We had been ambushed. I remember seeing Poze go down in front of me as if he, too, were diving in the ditch. The gunner was standing behind the hedge—the muzzle of his gun pointed through the bushes and he apparently had his weapon set on full automatic because when it started to fire it sprayed bullets all over the area.

Instantaneously shots started coming from the buildings in Saint-Côme-du-Mont and from the hedges that stretched out to the east and west, just outside of the town perpendicular to the road that we were on. Fortunately, there did not appear to be more than one gunner who was right on top of me. He had a greater field of vision across the road than he did right under him because of the thickness of the hedge. So while he could see me as I was standing up, he couldn't see me lying down—nor do I believe he could see Poze. After the first shot my patrol began to fire back—slowly at first, but building up their volume as they got into firing position. I could hear MacNeilly some 50 to 60 yards behind me shouting orders, but I was pinned down and couldn't move. I knew that if I stood up the man on the other side of the hedge could see me. If I continued to lie there, the Germans in Saint-Côme-du-Mont would finally pick me off. The grass was about a foot high in the ditch, but not very thick. It was still early summer and the weeds had not grown very high. They offered me some concealment, but not much.

The first thing I had to do was to get rid of that gunner right over my head. I knew I couldn't exist long with him there. He had probably seen me dive into the ditch, but he couldn't get a good shot at me until he climbed to the top of the hedge. I took a grenade out of my pocket, pulled the safety pin, and lobbed it over the hedge. I hoped that he didn't have time to throw it back. He didn't. After it went off, I heard no more firing from his position and assumed that that problem was out of the way for awhile.

I called to Poze and had no response. I lay there for a minute or so, but it seemed like a lifetime. I couldn't get my head up because every time I moved I drew fire. I yelled back to MacNeilly to tell him to cover me. He understood and so the fire from our patrol picked up. It was accurate enough to cause the German fire to slow down—and as soon as it slowed, I jumped up out of the ditch, took about six fast paces and took cover behind a concrete telephone pole. It wasn't very good protection, but it was better than I had had.

Of course, I was partially visible so I attracted a lot of fire toward me and the telephone pole. I couldn't stand there very long or they would have gotten me. I guess only luck saved me. It was clear then that the far side of the road offered better protection than my old or current position so I made a dash across the road and dove in the ditch again. How I escaped getting hit I will never know, but at least this ditch was deeper and no one could directly observe my movements as long as I stayed flat on my stomach. I slid down the ditch in the direction of MacNeilly. It was the easiest crawling I ever did. I had received such a shot of adrenaline I think I could have crawled a mile and I probably only crawled 50 yards when I slid under a low drainage culvert in the road and felt safe—or at least relatively safe. The firing continued, and I continued to crawl. After I had gone a short distance out of the culvert I had passed the crest of the low hill on which my patrol had taken up firing positions, and I was out of immediate danger. The first person I ran into was MacNeilly, and he was laughing a sort of nervous laugh. He said he had never seen me run so fast in my life and that I had looked like a jack rabbit going across that road with the Germans firing at me. I don't think he really thought it was funny, he was just uptight like the rest of us.

We began a visual search from our position for Poze. We could still see Saint-Côme-du-Mont—we were now about 300 yards from the town. We continued firing and would occasionally call for Poze and for the sergeant. Neither of them responded. We guessed that they were either out of action or so close to the German positions that they didn't want to give away their own positions.

By that time our patrol had taken up some good firing positions. Everyone was in the firing line except for the two glider pilots and their prisoner. The glider pilots couldn't have done much good anyway because all they had were pistols, and I could see them huddled over by the side of the road about 100 yards north of me. We slowed down our firing to conserve ammunition. It was obvious that we were badly outnumbered. We had at least two missing and one man reported that he was slightly wounded. I sent men out to the right and left to try to determine the extent of the German positions, but every time they moved they drew a lot of fire. It was more and more obvious that the Germans were well emplaced and had planned to defend Saint-Côme-du-Mont stubbornly.

So there we were, 200–300 yards north of Saint-Côme-du-Mont meeting superior fire from a major force. We had no automatic weapons, no radios—only our semi-automatic rifles and a few pistols. We hardly knew each other, but we were getting well acquainted, and we were working well together that day. Despite all the noise that we were making, we could not seem to attract the attention of any other Americans in the area. In fact, we had no idea that there were any more in the area. Before we decided to break off the fire fight, two of our men were killed. MacNeilly and I held a council. We called in a couple of the sergeants and decided that since the day was half over and since it appeared useless to try to attack the town, we just couldn't sit there for the rest of the day and wait for some miracle to happen. Also, I did not know what was building up behind us to the north because during our advance on Saint-Côme-du-Mont there had been intermittent firing from our flanks. We knew that there were Germans behind us, but we did not know where they actually were or how many they were.

I decided that the best thing to do was to split the patrol—leaving some with MacNeilly to continue firing into Saint-Côme-du-Mont—and for me to go northward to try to find some friendly force. We moved at a slow trot back toward Blosville. When we passed the spot where the wounded German had been, he was dead.

About an hour and a half after we departed the Saint-Côme-du-Mont area we reached the outskirts of Sainte-Mère-Église. We found a small unit of the 82nd had established a roadblock there near a crashed glider. The crashed glider was one of the bloodiest sights I saw on D-Day. It had been used by some units of the 82nd to attempt to bring in anti-tank guns and the pilot had overshot the field and crashed into a stone wall right off the highway. If there were any survivors, they weren't around. There were plenty of bodies. We turned over our prisoner and said goodbye to our two glider pilots who rejoined the 82nd. It was comforting to know that at least there were some American forces occupying the north and south ends of the stretch of road between Sainte-Mère-Église and Saint-Côme-du-Mont.

We headed for the designated glider landing zone, hoping that those operations which had been planned for D-Day evening would come off as scheduled. I had been designated to receive one of the six jeeps the 501st was to get. Jeeps were quarter-ton open trucks.

At Hiesville there were already gliders in the field—those that had come in about three hours after our initial parachute assault. General Don Pratt, assistant division commander, was killed in the landing of his glider. In fact, his body had not been removed when I reached the glider landing zone. There were other American soldiers from the 101st around. Not many—perhaps fifty. They were near a farmhouse, and I discovered it was the division command post, hardly the kind you might expect for a division. The farmhouse was large and substantial, surrounded by large trees that offered plenty of protection from overhead observation, but no brass [high-ranking officers] was around. Just a few men who had only begun posting maps on walls and preparing to get the command post in operation. They de-briefed me in about 10 minutes and entered the situation as I described it on their maps, and I headed immediately for the glider landing zone just south of Hiesville. I got there between 6:15 and 7:00 p.m.

Right on time the scheduled C-47s, towing two gliders apiece, appeared coming in from a northerly direction. As soon as they were in sight of the drop zones the gliders cut loose and began to land. What a mess! The fields were small, and there were still some of those anti-glider, anti-parachute poles in the field. There was small arms fire from the Germans directed toward the planes and the gliders. The gliders began to dive for the fields. Some hit short; some hit long; all of them hit hard. Some sheared wings; others ran into each other, but somehow they got down. I had seen glider landings before and knew that glider riders and pilots really earned their pay in that branch of the service, as those fellows did coming in that evening. I am sure some were killed, but we couldn't stay around to count bodies.

I am sure there were a lot of miracles on D-Day, but my own second miracle occurred when that glider assigned to carry my jeep landed right on time and right at the designated spot. I wasn't more than 50 feet from the spot where the glider landed—certainly within shouting distance—the glider nose opened and my jeep rolled out. I called the driver's name; he recognized me, and drove right over.

We had been isolated for about 18 hours that day. We had been shot at, taken some casualties, and inflicted a few ourselves but the arrival of this jeep was like a miracle. In this little landing zone 20 gliders had landed. Not one of them was in serviceable condition. Some were badly battered.

When I arrived back at the division command post, I was asked to help provide local security for protection of the command post because by that time darkness was approaching fast and there was still an awful lot of German firing going on. We organized a guard detail with others that had been arriving at the command post, and I was assigned a sector to the north about 300 yards from the command post. I took my small patrol to our sector and we divided the responsibility for the night. We posted the first guards, then moved into a well-built cluster of farm buildings—a milking shed, tool shed, hay barn, all clustered around a stone-paved courtyard. But it was home. There was already a small first-aid station operating at one end of the building and there were quite a few injured and wounded Americans, as well as Germans, lying on the ground. Some were resting up against the buildings. Others were just lying in the courtyard. In the dim light I could see some of our aid personnel bustling around but I didn't need their services, so I stayed out of their way.

I sat down in the equipment barn beside an old two-wheeled hay rake and opened my first K-ration: ham and eggs in a small tin can, a fruit bar, some biscuits that looked and tasted like I guess dog biscuits taste, and a hard chocolate bar for dessert.

The chocolate bar was so hard that if you had thrown it as a rock it would have been a dangerous weapon. Some kind of powdered coffee. I put the unopened powdered coffee back in my pocket, and I devoured my meal in record time.

I had the second shift of the guard detail that night so I went to sleep as soon as I finished eating. It was now dark and there was still plenty of firing going on. There was some moaning from the direction of the aid station, but I fell asleep so fast that by the time my turn came to pull my tour of guard duty it seemed like only 10 minutes had passed. I pulled my two-hour shift, woke up my relief and then went to sleep again. Once more I must have slept about an hour rather fitfully, but it sure felt good.

When the word came to wake up again, we were in contact with some other members of the 501st who had also shown up in the division command post area. I went over toward the direction of the command post, and found Colonel Harry Kinnard. I knew at least two people from the plane had survived. He said that we were moving out in a few minutes to join a force of the 506th. He asked me how many men I had and I told him about 35. I told him about MacNeilly being back at Saint-Côme-du-Mont with 15 others. Kinnard had about 150, I believe, I asked him about the rest of the regiment, and he said he knew where Colonel Julian Ewell was with his battalion, but he did not know where the rest of them were.

A parachute battalion at full strength consisted of three rifle companies and a headquarters weapons company with a total of about 600 officers and men. Ewell's battalion at that hour was hardly what you would call an organized, full-strength unit. He probably had 150–200 men, roughly organized along company lines. They had been very effective in the early morning hours of D-Day when they had been acting as division reserve—at that time he had no more than 50 men. But they had cleared out one of the four exits to the mainland from the invasion beach. The clearing out of these exits was essential to the successful passage of the seaborne assault forces from the beach to the mainland. Utah Beach was about 4 miles long. It had been designated as the landing beach for the seaborne elements of the Seventh Corps. The Seventh Corps was under the command of General J. Lawton Collins, who was later to become known as "Lightning Joe."

Ewell's mission that night was to act as division reserve and be under the direction of General Taylor for whatever purpose that Taylor wanted to use him. Because the drop had been so scattered, Taylor directed Ewell to use his small force to open up the nearest causeway and Ewell had proceeded to do so.

At about 4:30 a.m. on the first day after D-Day—or D+1—Ewell's battalion was again in division reserve. Kinnard was acting as regimental commander for our part of the regiment, which, excluding Ewell, was not more than 200 men. The situation of Colonel Howard Johnson, our regimental commander, and the exact location of the rest of the 501st Regiment was not clear to me. I learned later that the 1st Battalion had been badly mauled when landing near its drop zone—that the drop zone had been well and vigorously defended by the Germans and that the battalion commander, Colonel Robert Carroll, had been killed before he could get out of his parachute harness. Colonel Johnson had landed safely, had assembled a small force and had moved directly to one of the regiment's objectives, which was to secure a dam and locks across the Douve River about one mile downstream from the main highway that connected Carentan and Sainte-Mère-Église. Johnson and his command, which was probably not more than 100 men during the early hours of D-Day, captured the locks and crossed the Douve River so as to secure the locks. The locks were essential to the control of the depth of the water of the Douve and it was essential that the Douve be kept flooded so as to act as an anti-tank barrier to the German forces to the south. So one part of the regimental objective had been accomplished with dispatch and with great success.

We moved out from the division command post near Hiesville in the direction of Vierville with a mission of seizing the bridges across the Douve between Saint-Côme-du-Mont and Carentan. The advance from Hiesville to Vierville was relatively uneventful. There was some firing but it didn't stop us.

It was not until I had reached Angoville that the first serious action of that day began for me. When we reached Angoville there were already some other American forces there—apparently remnants of our 1st Battalion. We quickly exchanged information and no sooner than that had happened we came under heavy fire. I jumped into a barn adjacent to a farmhouse on the east side of the little road that we were on. It must have been about 9:30 or 10:00 o'clock in the morning. I felt safe in the barn with its heavy, sturdy stone walls and a tile roof. As first we received rifle fire and machine-gun fire, which we returned. Then mortar shells began to fall. This was the first time I had been under fire by mortar since the beginning of the invasion. After the third or fourth round hit in Angoville, one hit the roof of the barn. The roof was sturdy and covered with tiles about a half-inch thick, but when that shell went off, those nice, red clay tiles turned into lethal weapons. I learned then and there to stay away from barns with tile roofs—even if they do have good walls. I also learned later that same day that the first thing you do when you go into a house is to break out the glass windows. I had been in some houses on D-Day but there was no artillery fire directed at me and no mortar fire, and I felt safe with the glass windows but that day at Angoville I learned how dangerous glass windows and tile roofs could be.

We took some casualties. I don't remember how many. After an hour the firing stopped. With the 4th Division and some elements of our 101st pushing from the east with the only way across the Douve River and into Carentan being blocked by us, we were picking up one German unit after another as they were trying to move to a better position. There was too much resistance to the northeast for us to move in that direction. So we settled down after nightfall for some rest.

In the meantime I had almost started to like K-rations. I hadn't had a chance to try any of the powdered drinks, but the eggs and cheese were good. I couldn't get very enthusiastic about the rest. I was still nibbling on my first chocolate bar, and despite the fact that I had put it in my inside pants pocket, it hadn't melted! I think it must have been mixed with concrete.

Well, that takes you through two days of the invasion. The first day didn't seem like it would ever end and the second day went so fast I hardly remember it. Eventually we would take Saint-Côme-du-Mont. Instead of taking it with one company of the 501st, as had been our original plan of operation before the invasion—or with my small combat patrol as I had tried to do on D-Day, it took the whole division plus the fire support from the cruiser USS *Quincy* plus eight or 10 tanks that were assigned to us from the 5th Corps. It took plenty of lives, both German and American. But within three days we held Saint-Côme-du-Mont and control of the bridges, the line of the Douve River was secure and our first mission completed.

Near the end of the third day the 501st was ordered into division reserve near Vierville. I remember we counted heads that evening at Vierville on the third day and from our group of about 2,000 that came in by parachute, we now numbered no more than 600 to 700.

Fortunately, in the next few days more and more of our 501st men showed up and by the fourth day it seemed to me that we had about 800 to 900 officers and men. We reorganized as quickly as possible—reassigning duties, redistributing weapons, going out into the fields and finding the equipment bundles, getting what few radios we could find in action, and on the night of the third day I dug my first foxhole in France. It wasn't a very good one. The ground was hard and I was tired. But I scooped out a little place, covered myself with a parachute, and before I could count 10 I was dead asleep. Well, that night and the next day the war went on … we had more missions to accomplish—which we did.

So from a total strength of about 2,200 that went to France by parachute and by sea from the 501st, we brought back about 800. Some of the men were arriving back at Hampstead Marshal from hospitals but most of the rest were just gone.

CHAPTER 17

The Rangers on D-Day

I have chosen to explain the experience of each of the three Ranger task forces on D-Day rather than attempt to lump them together as is often done. Each had very different experiences and effect on mission. In that I was able, over time, to talk to veterans of each, I thought it most valuable to describe each independently which is how they were initially.

2nd Rangers at Pointe du Hoc

The formal mission statement given to the Ranger Group Commander, Lieutenant Colonel Earl Rudder, was:

> The 2nd and 5th Ranger Battalions are attached to 1st Division. They will destroy coastal defense batteries at Pointe du Hoc by simultaneous direct assault up the cliffs between Pointe du Hoc and Pointe de la Percée and by flanking action from Beach "Omaha." They will then, assisted by elements of the assault force, capture enemy batteries at GRANDCAMP and MAISY. Thereafter to operate against enemy positions along the coast between Grandcamp and Isigny.
> Operation Order of March 26, 1944 signed by Major General Gerow, commander of the V Corps

As in the 5th Battalion experience, the 2nd deployed to RAF Warmwell on 19 May and then embarked at Weymouth on 1 June. With the false start on 4/5 June, the 2nd joined the huge flotilla of floating steel headed toward the coast of France. With the dismissal of his executive officer, Rudder was now in charge of the assault.

At 0300 6 June, the British crew woke the Rangers for mess prior to loading the assault craft. Bud Lomell commented:

> None of us had really slept. The sea was rough and there was a lot of tension as might be expected. We were getting damn sick of the ship. The ventilation systems were shut due to the storm so the troop area was pretty rank. When the whistle sounded, I think we were all relieved that what we had been training for almost a year was finally getting started.

The channel steamers carrying the 2nd Battalion were large enough to load the Rangers from the deck rather than using a cargo net over the side. This helped, but not for long.

The Rangers were jammed into the British landing craft, which had been outfitted with steel sides. As in the 5th Battalion experience, this greatly reduced the freeboard in a rough sea, causing continuous waves to break overhead, soaking and chilling the men.

Many who had taken advantage of the British breakfast of eggs, pancakes, and sausages quickly lost it. Each Ranger had been given two waxed bags for vomit. These were quickly used and the remainder was tossed on the deck or over the back of the man in front.

Very quickly, the combination of puke and wave water overwhelmed the small bilge pumps. The coxswains told the men to bail with their helmets or the craft would be lost. The Rangers immediately did so, a task that lasted from 0430 until touchdown. In the words of Lomell:

> We bailed and barfed. Bailed and barfed. And we got increasingly mad at the Germans. We were cold and wet as dogs and just wanted to get out of the damn boats and up the cliff and start some payback.

Rudder joined the line of 12 assault craft with 260 men, the Rangers of D, E, and F companies. Each assault craft had six mortar-charged grapnels with ropes to be fired upon landing. Additionally, two DUKWs had the extendable steel ladders with top mounted machine guns. A third DUKW and assault craft carried supplies and 20 men led by the D Company commander.

Offshore, the battleship USS *Texas*, supported by the British destroyer HMS *Talybont* and the U.S. destroyer USS *Satterlee*, began firing on the point at 0600 as planned. By now, the assault craft were within 2 miles of the beach.

The flotilla was led by a British lieutenant who had both compass bearings, maps, and radar to assist. However, there was a very strong west–east current that carried the craft steadily east. With the low water horizon and limited visibility, it wasn't until almost 0615 that Rudder saw the error. The force was heading directly toward Pointe et Raz de la Percée, not Du Hoc. He and the lieutenant simultaneously realized the mistake and did a course correction, but it was too late for a 0630 touchdown.

At 0630, as planned, the bombardment lifted, allowing the Germans, now fully awake, to emerge and re-occupy the defense positions. Meanwhile, the Rangers began a slow right turn to the correct beach.

During the movement, the rough sea claimed both supply craft as well as the DUKW carrying the D Company commander and 20 men. Rudder now had only nine assault craft and no supplies. Bud Lomell recalled:

> The sudden change in direction woke us up and now we could see the problem. Both points were visible and we should have been heading to the one on the right, not left. Holy cow. Then the 20mm opened up with its white tracers. Thank God the Brits put steel on the side. It started to get loud over the waves.

On Pointe de la Percée, a German dual 20mm gun depressed and began to engage the line. Several Rangers were killed outright and others wounded. Quickly, the original plan for a two-sided assault on Pointe du Hoc was lost.

Signaling by hand, the boats hove into line, Rudder simply pointed toward a spot on the beach for each of the craft. This would be a simple linear assault against an aggressive defensive force.

During the lull in bombardment at 0630, the Germans had re-appeared on the cliff tops where they could clearly see the Rangers en route to them. Noting the re-appearance, the offshore destroyers re-initiated fire. The USS *Satterlee* moved within 2,000 yards of the cliffs and engaged it with machine-gun fire. The Germans returned fire, splattering the destroyer's gun tub. When they finally returned to port in England, the captain proudly displayed the pockmarks as visible proof of the close-in encounter.

Neither destroyer was able to depress its guns to hit targets within the battery position. Instead, they concentrated on the top of the bluffs where the Germans were most visible. This had two excellent effects for the Rangers: the cliff face was crumbled into a number of large debris fields on the beach, which would cut the technical climbing distance in more than half in some places; and many of the German defenders were either killed or retreated, leaving only pockets of resistance when the Rangers landed.

At 0710, the nine assault craft landed on a narrow, rocky ledge beach. The DUKWs were last in line and westernmost, and grounded just below the tip. The easternmost craft landed below the limit of the battery position. Each element executed what had been planned and practiced for months. Grappling hooks were fired and troops surged to the cliff base.

Less than a third of the ropes worked. The excess water from the ride in had heavily weighted the ropes and they fell well prior to making the top. Regardless, every craft had at least one grapnel that made the top, dug in, and allowed a Ranger climb to begin. As Lomell stated:

> After that ride in, we were wet, sick, and mad as hell. We were going to get up those cliffs and start killing Germans.
>
> As our ramp went down, I'm the first one off the landing craft. And as I did I was shot through the side above my hip through the muscle on the right side. Fortunately for me, my side was sore and hurt from the shot, but it didn't hit anything important. Bob, my radioman, was next to me on his rope and we're struggling and about to make the top when Bob says to me, "Len. Len, can you help me?" And I said, "What's wrong?" He said, "I don't have an ounce of strength left. I can't make it!" And it was only about a foot or two to the top of the cliff. And I said, "Bob, now that you mention it, I don't think I have an ounce of strength left either to make it. But you gotta hold on." I happened to see Leonard Rubin. He was a very husky fella. And I yelled to him, "Rube! Rube! Get over here." And he comes over, "What's up?" And I said, "Bob can't make it to the top, he's out of strength. Can you help him?" With that, Rube throws down his weapon, reaches over, grabs Bob and he is so powerful of a man he jerked Bob up over the cliff, slung him over. Bob's going through the air. In the meantime, I gained enough strength to get up. And I'm standing up there with

my submachine gun protecting Bob and Rube and the Germans and Rangers are being shot all around us.

There was no waiting around. We all knew our jobs and went about doing it though with a lot less than planned. It was a classic Ranger situation. We all did what we were trained to do without waiting for guidance or reinforcements.

Above, scattered German infantry rained potato masher grenades down, leaned over the bluff firing, and did their best to cut ropes from below. By 0715, greatly aided by the lessened cliff face, Rangers reached the top and began clearing the trench line. Additional ropes were secured to bring up the remainder. By 0730, Rudder had his total force of 200 out of a planned 400 men on top.

This was fortuitous as the Germans on Pointe de la Percée had depressed their gun to where it was now actively engaging the beach. The position was immediately engaged by the offshore destroyers with additional augmentation from cruisers and the *Texas*, rendering the mission of Task Force Charlie moot.

The DUKWs, upon touching down on solid ground, began to extend their ladders with a Ranger manning the top mounted machine guns. The rock ledge had been heavily cratered by prior bombing, creating large holes. Several of the wheels fell into holes, tilting the craft and making them extremely unsteady.

When the ladders were fully extended, each craft began to sway like a metronome. The Rangers would time their swing to fire when they crossed the top and then hold fire when the ladder dipped below. Rudder saw this and went down to them and told them to cease operations as being too dangerous. He returned to his craft, climbed the dirt pile, and established a command post in the ruins of a partially destroyed bunker on the cliff edge.

Rangers from all nine lanes began to independently go about their original tasks although with smaller elements than originally planned. Lomell added:

My job was to clear the guns and that's what we did. There was considerable fire crossing the battery field and the craters saved our asses. We could low crawl from hole to hole and make our way across the field to the casemates.

We got to the first one and it was empty except for a painted phone pole where the gun should have been. We picked up a lot of fire from a position on the flank, which pounded us continuously. This bunker was never cleared until the 8th and was a major problem for movement.[1]

---

1 The many Ranger veterans I talked to echoed the same points. They all said how focused they were on getting up the cliffs and doing their jobs. The cold and seasickness never changed that resolve. Once on top, they went about going to their objectives. They all stated what a life saver the craters were. The complex was inter-connected underground and Germans were constantly popping up like in a whack-a-mole. The bunker on the westernmost flank was a constant thorn in their side and seemed to have an endless supply of ammo.

Each Ranger party had a specific casemate to clear. Once that was done, they were to move to the road and block it. This they did but more as squads than the original company formations envisioned.

Arriving at the main road, the Ranger officers, four lieutenants and First Sergeant Lomell, assessed the situation with the assets they had and made a hasty organizational decision. They also confirmed to each other that the German guns were missing, for whatever reason.

The Rangers would establish three blocking positions, oriented west and east as well as south, the most likely avenue of approach for a counter-attacking force.

Lomell and his Company D personnel would orient on the western flank, with Company E on the hedgerow facing north, and Company F blocking the road to the east with positions on the left flank of Company E. There were fewer than 80 men within all three companies, requiring outposting rather than a linear defense.[2]

The Rangers dug in and awaited the Germans. But not before they did what Rangers do as a matter of course, which was patrolling. It was about 1500. Lomell recounted:

> As we rushed them we got to the gun positions that we were assigned and there were no guns. What was there were these phony poles making it look from the air as if the guns were in those positions. Well, I told my platoon sergeant Jack Kuhn, "You come with me." I said, "You and I are going to go find those guns. They gotta be here!" Down this one sunken road we saw what looked to be wagon wheel tracks. We came to a hedgerow that I had to look over into an apple orchard, a sunken apple orchard. And there, lo and behold, are the guns of Pointe du Hoc.

By chance, Lomell and Kuhn had positioned themselves furthest south from the point, about 500 yards south of the main road and at the first significant hedgerow between them and the likely German route to their position. Acting as a pair of scouts, they went less than 200 yards when they encountered deeply grooved tracks winding through an apple orchard. Looking through a small hedgerow, they spotted the five large artillery pieces, the objective of the entire endeavor.

Most fortuitous was that the position had no Germans. Lomell could hear some talking on the other side of the hedgerow, but the guns were alone. Ammo was stacked between each gun and they were pointed in the general direction of Utah Beach, ready to fire. Lomell said:

> It was the damndest thing. There they were all pretty in a line. Couldn't believe it. No Germans.
>
> Jack went to one gun and I went to the next one. We put our thermites on the breech, basically melting it so it wouldn't close. The thermite was a great weapon. Totally silent and burned white hot. Melted metal easily.
>
> I then went to the other guns and smashed the sights with the butt of my Thompson. We then hightailed it out of there to get more thermites from other Rangers.

---

2   When A/5th Rangers arrived around 1700, they replaced the F Company elements blocking the road to the east and integrated with E.

I don't think we went more than a hundred yards back down the same track when there was this tremendous explosion behind us. We were showered with splinters and mud. Some other Rangers had found what we did and blew the ammo. Anyway, the guns were found and destroyed. I sent a runner back to Colonel Rudder to say mission accomplished.

Independently from Lomell, a second group of Rangers, probably under Lieutenant Joseph Leagans and Staff Sergeant Lupinski of E Company, found the same position. They had a number of blocks of C2 explosive, a form of TNT. They placed these on the piles of ammo stacked between each gun, lit the fuses and left. This effectively destroyed the entire battery.

It was approximately 0900.

As Lomell's good fortune was developing and the road was being blocked, Rudder had separate issues to deal with at the point. The large concrete bunker that Rudder had landed against was declared the Ranger command post. Due to constant German fire, the command post was below the cliff line away from small arms fire. The side of the bunker, blasted by the destroyers, exposed a large open chamber connecting to other underground rooms. These became the combination clearing station and POW holding tank.

There were so few Rangers left there with him, less than 20 including his signal officer Lieutenant James Eikner and Dr. Walter Block, that he had to grab several Rangers, a lieutenant among them, to secure prisoners and provide some local security. The POWs, approximately 15, were quickly conscripted as medical support staff to move the wounded into rows where Dr. Block could begin treatment.

A machine gun bunker on the eastern flank, less than 150 yards from the command post, was a constant irritant, severely limiting local movement. Rudder ordered the lieutenant and an NCO to "Take it out." This the pair did, returning to command post to assume local security.

Rudder ranged up and down the cliff trench line assessing the situation and pondering what to do with so little. His greatest issue was lack of reinforcements, evacuation of the wounded, and dwindling ammo. He was greatly concerned about the situation with 5th Rangers and was anxious to have them join him, ignorant of the hold order imposed by Colonel Canham and General Cota.

He pestered Eikner to ask the Navy for reinforcements and resupply. Eikner's radio had been broken on the initial assault. It lost waterproofing and several tubes were broken. He did have two pigeons and a semaphore light. He was able to achieve recognition with the offshore destroyers with the semaphore and signaled Rudder's message.

The pigeons were released with unknown results. Later, it was determined that one had made it to England, but too late to assist. The other was considered killed or lost.

Meanwhile, the USS *Texas* continued to engage Pointe de la Percée and fired several "overs" that impacted on the Ranger position. One was a yellow dye marker that hit within 30 yards of Rudder, drenching his right side with the marker from head to toe. Additionally, he had been wounded by small arms twice, once on the beach and once in the trench line. Dr. Block bandaged the wounds but he could not fix Rudder's growing irritation and anxiety.

The Navy, responding to Eikner's signal, took it upon itself to assist Rudder with internal assets. The beachmaster at Omaha was notified to find and return Lieutenant Ben Berger with 5th Rangers to join 2nd Battalion. By 1600, he found Berger and brought him to the beach. As Berger's radio did not work and the 116th was beginning to coalesce with some artillery, Lieutenant Colonel Max Schneider did not object.

Accordingly, Berger, still completely ignorant as to exactly what was going on, embarked on a Higgins boat. He explained,

> I got a call from the navy to go to the beachmaster. He had a big sign so I could see him from the cliff top. I went down to him and reported. He said the Rangers at the point needed a naval gunfire officer and to send me. I told him my radio didn't work. He was very busy and just said, "Get in the boat."
>
> I had no idea what was happening. The beachmaster simply said orders. Move out. I was getting quite cold and grabbed a blanket from the boat locker and wrapped it around myself for the trip. I had my light uniform and the Aldis lamp and now empty musette bag.

It took about an hour to transit. The craft scraped against the edge of the stone beach, dropped ramp, and Berger ran off, alone. The boat lifted ramp and left. Berger asked a Ranger for directions to the command post. The Ranger pointed up the destroyed cliff face to the array of ropes and ladders. Berger went on:

> I barely got my feet wet, looked up, and there was this huge cliff face. Several Rangers were moving along the beach tending to the wounded. I walked to a small trail that had been made on the rubble pile and got to the ladders and ropes. I went up the small ladder and arrived at a ditch just below the destroyed bunker. It had a couple of very dirty Rangers. I could see some prisoners.
>
> I asked, where was Colonel Rudder? A Ranger said on the other side of the bunker. I got over the ditch into the concrete bunker and went to the room on the other side. There was Colonel Rudder, streaked in yellow with several wound bandages and I reported—all very formal:
>
> "Sir, Lieutenant Berger reporting as ordered."
>
> To say Rudder was unhappy would be an understatement.
>
> "Where are my reinforcements? Where are my supplies? I ask for help and I get a navy lieutenant? What are you good for? We need help"
>
> I explained my job and that I had no radio but would do what I could. I knew we had two destroyers for support and would try and bring them in for us.
>
> He softened a bit and told me to report to Lieutenant Eikner and work with him.
>
> I turned around and went back to the ditch and introduced myself to Lieutenant Eikner. Quickly, we compared notes and got out my Aldis lamp which was much easier to operate than Eikner's instrument. We had a tripod which made a steady spot. Quickly, we got a connection and began to plot fire.

Eikner and I set up a tripod with my Aldis and began to signal the destroyers. I knew who they were and what they had as well as the pre-planned targets. I had meetings with the destroyer elements in harbor before we departed England so we just used what we had developed in port. Eikner copied my target numbers. We got acknowledgements from both *Talybont* and *Satterlee*. Eikner then went to Rudder and got target data on his map which we transmitted to both. Morse was a slow system but we were able to use the pre-arranged targets and adjust from them.

A wire phone had been established by the Rangers on the road and they were talking to us. Eikner showed me the Ranger positions, which we transmitted to the ships so they wouldn't fire on them. The ships were very responsive and we developed a short code which helped.

Later, the Rangers landed a radio and we could directly voice transmit, which was much quicker. But for the afternoon through night the next day, it was all by Morse. We would call for fire. The destroyers would fire and we would wait for the phone adjustments and transmit to the ships. We were very busy. I would guess that both ships, in rotation, were firing near continuously for the first two days. In time, two more destroyers replaced them as they had fired almost all of their stocks.

Rudder came down to see what we were doing and was happy. In that we both were so busy, Rangers would hand us coffee or some rations while we worked. We tried a rotation system, but it didn't really work. Both of us seemed to be working all the time. By the time we were relieved, late on the 8th, we both were dead on our feet.

Throughout the day, Rudder was only able to get sporadic messages from the road positions. Runners would go back and forth but would have to dodge the constant firing from protected bunkers on the western portion of the position.

By 1700, a landline was established between the command post and the road. The line itself was a combination of light assault wire the Rangers brought and the heavier commo wire they pulled out of the bunker system. The phone was set on the road as that was the limit of available wire. This meant that Rangers would have to leave their positions forward of the road to make calls.

It was approximately 1800 when Eikner and Berger began their work.

Eikner and Berger established artillery grids for the forces forward. These were sent to the destroyers via Morse, as were all firing adjustments. By 2100, still reasonably light, the defensive fire was registered.

Concurrent with the landline, Lieutenant Charles Parker, commander of Company A, 5th Battalion, met 2nd Battalion elements on the road. He had 20 men including three mis-dropped 101st troops. He had started on Omaha with 65.

The persistent firing from several machine guns and snipers as well as random artillery impacts signaled to the Rangers that their assumption as to German intentions was probably accurate. They would be attacked across the fields to the north. This determined the Ranger dispositions.

The following map shows the forward dispositions of the Rangers on the ground in the photo.

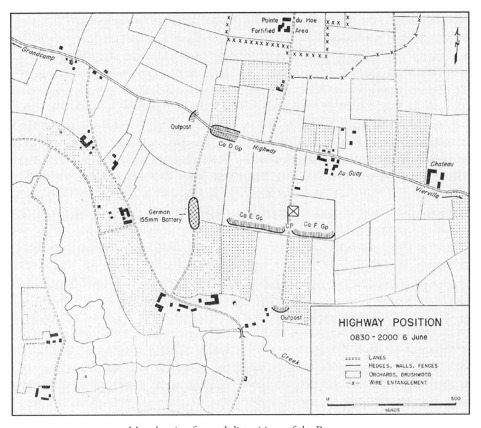

Map showing forward dispositions of the Rangers.

Company D, approximately 25 men led by First Sergeant Bud Lomell, would hold the road to Grandcamp with an outpost and place its primary defense on a north–south farm road connecting it with elements of Companies E and F dug in along the hedgerow facing north.

Between them they had approximately 80 men, who they deployed in a series of loose outposts. Several BARs were placed so as to cover the most likely German avenue of approach from the northwest.

Sergeant William Petty and two Rangers were placed in an outpost approximately 100 yards south of the hedgerow line. They had one BAR and reasonable observation.

All day, each group experienced intermittent fire. Small groups of Germans and occasional elements of 20 or more were observed traveling across the front, attempting to infiltrate the Ranger lines. These were engaged or ignored as common sense dictated. Lomell allowed a 50-man, well-armed and organized element to pass his front without engagement as they would have overwhelmed his position. He explained:

> We had about 20 men scattered in three directions. Germans were moving across us all day. They didn't seem to know where we were. Some looked like they were heading to the point and others just moving oblivious to our position. We took on everyone we judged moving toward us and ignored those that posed no real threat. I was very concerned about ammo and knew we would be in for a long night.
>
> In the late afternoon, there was a large force, well-armed, and in a strong tactical formation that crossed our front. I could see at least two machine guns and a mortar. They had about twice as many men as we did. I elected to let them pass and warned my men to lay low. The Germans passed by our front about 50 yards away and disappeared. I was sure if they attacked us, we would be done simply due to numbers. Combat forces choices.

As night descended, Rudder was in difficult straits. Of the 200 men landed, many were wounded and a number had been killed. He lacked reasonable communications with Omaha Beach and had no idea when 5th Rangers would join, reinforcements he desperately needed.

The battery position itself was held only at his immediate command post area and movement was very dangerous due to the bunker on the extreme west. Several attempts to take it had resulted in prohibitive casualties and Rudder ordered them stopped.

He knew the forward positions were routinely engaged from the sound of fire and the constant impacts of the destroyers firing in support. He had almost no information regarding the strength and status of the forward elements.

Rudder had to decide if the Rangers at the road should be withdrawn to the point to establish a strong defense of the position or remain in place. His choice, ultimately, was to hold what he had where it was. His reasoning simply was that to withdraw the road blocks, most likely under pressure, would allow the Germans unimpeded access to Omaha from the west and perhaps stop reinforcements that would use the same road. He would defend the battery with what he had, about 20 men, at least half of whom, including himself, were wounded.

The forward forces remained fairly widespread during the day but adjusted lines as darkness approached. Forward observation posts, less Sergeant Petty's forward of the main body, were withdrawn. Positions were tightened and held by pairs. Company D and Company E joined in mutual support along the trace that Lomell had established. The Rangers created a tight three-sided box and awaited the anticipated German counter-attack.

Throughout the day, the Germans had probed continuously and had a good indication as to the Ranger dispositions. Concurrently, the only reasonably concealed approach into the Rangers was from the south. Both sides planned for this approach.

About 2300, it was finally dark with a near full moon. The dense shrubbery and trees permitted only intermittent views along the orchard lanes and fields. Sounds of men and their equipment began to drift across the lines. It was 2330.

Near the junction of the D and E positions, the Rangers could hear Germans talking with several whistles sounding. Almost simultaneously, there was a blinding flash of light where the Germans guns were disabled, probably powder bags inadvertently ignited.

The light exposed numerous silhouettes which the Rangers immediately engaged. The fire fight was intense with action along the L shaped position of the two companies. During the skirmish, Lieutenant George Kirchner of Company D withdrew from his position to gather several Rangers to flank the Germans. Due to the noise of battle, his call for assistance was unheard. He traveled with a lone Ranger to the main road when the firing suddenly ceased. It was about 2400.

The net effect of this was that the corner position connecting companies D and E was lost or abandoned, essentially isolating each company to manage on its own. No attempt was made during the night to re-align into a coherent three-company position. Lomell said:

> It was damned dark where we were. We were reduced to firing at muzzle flashes and the occasional clear target. The Germans got through the juncture of our two positions and I had to pull my guys back in a defensive loop. I told them not to fire forward unless they had a target as I didn't want to hit any E company guys. It was impossible to talk due to the noise and the machine-gun fire kept everyone in their positions. I had no idea where Lieutenant Kirchner was and presumed him dead. It wasn't until the morning when we were able to reform.

At 0100, the Germans exploited this by assaulting the corner and pushing both D and E back, widening the gap. By 0130, firing had ceased and both sides held their positions in relative silence. At 0300, this would change.

The Germans, now holding the ground at what was the juncture of D and E, had effectively split the Rangers into four distinct groups: Company D along the highway and slightly south along the farm trace; Company E pushed back toward Company F but not contiguous; Sergeant Petty and his outpost well south of the main body; and Company F to the east.

There was no attempt to regroup at this point when the Germans launched their heaviest attack at 0300. They attacked on a small but weighted front where Company E had abandoned its original positions, allowing the full weight to fall on E's flank. They quickly rolled up the Rangers capturing more than 20 and killing and wounding another 10. The lieutenants in E and F decided to independently begin withdrawal to the main road, which they did, picking up stray Rangers en route while missing others.

Hearing the firing, Petty decided to withdraw his outpost. His movement triggered a meeting engagement where he hit the Germans from the rear, causing great momentary confusion, allowing his party to get to the road unscathed. Company D held its position and was ignorant of the others actions. The Germans held in place and did not pursue. Lomell recalled:

> We heard a lot of firing from the east but had no idea what was happening. We were also getting engaged. It wasn't until daylight we knew we were alone. I sent a runner back to ask for instructions and was told to hold in place. Most of the 7th, we were left alone but used a lot of naval gunfire to keep the Germans off of us.

Gathered on the road, the remainder of E and F moved back to the point where Rudder placed them within the battery casemates to hold a line facing south. Dawn was breaking.

Company D had 12 men on the road. Lomell and Kirchner moved everyone to the relative safety of the hedgerows where they hid the entire day of 7 June. Several other Rangers, abandoned by their elements in haste, remained hidden in the hedgerows to be finally reunited on 8 June.

By dawn on 7 June, Rudder's initial force of 200 was reduced to approximately 90 effectives. They were held in place by constant German pressure and rapidly running out of ammo, food, and medical supplies. Only the Company D element was forward positioned.

Eikner and Berger kept a constant salvo of destroyer fire screening the southern approach, isolating the battery from German penetration. Company D adjusted fire, much of it blindly by sound. All the veterans I talked to confirmed that the naval gunfire was absolutely crucial in saving their position.

Around 1700, 7 June, a re-supply Higgins boat landed on the beach. It had critical supplies and a Ranger platoon of 20 men who were quickly placed on line. Wounded were removed and everyone resupplied to some degree.

With the arrival of this element, Rudder directed companies E and F to return to the highway and set up positions astride the highway and facing south. The command post had just established contact with the relief force and wanted to be in position to link up.

Around 0800 on 8 June, the Rangers saw several tanks approach from the east accompanied by infantry. This was the composite force of 5th Rangers, the 116th Infantry, and the 742nd Tank Battalion. Rudder's Rangers were finally relieved.[3]

The cost had been significant. Of the original 225 Rangers who scaled the cliffs, 77 were killed and 152 wounded. Another 38 were listed as missing. Of the 90 effectives, 79 of them sustained wounds. In casualties also, Rangers sadly led the way.

---

3   I attended a number of Ranger reunions between the 2nd and the 5th, held at Grandcamp. It was evident that there was still considerable rancor between the two as to why the 5th didn't reinforce. While many of the 2nd understood why, they really, in their hearts, did not understand why they were not reinforced on D-Day.

Ranger Task Force Bravo

Task Force B, consisting of companies A, B, and C of the 2nd Rangers under command of Captain Ralph Goranson, offloaded from the HMS *Prince Charles* at approximately 0430 on 6 June. The force of 200 men had two separate missions. Companies B and C would move immediately inland and assist the Rangers in seizing Pointe du Hoc. Company B with 65 men would have a separate mission to eliminate the guns at Pointe de la Percée. All three companies would land together on Charlie Beach at the extreme right of Omaha Beach.

As all the Rangers experienced, they became dreadfully seasick and numbed by the constant crashing waves and churning in the rough seas. Quickly, everyone lost their heavy English breakfasts and had to begin bailing with helmets to prevent sinking. This condition lasted for more than two hours when the craft finally made the run in to shore.

The assumption prior to the event was that the 116th Infantry would have the beach cleared prior to the Rangers landing. It did not work out that way, as the enemy always gets to vote.

The Rangers landed approximately where the small pier exists today. They off loaded in the midst of burning Higgins boats, floating bodies, and a hail of fire. Getting off the beach to the relative safety of the cliff face cost more than 50 percent of the force.

Dragging what wounded they could, the remnants of three companies, now reduced to less than 35 effectives, moved further west, finding shelter from the fire in a narrow niche of the cliff. The leadership was reduced to two lieutenants and two platoon sergeants.

They noted that the niche, quite narrow, but of firm ground, opened all the way to the top of the cliff. This seemed to be a way off the beach. Quickly, the two lieutenants and NCOs took ropes and bayonets and began to climb using each other's backs as bracing up the narrow passageway.

Reaching the top, they noted that they were actually flanking the German defenses. There was a trench along the crest but it was unoccupied. They could hear the bunkers firing to the east and could clearly see the defenses as well as the beach itself. They lowered ropes and within 30 minutes brought up the remainder of the Rangers, leaving the wounded below with a medic.

The mission had been to move overland, west, to link up with the 2nd battalion at Pointe du Hoc. But in the words of a former lieutenant veteran: "We were damned mad and saw an opportunity to kill Germans. We decided we would do that and then go to the point."

The first thing they did was rope down the cliff face on top of the concrete bunker that was causing so much damage on the beach and had probably killed a lot of Rangers. They tossed in phosphorous grenades and cleared it with a Thompson submachine gun. That act alone created a significant drop in fire along the beach and removed a major anti-tank gun.

They then began to work along the trench, clearing several positions from the rear. It became a cat and mouse action as Germans would emerge in their rear and engage. Rangers would then have to fight in two directions, which they did.

By noon, the Rangers had progressed to the point where they could overlook the draw at Vierville and see other troops across the large concrete anti-tank barrier blocking the road. These were Rangers from 5th battalion.

Conducting a linkup, Lieutenant Colonel Max Schneider assigned them to his force and began to move out toward Vierville when they were halted by Colonel Charles Canham, regimental commander of the 116th. He ordered the Rangers to hold in place as they were the only viable fighting force he had after his regiment was decimated on the beach. General Cota quickly endorsed this order, forcing all Rangers to halt in place and dig in.

Task Force Bravo, landing with 200 men, was now reduced to less than 40 effectives, but it had been a major force in clearing the defenses and allowing follow on forces to land at Omaha. Selective disobedience to orders had made a good result.

5th Rangers at Omaha Beach

On 1 June, the battalion moved from its sausage to Portland Harbor and boarded its invasion ship, the HMS *Prince Leopold* (with the battalion headquarters, C, D, and F Companies). With the rest of the flotilla, it departed on late 4 June for the planned 5 June invasion. After a hasty callback in very rough weather, the Rangers departed the harbor again on the late evening of 5 June, arriving at their anchorage point midway between Omaha and Pointe du Hoc.

Private First Class Carl F. Weist, B Company, spoke of the cross-channel trip being like a ferry boat ride.

> We went aboard our transport ship on June 1st. For five days we had nothing to do except gab and speculate on our immediate future. Two one-hour periods each day were spent exercising and of course we had ample literature and maps available to review the whole invasion plan. This long period of idleness and confinement resulted in many rumors. The one I recall especially was this, all troops in the initial landings were green troops, and the landing schedule showed H-Hour. On the basis of this fact, it was said that the big brass expected 80 percent or more casualties during the first part of the landings. Naturally it figured they wanted to save the good outfits and were sending the green boys in to take the beating. Most rumors were of that type, bad.

The troops were wakened at 0300 and immediately fed a glorious English breakfast with all the trimmings. An event they would all later regret. By 0400 they lined the railings in boat order and began to descend the nets to their craft.

The sea was rough with low spitting clouds. It was less than 55 degrees Fahrenheit. The craft were barely able to hold station against the debarking ship, constantly banging against the hull and pitching in the wave action. It was a major task for each overburdened Ranger to guess the best moment to time leaving the cargo net for the leaping craft below. A mistake would break a leg or worse, tossing the Ranger into the sea for a pounding between the craft and the larger hull.

These were British commando assault craft modified from Higgins boats. They had large steel plates fixed to the side to provide small arms protection. The consequence of this had two parts modification was that the freeboard was reduced from about 4 feet to less than 2 due to the weight. The consequence of this was that waves broke steadily over the craft, requiring almost immediate bailing with helmets on the part of the Rangers.

The high sides blocked side vision which, in turn, created claustrophobia on top of the seasickness. The only vision was ahead to an array of helmets in the front or to the sky, which was indiscernible.

The craft, finally set loose from their mother ships, began circling around behind the bombardment group at 0500 for a touchdown at either Omaha or Pointe du Hoc, depending upon a signal from Lieutenant Colonel Rudder.

Lieutenant Colonel Max Schneider and his radio operator, Staff Sergeant Graves, were in the coxswain's position awaiting a signal from Rudder. No signal or the radio call "Tilt" would send the 5th to Omaha to conduct a landside linkup with the 2nd Rangers.

No signal was given at 0700. At 0710, 10 minutes beyond his deadline, Schneider ordered the three waves of 18 Ranger boats under his command to divert to Omaha Beach with a planned landing at Dog Green behind the 116th Infantry.

Once past the destroyer line, the last line of ships, Schneider could see the havoc wreaked on the first three waves on the beach. The disaster at Dog Green was particularly obvious as it had virtually no movement off of it, a mass of destroyed landing craft bobbing in the surf, and a constant arcing of German green tracers combined with the constant impact of mortar and artillery fire. No obstacles had been cleared. It was about 0730.

Schneider, using his experienced eye, directed the coxswain to shift to the left and land on Dog Red White and Dog Red. He could see this was a relatively unscarred beach area and free of much of the destruction that was piled up further west.

At approximately 0800, the 5th Battalion touched down. The beach presented about 300 yards of open sand and obstacles followed by a seawall and shingle rock to the roadway. Beyond that was about 30 yards of cratered ground to the cliff face.

Despite the lack of infantry defense there, the beach was enfiladed with machine gun and small arms fire. The Rangers surged off the beach, across the road, and gathered themselves in the protection of the cratered ground.

In a fortuitous mix-up, Company C, 1st Battalion, 116th Infantry landed with them, essentially part of the Ranger battalion. For the rest of the day, this company fought with the Rangers as an integral and welcome part.

Behind them, this section of the beach had a series of wooden groins from the high-water line to the low-water line. They were designed to contain the sand and maintain the beach. In this case, they saved a number of Ranger lives by providing protection from the machine-gun fire weaving across the beach. The remnants are still visible today.

As Schneider was collecting his command group, further to the west General Cota noted the reasonably organized line of craft landing and discharging infantry. Who were these troops? Cota walked calmly down the beach, fully exposed as an example for those 29th Division troops still not moving up the cliffs. He was initially greeted by Captain John Raaen, the 5th Rangers Headquarters Company Commander, who directed him to Schneider's position.

Cota moved to Schneider's position. The command group was arrayed in the depression as runners were sent to get the company commanders to organize for the next move up the cliffs. Lieutenant (JG) Ben Berger, the naval gunfire officer, noticed him first.

> This guy walks up behind us, calm as can be with a cigar in his mouth. He stands on the edge of our position and I see he is a general. He shouts over the noise, "Who are you guys?"
> Lieutenant Colonel Schneider turns around and yells back, "We are the Rangers."
> The general then takes the cigar out of his mouth and waves his hand at the cliffs and says, "You guys are Rangers. Lead the way." He then turns around and walks down the beach.

Staff Sergeant Graves, his radio man, years later, recounted the same story:

> This guy comes up behind us calm as a cucumber. Short guy with a beer belly and a cigar in his mouth. I see he is a general. Holy shit. I am next to Colonel Schneider and I jab him, pointing to the general. He turns around and sees him. The general asks who we are and Schneider says, "We're the Rangers." He then says, pointing up the cliff, "You guys are Rangers. Lead the way."
> I could tell Schneider was pissed as that is exactly what he was planning to do when the general showed up. It was all very calm. No big deal, but that is the origin of the Ranger motto.

It was now about 0800. Schneider immediately ordered the battalion to assault the cliffs. Bangalore torpedoes blew gaps and the Rangers began to climb the cliffs. The minefields on the cliff face were partially exposed by erosion from the initial bombardment which gave the Rangers some indication as to the locations. Engineer tape was laid along semi-cleared routes. Regardless, some Rangers lost legs in the climb.

Reaching the top, the Rangers found themselves in a maze of trenches and bunkers, much of which can still be seen today from the top. They began to fan out toward the west in the direction of the Vierville and met heavy resistance. A methodical cleanup process was required, which took the better part of three hours to accomplish until elements reached the draw itself.

As the original plan was to land and assemble at Vierville before going to Pointe du Hoc, Company A, commanded by Captain Charles S. Parker, assumed that was still the plan. He had landed at the extreme left/east of the main body, so he had to infiltrate his company, essentially in flank, toward Vierville. Facing sporadic but effective resistance, his force moved slowly toward the north, skirted Vierville and headed west where it eventually linked with the 2nd Battalion, the only Ranger reinforcements of the day.

When Parker reported to Rudder, he had only 22 of the original 65 and three of those were mis-dropped 101st troops. Rudder placed him on the road blocking the eastern approach. This was unknown to Schneider who understood Company A was missing, and had assumed they went to Pointe du Hoc but was not sure.

During this period, about 0930, the destroyers moved in and began to bombard targets on the cliffs. Schneider was very concerned about friendly fire and had a Ranger party on the cliff face move forward with a flag to indicate the Ranger position. The fire was extremely helpful in suppressing the major German strongpoints and no Rangers were known to be hit by friendly fire.

By noon, the cliff defenses were cleared between Dog Green and Charlie Beaches and subsequent waves began to land in orderly fashion and moved toward their objectives under less than effective enemy fire. The cliff defenses had been reasonably cleared by Rangers from 2nd and 5th Ranger battalions with augmentation from Company C, 1-116th Infantry, and individuals and small groups of the 116th, though neither Ranger element had that as part of their mission.

Upon reaching the draw, Schneider moved the 5th, now in a loose column, across the road to the west, approximately where the bridging material rests today. He linked up the remains of Task Force Charlie, reduced to less than 50 effectives and formed a single 2nd Battalion company in reserve. His plan was to clear Vierville and move toward Pointe du Hoc.

The Germans held Vierville and the road west in some strength. It took constant maneuver and fighting to clear the resistance nodes. By 1500 the battalion had moved less than a half mile from Vierville when Colonel Charles Canham of the 116th Infantry Regiment arrived at the 5th Battalion command post.

Canham ordered the Rangers to hold in place as they were the only cohesive element he had to hold Vierville until further reinforcements could be landed in relief. Graves explained to me:

> Schneider protested that Rudder and the 2nd needed him and that we had no idea even if the 2nd held Pointe du Hoc. Canham was calm but very clear: "You must hold here. I don't have anyone else."

Shortly after, Cota came up the road and reaffirmed what Canham had said. The colonel was mad but understood orders. He told the commanders to hold up and establish a defensive line until relieved.

5th Rangers spent the night of 6 June as the westernmost U.S. element at Omaha. The 116th Infantry was reduced to packets of men recovered after the beach was cleared and reconstituted on the high ground. Elements were tied in with the 5th.

During the day of 7 June, the Rangers were fully engaged in clearing operations at the Vierville complex as well as the several outlying farms that blocked access to the main highway. The Germans fought a skillful rear-guard action using the hedgerows and stone buildings to maximum advantage.

On the morning of 8 June, Canham ordered the 116th Infantry and the Rangers, augmented by armor, to begin movement west to relieve the Rangers at Pointe du Hoc, collect them, and then clear Grandcamp Maisey, a strongly held German headquarters and artillery complex.

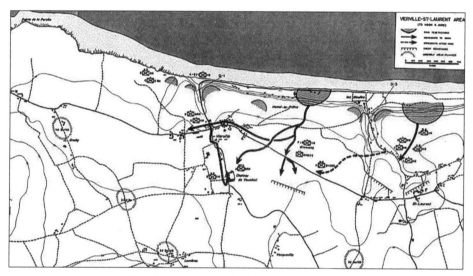

The advance position of 5th Rangers on D-Day.

CHAPTER 18

The British Airborne on D-Day

Getting In

I met and talked to the men behind these stories—Hill, Otway, Crookenden, and Howard. I was struck by their strength of character even through the clouds of 40 years. These were personalities that could and did lead through extreme adversity.

It took approximately 2,500 transport aircraft to drop three Airborne divisions. The Americans exclusively used the C-47 transport. The British used a combination of C-47s and converted bombers. Concurrently, the U.S. used no gliders in the initial assault whereas the British led with gliders for two surprise assaults on key German positions: Pegasus Bridge and the Merville Battery.

For these discrete events, the pilots picked were first class and trained with the assault infantry.

Brigadier Hill commented:

> The only way we could take Pegasus was with gliders. Parachuting was too problematical. We had faith in the pilots and they proved us right.
>
> Merville was a bit different. My intent was to initiate the assault with the glider landing which we had practiced. However, that part was not crucial, unlike Pegasus, which we proved. To this day, I cannot tell you why the pilots cocked up.

When loaded, the larger Horsa gliders required greater horsepower than the C-47 could comfortably provide. The U.S. planned for significant glider supply and reinforcement in the early morning and afternoon of 6 June.

The total force for the initial insertion had the three divisions scattered over 25 airfields. The troops had deployed to these airfields between 25 May and 4 June depending upon the element. This meant that each battalion of each regiment was usually assigned to a specific airfield. While this scattered the units within the regiments, their prior training and reasonable proximity to each other retained cohesion.

The challenge for the air staff was in coordinating this massive sky train of more than 2,500 troop carriers. The schedule had the first aircraft from Tarrant Rushton with the Pegasus force to be dropped at 0020 and the final assault lift for a 0430 drop of support elements of 9 Para from Brize Norton. In between, the fighting forces of all three divisions were lifted.

The challenge was in managing the stream to arrive at the right place at the right time within the entire flow. The British aircraft, depending upon type, were both faster and slower than the unbridled C-47s. The relative distance from each airfield combined with airspeed and objective time had to be precisely calculated with such a huge force in the airstream.

These calculations had to be managed with the fighter escort as well as the many bomber squadrons. In sum, between 2200 and 0430 of 6 June, more than 4,800 aircraft were flying on several relatively narrow streams more than a hundred miles in depth coming and going. Hill told me:

> It was a truly amazing experience to look out and see the mass going to France. It was inspirational to say the least. This was a big party and we could see the players for the first time.

Regardless of nationality or mission, the ultimate planeside experience was quite similar. Troops were assigned a specific "chalk" (plane), gathered their gear, and went to it. In some cases they walked, in others they were trucked. The gear was excessive by any measure, often doubling the weight of the jumper.

Each trooper had a weapon or weapons (rifles could not be used while in the air so many had a pistol or submachine gun in addition). Grenades, personal kit, lowering ropes, and ammunition ranging from small arms to machine gun to mortar rounds were added. Food, water, medical bandages, and morphine added to the weight. Specific tasks would add more, such as demolitions, medical supplies, signals, and Pathfinder gear, all attached in some form.

Beginning at 0020, the aluminum armada began to form and move toward France. It was still somewhat light and the men could see the naval elements below with their wakes, the many fighter escorts weaving through the formation and the tightly packed transport aircraft around them. The planes flew less than 20 yards between wingtips and less than 50 yards above and below other aircraft. Troopers could see the faces of their brothers through the portholes on the side.

Leading the entire pack were John Howard's Ox and Bucks.

Pegasus Bridge

Assembled at RAF Tarrant Rushton, the force moved to the aircraft on the afternoon of 4 June in pouring rain. John Howard wrote in his diary, "The weather's broken—what cruel luck. I'm more downhearted than I dare show. Wind and rain, how long will it last? The longer it goes on, the more prepared the Huns will be, the greater the chance of obstacles on the LZ. Please God it'll clear up tomorrow."

On 5 June, the weather had indeed improved and D Company prepared to board their gliders. Major Howard watched them: "It was an amazing sight. The smaller chaps were visibly sagging at the knees under the amount of kit they had to carry."

At 2256, still in daylight, Howard's glider took off, followed at one-minute intervals by the remainder of the coup de main force. Howard was prone to airsickness and had vomited on every training flight that he had participated in. He was not sick on this flight, because the prospect of going into battle for the first time was enough to steady his nerves.

The six gliders carrying the force were towed by Halifax bombers. Despite considerable pitching and yawing of the aircraft and general discomfort, the flight was uneventful and the tow aircraft made their release points exactly on time.

The pilots, trained to extreme, piloted their craft in several looping legs and turns to drop altitude and airspeed and to get a final fix on their very small target. An error could see a glider landing in water or woods.

The river and canal were easily spotted in the bright moonlight and there was no flak. On the final leg, the pilots called "BRACE" and guided their gliders into controlled crashes. Each aircraft save one landed exactly on spot or better. The sixth slightly missed but was close enough to do the job.

The three gliders for the Pegasus Bridge breached the wire defenses and stopped inside the German positions. However, the landings were extremely rough, with both of Howard's pilots thrown through the cockpit canopy and all its passengers left dazed.

Howard's seatbelt had broken and the impact threw him across the glider and the ceiling, which jammed his helmet down over his eyes. Later, on the 40th anniversary of D-Day, Howard recalled,

> I was knocked unconscious on landing. I lay on the floor and seemed to wake up but I couldn't see anything. I wasn't sure if I was alive or dead. I pushed my helmet up which was jammed across my nose and saw light. The bloody thing had blinded me. I recovered and scrambled out into the night to the sound of firing.

Upon recovery, Howard moved immediately to his planned location with his radio operator. He was able to receive information from the other gliders and see the first platoon in action as it cleared the bridge and moved across toward Benouville and the Gondree café. It was during this period that they sustained the first death, when platoon leader Den Brotheridge was killed.

Quickly, Howard received news that all three of the platoon leaders had been wounded and were out of action. However, the NCOs took charge and all the immediate objectives were taken. Soon, he learned that the Orne River bridge had also been successfully seized.

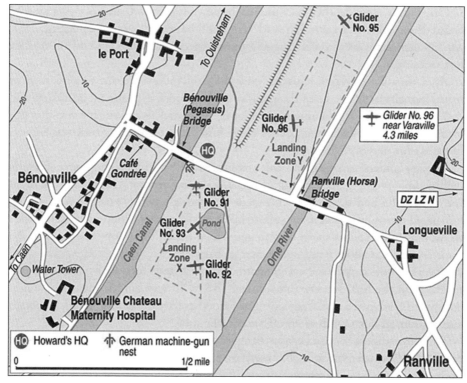

Ranville and Pegasus bridges.

He turned to his wireless operator, Corporal Tappenden, and directed him to send the success message, "Ham and Jam." Tappenden, sitting below Howard in the position, began to tap on his wireless. Howard, full of adrenalin, steadily beat on Tappenden's helmet saying Ham and Jam. Ham and Jam. Tappenden remembered,

> I was sending the message and the major was beating my helmet to the point that I couldn't concentrate on the Morse. I looked up and told him to quit beating on me, that I was sending the message. He looked startled, apologized, and stopped.

Howard made a quick assessment and saw that there was no resistance in the Orne Bridge area. Accordingly, he decided to focus on defending the road into Benouville as the most likely German counter-attack direction.

The initial assault force cleared the bridge and moved past the Café Gondree. Taking some casualties, the platoon leader, an NCO following the death of Brotheridge, went into the café to use it as a protected aid station. Monsieur Gondree and his family had been sheltering in the cellar and now came up. Upon hearing

English, the family went into temporary ecstasy and showered thanks on the men. Monsieur Gondree went into his garden and uncovered a cache of champagne he had been hiding since the occupation. He insisted all the men take a cup and it took some time to get the unit back to order. Meanwhile, Madame Gondree cleared an area for the doctor and medics to work. She and their daughter acted as nurses throughout the night.[1]

Howard directed an infantry platoon with a PIAT anti-tank weapon to defend the traffic circle just on the other side of the Café Gondree. He arranged a further 360 defense and waited for relief by 7 Para.

Shortly, the men could hear the clatter of tank tracks approaching. A tank emerged from the road and entered the traffic circle, searching for the defenders. The man on the PIAT had never fired it before and he would only get one shot. The range in the dark was less than 20 yards. He fired when the tank got within 10 yards and managed a miracle hit on the turret ring, the most vulnerable part. The tank stalled, caught fire, and the crew bailed out. The trailing armor pulled back, uncertain as to the strength and composition of the defenders. This respite would not last.

At approximately 0240, the 7th Battalion arrived at Pegasus Bridge. Major Howard was immediately informed and, setting off towards the bridge, he met Lieutenant Colonel Richard Pine-Coffin and gave him a full report on the situation. The arrival of the 7th Battalion allowed Howard to pull his force back tighter around the bridges and end their patrolling activities. In essence, the force became the 7th Battalion's reserve company. Howard explained:

> I was greatly relieved when 7 Para showed. The men were somewhat spent and I knew we had a tough road ahead. I ordered a more restricted defensive arrangement as we had lost so many officers. I wanted to be in a position to assist any if we got into trouble.

By 0800, the sky was clear and the sounds of the initial beach bombardment had passed. Aircraft flew overhead and did low flybys checking the status. No reinforcements had yet arrived.

At approximately 0900, Major General Gale, accompanied by Brigadiers Nigel Poett and Hugh Kindersley, approached the bridges from the direction of Ranville and, in spite of the sniping all around the area, casually strolled over, offering words of congratulation. They had a brief conversation with Howard and moved on. Howard added:

> Suddenly we had the division commander and several brigade commanders just stroll through our position as on a Sunday walk. I was a bit perplexed but the men took great comfort on their presence as did I.

---

1   In 1977, my wife and I visited the café and Madame Gondree walked us to the bridge and recounted in broken English the night and what it meant for her and her family. Even with the passage of time, it was clear the fervor and significance of the moment had not been extinguished.

Just after Gale and company left, the defenders were assaulted by German gunboats, more yachts with guns than formal naval craft. The Ox and Bucks as well as the 7th Paras opened up. Both were put out of action and several prisoners taken.

At 1000, the Germans made an attempt to destroy the bridges from the air. The first bomb scored a direct hit, but failed to explode. Shortly after, the Germans fired rockets from the Nebelwerfer rocket launchers. While impacting around the bridge and forcing everyone to cover, the bridge remained unscathed.

Meanwhile, 7 Para, at less than 50 percent assembled strength, was engaged in a major fight on the Benouville road. General Gale personally told Howard to send a platoon to assist 7 Para in holding the Germans. Howard did so immediately and reconfigured his defenses with the loss of a platoon.

Throughout the morning, German snipers constantly harassed the men near the bridge. A large multi-storied building on the other bank, less than 300 yards away, was their principal position. This was a mental and maternity hospital operated by an order of nuns. The Germans occupied the roof and the top floor.

Their fire was seriously impacting movement and Howard ordered a solution. A member of his command group swung a German 75mm anti-tank gun around and fired three rounds at the top floor. There was a heavy impact of the rounds and the sniping ceased.

Around 1300, the men at Pegasus could hear the skirling of the pipes as Lord Lovat's commandos made their way up from the beaches concurrent with another German infantry attack.

With rounds pinging off the girders, Lovat crossed the bridge and met Howard. Howard recalled:

> We heard the pipes and knew it was Lovat. What a relief. We could see the whole show was tricky at this point and their arrival did wonders for morale. We were no longer on our own.

Brigadier James Hill and Ranville Ridge

Hill and the 3 Brigade Headquarters departed from RAF Down Apney for a programmed 0056 landing. Hill had carefully studied the flight path over France and could see he was almost over Cabourg, several miles from his intended drop zone. There was considerable visible flak, so when the green light came on his stick jumped.

He described it as a cloudy but moonlit night as his parachute opened with a heavy jerk. To his horror, he saw he was over a clearly flooded area and would be in the drink. Depth unknown. He splashed in about 5 feet of water, initially going under and then pushing himself up as his feet found footing.

> I didn't know if I should be enraged or thankful I wasn't drowned. I was bloody mad as I knew we were not where we needed to be.

There was an immediate sound of gunfire. One of his bodyguards had accidentally shot another. To make matters worse, the many tea bags Hill had cached in his jump smock were thoroughly soaked. Hill explained:

> It was almost a comedy. My bodyguards shoot each other and I lose my precious tea bags. I took several hours to get to dry land and I was making tea the whole way.

Hill and his stick, along with several others, had landed in a large flooded valley. Prior to the flooding, it had been low pastureland delineated by numerous wire fences and ditches, all hidden underwater until discovered in movement.

The fences caught the troopers, struggling in 4 or 5 feet of water with full gear, as did the deep ditches. Hill instructed everyone, now about 40 men, to take out their lowering toggle ropes, each 10 feet long, and tie into each other. That allowed a snagged or underwater trooper to be recovered. In this slow and methodical manner, Hill's group finally reached dry land around 0600. Hill recalled:

> It was a bloody hard slog and I was extremely angry we were not where we ought to be. I controlled myself as best as possible and focused on getting out of the flood and about our business.

Finally free of the flood, Hill proceeded to his assembly area where he was met by the Canadian battalion who reported they had captured the German headquarters nearby. With no functioning radio, Hill focused on the result of the 9 Para Merville assault.

He took his sodden troops and moved toward where 9 Para was supposed to be. This would bypass his intended headquarters position on Ranville, but the priority in his mind was Merville. His party crossed the seaward side of Ranville in its movement.

Shortly after exposing themselves in passage, they were attacked by several Spitfires, who had mistaken them for Germans. A combination of bombs and machine guns wreaked havoc among the party, injuring or killing more than a third of the group. Hill himself was severely wounded on his back but still mobile.

Hill ordered a quick treatment of the wounded and ensured that all received morphine as needed as he moved toward 9 Para.

> It was simply awful and I hurt like hell. But I had to get on with it. I told the survivors to fix up the wounded as best as possible, strip the dead of medical kit. I was determined to find 9 Para and get on with the job. I looked back and the chaps were giving us a cheer as we moved off. I will remember that the rest of my life.

Around 1000, Hill and his party found the 9 Para aid station with the doctor, Major Watts. Watts reported that Merville had been successfully taken and Otway was moving toward his next objective. The doctor did not know any specifics in terms of casualties but did note that Hill looked quite poorly, a comment not well received.

They had an exchange and Watts surreptitiously gave Hill a shot of morphine while applying a bandage. Hill slept for more than two hours. Hill told me,

> Dr. Watts was a good man but I didn't appreciate being knocked out in the middle of the fray.

Coming awake, Hill determined he was immobile. The wound had stiffened his lower extremities. He decided that he needed to proceed to Division HQ near Ranville despite his condition. His men found a bike and pushed him to Ranville, a distance of more than two and a half miles. There, at 1300, he met General Gale, who informed him that his brigade had met all its tasks.

At this same meeting, the division doctor, Colonel Malcolm MacEwan, gave Hill a quick exam and demanded that he endure a short procedure to sew shut his wounds. As this would involve general anesthesia, Hill was very concerned that he would be evacuated. Accordingly, he extracted a promise that upon waking, the doctor would personally accompany him to Hill's headquarters, which he did.

En route in the doctor's jeep, several Germans crossed the road in front of them. The doctor and his assistant stopped and pursued the Germans to no avail. Proceeding on, they finally found Hill's headquarters at dusk. Hill, on being confronted by his administrative officer about his wound, established very clear instructions that no aid would be administered that rendered him unconscious or subject to evacuation.

Hill, with no radio yet, sent runners to his several battalions to obtain status reports and pass instructions. The Canadian paratroopers and the 9th were within a mile and 8 Para more than two miles. However, once everyone was aware of each other's location, things returned to near normalcy. Hill explained:

> It was a great relief to finally be in a position to be the commander. Muddled as it all was with mis-drops, lack of radios, and my injury, I felt some degree of comfort and confidence. It was rather like what being in a parachute unit was all about.

Hill was for the first time able to take stock of his brigade. 9 Para had about 90 men left of the 650-plus programmed to jump. The Canadian battalion was close to 75 percent strength and 8 Para had about 280 out of 500 men. Much of the support material, signaling, mortars, medical, and engineering equipment was lost. In sum, he had a weak brigade of less than 50 percent effectives.

The brigade mission, by late 6 June, was to occupy the high ground near Chateau Saint Côme once relieved by a commando battalion from division reserve. The commandos never arrived as General Gale had held them back due to strong German counter-attacks against his headquarters. Hill had no choice but to leave the chateau grounds to fate while he tried to reconstitute his forces.

During this period, just at dusk of D-Day, the primary glider reinforcement of the division occurred in plain view to everyone. Hill recalled:

It was a great sight and a major boost to morale. We knew we would be getting more of our missing materials and people and showed we were here to stay. I could now plan with some degree of confidence. It was a sight to remain forever.

Much of the brigade and division supporting elements did not land until later that day at approximately 2100. Crookenden noted:

> I was rather put out having to wait until the very last lift but that was my job. We had the long-distance communications, medical and logistical support, as well as what would be badly needed supplies. Due to aircraft limitations, the assault force was quite limited to just assault troops and minimal additions. The commanders were pretty much just themselves and a batman.
>
> We took off from Brize Norton in a Horsa and had an uneventful flight. We landed quite smoothly and went off to business. So far, it was more of an exercise than a war for me. That would change.

By the afternoon of 7 June, 9 Para was relieved and moved toward Chateau Saint Côme. Otway and Hill agreed that the intended area was far too much for his depleted battalion. Instead, the ground would be outposted and the gaps covered by constant patrolling. It was a risk but one they had little choice but to take. Beginning on the morning of 8 June, the risk would be demonstrated. Otway said:

> I made it clear that we were being asked to act as a full battalion when we were at best, 30 percent strength. General Hill understood but had no choice, nor did we.

During the period 6–7 June, the Germans were able to assess the nature of the invasion, its locations, and the relative strengths against them. It was also a period where the immediate German reinforcements could be sent to best effect. One of those units was the fresh 346th Panzergrenadier Division.

This division had a full complement of tanks and armored halftracks for the infantry, all supported by artillery and mortars. Its first task was to clear Otway's unit off of Ranville and unhinge 6th Airborne defenses.

Initial probing attacks focused on Hill's headquarters at Le Mesnil farm. These were unsuccessful but gradually depleted Hill's immediate defenses to the point where he had to ask Otway to send assistance in the form of 30 men. Only because of the timely arrival of these men in the rear of the attacking Germans was the position saved.

The tenuousness of the situation caused General Gale to send the 5th Black Watch Battalion to Hill. The plan was for the 5th to attack and clear the area on the ridge focused at Chateau Saint Côme, presently held by Germans. Hill then tasked a depleted 9 Para to seize and hold the chateau and pass through the Black Watch.

Otway attacked at dawn on the 11th, forced out the Germans, and established a thin holding line. The Black Watch passed through and attacked Breville where

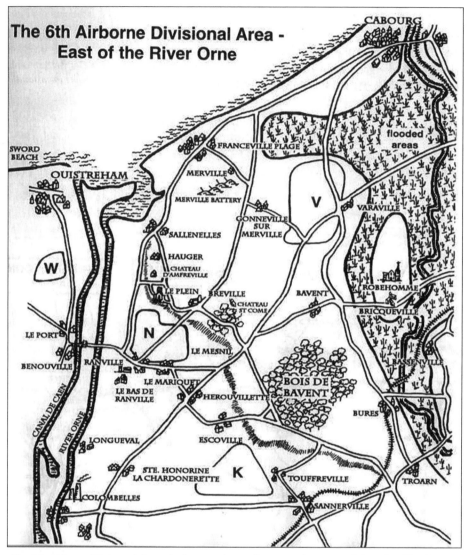

The 6th Airborne Divisional Area, the lower right quadrant was the responsibility of Hill's 3d Paras.

they were severely mauled. Hill ordered them back to Chateau Saint Côme where their depleted ranks joined 9 Para for an expected counter-attack.

On the 12th, the Germans launched a strong attack. Leading with artillery and armor, the German infantry mounted steady attacks against several points that Otway and the Black Watch held. Casualties began to mount and ammunition was running low. The pressure forced the British to slowly retreat until only the chateau defenses existed. At that point, Otway sent a message to Hill asking for assistance. Hill described this to us while standing in an open area at the chateau that overlooked the lower portion of Ranville:

> I had been quite anxious all day. The Germans were pressing us on all fronts and I was running out of manpower to respond. I got the message from Otway and knew immediately he must be in serious trouble. The chateau was the linchpin of our defense and we couldn't afford to lose it. I got a company from the Canadian paras and whatever I could find in my own headquarters and took them to the chateau.

Hill personally led this force, pistol in hand, to the chateau. There, the fighting was raging in the woods. Black Watch troops were giving ground. Hill led his men in flank and began to restore the position. He then went back and gathered a sapper element he had at his headquarters and brought them up to bolster the defense.

It was apparent that the Germans would counter-attack very soon. A naval gunfire element was brought up and began to provide heavy fire in support of the defenders. This caused the Germans to back off for the moment. Hill had retained his position, but at a cost. The ability to hold the ground was quite tenuous. Hill went on:

> The naval gunfire was a godsend. It completely disrupted the Germans, allowing us to hold. I was now able to manage the brigade, but I was seriously concerned as to what we could do with a major German counter-attack. I had run out of forces and we were very thin.

Key to the German ability to mount attacks against Ranville was the village of Breville, which held the core of the 346th Division. Gale coordinated a massive artillery barrage against the position and sent in 12th Para from 5 Brigade. Taking heavy casualties, the village was cleared and the division settled down to a holding situation. While resupply was available, virtually no replacements arrived to fill the units. Some stragglers were recovered over time but not in significant numbers. Hill added:

> We held but barely. I redistributed men as best I could and made some adjustments as to the ground. The Germans took very heavy casualties and I was quite pleased with the work we had done.

Merville Battery

Much of the discussion below came from the staff ride conducted by Brigadier General James Hill and Lieutenant Colonel Terence Otway on site in June 1984. After, he and General Napier Crookenden talked to my officers and those of the Parachute Regiment in greater detail. Their consummate strength of personality and command was well exhibited.

Everything that could go wrong did.

Otway's lead element, a Pathfinder unit jumping ahead of the main body from RAF Harwell, landed correctly, but broke most of the Rebecca gear upon landing.

Concurrently, a major heavy bomber attack raised huge clouds of dust over the drop zone area, making it very difficult for pilots to see landmarks.

Jumping with the Pathfinders, the recce and clearing parties also landed relatively intact. They immediately moved toward Merville as planned.

German flak opened up in strength, further effecting pilot performance. Once the Channel was crossed, facing the fire and the obscured ground, planes made their own decision regarding the green light location. The formation quickly dissolved over land.

At 0045, Otway's force arrived in the area. Making independent decisions, planes jettisoned troops as they saw fit. One stick was dropped 30 miles from the drop zone and others were scattered over a very wide area. Any semblance of an organized drop was lost but Otway did not yet know it. Otway recalled:

> We could see the flak everywhere and the plane pitching about. We got the red light and then the green light and got out. I found myself landing almost in a German headquarters. We fired on the way down and put it out of commission. But it was clear to me were mis-dropped. It took me more than an hour to get to our assembly area and we had almost nothing there.

The glider forces, loaded with the heavy equipment for breaching and demolitions as well as the supporting mortars and machine guns, had a similar experience. Several were lost over the Channel and most of the others were scattered well away from the drop zone.

By 0230, there were about 150 men assembled of the 700 planned. They had recovered some para-pack bundles with ammo and some Bangalore torpedoes but nowhere near the programmed amount.[2]

Otway waited until 0250 and then moved out. The requirement to take the battery before 0430 was foremost in his mind. He explained:

> We had a dog's breakfast at that point but I was determined we would do what we had to do even if it was only my batman and myself.

The party moved through flooded fields and occasional German patrols but finally arrived at the intended crossroads. It was marked by a large concrete calvary cross and had been picked from aerial photos due to its obvious visibility. To the rear were the woods of Ranville Ridge and to the front, somewhat lower, was the battery and the town of Merville. In the moonlight, the battery was completely visible.

At the cross, Otway met Major George Smith, the advance force commander. Smith had cut four paths through the outer concertina and cleared them of mines

---

2   At this point in the staff ride discussion, one of my men asked: "Sir, what were you thinking at this moment when you knew your force wasn't there?" Otway looked at the man with the full command of his personality and said: "Failure is not an option in the Parachute Regiment. We would go with what we had." With that, he turned to us and continued his discussion.

through hand probes. There being no marking tape, boot tracks indicated the way in. There was one Vickers heavy machine gun. No other heavy weapons were available.

Smith reported this as well as the fact that the Germans were fully awake and in their positions, as the earlier bombing runs and flak had put them on alert. Otway now had to decide how to take the battery with a vastly depleted force.

> At that moment I knew any change to the basic plan would be a mess. I was determined to stick with the original which we all knew by heart but just to do it with less. It would either succeed or not. It was that simple.

Otway's plan was simple. The infantry would advance in two elements on the cleared lanes, each divided into two assault elements; in sum, one for each of the four casemates. The Vickers would provide support on the flank. Otway and his batman would be the diversionary force at the gate.

As soon as the gliders landed, the party would blow the inner wire and assault. Otway's hope was that speed and violence would make up for numbers.

He briefed his force, which quickly moved out and awaited the gliders.

At 0415 the gliders appeared and disappeared. One crash landed well into the woods more than a mile away. Another flew over the battery and continued on to a field well outside the perimeter. The third broke its tow in England and never appeared. At that point, Otway ordered the Bangalore torpedoes to be fired, shouting: "Everybody in! We're going to take this bloody battery!"

The men arose, running and firing at their assigned casemates. German machine guns cut into them but were quickly silenced by the heavy Vickers. The great emotion and élan carried the survivors to the battery positions, which they grenaded and occupied. It was approximately 0455. Hill said:

> Well, we did it. I knew we had considerable casualties but my focus was on getting a signal out to *Arethusa* before it fired on us.

The battalion signal officer, Captain Loring, released a pigeon with the success message. It circled and then obediently flew toward England where it successfully landed. Loring also undertook a timelier signal by firing a yellow Very flare skyward. It was not the agreed upon green star cluster from the non-existent mortar but the *Arethusa* understood and did not fire. Now the force had to destroy the guns and move out.

The guns, thought to be the Skoda 150mm howitzers, turned out to be older Czech 100mm guns. Missing the major engineer demolition kits, the men improvised using the Gammon grenades against the sighting and traversing mechanisms. Otway then gathered up his men and 20 German prisoners and moved toward his next objective, the town of La Plein.

The cost had been high. Otway had only 75 left of the original 150 who were reasonably fit to fight. More than 65 had been killed or wounded. Otway had the physically able carry the wounded to the calvary cross and a nearby barn where the surgeon and medics could begin to care for them. The surgeon, who had lost much of his kit on the drop, operated with a razor blade.

Within the battery position, now abandoned by the paras, the Germans began to emerge. Most of the men had retreated to within the underground tunnel complex, which was not cleared by Otway in his haste to get out. The position was littered with more than 80 dead and wounded.

The German battery sergeant major, the ranking man present, quickly re-organized the position and went about attempting to restore some of the guns.

Knowing that the battery was still formally uncleared, General Gale ordered its occupation. 3d Commando from the 1st Commando Brigade attacked on 7 June and was severely repulsed. Repeated attempts to breach failed and the commandos fell back.

General Gale, aware that the battery was not in a position now to do extreme damage, decided that an isolation of the position was the best approach. No further attacks were ordered. The battery held out until 17 August with its personnel retreating with the main German army.

Meanwhile, a severely depleted 9 Para moved toward La Plein and attacked as planned. The objective was strongly held and Otway could only take half the village and had to hold in place. Later that day, 6 June, the 1st Commando Brigade relieved Otway. Otway concluded:[3]

> Well, we did it [Merville]. Brigadier Hill was unaware at the time of the extent of casualties and mis-drops until I was able to see him face to face. I was getting these messages from people to do this, do that, as if I was a full up battalion which I bloody well was not. He was quite understanding and gracious as we had to get on with it [the war]. I picked up some stragglers and moved off to my defensive position on the ridge. I was damn proud of the men. I just wished there were more.

---

3   At this point in his discussion with the officers, I could see he was thinking about his next words as Hill and Crookenden were present.

CHAPTER 19

Mayor Renaud Makes a Decision

The mayor of Sainte-Mère-Église, Monsieur Alexandre Renaud, was awake with the light. He and his wife and three sons had spent the night huddled in a deep trench behind the church, overlooking the town spring. They had been sleeping there for two nights, since the early morning hours of 6 June. A woman, less than 10 feet from the family, had been killed by a German artillery round and in the full sight of the children. Paul and Henri-Jean would remember this. The youngest, Maurice, clutched his mother in silence.

The mayor had spent the night fighting the fire that engulfed a building on the east side of the square and was a crematory for a trooper who fell from the sky into its burning interior. He noted the dead bodies of other paratroopers, hanging limply from the many sycamore trees that graced the church square. He wanted to cut them down, but the fighting was still too intense and he returned to his ditch to await dawn.

Much later, in a liberated Sainte-Mère-Église, he would write a letter to the President of France, Charles de Gaulle, who would agree to award the French *fourragère*, an award in the form of a braided cord, to the 82nd Airborne liberators, a decoration worn today by all members of the division. His wife, Simone Renaud, tended the graves of the liberating soldiers for the rest of her life and rightly earned the title "Mother of Normandy," the mother none of the fallen would ever again know. Renaud's oldest son, Paul, would go on to design the memorial stained-glass windows of the church; the middle son, Henri-Jean, would manage the Airborne Museum and be the principal host for all returning veterans. The youngest son, Maurice, would be chairman of the AVA (Les Amis des Vétérans Américains), the local citizens' group that hosts and feeds every returning Airborne soldier every year.

On 7 June, 1944, the citizens sensed greater security though the fighting was still close-by, as evidenced by the rattle of small arms as well as the boom of occasional German artillery rounds. Regardless, fueled by a combination of anxiety, exhaustion, and curiosity, they begin to leave their basements and protective crannies to see what had transformed their lives. The mayor was determined to gather them and to lead them. He was a veteran of Verdun and tapped into his well of experience and competence in managing difficult situations.

The church was a very busy place. The Airborne doctors and medics had converted it to a hasty clearing station. The pews were beds with plasma bottles hanging throughout the cloister. The doctors had created a small surgical ward where the light was best flowing through the stained glass above, the dove departing in flight, which seemed wholly appropriate. Outside, to the rear of the nave, was a small door opening onto the eastern side of the square. Here and in the recesses of what passes for a garden, the dead were laid in the shadows of the buttresses.

The mayor, mindful of the shadowed remnants of youth he saw in the square earlier, had made a decision and went about implementing it. He walked the streets talking to the emerging citizenry, offering both hope and the simple norms of human communication, which were suppressed for many dark years.

The streets were covered with the trash and debris of close combat. The windows were shattered, walls crumpled, doors smashed, and furniture scattered. The reconstitution of the town will have to await the reconstitution of their spirit.

Close by, he saw the body of a paratrooper, jammed against a telephone pole, a point of curiosity to the citizens. The mayor reflected to himself:

The soldier is young. He has not yet lived his life. But in dying, he has fulfilled the meaning, the future, and the salvation of life for all that he saved this day of days.

He brought a message of hope and future for a humanity that had lost hope. He gave his life that all others could live.

His body was lifeless in the street as the sun rose over the newly liberated citizens. They crept out of their cellars and safety to awaken to the first dawn of freedom in many years. Some walked next to him, stopped, crossed themselves, and gave a silent prayer for the deliverance he and his brothers had given them. An older widow, dressed in black, stopped by a garden on the street and picked some flowers. She stooped by the young soldier's form and gently arrayed them over his chest.

Another person gently shifted the young soldier to his back, untwisted the last agony he endured for them and crossed his stained and dirt-encrusted hands on his belt. They had not yet been wrinkled or freckled with age, nor would they ever be. Empty cartridges are brushed aside.

Down the street, the church padre, who was also tending his flock, joined the mayor, who quietly talked to the citizens he encountered. Behind the mayor was his wife, dressed in a simple cotton dress, and holding her three young children's hands. All were oblivious to the stains of mud and dirt covering them from the night's events, which had been observed from a soggy but protective ditch behind their shop and house on the square. The sensitivities associated with cleanliness and appearance, so endemic in the people, were ground away and forgotten in the events of the night.

The mayor and padre came upon the young soldier and the pair attending to his body, in their way performing an act of contrition and cleansing to a body and spirit that truly needed no such help.

The priest and mayor spoke for a moment and then the mayor quietly moved to several other citizens who had gathered at the scene. Together, they all grasped the body of the fallen paratrooper and his now limp parachute canopy and carried it all to the church. Other parishioners secured the white rectangular box that resided on the edge of the square to accommodate occasional speakers and ceremonies. The box was placed just outside the church door so as not to disturb the hospital within.

The soldier was gently laid on the box and the parachute draped over his body. A breath of wind coursed through the square, lifting the shroud from his face, revealing the youth and vibrancy of this man, among the many who had brought them this moment. The weight slipped the silk past the jumpboot tops, revealing the one part of the soldier uniquely identifying him as one of a very few numbers of delivering angels. He would be symbolic of all those angels that descended that night.

The mayor and the padre smiled. This silent soldier had brought them a life-liberating joy that none there and their future generations would ever forget.

On 8 June, a special mass was held at the front of the church. The padre stood behind the bier and delivered the service. At its conclusion with the communion, each parishioner took a wafer and touched the catafalque silk as they walked to their newly liberated homes.

PART V
Postwar Normandy

CHAPTER 20

A Special Place

The passage of time has done little to diminish the significance of the invasion. If anything, its magnitude in human, physical, and strategic import has never been better appreciated. Without Normandy, there would likely have been a far different Europe and United States than we know today.

The appreciation of Normandy can be felt in two ways—the people and the place. The people were the veterans who landed here and the civilian population they liberated. The few veterans still alive return yearly to visit and to walk the long white marble rows of the cemetery at Omaha and commune with their buddies who didn't go back home. They walk the terrain where they fought and mingle with the ghosts in their mind.

Initially, they came in droves and represented all the ranks from senior generals to privates. Now the ranks are almost empty, with an occasional former 17- or 18-year-old private reminiscing with much younger visitors. If they listen carefully, the tourists will learn something not written down and sense the deep human emotions felt by each soldier who served that day. They all knew they were part of something of over-arching significance and were exceptionally proud that chance placed them there. Their memories are primarily of the soldiers with whom they served, but there is an underlay of the immense stage on which they played. For one brief moment, all were stars and all were heroes—never to be repeated. These were ordinary people doing extraordinary things.

The other people were the French whom they liberated. This is a part of France that is far from the culture and lights of Hollywood France. It is not Paris or Marseille or the warm wine hills of Burgundy and Bordeaux. But it is France and they were the first to be free that cold windy day of 6 June 1944. And they have not forgotten. A visit to Pointe du Hoc, Omaha Beach, Sainte-Mère-Église, Pegasus Bridge, Ouistreham, and the various national cemeteries will find copious numbers of local Normans and school children paying homage to the debt they feel they owe.

Today, the anniversary period is so huge that a large part of the French military and foreign service is engaged. Over a million visitors crowd into the area during the week of events to observe the huge array of memorial ceremonies. These range from the President of France at Utah Beach to the President of the United States at Omaha—with hundreds of lesser stops at all the small villages and isolated farm yards where soldiers came, some to depart and many to stay behind. They are graciously and sincerely remembered.

The physical place of Normandy is equally unique. The population descends from Caesar's legions and Viking raiders. They are quick to point out they are not metropolitan French. They are hefty, strong, hard-working farmers and small business people with strong appetites and equally generous hearts. The relative poverty and isolation of the land has caused many of the battle sites to be almost exactly as they were on D-Day. There is no parking lot covering Antietam here.

The route up the cliffs to the right of Omaha taken by a platoon of desperate Rangers is easily spotted as are the trench works and bunkers once filled by the 352nd German infantry division. If you walk to the edge of the cliff at Pointe du Hoc and look back, you will see what First Sergeant Lem Lomell saw as he led the 2nd Ranger Battalion up those cliffs. The only difference at Brécourt Manor, famous for *The Band of Brothers*, is the missing artillery pieces. Precisely where they were is instantly recognizable. La Fière Bridge, the location of what the Official U.S. Military Historian called "the bloodiest combat per square foot in the war," is almost exactly as it was less the casualties covering most of the visible ground. At Neuville-au-Plain, one can precisely see the ground and its effect on combat as Lieutenant Turner Turnbull and his platoon held off a German regiment the morning of 6 June 1944 and in so doing, saved the 82nd Airborne.

Throughout this land, there are isolated markers, memorials, and plaques. Each identifies a particular unit or person who fought and died for that land so far away from their own. These were placed by both U.S. military and the local French over time. The Normans now tend them full time. Throughout the year they clean the grass, wash the monuments, and place flowers by it. Many are in very isolated, hard to reach places such as the sign which reads: Here Corporal DeGlopper, was awarded a posthumous Congressional Medal of Honor 9 June 1944; or where Lieutenant Colonel Timmes was surrounded in an orchard; or where Private First Class Marcus Heim won a Distinguished Service Cross stopping three German tanks; or where the aid station for the 505th Parachute Infantry Regiment was located on 6–8 June.

These monuments are largely lost to all but the family that owns the land. Regardless, when found by the dedicated tourist, they will be clean, repainted, re-mortared, and usually adorned with flowers. Very few people will know that, but that is irrelevant to the family that tends the ground where others once stood.

Normandy is not just a place and 6 June is not just a date. That small space and date in France is the sepulcher that holds the spirit of what being a soldier is all about. There is no other place like it on earth. It is a well where its visitors, and particularly soldiers, can quench their thirst for pride, purpose, and dedication.

Any trooper that ever wore a uniform will depart with stronger steel in the soul and a recognition of what it took to make that date in time. It resides within them and can be drawn upon to strengthen the soul in whatever place requires a supreme effort for a goodly purpose.

Normandy writ large shows that ordinary people can do extraordinary things. It is the repository of that spark within anyone carrying a rifle with the American flag on his or her shoulder that permits uncommon valor to be a common virtue.

Angels descended from the sky and Olympians ascended from the waters to embody what is best and good about our nation. It is a bond carried within all of us, to be drawn upon when needed in good and noble purposes, the greatest of which is the strength and camaraderie of our participants under the greatest stress on our varied battlefields.

Normandy will not let us forget that bond. The men of D-Day embodied the holy virtue of sacrifice. Despite all of the challenges, these men came again and again to fight and die, if necessary, to achieve victory. They would accept nothing less. In this single expression of the warrior's character, these men embodied the noblest and highest of virtues, the willingness to die for another.

These men marked the point where we all can begin our journey to goodness rather than greatness. The track has a start point, but no end point. Normandy transgresses geography and accompanies any trooper, anywhere—whether in uniform or out.

Normandy connotes both the price and purpose of citizenship.

It is one of the noblest undertakings of our civilization and lives with us today.

The Normans of today have guaranteed that. They preserve the place and spirit for all of us to draw upon.

Thankfully so.

The lack of physical interference since 1944 allows the visitor to become much more deeply engaged by events that occurred at a given piece of land. One can easily visualize where the combatants were, how the ground effected the action, and where casualties were bound to lie. No one who visits Normandy leaves without knowing that this is a special place, made so by special people.

Sainte-Mère-Église

The town of Sainte-Mère-Église, arguably the first town liberated on D-Day, has done two things that epitomize the depth of feeling and generosity of spirit toward their liberators. The city heraldry, drawn some thousand years ago, was changed in 1946 to reflect the recent events. One of the stained-glass windows in the church, made famous by the movie *The Longest Day*, depicts the new town seal. It is that of an 82nd Airborne paratrooper descending from the sky into a burning town square.

Every year, the town hosts active duty and reserve soldiers en masse. Beginning with the 40th anniversary, the town has accepted the soldiers into their homes as billets and fed them for the entire period—usually a full week. A soldier cannot buy a drink or a meal without a French family paying the tab. Recently, this has included airborne soldiers from England and Germany, now a NATO ally. Sainte-Mère-Église would be considered a poor rural town of no particular note but for the immensity of its spirit and generosity. This is not a commercial enterprise. It is led by no one but by everyone.

Each year there is a memorial service at the church of Sainte-Mère-Église. It has honored as few as two Americans and as many as the entire command group of the 82nd Airborne Division. To the French, gathered within the church, it is current events and a recognition of the price paid by hundreds of nameless troopers whose actions allowed these services to be held. This is a joint ecumenical service with the padre and a U.S. Army chaplain. Listen to what is said in both languages. After each mention of casualties, the French will say in strident voice, "Mort pour la France," *We died for France.* They understand.

The church is crammed to capacity. Families from the town and area fill the pews not reserved for the veterans and active-duty troopers. To the side, the church choir sits awaiting their moments. The flags of the Resistance, France, the United States, the U.S. Army and the representative U.S. Divisions are arrayed on both sides of the central nave. This is a relatively small church, dating from the 1200s and stoutly built.

A transfixing sight are the several stained-glass windows emitting a muted light within. They were designed by Paul Renaud, the eldest son of the wartime mayor, at age 19. One depicts St Michael, the patron saint of paratroopers. Another depicts the men descending upon the square and church. *Nous restons ici.* We remain here.

The following is a speech I gave at the Sainte-Mère-Église church on the 75th anniversary of 6 June in a joint service between the citizens of the town and the 82nd active-duty troops and veterans. The Chairman of the Joint Chiefs of Staff, Supreme Allied Commander, Europe, and the commanding general of the 82nd Airborne Division were all in attendance along with a large group of French politicians. Also present were units from the French Foreign Legion and the French military academy, Saint-Cyr, along with Susan Eisenhower and Helen Patton.

> We are here today to commemorate the Airborne soldiers of the 82nd and 101st and what they were and what they did and to express our gratitude for them and their sacrifices. Some died here, some died much later, and all lived for the cause of liberty. Some are precious to the memory of the citizens of Sainte-Mère-Église and the people of Normandy, some are known and precious to only their families, but all are precious to us.
>
> Some still live and carry the flame of remembrance; they are a precious few but we gather here for both the living, the dead and the future of our two nations; here in this exact place, where freedom began 69 years ago today. The price of that freedom, calculated after return to England, was 2,150 killed and 7,436 wounded.

In order to understand the enormity of their accomplishments, let us go back to noon, 6 June 1944, at this very place. The church is full, full of the wounded of the 82nd and 101st, who were felled within walking distance of where we sit. The pews are beds and corpsmen and doctors walk between the aisles fixing plasma bottles, changing bandages, and silently signaling others to carry a deceased soldier to the back street and lay him with all the others gathered that day.

Immediately east of here, less than 300 yards at the fountain, Mayor Renaud's family lies huddled in a trench. The children, Paul, Henri-Jean, and Maurice, are with us today because of that trench.

Earlier, 36 soldiers had jumped into and drowned in the Merderet and 63 others had been wounded and captured. Many more were wounded and still fighting. An entire stick of 23 jumpers simply disappeared—their fate known but to God. The nearly 12,000 jumpers from both divisions were scattered literally from Cherbourg to Omaha Beach. At approximately 0430 that morning, the first reinforcements of more than 1,000 soldiers began arriving by glider for both divisions. They suffered more than 60 percent casualties upon landing due to stone walls and hedgerows. Among the dead was Brigadier General Don Pratt of the 101st, killed less than 4 kilometers from here.

It was not a bright beginning but it began.

To the immediate north at Neuville-au-Plain, Lieutenant Turnbull and 40 others are holding off a reinforced battalion in an action the army historian will call the greatest single small unit action of World War II. Lieutenant Turnbull would return with 16 soldiers, all of whom were wounded. One of those that will not return is Staff Sergeant Robert Niland, who will die at the town, and be the catalyst for the movie *Saving Private Ryan*.

To the immediate south, Major Krause is fending off a German counter-attack, an action that will consume most of the day. He will suffer more than 30 killed between noon and 1800. Before, he had cut the communications cable at the Hotel De Ville, raised the American flag, and removed the bodies of five soldiers hanging from parachutes in this square, killed before they left their parachutes. Inside the burned remnants of the barn across the square are the two bodies of 82nd troopers who flew into the fire that had called the townspeople out and lit the sky for all to see the first descending parachutists. To the west, General Ridgway has just established his command post on the farm just to the west of the present underpass of M-13 and the fork to La Fière. Brigadier General Gavin is just returning from his initial assault and clearing of Chef-du-Pont, which at this moment is not yet secured but under assault from Captain Roy Creek and 36 other soldiers. Captain Creek will secure the bridge at the cost of 14 dead and 23 wounded.

Slightly to his northwest, Lieutenant Colonel Shanley is just moving into a defensive position at Hill 30 with 206 soldiers, including several mis-dropped soldiers from the 101st. He will emerge on the 10th of June with 58 dead and 82 wounded.

To his immediate north around 5 miles away, Lieutenant Colonel Charles Timmes is also digging into hasty defensive positions with his 142 troopers. He will also emerge on 10 June with 65 dead and 45 wounded.

And to our immediate west, and within easy earshot of where we are, a battle has been waged since 0400 that will not cease until noon on the 10th: that of La Fière Bridge and the area of Cauquigny church. Ultimately this action will account for more than 300 dead and 600 wounded. Two battalion commanders are already dead.

To our immediate east, Lieutenant Dick Winters and 30 soldiers have now just cleared Brécourt Manor at a cost of four dead and six wounded.

Further to the southeast, Major General Maxwell Taylor and 65 men have just been met by a captain, the lead element of the 4th infantry division at Pouppeville. After badly scattered drops General Taylor has less than a regiment remaining from what was his division.

At Saint-Côme-du-Mont, Lieutenant Colonel Julian Ewell is attacking the defending *Fallschirmjägers* of the German 6th Parachute Regiment. He will suffer more than 20 dead and 60 wounded in this action.

Well to our south, more than 100 soldiers from the 507th are coalescing out of the swamps upon the small church at Graignes. Some will be executed by the eventually victorious German force.

Much further to the south and west, out of our earshot, there are four mis-dropped soldiers from the 101st. They are hiding in the hedgerows between Omaha Beach and Pointe du Hoc. By 1630, they will encounter 20 U.S. Rangers moving overland from Omaha to reinforce Colonel Rudder at the Pointe. One will be immediately killed and the other three will fight with the Rangers and be wounded.

The names are now forgotten to all but the families. We remember them always for what they did for France and the world. Their average age was 19, but they became family to us all, French and American. Some with blood, all with sweat, and the knowledge that they were part of something much greater than themselves. They gave their all so that we both French and American could be here today. We will not forget them or what they did for all of us—the living and the generations to come.

Amen.

Hémevez

Each year, I go to a special place that encapsulates what Normandy was all about. As time passes, the memories diminish and the significance ebbs into oblivion. There are occasional bursts of "remembrance" that capture a moment in time and permit some symbolic gesture for an historical event largely lost in time. In 2019, presidents, prime ministers, and the panoply of civilization assembled on the week of 6 June to commemorate acts of long ago and to pledge fealty to that spirit and sacrifice. The invasion beaches were be serenaded by bands, banners, and pomp and circumstance. Speeches were made by the elected and appointed leadership of many nations recounting the events and meanings that took place there many years ago. Quickly, the crowds disappeared, the tides continued, and the events forgotten. But the real meaning of Normandy, 6 June 1944, lives on in the obscure rural towns and villages of the Cotentin Peninsula and more honestly reflects the true meaning of the event.

For these people, 6 June 1944 is a current event and a moment and spirit to be honored in perpetuity. This is the French honor to what is truly Memorial Day. Their selfless and profound reverence is the exact point of what our Memorial Day means. It is repeated in virtually all villages of Normandy in honor of those of our nation that died on their behalf. Such a place is Hémevez.

Hémevez is a very small obscure farm town near the more populated city of Picauville. One would have to have an acute desire to visit and a great sense of navigation or be hopelessly lost in order to encounter its environs. Yet, on the slight high ground of the village center resides what the inhabitants believe Normandy and the invasion of 6 June was all about. The hill is dominated by a small church and copse of trees. The church is encompassed by a graveyard several hundred years old and several monuments to the various wars that the men of Hémevez have served in and sacrificed for. The monuments are close to an open farm field and gathered together, much like gravestones of the past. On one edge, in an open sunny place, is a unique stone. It is polished black granite with gold letters. Unlike the others, it is not an obelisk but rectangular. There are words and names incised on it and lettered in gold. Also unlike the others, it has a small gravel walkway leading from the church directly to its front. It truly stands alone among the others and is treated with reverence.

Across the top are the simple words in French, In Remembrance Of The Fallen Soldiers 6 June 1944. Under are seven names—all members of the 507th Parachute Infantry Regiment, 82nd Airborne Division, 6 June 1944 that were executed by the Germans. On that night, at around 0240, 14 soldiers of Headquarters, 1st Battalion, 507th Parachute Infantry Regiment, were mis-dropped over the small village of Hémevez. Seven were captured and executed by the local German unit and seven evaded capture and eventually returned to U.S. lines. One soldier observed the execution from a hidden shell crater. On the back of the monument is the statement in French,

> In memory of the 7 American Parachutists of the 82nd Airborne Division who were executed in the vicinity of this community 6 June 1944

The seven captured were lined up and shot in a field close to the church. The villagers buried those seven within the grounds and later, as the Allies cleared the area, repatriated those bodies. However, the villagers did not forget them or what they signified and built this monument in their memory. Each year, at the anniversary period, the entire village gathers in the churchyard and remembers those teenagers of long ago and what they meant for their grandparents, for them, and their succeeding generations.

This is not a contrived event, as the town is as obscure as a distant rural small village can be. No persons of import, French or American, present themselves except on the rarest of occasions and then often by chance. It is not important to the village. They know why they have assembled and it is important to them.

The sun peaks over the roof of the church. Next to the monument, the mayor stands. A farmer amongst them, he is wearing his best and only suit and tie with a stained shirt and shoes still muddy with the residue of his livelihood. The prefect of the church has a small antiquated CD player. Next to them, in line, are the local historical representatives of the FFI (French Forces of the Interior, which were resistance units during the war), army units, and Foreign Legion with their flags, dressed as simply as the mayor. If there are attendees other than the villagers, the mayor brings them forward in a place of honor. He begins by playing the U.S. National Anthem on the CD, somewhat broken and stuttering in reproduction.

Following protocol, he then plays *La Marseillaise*. Every citizen, as is the French custom, including the flag bearers, sings somewhat lustily and with emphasis. At the conclusion, several of the donkeys in the adjacent field begin to bray, lending a concluding chorus to the affair.

The mayor signals for the CD to be stopped and, ignoring the braying, quietly recounts the events of that night so long ago. It is a simple statement of facts. The villagers stand mute and without gesture, thinking about those words. The mayor then pauses and begins again.

He quietly but clearly reads each name engraved in gold:

PFC Elsworth M. Heck

Private Anthony J. Hitztaler

Private Andrew W. Kling

Private Delmar C. McElhaney

PFC Daniel B. Tillman

Private Robert G. Watson

Private Robert E. Werner

At the conclusion of each name, the villagers in unison and a firm voice state, "Mort pour la France."

After the seventh name is read, the mayor turns to the village priest who issues a short prayer. The villagers cross themselves, quietly turn around and depart. Some linger and drop a flower or bouquet by the monument. The cattle peer through the wire at the event, the donkeys feed in the tall grass, and the sun settles behind the church. Every year the village repeats this ceremony. Every year the villagers repeat the names and remember what they mean to them. This ceremony is unseen by the thousands who visit Normandy, but that is of little importance to the village. They know why they come together and they always will. It's what they do.

Picauville

The small and obscure town of Picauville lies in a beautiful and tranquil valley. It is surrounded by the lush grasses and watercourses that nurture Normandy's cows and horses, both famed throughout France. It is a small oasis of urbanization in an area of rural isolation. Its location causes a spider web of roads to run through it connecting the larger, more prosperous towns and cities of the region. Cars and trucks hurry through to their destinations slowed only by the occasional pedestrian or tractor traversing the main street. But every person and every vehicle that courses on its way must pass what the citizens believe is the soul of their city, its collection of monuments and memories.

One honors the dead of World War I with the names of each loss—losses that must have had a dramatic impact on what was then a very small place. Near it and by the road, inescapable to view, are several others—erected after

World War II and remembering those Americans who fought and died for this small obscure property which for a few mortal moments for them became the most important place on earth.

The town is located on a confluence of roads and rolling hills that lead to greater prizes—the key town of Sainte-Mère-Église, Cherbourg, Utah Beach, and to the south, Omaha, and Saint-Lô. To the villagers at the time, life was tranquil with the rural quiet and loose occupation of German forces. In England, photo interpreters scoured the deluge of images pouring in and became aware that Picauville had far greater importance than the local population imagined. They wrote their notes and assigned priorities for management, notes to be paid in blood.

On the night of 5/6 June 1944, its importance became known to all its inhabitants and is registered by the monuments one sees today—it is largely ignored by visitors but honored by its citizens who recognized the price paid for their liberation by soldiers and airmen who probably could not pronounce the name with any accuracy but paid for it with their blood.

The Germans were equally mindful of Picauville's significance. Sometime around 15 May 1944, the primary German response unit, the 91st Airlanding Division, moved from its previous location at Saint-Sauveur-le-Vicomte to Chateau Bernaville.

Its commander, General Wilhelm Falley, entertained Rommel at the chateau and explained the local defense posture. On the evening of 5 June, he motored to Rennes for a long-planned war game. Notified of the invasion early in the morning of 6 June, he returned to Picauville and the chateau to command the heart of the German defense of the area.

Sometime in the very early hours of 6 June, First Lieutenant Malcolm Brannen stood in the door of his C-47, jumped into the dark, and landed within a mile of the chateau. His particular jump element of 22 soldiers, all members of the 1st Battalion, 508th Infantry, landed in the hedgerows, several miles from their intended location. Many were separated, not to be rejoined until days later, if at all. Lieutenant Brannen gathered those soldiers he could find, some from other units equally mis-dropped, and moved slowly north of Picauville along a small rural road and farmhouse complex that bounded the north side of the Chateau property. Here, in a surge of exhaust smoke and engine noise, he and his band staged a hasty ambush of a staff vehicle and killed arguably the most important German of the moment in all of the Cotentin. Unaware of the significance of his act, Lieutenant Brannen moved on toward the sound of the guns further to the east—now carrying the area defense plans and maps recovered from the general's vehicle.

Further to the east of Picauville and about 7 miles west of Sainte-Mère-Église, a different and more prolonged story was playing out. Hill 30 is nearly indistinguishable from the rest of the terrain that lies just west of the Merderet River, then the flooded basin selected as the drop zones for the 507th and 508th Parachute

Infantry Regiments of the 82nd Airborne Division. To the casual observer today, it is just a rough tree-covered hillock not particularly noteworthy. On the early twilight morning of 6 June, it was a relatively defensible piece of ground for a patchwork organization of mis-dropped troops and became extraordinarily valuable for those assembled there and a major problem for the Germans determined to destroy them.

The 508th Parachute Infantry Regiment jumped in darkness, confusion, and disarray. Only a quarter out of more than 2,000 men landed on the designated drop zone or nearby. Lieutenant-Colonel Shanley, commanding the 2nd Battalion of the 508th Regiment, gathered about 300 paratroopers near this same quiet village of Picauville. Recognizing his dilemma, he and a small group, less than 20, decided to move toward the regiment's assembly area, roughly centered by Hill 30.

On the way they were joined by bits and pieces of small groups of equally distressed soldiers until he had accumulated more than two hundred men. Traveling quietly and with great caution and occasional combat, they reached the hill around 2100 on the night of 6 June. The Germans of the 91st Airlanding Division, now fully alerted, launched counter-attacks against Hill 30, but were continuously pushed back by the hodge-podge group of Airborne troopers. The Germans, greatly concerned the Americans would establish a bridgehead west of the Merderet, quickly encircled Hill 30 and maintained constant pressure against the isolated Airborne contingent. The residents of Picauville went to bed with the sound of gunfire ringing throughout the village.

On 8 June, the Germans were once again kept from seizing the hill but their artillery shelled the position continuously, creating numerous casualties among the surrounded troopers. During the day, through an intermittent radio contact, Lieutenant-Colonel Shanley was able to establish communications with troopers from the 507th and 508th holding Chef-du-Pont, less than a mile away but through two belts of impenetrable German infantry. Lieutenant-Colonel Shanley's situation became critical, with a serious shortage of water, munitions, and plasma. Small patrols crept through the swamp to bring back plasma and ammo but in quantities too small for real relief.

On 9 June at about 1000, just to the north, less than a half mile away, a distance greatly magnified by the force necessary to traverse, elements of the 325th Glider Infantry, reinforced by 1st Battalion, 507th Infantry, managed to seize the causeway at La Fière Bridge and move toward Shanley and his surrounded band on Hill 30. The Germans withdrew to Picauville to prepare for its defense. General Gavin was one of the first Airborne soldiers to climb Hill 30 and welcome its soldiers back into the 82nd. In his report, he noted that he walked the small tight perimeter on the hill top and noticed that in almost every position there was a wounded soldier still holding his place. From 6 to 9 June, evacuation was not an option.

By 10 June, the 358th Regimental Combat Team of the 90th Infantry Division attacked toward Pont-l'Abbé and Picauville. The main street of Picauville was jammed with burning vehicles, bodies, and clashing forces. The quiet of the village had been replaced by the noise and detritus of combat. Where the monuments stand today would have been considered a key objective to seize or defend by both forces.

By 20 June, the mortal aspects of combat had passed through Picauville, and the infrastructure of a much larger plan began to take shape. The U.S. Army Air Forces established a temporary airfield within a mile of the Chateau Bernaville just to its north and on what is now a connecting rural road. Its size and signs are lost to time and the normal progress of farming and agriculture. But it holds the record of being one of the first established forward fighter fields in the liberated area of Normandy. It was constructed by the IX Engineering Command, 826th Engineer Aviation Battalion. There is a monument to that unit.

Known as Advanced Landing Ground A-8, the airfield consisted of a single 5,000-foot Prefabricated Hessian Surfacing runway aligned to 25 degrees. Tents by the open pasture were used for billeting and support facilities. An access road was built to the existing road infrastructure, which is now incorporated into the existing road network. With local labor, a dump for supplies, ammunition, and gasoline drums, along with water storage and a small electrical grid for communications, were established. The chateau was converted from German headquarters to an area signal center.

The primary combat unit stationed at the airfield was the 405th Fighter Group, flying P-47 Thunderbolt fighters from 30 June through 14 September 1944. As you eat cheese and drink wine from the Picauville area, remember that the returning fighter pilots enjoyed the same local production made by the grandparents of those providing today's fare.

As the Allied armies swept across France, Picauville became too distant from the front to be useful. On 15 September 1944, the airfield was shut down and the field reverted to pasture. In time, the marks of combat and military infrastructure reverted to invisibility. The population went about the business of living but they did not forget.

Some of the American veteran associations built plaques and dedicated monuments to their brief exposure to this small village and its inhabitants and then went back to their homes and lives. But to Picauville, then is now and is always current events. During the memorial period, the town turns out in mass to the small spot where the monuments and memories reside. Regardless of the month, the place is kept pristine, trimmed, and immaculate by the town. Sometimes returning veterans are present, more often now, there are none. It makes no difference to the village. They know why they are there.

CHAPTER 21

The Children

The cemetery at Omaha Beach is a lodestone for the human soul. Its vast and manicured marble garden is an attractant that no pheromone can match. Each visitor takes away a deeply personal view of the precise survey-aligned monuments. For some, it is a chance to re-visit a friend from a moment many years ago. For others, it is a simple statement of the strength of the human spirit, and the ultimate good deeds that the interred achieved. For all, its sanctity is affirmed.

Perhaps the most impressive scene is the endless groups of children that course between the marbles stones. Stopping at a particular point, they gather to view a name, a unit, and a date, as their teacher or guide indicates. They show boundless curiosity, enthusiasm, and interest, yet they are not Americans, and they have no blood relative within the immaculately trimmed borders. These are French children surveying and studying the price paid for their freedom. The limitless energy, questions, and note taking indicates a strong, genuine interest in the events the marble implies. They note the dates and the volume for specific weeks or days years ago that brought the name on the cross to this place. They discuss the unit of the deceased and recall its history on their soil and remember that they live where he died. Altogether, their presence is a profound statement of gratitude for those whose presence then is established by their presence now. These children know what our American children do not.

Nearly 80 years ago, a generation of Americans conducted the largest single-purpose operation our civilization has ever undertaken and probably ever will. The vast majority of those participants have died leaving only a miniscule number of then-teenagers, now nonagenarians. How will that day of days be remembered and commemorated? Will it be forgotten in the course of time? If 2019's anniversary events are any indication, that day and those that were there will be remembered by succeeding generations of Norman school children—the true symbols of the purpose and goodness of the event now so long ago.

Every D-Day, hundreds of children present songs and poems at each ceremonial location in honor of the soldiers who fought and died there. Every small village in

THE CHILDREN • 263

the peninsula that saw action has a memorial club and celebrates each anniversary with a town remembrance followed by a lunch or dinner with the modern-day U.S., British, and German soldiers.

During the anniversary period, virtually every village, large and small, holds a commemoration and memorial of the event and specifically of what occurred at that location. Plaques have been placed describing the actions of that period and identifying the specific U.S. elements engaged. In many cases, names of specific participants have been indicated as well as their actions and how they liberated the local population. Depending upon the size of the village, dignitaries at several levels within the political structure will make short speeches to honor the U.S. personnel brought by fate and chance to the location. This is not a commercial enterprise, but a deep, sincere, and lasting recognition of who freed their grandparents and the sacrifices we, the U.S. and Allies, made on their behalf. "Mort pour la France" accompanies the mention of a specific name. To the French, they died for us.

They see in the soldiers of today their grandparents in uniform, then so young, so strong, and so important. Through the disciplined formations at the memorial services, they also see the rows of crosses in the many military cemeteries that dot the once troubled land. After the ceremonies, many will approach a soldier, grasp his or her hand, and thank them with broad smile, a firm handshake and a strong "Merci." The soldiers are initially mystified by this repetitive event but soon they realize the sincerity and the importance. Most, on later describing their experience, will say this was the most profound and meaningful moment of the trip.

Most of the ceremonies do not include U.S. personnel other than by chance. Should active duty troops be able to provide a color guard or a senior officer to speak, they will be given a place of honor at the front and treated as the liberators of the past. The depth and sincerity of the gestures is without precedent to anything they have been experienced. It goes far beyond applause at an airport or perfunctory "Thank you for your service." It comes from the heart.

The bearers of this gratitude are invariably the children of these villages. They will present flowers or tokens to the troops. The ceremony often involves a small children's chorus from the local school, and more often than not, includes a unique rendition of the *Star Spangled Banner* or *America*. It is hard not to tear up. Later, the children will tug at the soldier's sleeves and ask for a souvenir patch or unit insignia and an autograph.

Forewarned, most troops come armed with a pocket full of Airborne, Ranger, or unit insignias. The child will proffer a piece of paper for the celebrity soldier to sign. He or she will invariably be asked to indicate his or her unit. If it is one that was there on D-Day, a large smile will erupt on the face and often as not, in broken English, the child will recount what that unit did that day.

In Normandy, the Liberation (not invasion) is embedded in the elementary and high school curriculum. Students are given specific units to study, usually those that participated on 6 June. These range from the expected—Airborne—but often include the air transport, fighter commands, or bomber units, especially if they crashed nearby, as many did. Should a veteran be present, usually in a wheelchair or walker now, the more senior students will recount the history of a veteran's unit as introductions are made. In many cases, the child will know more than the veteran as to the organizational events of that period.

Consider that this has been the case from 1945 to today. The grandparents and great grandparents have died. The parents are of middle age. Yet the fervor and energy of the children has remained well past any first-hand memory. The children will always be there.

The children laying flowers at the small town monuments, tugging on the fatigue shirt of a soldier asking for an autograph, or walking between the rows of marble crosses in the cemetery ensure what happened those years ago will always be remembered and appreciated in succeeding generations. Any veteran of that period, resting in a wheelchair or holding a proffered arm, would be the first to say that it was all for the children. Somehow, the children know that.

CHAPTER 22

The Return

Memories and memorializations can be both melancholy and uplifting. So it was on 6 June 1984. As Commander of Troops, I returned to Sainte-Mère-Église, Normandy, with 350 selected troops from the 82nd Airborne Division. This was the first time the division had been to Normandy since the actual invasion.

Only one American, Bob Murphy, Pathfinder on D-Day with the 505th Parachute Infantry Regiment, returned annually with his French companion, Yves Tarriel, to make a HALO (high altitude low opening) jump into the city square. Other than that, the town was bereft of outside recognition. The lack of outside attendance did not matter much to them.

On a clear, beautiful June day, we jumped near the town and marched into the city square. There, in a large U-shaped formation, was the entire population of the immediate area, as well as dozens of the original veterans at the base of the U. In front of them were the mayor and the town priest. Our commanding general made short remarks followed by the mayor and a final benediction by the priest.

We marched out of the city to wild applause. In time, we crossed through an underpass west of the city and retraced the steps of our brothers, 40 years past, along the linking road that brought us to Drop Zone O, where at approximately 0115, 6 June 1944, Bob Murphy and his small group of Pathfinders brought in the entire 505 Parachute Infantry Regiment, the only one of six regiments to land where intended.

Continuing, we followed the small rural road the Originals traced, to La Fière Bridge and the fated causeway. Here, on the following morning, General Gavin, lifting his walking stick, pointed to a small projecting piece of land west of the Merderet, indicating where he had landed and begun the war. There, we would camp.

Across the causeway, we came to Cauquigny church, located at its western end. As this was the last stronghold of the German defenders on 9 June 1944, it was severely contested.

Where then the waters of the Merderet meadow lapped at the narrow edges of the causeway—severely restricting maneuver—today, the previously inundated land was dry to the edge of the now innocuous stream. A broad grassy meadow in the glowing sunlight now, on 6 June, it hid the many bodies of the troopers that had drowned in its inundated confines.

The pre-assault maps marked this area as "boggy ground." The bog was between 3 and 12 feet deep. In the darkness of the assault, burdened by weight greater than the body, Airborne soldiers quickly learned the error of the designation. More than 30 troops were drowned within its grasp. Later, the flood lapping at the causeway created a more effective maneuver obstacle than any stretch of barbed wire.

The narrow road leading to the church became a causeway of death and a machine gunner's dream. Where we walked unimpeded, General Gavin recounted we could have walked end to end and never touched pavement for the carpeting of bodies. He was there and he did and he never forgot.

Now, mindful of this land and its past, the troops marched in reflective silence another kilometer along the edge of the Merderet meadow. In time, we came to the narrow projection of land that General Gavin had indicated. This was where he estimated he had landed. Less than three hundred yards away, slightly inland, lay a large apple orchard—now named Timmes Orchard—which was our bivouac site.

I selected this based on the history of the event and the moment. I talked extensively with then retired Major General Timmes, and he had given me extensive matter of fact history of his trials there 6–9 June. From his badly mis-dropped experience, collecting less than 250 men of what should have been 600, he fought the Germans in an increasingly uneven battle. This orchard, our camp site, would ultimately contain less than 160 soldiers with their backs to the water. Operating in isolation until 9 June, then-Lieutenant-Colonel Timmes and his scratch force held much of the Germans off of the causeway and diverted them from the main body of a weak Airborne force.

When finally relieved in mid-afternoon of 9 June, he had 155 troops including himself in the perimeter; 64 were dead and 45 wounded. We would sleep on their soil.

On the night of 6 June, on this hallowed ground, we would conduct our own memorial of the events and our remembrance of 40 years ago. This would be a soldier-to-soldier moment unimpeded by the panoply of civilians, dignitaries, and protocol.

At 0115, the approximate time the Pathfinders jumped over Sainte-Mère-Église, we assembled on General Gavin's ground. It was a bright moonlit night, much as the original night. Fog hung over the Merderet meadow reflecting a silvery sheen on the troops, unusually quiet and reflective. They understood the moment and why they were there.

Later, on that drizzly, cloudy morning at the 0820 assembly at La Fière, General Gavin would recount his memories of the moment and place we stood.

From the ground on which Gavin had stood, 40 years later, I and the 82nd Airborne Division would honor its past, as well as its future. After a short discussion of the place, the meaning, and the moment, I directed the buglers to play *Echo Taps*. With the first note, a flare was projected across the meadow.

Taps is an elegiac sound that is instantly recognizable, weighted with both clarity and symbolism. As the last sounds reverberated across the water with the shimmering glow of the flare, the sound and light were lost in the fog and mist of the place, silence and velvet darkness shrouded us all. I did an about face, and saluted the troops. The 40th generation of that day of days, without a word, returned to their earthen beds in the midst of Timmes Orchard. The sights and sounds would be forever retained in their memories.

Bradley at Pointe du Hoc

I had the privilege of being at General Bradley's presentation of events at Pointe du Hoc in 1979. He was frail and it was a typical day at Pointe du Hoc—windy and cool with intermittent sunlight. Though he did not focus on the events of Pointe du Hoc, his selection of the spot was symbolic of his belief that the Rangers did something very special that day. I have included General Bradley's remarks as I recalled them.

During the anniversary celebrations in 1979 then-Lieutenant John Cal and I went to Pointe du Hoc from Vicenza as part of the anniversary celebrations, at that time considerably more low key than now.

At the time, Pointe du Hoc was noticeably wilder and more undeveloped than it is today. A visitor had uncontrolled access to the entire site including the beach below. It had not yet been acquired by the American Battle Monuments commission and the French chose to let the ground lay fallow as much in tribute to what had occurred there as a cost-saving measure. The original barbed wire only partially kept wanderers from the edge. No markers or developed trails existed less the single stone Ranger memorial on the observation bunker overlooking the beach and the tethered steel London ladder at the base. The ground originally projected several yards from the bunker toward the sea but is now presently eroded to leave the floor of the bunker literally leaning in air. It was not until President Reagan spoke in 1984 that the land was given to the U.S. and turned into a living memorial complete with bleachers, trails, bathrooms, and safety features.

For the purposes of the ceremony and in consideration of the general's age, a dirt road had been bulldozed from the highway to the memorial to permit a single vehicle to traverse. Temporary bleachers had been erected in front of the new road facing the memorial where several hundred of us either sat or stood, mostly French families with a scattering of uniformed U.S. personnel as well as considerable media and U.S. embassy staff.

Eventually, from the right rear, a U.S. Army olive drab sedan slowly wound its way toward us. The vehicle stopped directly in front of us and two aides emerged.

One opened the trunk and extracted a portable wheel chair while the second opened the rear door and adjusted the passenger's uniform. The green army dress uniform was covered with stars, badges, and ribbons that glittered and shimmered in the sun, reflecting a half century of America's turbulent history—General Omar Bradley had arrived.

The general was fixed in the sunlight, half in the shade provided by the sedan roof, head slumped down and jaw slack, apparently unaware of our presence. The aide gently turned the general around to where he faced us and placed his legs outside the car. Both aides then assisted him out of the car, placing him gently in the wheelchair. There was almost total silence save for the constant blowing wind of the point. Bradley once slowly looked up at us but made no sign of recognition or change of emotion. We lost sight of his face as an aide placed the gold embroidered service hat on the general and centered it on the now slumped head as one would aid an invalid about to have an outing. Meanwhile, the other aide had gathered a portable microphone and placed it in the grasp of both of the general's hands.

John and I looked at each other and one of us whispered words to the effect—this is going to be a disaster. Here we had one of the most revered figures of the war, a national military icon placed in front of hundreds of people and the media of several nations, about to be personally embarrassed by his lack of mental acuity and gross physical infirmities. This Omar Bradley was a far cry from the day he stood on the USS *Augusta*, staring toward Omaha Beach, and commanding the forces of western civilization on their most momentous of days.

There was a short pause while the aides departed and the general was left alone to our front, mic in hand and head bowed with the hat covering his face. It seemed the collective audience held its breath and was preparing to be embarrassed and sad and filled with pity for what the man had become. We need not have worried.

General Bradley looked up slightly at us and gestured for an aide to turn the chair half left so he could view the beach. When turned, he proceeded to speak uninterrupted for 45 minutes. Though his voice was low and somewhat breathless, his diction was clear and his words unslurred. His mental acuity and recall of the events of that day were as if they had just occurred. It was an amazing tour de force of the power of the human mind to overcome physical infirmities at a point of great import and a great lesson in personal discipline and purpose.

He began by relating the background to the invasion—the rationale for the location of the landing, the selection of troops to attack Omaha (one veteran division, the 1st Infantry, and one untried, the 29th Infantry), the anticipated enemy, and the briefing at St Paul's School with the king, Churchill, Monty and Ike.

> We knew this was the most important moment in our history. I marvel at it now. The king spoke very well but Churchill—he was inspiring. A truly great man and a good friend.

He then described his last meeting with Ike in England—"We played bridge and ate dinner"—and his boarding the cruiser at Southampton. He noted the vast armada of ships to all sides and said with emphasis, "We had to win here to win the war. We all had the greatest confidence we would."

His description of the senior leaders was plain and without emotions.

> General Montgomery was a thorough professional who gave us a mission and left us alone. I never had an issue with him throughout the battle. Ike was, as always, calm and supportive. We were old friends, classmates, and he never refused me anything and I was very careful not to add to his burdens. I couldn't have asked for a better set of bosses.

Bradley discussed the selection of Omaha, why its position in relation to all the other beaches made it essential and how they early on recognized it was going to be the toughest.

> I had the greatest faith in General Collins at Utah. He was a go-getter who proved to be a magnificent commander. I had no worries there. It was Omaha that was always on my mind. We picked the 1st Division, real proven veterans of Africa and Sicily, as we needed extra insurance here and we certainly did.

The Airborne operation was then addressed.

> We had to put the Airborne on the flanks of Utah to seize the peninsula and ensure the safe beach landings. Nothing gave me more agony than the discussions with Air Chief Marshal Sir Trafford Leigh-Mallory and his belief of the slaughter that would ensue. However, I talked this over at length with Generals Ridgway and Taylor and my staff and in the end concluded we simply had to have the jump. I went to Ike and he concurred. I am forever thankful that Air Chief Marshal Sir Trafford Leigh-Mallory was wrong—and he quickly noted that to me—a real gentleman.

There was a momentary pause as an aide brought a glass of water. He returned the glass, slowly looked around, and went on.

> This piece of ground was the most important objective of all for the Americans on D-Day. It had to be taken. German artillery here could control both Utah and Omaha. It was a very tough objective but we assigned some very tough people to take it. The Rangers were the best assault soldiers we had. I had viewed them train in Scotland and knew we would need every bit of their skills and courage to take this place. It had to be taken and it was. I didn't appreciate the true difficulties they faced until several days later and I still marvel when I look around that it was done at all. When the chips are down, there is no better person for the tough jobs than an American soldier.

He then went on to relate the events of the landing itself. He described the low clouds, cold wind, spitting rain, the high seas, and his concern for sea sickness of the invading troops, the tremendous noise of the bombardment, and how he had to stuff cotton in his ears as the *Augusta* fired. He described his increasing agitation at having no information regarding success or failure on the beach and his dispatch of the captain's gig with General Thomas Handy and an aide to get a closer view and their report: "They couldn't really see and I still didn't know other than second hand reports, all of which were bad."

In a low but steady voice he recounted his instructions to the staff to consider how to use the nearest British beach should Omaha be untenable and then explained how he just resigned himself to wait. Then with a pause and emphasis, "Then, I got the Navy report—they could see our soldiers on the bluffs. We were winning."

Throughout this recounting, he recalled specific names, call signs, and beach designations and provided detailed sound bites of the conversations.

> "Get me Shellburst [Ike's HQ]" I asked the radioman.
> "Ike, I think we have it. I am sending in Gee [Major General Gerow the V Corps Commanding General] and the corps headquarters."

At last he sighed and looked up and described his personal feelings of that day and his thoughts of the thousands of casualties: "We took this beach. It was an awful price but we had to pay it."

There was a momentary pause as he collected himself and then began what were his closing comments—a paean to the American soldier.

> Omaha Beach and this objective were bought by the blood of thousands of Americans who proved that morning they were the best in the world. They never let me down. In history, it's the seniors who get the publicity and the credit but it's the soldiers who do the work and take the casualties. I have never been prouder or more grateful than as their commander. We must never forget how we got here and who did this job for us and our future generations.

There was a moment of silence and then a smattering of applause which then grew into a roar—sustained and blowing past him with the wind. For the first time, he looked up, gave a half-smile, and waved his hand—paused and then rendered a shaky salute which re-invigorated the applause—all of us now standing as he was wheeled to his car.

John and I looked at each other and sat down as the general disappeared down the road. WOW! Whatever had transpired with General Bradley mentally and physically between D-Day and this day had been wiped out for those 45 minutes. We should all be taking his medicine.

Gavin at La Fière

As an eloquent example of "paying it forward," this is a photo of Lieutenant General Jim Gavin, the heart and soul of the 82nd and 505th during World War II. This was taken on 6 June 1984 at La Fière Bridge, Normandy—the Gettysburg, and soul of the 82nd Airborne. It is truly hallowed ground. On 9 June 1944 at 1030 in the morning, virtually every numbered unit in the division was there, engaged in clearing a seemingly inconsequential causeway that had defied capture to that point.

Lieutenant General Gavin at La Fière. (Author's photo)

The commanding general, Major General Ridgway, personally stood on the bridge trying, with a combination of physical force and presence, to will the soldiers across this narrow 200 yards of fire-swept ground to seize the other side. Failure would have halted the entire eastern side of the Normandy invasion area from its required tasks, placing the entire operation in jeopardy. Brigadier General Gavin—as he was at the time—was tasked with assembling and commanding the actual assault as three reinforcing divisions pressed up from Utah Beach to transit the causeway which should have been taken on 6 June.

The 1-505th had continuously attempted to clear it but the better part of a first-class German regiment held firm and denied passage. Indicative of the intensity was that by 8 June, the battalion had less than 200 effective troopers. Company A, the point of the bayonet, had a foxhole count of 40, which included Lieutenant Red Dog Dolan, the acting battalion commander. Two previous battalion commanders had been killed leading assaults.

This point of land was so crucial that the corps commander and the commanding generals of both the 4th and 90th Infantry Divisions observed from the high ground less than 300 yards from the conflict point, wishing the force forward. Major General Ridgway assembled every single senior officer and NCO in the division that he could muster to assist in any way possible. This assault would be carried by a combination of Airborne spirit and the pure personal will and dedication of the troopers engaged. This was a moment that memorialized what Airborne truly meant. The leader would be Brigadier General Gavin, the previous commander of the 505th Parachute Infantry Regiment and now assault commander for a piece of ground less than 5 yards wide and 200 yards long. The lead element, as much by chance as by design, was Company G, 3-325 GIR, led by Captain John Sauls.

By 1130 that morning, the division counted 254 killed and 525 wounded, and two Congressional Medals of Honor awarded—the price of the capture of this causeway. With the causeway cleared, the division and the rest of the force continued west into Normandy, not to return here until 1984.

On the 40th anniversary of D-Day, the commanding general of the 82nd Airborne, Major General Jim Lindsay, created a package from the division to return to Normandy for the first time since 1944. Every numbered unit in the division had slots for the trip and sent their very best troops as representatives. The actual jump into Normandy was a huge event unanticipated by either the division, the U.S. embassy, or the French themselves. More than 10,000 civilians crowded the entire drop zone at La Londe and greeted every troop recovering from his parachute landing fall (PLF) with hugs, handshakes, kisses, and calvados, an apple-based spirit of unusual strength. A bridge had truly been built from 1944 to 1984.

The troopers would be in Sainte-Mère-Église for 10 days, placed and fed in private homes throughout the small town. During the day, they engaged in staff rides throughout the Normandy area. They were joined by elements of the British Parachute Regiment and conducted joint staff rides to include Pegasus Bridge and the Merville Battery with the original commanders and veterans.

A highlight of all the terrain discussions was that many of the original 82nd and Parachute Regiment members (officers, NCOs, and junior enlisted) were present and spoke of the events at that spot. To listen to then-Lieutenant-Colonel Ben Vandervoort recount the events at Neuville-au-Plain or Pathfinder Bob Murphy talk about being the first trooper on the ground made an indelible impression. The spirit, drive, and resolution of the precursor force made a lasting lifelong impression on all the active-duty soldiers. But the best was yet to come.

The 6th of June 1984 was a cold, rainy, dismal day. This was the day for the La Fière Bridge staff ride and not entirely welcome due to the weather. This was originally planned to be a unit staff ride with some veterans, as the principals on the original action were either dead or unavailable. But the Airborne gods provided an example of their powers. The previous night, Lieutenant General Gavin had a casual conversation at a dinner with the 82nd troop commander and learned of the La Fière event the following morning. He agreed on the spur of the moment to "be there if I could make it." He was scheduled to be interviewed by Walter Cronkite at Omaha Beach mid-morning and a diversion might not be possible. Further, he was in an advanced stage of Parkinson's and had difficulty both moving and speaking. If he did participate, it could be painful for both him and the troops watching him.

La Fière is the site of the Iron Mike paratrooper statue established and paid for by the citizens of Sainte-Mère-Église in memory of those troopers who died liberating that town. It rests on the side of a grassy plain overlooking the causeway and the Merderet River watching over this truly hallowed ground. Assembled that morning next to the statue, 40 years after the event, were the entire 82nd Airborne Division package wearing ponchos all around but distinguished by their red berets against the grey sky.

At approximately 0700, a grey Mercedes sedan came around the narrow road and parked just below the field. In the back seat was Lieutenant General Gavin, stoop shouldered with head forward, visible through the window. His World War II aide, Hugo Olson, exited the front passenger seat and opened the general's door.

The opportunity to be with his old unit had been too powerful to ignore. He was clearly determined to re-establish the bonds that had welded him to his unit and its heritage on that difficult Normandy morning 40 years ago. The open door revealed him looking somewhat shaky and infirm; clearly every fiber of his being had to be brought to bear to manage this moment. The troop commander stood by the open door and saluted.

General Gavin finally acknowledged his presence and for the first time looked up and out the door as he must have on that night 40 years before. He saw the assembled troops in their fatigues and berets and his whole body changed. He quickly put on his service cap, turned out of the car, stood erect, and fixed his gaze on the assembled troopers and the sea of red berets.

He walked directly in front of the troops and without introduction began to lucidly explain what had happened here on this ground in intimate detail and then, entirely unplanned, took the entire body down the causeway, stopping to explain what had happened at each stop along the causeway itself. The soldiers were transfixed by the extraordinary demonstration of both will and command presence. The walk took about an hour and a half and Walter Cronkite was toast to Gavin's priorities. For that moment in time and in the mind's eye of every trooper present he was every inch the Assault Force Commander. Everyone present clearly understood why his troops would follow him anywhere. There are some aspects of leadership that cannot be taught or trained.

That day was but one of many similar experiences his soldiers recalled many years after the events. If any one person could be truly loved by his unit, General Gavin was the one. He had an essence others did not and it made all the difference.

CHAPTER 23

The Sounds of Deliverance

Medical experts say that the sense of sound is usually the last to go among the living. What did the veterans of D-Day hear as their last memories faded away? At the hôtel de ville, the city hall of Sainte-Mère-Église, the last memorial ceremony highlighted how tenuous is our hold on these Originals. A single short row of only six veterans was the focus of the best we had to offer on 5–6 June 1944. What did they hear?

The drone of the more than 4,000 aircraft taking off from the south of England on that ebbing twilight day? The sound of the wind loudly coursing by the open door frames with a mix of moisture, exhaust, and gasoline with a partial view glimpsed by the six in the waning kaleidoscope of light across the English countryside? Unheard and unseen by them were the thousands of faces upturned throughout the land, knowing that the source of the endless noise was the beginning of their final deliverance. The six soldiers were an integral part of that noise. For the seaborne elements it was the coalescing of more than 4,500 vessels in a relatively narrow passage each throbbing and grinding away in the surging indigo-black sea, moving as swiftly as possible to meet the paratroopers passing above.

Unheard by both elements would have been the church bells, rung all over England on Churchill's order, calling the congregations to prayer for this final endeavor. A bit later, on the American East Coast, beginning around 0400 Eastern Daylight Time, a similar event was occurring, a reaction to the initial news broadcast by the Germans of the invasion and confirmed by CBS. However, as the American peals rang out, almost half a day had passed and the beaches, fields, and watercourses had already been littered with the shattered detritus of battle. Our six veterans would have been engulfed by those fatal sounds.

The cacophony of noises generated by the aircraft engines began to be interrupted by the random slap of shrapnel on the fuselage. As gravel or rain on a tin roof, it ebbed and flowed. The individual anxiety of the men within each aircraft could not be heard but was felt by all. The jump commands broke the rhythm, curbed the anxieties, and suppressed for a moment the sounds outside. Each of the six veterans would have heard the rough rasp of the static line snap fastener against the cable and the clunk of boots against the floor as each of them moved toward the door. A bright green light followed by the loud command of GO released the six and their companions, uniformly rasping along the cable.

For a very brief moment, the exit sounds broke the internal fears, the wind and noise wrapping each soldier in his own cocoon. Then, the parachute serially snapped out of the container, the sound lost to the six but bringing each to a uniformly sudden stop. A loud grunt of compressed air and a pop of the now inflated canopy swung each below his suspension lines. Moments before, he may have heard a tearing sound as his equipment bag or other gear was ripped from his body by the combination of airspeed and the violence of the opening shock. For a very brief interlude, the sounds of silence at this moment brought a mental focus as the long prior training and experience was activated.

The next sounds could have been the quick pop of a bullet passing through canopy or snapping by an ear. For many of their brothers, it was the dull thunk of a strike on flesh, unheard except by the recipient who would hear no more.

Next came the contained slam into the soft Norman earth or a splash into the Merderet and the sounds of water and air quickly closing overhead. Some of the fortunate would exhale loudly as lungs collapsed and recovered. Others, at least 32 underwater, would never breathe again.

Perhaps a cow was deeply snorting and investigating this incursion into the herd, its breath, grunts, and steps communicating to others. Soft ripe apple blossoms, disturbed by the soldier's descent, would, like snow, fall unheard. The parachute would softly encompass the area; its existence more sensed than heard. Now the sounds of soldiers at work would begin.

Initially, it is the grunting, snapping, and rasping cuts of a soldier getting out of the parachute. Then a moment of silence as he tries to orient himself, find a friend, and locate the foe. The sound of movement through the nettles, hedges, and vegetation is equal and neutral to both. The sound of human voices, shattering in the stillness but truly low in volume, override the non-human sounds of the night. A friendly accent, a familiar language, or metallic click, or the sliding and closing of a bolt, signal friend or foe.

The whole experience and the overload of adrenalin is draining. Some, after divesting the parachute, reach for a canteen and quench a newly generated thirst. The black Bakelite cap, if not carefully held, knocks against the aluminum container and makes a loud clang, sounding like a dull church bell but probably lost within several feet. The water is drunk and the canteen returned to its pouch with the grinding sound of newly emplaced grit between the cup and the container.

A German Mauser rifle has two or four distinct sounds, depending on whether or not it has been fired. The supremely lethal MG-42 has a distinctive ripping-cloth sound—it is a sound that sticks. Chance encounters are sudden stabbing sounds laced with the heavy breathing and adrenalin-filled shouts of the respective participants. This is followed by a moment of relative quiet as the combatants sort out their mortality and the results.

For some, the encounter can be fatal with the tenuous sounds of ebbing life. The impact of a bullet striking flesh is a distinctive thud, often unheard by others but overwhelming to the recipient. Blood hisses and bubbles slowly from a lung shot and speaking is difficult. For the deeply visceral wound, there is little in the way of sound with the occasional exception of a slow death rattle of air bubbling by the trachea.

An M-1 has a capacity for eight rounds in the clip, which can be very satisfying to the firer with its comforting repetitive fire. But, at the end of the sequence, it emits a sound unique to it—a sharp metallic clank as the empty clip is ejected. A deep and excited exhale is emitted as the user slams a new clip into the open bolt face and closes it, renewing its capacity in the endless cycle of close combat. Our six would have great experience with this sound.

All this recedes in the minds of the six old soldiers. Assisted by hearing aids and canes to limit the effect of life's infirmities, they sit in silence and polite attention as the ceremony honors their life. Massed bands play respective national anthems—this time including Germans in their distinctive *Fallschirmjäger* uniforms—friends and fighting allies now. Enemies of high professional regard earlier. The six remember and respect.

In time, the program reaches its conclusion. The six old soldiers arise and stand as the bands leave in mass. All march in silence but one, that of the Germans. Reverberating through the narrow streets and softened by the effect of more than 10,000 people from a myriad of nations, the strains of the 5th Movement of Beethoven's Ninth, *The Ode to Joy* with its paean to faith and hope, lifts over the scene and flows past the six standing soldiers. They knew at this moment, with the sights and sounds of the scene telling them, that they ensured everyone had won.

CHAPTER 24

Visiting the British Sector

As part of the 40th Anniversary visit to Normandy, we were paired with the British Parachute Regiment. We spent a week with them at Aldershot, doing balloon jumps, cross-briefings, messing, and visiting the sites. Copious quantities of beer were consumed as the Brits led our troops through the traditional pub crawl. Morning was always problematic, with the officers doing as best they could and the enlisted of both sides barely surviving parade.

As the British do best, they planned to match our staff rides with their own, both in joint attendance. We went together to our departure airfield at RAF Lyneham, chuted up, and in intermixed sticks flew into our jump at Normandy.

We rolled up together and spent the first night, at my direction, in Timmes Orchard, where we held a 0115 memorial service—coincidental with the first drop of the assault force 40 years prior. The next three days were spent at the U.S. objectives, each led by busloads of veterans as organized by General Gavin. On the fourth day, we deployed to the British sector.

We began at Ouistreham and Sword Beach. We were placed in chairs overlooking the beach and a succession of veterans briefed us on events. A member of General Dempsey's staff addressed the "why" and "how" of Sword Beach and the planning issues and complications. He brought out a stooped individual who was introduced as an engineer for the famous Mulberry port system, which lay in distinct outline in front of us.

Despite his obvious infirmities and sitting in a chair, he clearly described the process of constructing and transporting the immensely complex parts across the Channel and dropping them in place. He described the constant din of ships being scuttled for the breakwater, whooshing air and water jets as the giant Phoenix caissons were sunk, and the constant grinding and heaving of the floating causeways as they moved up and down with the waves. He concluded by looking up and stating in a clear voice: "It was a bloody hard piece of work, but we did it. And here it is today."

We rose as one and applauded.

Then a well-spoken French veteran of Lieutenant Commander Philippe Kieffer's commandos discussed the assault on the casino just to our left, made famous by *The Longest Day*. He paused a moment in his talk and then described the entrance of the French nuns to the position. Their flowing habits, tightly packed formation, and hard stride had brought all firing to a stunned halt.

Before the Germans could recover, the nuns were within the rubble of the buildings and, after seeking directions, went straight to work with Kiefer's casualties. He reported that the sound of French civilian voices ashore sent a huge boost of energy through the defenders. He then introduced a member of the same order. More applause.

Next, and clearly intended to be the ringing conclusion, our guide introduced a veteran who was a member of Lord Lovat's commandos. He had a deep, but generally understandable brogue and an obviously polished presentation. He described their initial sodden landing and march to relieve Major John Howard at Pegasus Bridge and the sight of Lovat, tall and in casual hunting gear with a deer rifle slung over his shoulder, striding just behind the lead elements as they made their way off the beach and onto the road guiding north. The intensity of his men then was quite evident within him even with the shroud of 40 years.

At this point, the commander of the Parachute Regiment took the stage and discussed the next guest—Bill Millen, the piper for Lord Lovat. He explained to us, the colonials, how important the pipes were for the Scots in battle and that each battalion had at least one piper. In the Parachute Regiment, they would provide the assembly aid as well as the morale boost at the height of conflict. With that, Bill Millen came upon the stage and began to play "Blue Bonnets Over Scotland," the tune he had played as they traversed the road to Pegasus.

We sat in mesmerized silence as the sounds skirled over the assembly. More than one of our Para friends would lean over, nudge his Yank counterpart and whisper: "Bloody awful, isn't it?"

Most of us just absorbed the effect, reflecting upon its importance long ago and the history that went with the fading notes.

With that, we were directed to stand. A massed band of Argyll and Sutherland Highlanders, the Black Watch, and the Parachute Regiment played "God Save the Queen" as only such a massed band can do. With that, we piled into the busses and headed to Pegasus. It was our first true immersion in the British military culture and decidedly striking. They had done, as always, a first-class job.

CHAPTER 25

A Uniform Item—The *Fourragère*

Every soldier who serves in the 82nd Airborne Division wears a *fourragère*. Very few really know why and even less fully understand.

As a brand new second lieutenant in 1965, I joined B Company, 2-505th of the 505th Parachute Infantry Regiment. I knew it was a proud unit with a great history, one of the reasons I chose to go Airborne and join the 82nd. If I was to be infantry, I wanted to be with the best. One of my first requirements was to visit the supply sergeant and get my basic equipment, which included two uniform items, a blue infantry cord and the green and red braided *fourragère* awarded to the division after Normandy. Both were wrapped in a simple plastic bag by the manufacturer. I dutifully went home and put them both on my Class A green dress uniform, the *fourragère* on the left shoulder with the brass tip touching my jacket pocket.

Later, I was introduced to the several platoon sergeants, all World War II veterans. Two were from the 82nd and one was from the Wehrmacht. He joined the postwar 82nd when it was in Germany on a rotation. He had similar background compatriots in the anti-tank platoon sergeant and the supply sergeant, the man that had issued my equipment and was fastidious in filling out the forms and making me sign for the issued materiel. At the time I thought it interesting that the previous foes were now all together in the same unit and all engaged in trying to teach me how to be an officer.

I thought nothing of this until the next Saturday when we had our usual half day inspection: everyone in Class A uniforms. I arrived on the company steps in my spit-shined jump boots, polished brass, and green leadership tabs. I had not done anything with the brass tip of the *fourragère* other than take it out of the wrapping. It still had a semi-shiny brass appearance through the factory protective coating and I thought nothing of it, just another part of a not very impressive uniform of an officer with less than six months' service.

Waiting inside were all the NCOs, getting ready to move to their respective elements in the billets. Immediately, as if rehearsed, the two World War II 82nd NCOs closed in on me at the door. One expertly unbuttoned my shoulder tab, removed the *fourragère* and passed it to the other NCO. He disappeared down the hall with my cord in hand while the other propelled me through the first sergeant's door and told me to wait there. I was perplexed but obedient. They had been very solicitous of me and gone out of their way to educate me and ensure I was a success in front of the troops. I knew something was amiss, but I wasn't bright enough at the time to know what and too surprised to ask.

Shortly, both NCOs walked into the room. As I stood up, still somewhat confused, they both attached the *fourragère* to my left shoulder, straightened up the cord, and said, "Airborne, sir. You are ready to go." Before I could say anything else, one looked at me and spoke.

> Sir, note the brass tip to our *fourragères*. We won this in Normandy and we know what it cost—a lot of men who can't be here in this formation. Every 82nd vet in this division has a brass tip as shiny as it can be made. We know what it cost to get it and we want to make sure you look like you ought to command this outfit. Go out and bring the unit to attention.

That Sunday I went home and did some research on the 82nd at Normandy and its casualties. When the 82nd returned to the England in July 1944, it calculated its losses.

Total division strength in Normandy including the 325th and the sea tail. 11,770
Killed	*1,142*
Wounded	*2,373*
Missing/Captured	*840*
Sick/evacuated	*1,801*
TOTAL CASUALTIES	*6,156 or 52 percent of deployed.*

This was a very expensive uniform item and deserved the best of care. The NCOs were ensuring that both the cost and the symbolism remained well past their retirement.

Much later, well after my own retirement, Maurice Renaud, the youngest son of the wartime mayor of Sainte-Mère-Église took me aside during the 67th Anniversary and showed me a yellowed typewritten page he had found in his father's materials. It was a letter from his father to General de Gaulle in September of 1944:

> September 1944
>
> From the mayor of Sainte-Mère-Église, Mr. Alexandre Renaud to Monsieur le commissaire du gouvernement du General de Gaulle
>
> Subject request for a French "citation" for the two U.S. Airborne Battalions which landed in Sainte-Mère-Église on June 6th 1944.
>
> Monsieur le commissaire,
> Monday 5 June, around 2330, in the thundering noise of large aircraft flying at low altitude, in the light of a house fire, the American paratroopers landed in Sainte-Mère-Église.
> They were the first Allied troops to set a foot on the soil of our enslaved country. They mainly belonged to two battalions, the 2nd and the 3rd of the 505th Parachute Infantry

Regiment of the 82nd Airborne Division under the command of Lieutenant Colonel Benjamin Vandervoort and Lieutenant Colonel C. Krause.

Upon their landing, they were machine gunned by a group of flak soldiers who camped in a park located near the city square. At dawn these flak soldiers were pushed out of the town and settled in the village of Fauville, south of Sainte-Mère-Église.

The first night these two battalions suffered heavy casualties. Then it became even worse. More than 8 kilometers from Utah Beach, they were completely surrounded by German units.

To the south in Fauville, to the north in Neuville-au-Plain with two battalions of the 91st Airlanding Division well equipped with cannons and tanks, to the east, in direction of the sea, by two companies of fanatical Georgians who will fight to the last man. These two battalions resisted alone with their guns, two heavy machine guns, and two small cannons later delivered by gliders.

These American paratroopers (I was able to observe them closely during the battle) were very quiet and self-controlled as if they were doing maneuvers. They walked quietly close to the walls of the houses, smoking or chewing their gum under the constant shelling of German guns located in Azeville and Saint-Martin-de-Varreville.

In the evening of June 6th, from the ditch where I took refuge with my family, I sensed that the front line was getting closer to us. The two German battalions and the troops of Captain Keller attacked. All the night of June 6th the battle was ferocious. The Germans got very close to the northern entrance of the town. The paratroopers were fighting with their knives. One paratrooper I talked to told me: "We will attack. Reinforcements from the sea will get here around 0600. Everything is ok." That was not to happen. That same evening, they were still waiting for the reinforcements from Utah Beach. One soldier told me: "There is some delay. The sea is very rough" and as the women were crying and saying "Please don't abandon us," he replied with a large smile, "We never give up, we would rather die here."

A witness told me that he saw some paratroopers riding horses at full speed to rush to the defense of a threatened part of the town. After the battle several horses were dead in the center of the town. Before the troops arrived from the sea, the paratroopers were running out of ammunition. They told me: "We can only use our guns when we are very close to the target and we cannot waste ammunition. After that, our only defense will be bayonets and knives."

48 hours after their landing the Airborne men had achieved a fantastic success. Those two Airborne battalions had destroyed the German troops; in the north two battalions, in the south one battalion and one flak group, in the east two companies of Georgians who fought to the death sheltered in the castle of Beuzeville-au-Plain.

They also destroyed eight tanks.

The paratroopers suffered very heavy casualties. During all that time, the battalion medic, Captain Lyle B. Putman, was taking care of our civilian wounded as if they were American soldiers.

So I am asking you, Monsieur le commissaire du gouvernement, if it would be possible to solicit General de Gaulle, who knows what bravery means, to give to these tough soldiers who were the first to have defeated the Germans on French soil, a citation which gives them the right to wear on their uniform the French *fourragère*.

I believe that their sacrifice will feel lighter to them if they get the right to put on their regimental flag this sign of the French gratitude.

In their coming battles, these paratroopers will fight with even more bravery, proud to be the airborne troops which France has distinguished as

"Bravest among the brave"

Signed Mr Alexandre Renaud[1]

---

1 Translation by Maurice Renaud.

To this point, I had no idea as to the origin of the *fourragère*, but here it was. General de Gaulle approved and the citation with *fourragère* was granted to the 505th. This was not a request made on emotion or to curry favor. The mayor had an experienced eye and judgment for combat worthiness. He was a World War I veteran of the battles of Verdun, Ypres, and Chemin des Dames as well as other engagements. He commanded a machine gun platoon and finished the war as a prisoner of the Germans. His narrative was written with a war-weathered eye that makes it all the more noteworthy.

At the time the letter was written, Sainte-Mère-Église had the largest military cemetery in the world with more than 35,000 soldiers interred. It was not until 1948 that the bodies were re-interred either at Omaha Beach or sent home to families. His wife sent hundreds of photographs of individual graves to grieving families. She accompanied each with a personal letter written on an ancient typewriter at the kitchen table. One of Maurice's earliest memories is that of his mother bent over the table at night, often with a candle, two-finger-typing the letters. While the electrical infrastructure of Normandy had to be replaced, the spirit of its people always burned brightly.

All this and much more was and is reflected by the brass tip of the *fourragère*. Today, it hangs on my uniform in the closet with the tip wrapped in cotton and sealed in plastic. It will be displayed once more the last time it will ever be worn.

CHAPTER 26

A Nice Moment

The sun was crossing the narrow stone alley that is the conduit of Mont Saint-Michel. The cobbles were glistening from the evening's light rain and the awnings of the shops still dripped. The light played with the colors, the shined copper and the polished windows.

For a moment, it fell on the faces of the men in front of me. I thought it beatific in light of where we were and who they are.

Former privates Bob Murphy and Bill Sullivan, late of Headquarters Company, 1-505th 82nd Airborne, had agreed to the mayor's request for their attendance to receive the annual tribute to the Normandy veterans proffered by the city. We were in Sainte-Mère-Église and my task was to drive them there, enjoy a good lunch at Madam Pouillard's, and drive them back.

They were my near constant companions every anniversary period. We would gather at the STOP Bar with their families, be surrounded by the active duty Airborne in their fatigues and red berets, and just enjoy the moment. The 50-plus years washed away from them and they were once again Airborne privates with all the irresponsibility and energy of youth.

Each year and each visit was an elixir to their lives that seemed to provide the necessary reservoir of strength for the next year. As it was for mine.

I always had them speak at La Fière Bridge to the troops, an engagement that energized both the audience and the narrators.

Sullivan, the three-time prisoner of war after landing on a German headquarters, described being marched off at rifle point, only to escape at a train station, be recaptured, escape again, and finally to be shipped in chains to Austria to a special camp for the difficult soldiers. His multi-angled nose, piercing blue eyes, and heavy Boston accent conveyed the message, *I am a tough soldier*. His strength was not diminished by his 92 years.

Murphy, who had been a 17-year-old Pathfinder on his third combat jump, explained the defense of La Fière Bridge and the experience of sharing a foxhole with

Sergeant Bill Owens at 1600 on 7 June when the position was almost overrun. He remembered Owens instructing him to tell the acting battalion commander, First Lieutenant Red Dog Dolan, of their dire situation and Dolan writing a note for Murphy to carry back, "There is no better place to die."

As he related the tale, Murphy would point to his position, Dolan's position, and the sight and sound of impacting bullets and mortars on the path he took. They were still plainly visible. The troops were transfixed and deeply moved. And these were troops that had multiple tours to the sandboxes of the Middle East.

I knew Murphy and Sullivan in a much deeper sense and understood their humanity aside from the combat narratives. I learned how to eat from a mess kit in the pouring rain, how to heat rations in a foxhole so the light wouldn't shine, to open a locked Dutch rabbit hutch, and to move prisoners who outnumbered you 10-to-1.

Sullivan demonstrated how to quietly kill a man and would then show off soccer kicks for the dozens of French children who attended the annual lawn party for the veterans. These were men who became better citizens for their experience, the harder truths submerged by the softer desires the future held. In sum, these were special people that I was attracted to as a magnet to the poles.

A great deal of exceptionally good and bad food was shared at the tables, a lot of wine, tea, and Coke consumed and a special spirit passed between us all, built over both shared and common events in our lives.

During the long drive from Sainte-Mère-Église to Mont Saint-Michel, we laughed, told stories, reflected, and just generally acted as great friends, which we surely were. They kept me supplied with cold beer and watched out for the gendarme hiding posts. In sum, we were three Airborne privates having a great day together.

Murphy rehearsed his speech, Sullivan insulted most of the phrases, and I gave corrections. This consumed the better part of the early morning.

We plied our way across the water-soaked causeway and with our laissez-passer, parked in the central courtyard where the mayor met us. He warmly greeted Sullivan and Murphy, acknowledged my presence, and "suggested" to me that I occupy them for an hour as there was a delay.

After huddling, we decided to walk into the town and find a café. Murphy thought we could do this from the top, Sullivan just looked askance. It was quite cool and both had the florid faces of the Irish exposed to either too much whiskey or cold air.

We passed through the portals and began to wind our way along the very narrow shop-lined trail that delineated the path. Sullivan and Bob walked ahead and I trailed behind.

Less than a hundred yards along the steepening grade, they stopped, a mutual act. Bob turned and looked at me and said, "Let's do coffee and warm up." Sully smiled in hidden satisfaction.

I slid into the door of the first café. Knowing both the taste and my role, I ordered three *cafés au lait* and two waters.

We sat huddled around the table, just enjoying the place, the moment, and the company. They became transfixed on a subject, leaned across the table, and became lost in deep conversation. I sat back and watched the piercing soft light of the morning reflect on their faces. I thought it a special privilege to be there and to share the space. A special picture of special people. My brothers.

CHAPTER 27

Zane's Last March

Sergeant Zane Schlemmer returned to Normandy almost every year after retiring. He would find a secluded room for rent and just walk the land he had helped liberate so long ago. In time, people would recognize him and he would be invited to be honored by the local mayors during the anniversary period. He would, somewhat reluctantly, retire to his room and don his original jump uniform which still fit.

He would sit in the front row, stand when appropriate and salute the several flags and dignitaries. If asked to speak, which was often, he would make very short, easily translated comments. They always had two themes: how grateful he was that the Normans recognized the men of that moment and how happy he was to see the children. Children were very special to him as he saw them as the purpose of his efforts and the reason he and his companions came so many years ago.

In time, nature took its toll. His walk was slower and his visits more private. His children would frequently escort him and were wise enough to leave him to his time and thoughts.

He took walks in the morning along the same road he had liberated and the field he had landed upon. It gave him solace to see the new crops and the several monuments in the area. Villagers would smile in acknowledgement. Children would tug at his sleeve with great smiles and adults would step aside to let him pass. His uniform was his credentials as to place and everyone honored his passage. He always said that the acknowledgement was for all of them that day rather than for him. It was surely for both.

As was our usual practice, I met him for afternoon cocktails at his place of choice and we would talk about everything: his children, his walks along the road in Hawaii picking up trash, the load-out on D-Day, and his observations of people and events during the invasion. He was energetic, lucid, and fully in control, though it was clear he was straining to hold back the effects of time. Our departure that evening was melancholy as we both knew the cancer that was ravaging him within would ultimately win and in a fairly short time.

The next morning, about 0630, I was having coffee in the town square near the church. Lining the path to the church was a row of green leaved sycamore trees, Plain trees to the Europeans. Out of the corner of my eye, I saw a single figure advancing along the path. It was Zane in full Airborne dress including polished jump boots. He strode purposefully toward the church doors, opened them, and stepped inside to render his last thoughts of this place and the people he had arrived here with all those years ago. People he would soon join.

I felt extraordinarily privileged to have shared this moment. Zane is most fitting as both the beginning and the end of my work. As much as anyone who arrived in Normandy that day, he represented them as well as a human being can. Upon notification of his passing, the town held a Sunday mass for him. This was not a small thing. We will miss Zane and his type and hope we have a deep well of people prepared to make the first jump and the last walk for us all.

Appendices

APPENDIX A

Summary of D-Day

What may we have forgotten with the passage of time?

D-Day was the largest single concentration of manpower and logistics in the history of Western civilization.

D-Day was the most crucial and significant battle for the U.S. since Gettysburg.

D-Day would largely decide the outcome of the war with Germany. Who would own the European Continent—Germany, the Allies, or the Soviet Union? Between 2330 5 June and 1200 6 June, the issue would be decided.

The U.S. had been pressuring the British since 1942 to invade the French Coast in order to get to Germany. Ultimately, all roads had to lead to Berlin and they would begin in the France. It was not until 1944 that the Allies were able to muster sufficient will, manpower, and landing craft to attempt the invasion. Even then, it was felt by all to be a chancy thing.

How many Allied troops were involved in D-Day?

On D-Day, the Allies landed around 156,000 troops in Normandy. The American forces landed numbered 73,000: 23,250 on Utah Beach, 34,250 on Omaha Beach, and 15,500 Airborne troops. In the British and Canadian sector, 83,115 troops were landed (61,715 of them British): 24,970 on Gold Beach, 21,400 on Juno Beach, 28,845 on Sword Beach, and 7900 Airborne troops.

11,590 aircraft were available to support the landings. On D-Day, Allied aircraft flew 14,674 sorties, and 127 were lost.

In the Airborne landings on both flanks of the beaches, 2395 aircraft and 867 gliders of the RAF and USAAF were used on D-Day.

Operation *Neptune* involved huge naval forces, including 6,939 vessels: 1,213 naval combat ships, 4,126 landing ships and landing craft, 736 ancillary craft and 864 merchant vessels. Some 195,700 personnel were assigned to Operation *Neptune*: 52,889 U.S., 112,824 British, and 4,988 from other Allied countries.

By the end of 11 June (D+5), 326,547 troops, 54,186 vehicles, and 104,428 tons of supplies had been landed on the beaches.

As well as the troops who landed in Normandy on D-Day, and those in supporting roles at sea and in the air, millions more men and women in the Allied countries were involved in the preparations for D-Day

How many Allied and German casualties were there on D-Day, and in the Battle of Normandy?

The Allied casualties figures for D-Day have generally been estimated at 10,000, including 4,700 dead. Broken down by nationality, the usual D-Day casualty figures are approximately 2,700 British, 946 Canadians, and 6,603 Americans. However, recent painstaking research by the U.S. National D-Day Memorial Foundation has achieved a more accurate—and much higher—figure for the Allied personnel who were killed on D-Day. They have recorded the names of individual Allied personnel killed on 6 June 1944 in Operation *Overlord*, and so far they have verified 2,499 American D-Day fatalities and 1,915 from the other Allied nations, a total of 4,414 dead (much higher than the traditional figure of 2,500 dead).

Casualties on the British beaches were roughly 1,000 on Gold Beach and the same number on Sword Beach. The remainder of the British losses were amongst the Airborne troops: some 600 were killed or wounded, and 600 more were missing; 100 glider pilots also became casualties. The losses of 3rd Canadian Division at Juno Beach have been given as 340 killed, 574 wounded, and 47 taken prisoner.

The breakdown of U.S. casualties was 1,465 dead, 3,184 wounded, 1,928 missing and 26 captured. Of the total U.S. figure, 2,499 casualties were from the U.S. Airborne troops (238 of them being deaths). The casualties at Utah Beach were relatively light: 197, including 60 missing. However, the U.S. 1st and 29th Divisions together suffered around 2,700 casualties at Omaha Beach.

The total German casualties on D-Day are not known, but are estimated as being between 4,000 and 9,000 men.

Naval losses for June 1944 included 24 warships and 35 merchantmen or auxiliaries sunk, and a further 120 vessels damaged.

Over 425,000 Allied and German troops were killed, wounded or went missing during the Normandy campaign. This figure includes over 209,000 Allied casualties, with nearly 37,000 dead amongst the ground forces and a further 16,714 deaths amongst the Allied air forces. Of the Allied casualties, 83,045 were from 21st Army Group (British, Canadian, and Polish ground forces), and 125,847 from the U.S. ground forces. The losses of the German forces during the Battle of Normandy can only be estimated. Roughly 200,000 German troops were killed or wounded. The Allies also captured 200,000 prisoners of war (not included in the 425,000 total, above). During the fighting around the Falaise Pocket (August 1944) alone, the Germans suffered losses of around 90,000, including prisoners.

APPENDIX B

Cover and Deception

From the beginning, the British had recognized the need for two things: the necessity to cut off the ability of the Germans to spy in England; and to protect the ultimate invasion forces and locations, by using deception. These imperatives evolved into two major operations:

- *Double Cross*, which was the capture and flipping of German spies in England; and
- *Fortitude*, which was the creation of a grand deception to fool the Germans into believing the landing would occur somewhere else than Normandy.

Churchill, upon being briefed on the creation of *Fortitude* to protect Normandy as the true landing site said that the truth must always be protected by a bodyguard of lies. *Double Cross* and *Fortitude* did exactly that.

Double Cross

Operation *Double Cross* was initiated by MI5 (the British security service) shortly after the outbreak of war. It was designed to capture German espionage agents sent to the England and to flip them to support deception operations. This program continued throughout the war and was highly successful.

Location and capture were accomplished by a variety of means. The primary cause for exposure was the use of radio transmissions. They could be located relatively easily due to the extensive radio transmission monitoring in country combined with poor tradecraft on the part of the agents.

Mail intercepts were the next most useful tool in detecting agents. Unknown to the general public was that all mail was subject to review by MI5. Most foreign-bound mail was checked. Microdots, invisible ink, and other techniques were discovered and the sender immediately surveilled until sufficient evidence was established to capture him or her.

Fifty-one German agents were captured, of which 20 were ultimately used to support Operation *Fortitude* and the cover programs for the invasion. The rest were either executed or imprisoned. This actually accounted for 100 percent of all German agents sent to the England.

Interrogation determined the relative value of the detainee for purposes of the program. Once he or she agreed to assist and was deemed relatively reliable, carefully worded messages were provided to send back to the Abwehr (the German military intelligence service).

The messages had just enough factual data to appear reliable if checked by an alternate source. In time, it was clear by intercepted Enigma messages that the Germans believed what their agents were sending.

By 1944 MI5 was sufficiently confident of its double agents to be entrusted with *Fortitude,* the principal deception campaign intended to persuade the enemy that the widely expected Allied invasion of France would occur in the Pas-de-Calais region instead of Normandy.

A secondary objective was to convey the impression that the landings in Normandy were merely a diversionary feint that could be safely ignored. The task of supplying this information rested with a key flipped agent called "Garbo," who was highly regarded by the Abwehr; "Brutus" a former Polish Air Force officer who had been allowed to escape from German captivity in France; and "Bronx," the daughter of a Peruvian diplomat who had travelled to Vichy for the Secret Intelligence Service.

These agents had great credibility with the Germans. Hence, their input was a material factor in the German appreciation for the site of the invasion. They wished to believe that the Pas-de-Calais was the true invasion area and their agents reinforced that belief.

Messages were prepared for transmission that reinforced the location of the main Allied army, First United States Army Group (FUSAG), as being in East Anglia and the northeast ports across from the Pas-de-Calais. The messages contained some truth and much fiction, but they were regarded by the Germans as highly plausible.

General Patton was believed by the Germans to be the logical choice as the overall commander. Hence, his presence was routinely reported by the *Double Cross* agents. This was further reinforced by Patton's very public visits to the local towns. These were dutifully recorded in the local press, copies of which the Germans routinely acquired from a variety of sources.

The agents were worked during and after the actual invasion and were a factor in Hitler deciding Normandy was a feint, refusing to transfer divisions to the invasion area until late June when it was too late. *Double Cross,* as a critical cog in *Fortitude,* was an unqualified success.

Fortitude

Fortitude became a textbook example of how strategic deception should be conducted, and captured documents demonstrated that the enemy was duped not just about the date and place of the main Allied offensive, but even accepted that an entirely fictional army, FUSAG, had assembled in southeast England in anticipation of crossing the Channel from Dover.

The French Resistance and Underground

The actions of the French within France were extremely important for the overall success of the invasion. They provided critical intelligence, tied down thousands of German troops, and isolated the battlefield. While they had internal political agendas, they were universally helpful to the invasion before and during the event.

From the very beginning of the war, association by the British and U.S. with "The Resistance" was a continuous minefield of personalities, politics and competing agendas. In this dark morass, General Eisenhower had to tread lightly while attempting to utilize the potential of French elements to assist the overall Normandy campaign.

The first issue was that the French Underground/Resistance, a broad term, actually encompassed a byzantine puzzle of assets controlled by disparate personalities acting largely as independent entities. Major players were French Communist elements more loyal to Moscow than Paris, anarchists loyal to no one, de Gaulle loyalists, French regional players operating on local priorities, and French simply disaffected by the Germans wanting to play a part to regain independence.

No single entity could control/command this hodge-podge of groups. Closest to do so was General de Gaulle and his Free French operating from North Africa. However, he was anathema to the Communists and they likewise to him. Compounding the problem was that de Gaulle was loathed by Roosevelt, who refused to provide any sort of formal recognition despite Eisenhower and Churchill's desire that he do so.

Exactly what the overall Resistance assets were composed of, fell into three broad categories only vaguely organized as such:

French Forces of the Interior (FFI). A very loose tag that encompassed saboteurs, intelligence operatives, armed forces, and guns for hire or other purposes. These were largely locally based and operated independently of each other. On some occasions, with sufficient motivation, two or more elements might act together in common cause. No single command authority existed for their operational guidance despite de Gaulle's best efforts to impose order.

French Resistance. The "resistance" was an equally broad blanket that was more shadowed than the FFI, and composed of individuals and small clandestine elements that specialized in intelligence, downed pilot recovery, sabotage, or any arcane task that appealed to a personality. Over time and the influence of de Gaulle and Allied aid, this element was subdivided into a structured management: Air, Ground, Support, Intelligence, etc., and became the most effective blanket organization.

The Maquis. These were armed groups of personnel that might be FFI or Resistance or entirely independent, depending upon local leader desires. They were composed largely of disaffected or alienated/threatened personnel that lived and acted as guerillas in the country. They could be a formidable force and were aggressively hunted by the Germans as the most potentially dangerous.

Regardless, Eisenhower had to make use of their skills, talents, and intelligence potential. In this, he was materially aided by British experience and Allied aid to de Gaulle's Free French.

Since the start of the war, the British, initially by MI6, and later by military "Special Operations Executive"(SOE) elements, developed, trained, and supported the overall resistance entities in France. French were recruited, trained, and inserted back to France with radios or other communications systems.

Early on, these personnel were primarily used for intelligence or specific spot missions. In time, and by 1943, they became more formally managed by the Jedburgh program. It was this that was the primary tool for Eisenhower in developing support by the interior French for the invasion.

The Jedburghs

The British Special SOE and its American counterpart, the Office of Strategic Services (OSS), came up with the concept of the Jedburghs in May 1943. The idea was that small groups of military personnel would be inserted by parachute inside territory occupied by Germany to assist local resistance forces and to carry out military operations. It was these teams and others that Eisenhower utilized for a variety of tasks before, during, and after the invasion.

Unlike SOE agents who worked in occupied Europe, the Jedburgh teams would be armed and uniformed military personnel. Fluency in French was required, although the language requirement was reduced for radio operators. The "Jeds," men and women, were all volunteers.

Once selected, they were sent to Scotland for two weeks of paramilitary training and then moved to the airfields from which they were to be launched into France. While initially used to support a variety of Allied tasks, by the spring of 1944, it was hoped they could bring some order to the FFI/Resistance/Maquis in direct support of the invasion. A key component to persuasion was the promise of weapons, supplies, and funds, which would be doled by the Jedburgh teams.

Teams were provided specific operational tasks ranging from sabotage to intelligence development to pure paramilitary strike plans. Neither the Jedburgh teams nor their French counterparts were aware of either the invasion location or the dates. Simple code messages would indicate the strike date and the times for execution of planned tasks.

Teams were inserted throughout late 1943 and early 1944 to develop contacts, distribute resources, assess capabilities, and develop skills as required. The first team in direct support of the invasion was inserted in less than 24 hours prior to D-Day. It was met by FFI elements, that were supplied with specific targets and times for actions. These consisted primarily in cutting telephone cables and destroying railroad switch systems.

In many cases, the local French elements did not fully cooperate with the Jedburghs or only so far as Jedburgh resources and participation carried influence. De Gaulle never gave his full support to Jedburghs in that he was not permitted to control them other than by cooperation with his London headquarters and was concerned they would agnostically support non-loyalists such as communist and anarchist elements. This conflict was never resolved until the Free French Government and de Gaulle's leadership was formally established.

Regardless of the complexities associated with managing French elements, they were used extensively by Supreme Headquarters Allied Expeditionary Forces (SHAEF) as part of the Normandy support programs. Two key operations serve to demonstrate the value of the French elements specifically for Normandy.

A crucial question was the ability of the selected beaches to handle tracked and wheeled vehicles. Old anecdotal input was useful but not decisive. This could only be achieved by retrieving soil samples. FFI elements were provided with core sampling tools and specific beaches to extract materiel. This was virtually 100 percent of all coast beaches, to disguise specific points. These, spirited out by either liaison, fishing boats, or night air extraction were extremely valuable. British swimmer commandos performed like extractions on mission beaches to validate FFI materiel.

In May, a member of the resistance was spirited from Carentan to the England. He was a repairman for the local telephone system and intimately familiar with the German operational communications network. These were major underground cable conduits between the command nodes and not discernible from the air. He provided detailed drawings of the cable box locations and configurations. These were provided to the 82nd, 101st, and 6th Airborne prior to the assault. In all cases, this resulted in a severing of land line communications within an hour of the Airborne assaults.

Concurrent with this, Allied intelligence and operational elements provided specific targets for the Resistance to be executed upon command. These were to be transmitted by either radio code or Jedburgh teams. This resulted in numerous demolitions of rail and communication nodes as well as some ambushes of couriers as the invasion unfolded.

In sum, the many complexities, parts, and pieces of the French Underground did provide excellent service toward invasion objectives. SHAEF was able to gain significant advantages for the invasion by using the entire spectrum of French resistance elements despite the lack of a centralized command.

De Gaulle's loyal elements in Resistance cells provided the bulk of support while the Jedburgh associations with the Maquis and others materially augmented the whole. De Gaulle ignored non-loyalists in his support and control and would not attempt to do so. The communists, anarchists, and other non-de Gaulle supporters operated on their own local agenda and were utilized by SHAEF as requirements dictated.

In Eisenhower's view, the combined elements of the French Resistance were particularly valuable post-invasion where they provided the only control mechanism for the population, freeing the Allies of having to provide general police and security forces.

Eisenhower's larger problem was in managing de Gaulle in support of the invasion from both a political and a military viewpoint. Absent having a recognized French actor working under SHAEF control, Eisenhower understood he would have major issues once the Allied forces landed.

The Transport Plan

Isolation of the battlefield was a paramount requirement. The issue tested Eisenhower's resolve and was one of the few times he put his stars on the table to get what he needed.

By early February, SHAEF had examined German reinforcement capabilities for Western Europe. Studies indicated that the Franco-German rail network was the primary route for reinforcements and supplies to the invasion area. The issue in Eisenhower's mind was quite simple: stop rail transport and German reinforcement becomes a manageable issue. Isolation of the battlefield became a key priority for the pre-invasion planners. The issue then was where and how.

Extensive overhead photography coupled with analysis indicated that the key rail choke points were the rail marshaling yards in France and the multitudinous bridges over major water barriers. Kill the rail yards and drop the bridges and significant German reinforcements could not arrive.

At the time, accurate bombing was as much a factor of luck as skill. The Norden bombsite was reasonably accurate within a 1-kilometer box. Using dozens to hundreds of bombers for a mass drop compensated for inaccuracies through sheer mass. This might work for a large rail yard but was highly problematical for such a small point target as a bridge.

In the England, the Allied bomber units, commanded by Air Chief Marshal Leigh-Mallory had two major components:

- Strategic bombers, the B-17s, B-24s, and British Halifax and Lancaster bombers
- Tactical bombers, the A-20s, B-25s, B-26s, and the British Wellingtons.

The strategic bombers, under command of British Air Marshal Hugh Dowding, concentrated on key targets well within Germany and Central Europe—oil refineries, synthetic gasoline facilities, ball bearing plants, factories, and other manufacturing nodes.

The tactical bombers were used for more close-in targets in France and the low countries as well as direct troop support when they were engaged.

In February, Eisenhower's deputy, Air Chief Marshal Tedder, in conjunction with British scientist and close friend of Churchill, Solly Zuckerman, recommended that almost 100 percent of all bombers of all types be devoted to isolating the battlefield by destroying the French rail infrastructure.

Eisenhower and Montgomery immediately bought into the plan and asked Tedder to manage it. In this, he ran into a buzz saw of opposition from all the bomber generals.

They were adamant that the strategic bombers not be diverted and that the results of their efforts would be more beneficial for the invasion. Ike could use the tactical bombers but not the strategic bombers.

This created a delicate problem as Eisenhower, did, in fact, not command the strategic bombers. They were under command of Army Air Forces (AAF) Lieutenant General Tooey Spaatz, who reported directly to the Air Force Chief of Staff, General Hap Arnold. Arnold initially declined to make a decision.

Eisenhower met personally with the bomber commanders but could not persuade them to divert assets. Increasingly frustrated, he sent a detailed and strongly worded message to General Marshall requesting they be directed to support the Transport Plan and operate under SHAEF for the build-up period. In essence, he said inclusion of the strategic bombers was imperative or he could not assure success. His stars were on the table.

Marshall met with the U.S. Chiefs of Staff and messaged the British Chiefs as to the imperative nature of the diversion. In this, Arnold slightly demurred, but Leigh-Mallory, despite being subordinate to Eisenhower still strongly objected. Eisenhower met with Churchill and got his informal blessing. With that, Ike went back to Marshall requesting a clear command decision.

The Combined Chiefs directed that the strategic bombers, from March through the invasion, respond to SHAEF and bomb targets as directed in conjunction with the tactical air forces. A small caveat was inserted where the strategic bombers would respond to SHAEF directives as requested, but would not be placed within Eisenhower's chain of command, a distinction without a difference, considering the point.

Accordingly, by early March, in what is known as "the Transport Plan," almost all the available bombers began saturation bombing of the French rail infrastructure and key river bridges. These were more than 100 bomber raids that operated around the clock in order to disrupt the very efficient rail repair crews.

Tactical fighters were also employed in this scheme. Finding and killing trains and specifically locomotives became a key priority for either dedicated missions or post escort tasks. Imagery analysts would provide photos of parked engines and repair facilities and pass them on for immediate targeting.

In order to maintain the Pas De Calais deception, more attention was paid to that area than to Normandy. For every bomb dropped in the Normandy area, two were dropped on the North. This added to the German analysis as to where the invasion would come.

By 6 June, the entire west coast of France was essentially isolated. German intercepts were clear that the Transport Plan was a major disruptive event and had more than materially assisted in isolating the battlefield. By the first week of the invasion, the only way German forces could be inserted was by road where they were quickly interdicted by ubiquitous fighter coverage.

Within the battle area, the constant rail and road interdiction had robbed Rommel and Von Rundstedt of badly needed supplies, especially construction material and gasoline. Lack of mines, cement, and barbed wire left many positions unfinished or not even started as the material languished in Germany, unable to move forward. Despite the best efforts of Rommel's construction coordinator, Admiral Friedrich Ruge, schedules were either greatly delayed or simply ended.

The lack of gasoline reserves became a major limiting factor in German counter-attack planning. Panzers ate huge quantities of gas that could not be provided. As a result, many tanks were limited to local movement only in order to divert fuel to a smaller quantity of attacking armor. By the time of the breakout at Saint-Lô, many German vehicles simply were abandoned with empty fuel tanks.

The Transport Plan was an unqualified success and clearly merited Eisenhower's willingness to put his stars on the table.

Higgins Boats—American Ingenuity at Work

Nothing was more important for the invasion than the Higgins boat. It became the core of all amphibious operations in all the theatres. Its development overcame an intransigent bureaucracy. Without the Higgins boat, there would not have been the invasion.

Some of the hallmarks of the essence of America are ingenuity, inventiveness, and perseverance. Normandy required all that in spades, but no more than in the unique materiel required for a landing of such magnitude.

General Eisenhower said after the war that the three items that contributed the most to victory were the Higgins boat, the jeep, and the LST (Landing Ship, Tank). None of these existed before 1940 when the first prototype jeep came off the Willys Motor Corporation assembly line. Each were major assets in the constant appetite for transport. Once the Navy brought a force to a given shore, how did that force effectively land in a combat configuration, move key items off the beach and remain sustained? The solutions ultimately achieved were not easily acquired, especially in the amphibious landing capability. At the outbreak of World War II, the Navy Bureau of Ships was a highly structured, bureaucratic organization that claimed total primacy over what ships would be designed and produced. Outside ideas were not welcomed.

It quickly became apparent to the Service Chiefs that a vast quantity of amphibious craft would be essential or all the newly created forces could not be employed. The landing fleet was primarily traditional V-shaped hulls with troops off-loading over the sides, which was completely impractical for modern warfare on a contested beach. Further, the vast array of tanks and other heavy equipment could not be employed unless offloaded from traditional freighters in a deep-water port, again totally impractical in light of reality. Bureau of Ships was approached by myriad civilian organizations suggesting certain designs and architecture, all of which were Dead on Arrival as Not Invented Here. Into this situation came a combination of overwhelming requirements and two personalities, Andrew Jackson Higgins and Henry J. Kaiser.

The mass of issues facing the Allies was stark at the first joint meetings between the British and American military leadership. The British had considerable experience in the amphibious design area and had a significant array of different landing vessels ranging from small beach landing craft to major flat-bottomed designs hauling a dozen plus tanks. The British passed their designs to Admiral Ernest King, the U.S. Navy Chief of Naval Operations. In turn, he gave them to the Bureau of Ships with orders to initiate a huge ship building program. Finally, exhausted by the struggle to retain design authority and unable to retain construction autonomy, the bureau began to solicit outside ideas. The first and most vocal personality to respond was a Louisiana oil rig supply businessman, Andrew Jackson Higgins.

For nearly 30 years prior, the boat building company founded by Andrew Jackson Higgins was an important fixture in New Orleans. What began as a sideline to the petroleum industry in 1930 soon developed into a thriving commercial concern. Higgins specialized in shallow-draft boats suitable to the bayous of Louisiana. Higgins briefed the bureau on his craft and their design and volunteered to produce them in great quantity. The bureau strictly limited his initial production and ignored his other designs and entreaties.

Despite the opposition, Higgins managed to have several hundred of his modified oil patch craft manufactured and used by the Marines at Guadalcanal. General Vandergrift, the 1st Marine Division Commander, praised the craft and wrote a letter to that effect to Higgins who quickly used it to advantage. He initially took it to the Navy, who ignored it and continued to resist a flat-bottomed design.

Not to succumb to an entrenched bureaucracy in the face of a clear need and with the strong support of the Marine Corps, he traveled to Washington, lobbied Congress and through the efforts of several senators and congressmen, forced a meeting with Roosevelt. Higgins was an Irishman of temperament and a hard drinker. His press conferences in Washington were about the most colorful on record. Roosevelt, in his usual manner, saw a personality that could get things done when in need and he overrode the Bureau's limitation on Higgins boat production. Higgins was eventually authorized to build as many as fast as he could with no limits. Only by 1945 were production quotas established, so valuable were these craft.

That authority enabled Higgins Industries to become one of the largest manufacturers of U. S. naval combat boats during World War II. The ability of the company to design and produce vessels in record time meant that during the war they produced 20,094 boats, employing 20,000 workers at seven plants in the New Orleans area. On D-Day, slightly less than 140,000 men were afloat in Higgins boats of various designs across all five beaches. Each craft could hold about 36 men or 8,000 pounds of cargo. They were the jeep and truck of any assault. Many variants were created by the users to meet specific local needs. Plywood and sheet steel were the only materials needed.

Higgins was also highly unusual other than in terms of personality. In his seven plants in the heart of the Old South, he mandated a completely integrated work force to include all aspects of the assembly line, mess halls, and sleeping quarters. He also paid the unheard of minimum wage of $5 an hour, which could quickly escalate with worker bonuses for exceeding quotas. Pay was equal for all doing equal tasks regardless of gender or color. The local newspapers chose not to advertise any of this as being disruptive to society but word of mouth brought thousands of workers to his plants.

The equally important LST and LSD took a similar path.

In 1941, the Navy had zero across-the-beach capability for heavy equipment. Again, the British proffered their designs, which served as the basic architecture for an entire array of various flat-bottomed purpose-built ships. These ranged from tank and truck carriers to infantry transport. The key in all was the ability to move large quantities of materiel and land them on a shallow beach. These designs were for considerably smaller ships than the need. Regardless, in that they were British designed and clearly valuable and that Churchill offered them gratis, and Admiral Ernest King directed Navy Ship and Design to develop a U.S. model.

The U.S. design(s) were considerably larger than the British. This was primarily because Roosevelt had asked Henry J. Kaiser, the car manufacturer, to examine the possibilities for production. Kaiser saw a number of improvements that could be made to the original design as well as some manufacturing shortcuts. While the Bureau of Ships vigorously opposed the Kaiser manufacturing model, Admiral King saw merit in them and squashed opposition, so desperate was he to get meaningful forces into the Pacific fighting.

The design concept was to provide for a large portion of a Marine infantry battalion aboard. A then revolutionary well-deck was developed allowing the units to load aboard amphibious craft within the hull in relative protection and then proceed to shore, the returning Higgins boats or amphibious tracked vehicles to return for subsequent loads. When the beach had been secured, the ships could land on the beach and act as an instant shelter and supply point. Until late 1941, the Navy had nothing remotely capable of doing this.

The LSD (Landing Ship, Dock) was of a common hull design, but with significant differences topside and in the well deck. As a dock ship, landing on a beach, it had a number of gantry cranes on both sides as well as portable wharf material. The well deck had fabricated tread ways that could be dropped to accommodate wheeled vehicles as well as compartments for dry cargo storage. Very soon into the war, a number of LSDs were outfitted as refrigerator ships as the standard design V hulled ships could not get close enough to some of the islands to be efficient. In time, these were used as off-shore deep water floating piers for deeper draft vessels to offload their cargo for run-ins to shore, greatly improving supply by eliminating individual lighterage time.

The keel of the first LST was laid down on June 10, 1942 at Newport News, Virginia. The overall length of the ship was 328 feet with a 50 foot beam and a minimum draft of 3 feet 9 1/2 inches. As eventually modified, an LST could carry a 2,100-ton load of tanks, vehicles, or a reinforced infantry company The ship's armament usually consisted of multiple 20mm and 40mm anti-aircraft guns along with a 3-inch .50-caliber gun.

Perhaps Kaiser's most valuable contribution was in his manufacturing design system. Based on his radical car assembly system, he suggested that the landing ships be built on an assembly line design with rail bringing in pre-manufactured parts to be assembled "by the numbers." He further stated that the assembly points be arrayed sideways along the banks of large rivers as opposed to the traditional perpendicular-to-the-harbor method. This allowed for essentially unskilled labor to do the work in a very rapid fashion and without the necessity to build a large dry dock/slip. Ships, once generally hull finished, would be slid sideways into the river, tied to the bank, and the finishing work performed in a series of progressions down the shore.

This violated all sorts of traditional norms, but was very efficient. Small portable rail lines would be laid down next to the assembly area and parts from all over the U.S. slid into place as needed. The Bureau of Shipbuilding fought this approach as a violation of contract regulations. Kaiser simply had Congress re-write the regulations, bypassing the bureau.

During some of the initial planning sessions for Normandy, it was clear that there were insufficient LSTs to lift the needed force. Even by moving assets from the Mediterranean (which was strongly opposed by Churchill), there simply were not enough. Eisenhower explained the problem to General Marshall such that a May invasion date was impossible without the necessary transport. Marshall met with King and Roosevelt. Roosevelt directed that manufacture of the landing ships be given top priority for all resources. Even so, the fastest production would not meet the need until late May. Accordingly, the invasion date was shifted from May to June. Churchill said, "The success of the entire war seems to depend upon some damn thing called LSTs."

And it did. Many of the ships facing the five beaches on D-Day had been commissioned on the Ohio River less than 30 days before. They were crewed with a polyglot of just graduated junior officers and enlisted, grizzled merchant mariners and whatever excess personnel the Navy could find to reasonably safely con the ships.

We all owe Higgins and Kaiser a huge debt of gratitude. Neither of them saw their ships in action, but that made no difference; their perseverance and creativity was arguably one of the most significant tools in our arsenal.

APPENDIX F

Gliders

Gliders were a new tool on the battlefield and a crucial part of the Allied Airborne capability. Their development ensured the success of the Airborne. They provided a variety of employment choices that did not previously exist and that we exploited to advantage.

Gliders were a new phenomenon in the beginning of the war and became an inclusive part of the Airborne divisions through necessity. Though the Airborne units had vehicles, guns, and all the materiel associated with divisions, these could not be delivered by parachute with few exceptions.

Para-packs, containers with parachutes, were provided to each aircraft with jumpers. These were sufficient to carry the crew-served weapons, small arms, ammunition, and light man-portable supplies.

Jeeps, artillery, medical supplies, and signal material as well as follow-on ammunition and food and other cargo had to come by glider or not at all.

The British had two basic designs which they built in quantity: the Hamilcar, which was a very large glider with a capacity in excess of 17,000 pounds; and the Horsa, which was a medium glider with a capacity of 15,000 pounds.

The U.S. had a single design, the Waco, which was a small to medium glider with a 7,500 pound capacity.

Due to the fact that a C-47 could haul only a Horsa or Waco, these became the workhorses of the glider fleet. Type loads for a Waco included:

- 13 troops and 2 pilots
- Jeep and 4 troops and 2 pilots
- Trailer and 7 troops and 2 pilots
- 75mm howitzer, 3 troops, 2 pilots, 18 rounds of ammunition
- 57mm anti-tank gun, 3 troops, 2 pilots, ammunition
- 3 mules and 3 troops, 2 pilots

In the U.S. Airborne Divisions, a Glider Infantry Regiment (GIR) was added to the two Parachute regiments, later expanded to three for Normandy. The glider infantry were draftees and received no additional pay incentives nor were they allowed to wear the distinctive Airborne uniform and patches.

The pilots for the British gliders were for the most part RAF NCOs who underwent extensive training. As part of the buildup for D-Day, and in recognition of the much-enlarged glider requirement, troops were taken from the units on a volunteer basis and placed in the right seat for basic training.

The U.S. gliders were piloted by a combination of Army officer pilots and volunteers from line units. In either case, British or American, riding in a glider being towed by a C-47 was a sickening and dangerous experience.

Attached by a tow rope and telephone cable, the glider bucked and yawed 100 feet behind the C-47. The glider rose and fell continuously as well as jerked and stopped as the tow rope slacked or stretched.

Practice with gliders was predominately for the pilots and with experimental loads. Due to the frequentness of accidents, troop insertions were only occasionally practiced.

The 82nd and 101st integrated a large number of Horsas into their program due to the increased load capacity compared to a Waco. It could carry 30 troops as opposed to 12 or 13. The Horsa could accommodate the new snub-nosed 75mm howitzer, its tow jeep, and crew. The Waco would be very dangerous to land with such a load.

By early May, both the 82nd and 101st settled on using the Waco for initial troop and supply insertion with the Horsa for the heavier equipment and resupply. While the Airborne trained they were rarely integrated with the glider forces. Concurrently, most glider infantry training was conducted out of the back of a truck due to the limited supply of gliders and the tendency to crash, especially with limited pilot quality.

For D-Day, the gliders had a crucial support role. The British 6th Airborne would have a mix of glider and Airborne forces at H Hour. The 82nd and 101st reserved the glider support for post H Hour choosing to being in the first lot at 0400 5 June. Each had a reason for their choice.

The British felt they could get much larger and more robust forces on the ground by using gliders with the Airborne assault. They were prepared to take a high rate of accidents to do so. Concurrently, their primary glider landing zone was a very large open area on Ranville Ridge they felt could safely accommodate such forces.

Unlike the Americans, they also planned to use gliders to execute two coup de main assaults: Pegasus Bridge and the Merville Battery. For these discrete events, the pilots picked were first class and trained with the assault infantry.

The 82nd and 101st viewed the gliders as primarily logistics, support, and follow-on elements after primary objectives were achieved. Both Ridgway and Taylor felt that landing them in relatively close terrain required daylight. Neither envisioned tasks for gliders at H-Hour. Further reducing glider requirements, the sea tail of the 101st with the 327 GIR would land intact at Utah Beach.

The 82nd would bring in the 325th GIR beginning at 1600 on D-Day and that would be on a large open area south of Sainte-Mère-Église, Landing Zone W, which was also being used by the 101st. No glider support was projected for either the 507th or 508th Parachute Infantry Regiment west of the Merderet. All supplies and support would be centralized at Sainte-Mère-Église.

To Supreme Commander Allied Expeditionary Force

To Supreme Commander Allied Expeditionary Force
(Issued 12 February 1944)

You are hereby designated as Supreme Allied Commander of the forces placed under your orders for operations for liberation of Europe from the Germans. Your title will be Supreme Commander Allied Expeditionary Force.

Task—You will enter the continent of Europe and, in conjunction with the other United Nations, undertake operations aimed at the heart of Germany and the destruction of her armed forces. The date for entering the Continent is the month of May 1944. After adequate channel ports have been secured, exploitation will be directed towards securing an area that will facilitate both ground and air operations against the enemy.

Notwithstanding the target date above you will be prepared at any time to take immediate advantage of favorable circumstances, such as withdrawal by the enemy on your front, to effect a reentry into the Continent with such forces as you have available at the time; a general plan for this operation when approved will be furnished for your assistance.

La Fière Plaque

The Battle for La Fière Bridgehead 6–9 June 1944

The area encompassing La Fière bridge and the causeway together with the sister bridge and causeway at Chef-du-Pont were strategic objectives for the entire eastern portion of the Normandy invasion. From 6 to 9 June the battle raged within sight of this place. As a final "all in" assault at 1030 on 9 June the causeway and bridgehead at Cauquigny church were seized by elements of the 82nd Airborne supported by elements of the 4th and 90th Infantry Divisions and the 746th Tank Battalion.

For the Normandy campaign the 82nd Airborne awarded an estimated 38 Distinguished Service Crosses, 271 Silver Stars, 925 Bronze Stars, and 5,209 Purple Hearts.

One Congressional Medal of Honor was awarded To Private First Class Charles DeGlopper for actions within sight of this monument.

Primary units engaged within sight of this location include:

1st Battalion, 505th Parachute Infantry Regiment

2nd and 3rd Battalions, 507th Parachute Infantry Regiment

2nd Battalion, 401st Glider Infantry Regiment/3rd Battalion 325th Glider Infantry Regiment

307th Airborne Engineer Battalion

80th Anti-tank Battalion (57mm)

325th Glider Infantry Regiment

Command Group, 82nd Airborne

Elements of the 4th and 90th Infantry Divisions

C Company 746th Tank Battalion

Approximate casualties at and near this location: Killed 254 Wounded 525

The most hotly contested piece of ground in the European theatre (S. L. A. Marshall, U.S. Army historian)

The soul of the Airborne resides in this place

Sources

Some of interviews were either done with others, e.g., John Brannen, or simply informal walk-about discussions, e.g., O. B. Hill. Most were simply informal conversation rendered on site.

Susan Eisenhower, Dwight Eisenhower's granddaughter.
  Extensive discussions regarding Ike's leadership style and difficult issues he managed.
Lieutenant General Omar Bradley, Commanding General American Forces for the invasion
  His recollection of events of D-Day and Pointe du Hoc as presented by him.
Major General Lawton Collins, VII Corps Commander
  Discussion of background to invasion, training and Airborne controversy.
Major General Matthew Ridgway, Commanding General, 82nd Airborne
  Extensive discussions on all aspects of the invasion.
Major General Maxwell Taylor, Commanding General, 101st Airborne
  Comment to his aide regarding the flight into Normandy.
Brigadier General James Gavin, Assault Force Commander, 82nd Airborne
  Extensive discussions of all aspects of the invasion, leadership issues, and specific discussions of events at Chef-du-Pont and La Fière Bridge.
Brigadier General John Hill, Commanding General, 3 Brigade, British 6th Airborne Division
  Discussions regarding landing and issues on Ranville Ridge as well as Pegasus and Merville.
Lieutenant Colonel Tom Timmes, Commander, 3-507th.
  Extensive discussions regarding his stand at Amfreville and subsequent siege at Timmes Orchard.
Lieutenant Colonel Ben Vandervoort, Commander, 2-505th.
  Extensive discussions regarding pre-invasion training, the flight into France, and actions at Neuville-au-Plain.
Lieutenant Colonel Frank Norris, Commander, 345th Artillery Regiment, 90th Infantry Division
  Extensive discussions regarding La Fière Bridge.
Lieutenant Colonel Terence Otway, 9 Para Battalion, Assault Force Commander, Merville Battery
  Discussion regarding capture of Merville Battery.
Major Napier Crookenden, 6th Parachute Regiment
  Extensive discussions regarding the Airborne plan and subsequent actions.
Major John Howard, Commander D Ox & Bucks, 5 Brigade at Pegasus Bridge
  Discussion regarding capture of Pegasus.
Captain Bob Piper, Headquarters Commandant, 82nd Airborne Division
  Extensive discussions regarding pre-invasion training, the jump. and leadership at La Fière Bridge.
Lieutenant John Brannen, 508th Parachute Infantry Regiment, Chateau Bernaville
  Interview regarding his ambush of General Falley.
Lieutenant (JG) Ben Berger, Naval Gunfire officer, 2nd and 5th Rangers Discussion regarding experience at Omaha and Pointe du Hoc.

2Lt Vince Baker, Duplex Drive Tanks
   Gunfire plan for Omaha and the floating tank performance.
First Sergeant Lem Lomell, Company D, 2nd Ranger Battalion
   Extensive discussions regarding pre-invasion Ranger training, assault, finding the guns, and actions on the road.
Staff Sgt John Hall, halftrack 105mm Crew Chief
   Pre-invasion training and actions at Omaha Beach.
Staff Sergeant Otis Sampson, 60mm mortar platoon sergeant, 2-505th
   Discussion of actions at Neuville-au-Plain.
Sergeant O. B. Hill, Squad Leader, 1-508th
   Discussion of his landing in a swamp and actions after being mis-dropped.
Technical Sergeant David Jones, Headquarters and Headquarters Company, 1-508th
   Discussion of being mis-dropped into a swamp, recovery of other troops, and actions well away from his unit.
Technical Sergeant Pinky Pinkston, 1-505th Medic at La Fière Bridge
   Discussions of events at La Fière Bridge.
Sergeant Tom Brown, 105mm Howitzer Gunner, Omaha Beach
   Discussion of landing and engagement.
Technical Sergeant Graves, Radio Operator with the 5th Rangers on Omaha Beach
   Interview regarding landing and actions at Omaha and remembrances of General Cota saying the Ranger motto.
Private First Class Bob Murphy, Pathfinder, probably the first 82nd trooper on the ground
   Extensive discussions regarding pre-invasion training, the sausages, initial drop, and La Fière Bridge
Private First Class Bill Sullivan, Headquarters and Headquarters Company, 1-505th, three-time escapee from the Germans
   Discussions regarding initial jump and POW experiences.
Private First Class Howard Manoian, Company A, 1-505th
   Discussions regarding initial jump and events at Sainte-Mère-Église.
Private Silvio Marcucci, Radio Operator, 1st Infantry Division, First Wave
   Interview on his landing at Omaha.
Maurice & H. J. Renaud, sons of the mayor of Sainte-Mère-Église
   Extensive discussions regarding events at Sainte-Mère-Église and postwar impressions.
Yves Tarriel, a child on D-Day
   Remembrances of 6 June.

Glossary

Bangalore torpedo. An explosive charge placed within one or several connected tubes. It was used by combat engineers to clear obstacles that would otherwise require them to approach directly, possibly under fire.

BAR. Browning Automatic Rifle. An American fully automatic light machine gun with a 20-round magazine.

Benzedrine. An amphetamine issued to soldiers to increase alertness. It also had the added benefit of reducing appetite and fatigue.

Bigot. BIGOT was a World War II security classification at the highest level of security, above Top Secret.

Bren gun. The standard British light machine gun, firing .303 ammunition from a 30-round magazine.

British Double Summer Time. Britain changed to British Double Summer Time during World War II, with clocks two hours ahead of Greenwich Mean Time in the summer and one hour ahead in the winter.

DD tanks. Duplex-drive amphibious M-4 Sherman tanks.

DUKW. Amphibious truck universally dubbed Duck.

FFI. A very loose tag that encompassed saboteurs, intelligence operatives, armed forces, and guns for hire or other purposes. These were largely locally based and operated independently of each other.

Gammon grenade. An improvised hand-thrown bomb especially suitable for the destruction of vehicles. An explosive charge was wrapped in fabric and sewn to an impact fuse that detonated on sharp contact.

GIR. Glider Infantry Regiment.

Higgins boats. The landing craft, vehicle, personnel (LCVP) or Higgins boat, was a landing craft with a forward ramp that was used extensively in amphibious landings.

Jedburghs. Jedburgh teams, military personnel parachuted into France behind German lines, were employed to coordinate French resistance actions with the allied strategic and tactical plans in order to slow down German forces during the Normandy landing.

JG. Naval Junior Grade rank as in lieutenant LG. The equivalent of an army first lieutenant.

LCT(R). Landing Craft Tank (Rocket). An LST modified to fire a barrage of rockets.

LGOP (Little Group of Paratroops). The concept that wherever a paratrooper is dropped, regardless of error, or how isolated he might be, he does whatever he can to wreak havoc on the enemy.

LSD. Landing Ship, Dock. Support vessels designed to transport loaded landing craft, amphibious vehicles, and troops into an amphibious landing area.

LSI. Landing Ship, Infantry. These vessels were several classes of seagoing amphibious assault ships used to land large numbers of infantry directly onto beaches, and in size fell between the Higgins boat and the LST.

LST. Landing Ship, Tank. A large flat-bottomed amphibious ship capable of landing vehicles and infantry directly to the beach via a ramp.

Maquis. These were armed groups of French citizens that might be FFI or Resistance or entirely independent, depending upon local leadership.

MP. Military Police. Responsible for traffic control and prisoner management.

MG-42. Standard German belt-fed machine gun.

Oboe. A bomb drop plan.

PIR. Parachute Infantry Regiment.

PIAT. The Projector, Infantry, Anti Tank was a British man-portable anti-tank weapon.

PRG. Provisional Ranger Group.

Rhino ferries. Essentially, large rafts with outboard motors.

Sausage. Military encampments in Britain, often shaped like a sausage.

SHAEF. Supreme Headquarters Allied Expeditionary Force.

SOP. Standard Operating Procedure.

Sten gun. Mass-produced British submachine gun, used by British forces and widely distributed to resistance forces.

Index